D0862039

Unwin Critical Library
GENERAL EDITOR: CLAUDE RAWSON

LOCKE'S
TWO TREATISES
OF GOVERNMENT

Unwin Critical Library
GENERAL EDITOR: CLAUDE RAWSON

LOCKE'S TWO TREATISES OF GOVERNMENT

Richard Ashcraft

*Department of Political Science,
University of California, Los Angeles*

London
UNWIN HYMAN
Boston   Sydney   Wellington

Published by the Academic Division of

Unwin Hyman Ltd
15/17 Broadwick Street, London W1V 1FP, UK

Unwin Hyman Inc.,
8 Winchester Place, Winchester, Mass. 01890, USA

Allen & Unwin (Australia) Ltd,
8 Napier Street, North Sydney, NSW 2060, Australia

Allen & Unwin (New Zealand) Ltd in association with the
Port Nicholson Press Ltd,
60 Cambridge Terrace, Wellington, New Zealand

First published in 1987
Second impression 1989

British Library Cataloguing in Publication Data

Ashcraft, Richard
  Locke's two treatises of government.
(Unwin critical library; 17)
1. Locke, John, 1632–1704
I. Title
192   B1297
ISBN 0 04 44538 8

Library of Congress Cataloging in Publication Data

Ashcraft, Richard
  Locke's two treatises of government.
(Unwin critical library)
Bibliography: p.
Includes index.
1. Locke, John, 1632–1704. Two treatises of
government. I. Title.   II. Series.
JC153.L853A84   1987   320   86–17293
ISBN 0 04 44538 8   (alk. paper)

Set in 10 on 12 point Plantin by Columns, Caversham, Reading
and printed in Great Britain by Billings & Sons Ltd,
London and Worcester

GENERAL EDITOR'S PREFACE

Each volume in this series is devoted to a single major text. It is intended for serious students and teachers of literature, and for knowledgeable non-academic readers. It aims to provide a scholarly introduction and a stimulus to critical thought and discussion.

Individual volumes will naturally differ from one another in arrangement and emphasis, but each will normally begin with information on a work's literary and intellectual background, and other guidance designed to help the reader to an informed understanding. This is followed by an extended critical discussion of the work itself, and each contributor in the series has been encouraged to present in these sections his own reading of the work, whether or not this is controversial, rather than to attempt a mere consensus. Some volumes, including those on *Paradise Lost* and *Ulysses*, vary somewhat from the more usual pattern by entering into substantive critical discussion at the outset, and allowing the necessary background material to emerge at the points where it is felt to arise from the argument in the most useful and relevant way. Each volume also contains a historical survey of the work's critical reputation, including an account of the principal lines of approach and areas of controversy, and a selective (but detailed) bibliography.

The hope is that the volumes in this series will be among those which a university teacher would normally recommend for any serious study of a particular text, and that they will also be among the essential secondary texts to be consulted in some scholarly investigations. But the experienced and informed non-academic reader has also been in our minds, and one of our aims has been to provide him with reliable and stimulating works of reference and guidance, embodying the present state of knowledge and opinion in a conveniently accessible form.

C.J.R.
University of Warwick,
December 1979

ACKNOWLEDGEMENTS

I want to thank Sage Publications for granting me permission to reprint material from my article, 'Revolutionary politics and Locke's *Two Treatises of Government*', *Political Theory*, vol. 8, no. 4 (November 1980), pp. 429–86. I also want to thank the American Political Science Association for permission to reprint material from my article, 'Locke's state of nature: historical fact or moral fiction?', *American Political Science Review*, vol. 52, no. 3 (September 1968), pp. 898–915. Princeton University Press kindly granted me permission to make use of some material from my *Revolutionary Politics and Locke's 'Two Treatises of Government'* (Princeton, NJ: Princeton University Press, 1986).

I am grateful to the Academic Senate of the University of California at Los Angeles for its assistance in funding the research for this book and to the staff of the William Andrews Clark Memorial Library (UCLA) for their courteous and efficient help in the execution of that research. A special thanks must go to my research assistant, Susan Matthews, whose dedication and perseverance made a valuable contribution to the completion of this project. I am also indebted to the Keeper of Manuscripts of the Library of the Inner Temple, and to the staffs of the Bodleian Library, Oxford, and of the British Library for allowing me to consult manuscripts in their possession.

I am appreciative of the advice and suggestions I received from Ian Shapiro and C. J. Rawson, though the responsibility for whatever errors remain in the text is mine.

CONTENTS

ABBREVIATIONS

Works	*The Works of John Locke*, 12th edn, 9 vols (1824).
ELN	*Essays on the Law of Nature*, ed. W. Von Leyden (Oxford: Clarendon Press, 1954)
I:1,1	*An Essay Concerning Human Understanding*, ed. Peter H. Nidditch (Oxford: Clarendon Press, 1975)
I,1 or II,1	*Two Treatises of Government*, ed. Peter Laslett, 2nd edn (Cambridge: Cambridge University Press, 1967)
STCE	*Some Thoughts Concerning Education*, in James L. Axtell (ed.), *The Educational Writings of John Locke* (Cambridge: Cambridge University Press, 1968)
FTG or STG	*Two Tracts on Government*, ed. Philip Abrams (Cambridge: Cambridge University Press, 1967)
Early Draft	*An Early Draft of Locke's Essay*, ed. R. I. Aaron and Jocelyn Gibb (Oxford: Clarendon Press, 1936)
Correspondence	*The Correspondence of John Locke*, ed. E. S. De Beer, 8 vols (Oxford: Clarendon Press, 1976–85)
MS	Locke manuscripts, Bodleian Library, Oxford University

LOCKE'S
TWO TREATISES
OF GOVERNMENT

INTRODUCTION

Thirty years ago, Locke's *Two Treatises of Government* was viewed as the classic expression of liberal political ideas. It was read as a defence of individualism and of the natural right of individuals to appropriate private property. The *Two Treatises*, it was argued, stated the fundamental principles of the Whigs, and thus served as an intellectual justification for the Glorious Revolution of 1689. The *Two Treatises of Government* provided, in short, a general philosophical defence of the rights of property-owners to institute and defend a political system based upon their consent, and a specific historical defence of the actions of the landed gentry and aristocracy in placing William and Mary on the English throne in 1689. Moreover, Locke's work, and especially the *Second Treatise*, was often characterized as the first secular expression of political theory in the modern era.

In recent years, every aspect of this long-accepted orthodoxy has been challenged by Locke scholars and historians of Restoration England. The communal, religious and traditional features of Locke's political thought which derive from his acceptance of the primary assumptions of Aristotelianism and Christianity have received considerable attention. The general thrust of this interpretative approach has been to see Locke more as a lineal descendant of medieval and Reformation political thought than as the founder of modern political theory.[1] At the same time, greater emphasis has been placed upon Locke's political activity and commitments, and especially upon the radical dimensions of his political ideas in the *Two Treatises of Government*. That work, it is now argued, was not accepted by the Whigs who came to power in the wake of the Glorious Revolution as a commonsensical expression of their political beliefs; on the contrary, they generally dissociated themselves from the anonymously authored *Two Treatises* because it contained radical ideas which were alien to their own conservative perspective.[2] Locke's political thought has simultaneously moved much closer to that of Hooker, Suarez and Aristotle on the one hand, and to the Levellers, Sidney and the Republicans on the other. Indeed, an almost complete reversal of emphasis has occurred. In place of the modern secular Locke, we are offered a traditionally religious thinker, and in place of the conservative spokesman for a landed oligarchy, contemporary interpreters have unearthed a politically revolutionary Locke surrounded by artisans, tradesmen and old Commonwealth army officers. The *Two Treatises of Government* has become a work which is at once philosophically more conservative and politically more radical.

There are other political theorists about whom more has been written, but with the possible exception of Marx it would be hard to think of an example of one who has undergone a more radical transformation than Locke within the last generation with respect to the characterization of his political thought in the secondary literature. Various aspects of the older orthodoxy still persist, of course, and are defended in books and articles on Locke published during the last decade. Nevertheless, it is fair to say that the tide has shifted in favour of the new orthodoxy – which, however, is not quite so internally homogeneous as I have sketched it above. If the latter has not yet scored a complete triumph, it has seriously undermined the foundations of the older intellectual structure. While this fact says something about the dynamic dimensions of Locke scholarship, it also reveals the perils of interpretation. All that seems solidly grounded to one generation of interpreters may melt into the air for the next.

The tension produced by these co-existing interpretative frameworks will necessarily emerge at almost every crucial point in our discussion of Locke's argument in the *Two Treatises*. Quite apart from the disagreements among various scholars as to the interpretation of a particular passage in the text, therefore, the reader needs to be aware of the broader dimensions of the controversy over the meaning of the work, viewed as a whole. The range of this controversy extends beyond any possible substantive consensus among the participants with respect to the basic precepts of Lockean political theory. For underlying the opposing interpretations of Locke's political thought are fundamental disagreements concerning the definition of political theory, the methodological principles one ought to employ in order to interpret political theory, and the epistemological ground upon which the arguments pertaining to both of these questions must ultimately rest. Our preoccupation with reading one particular text of political theory, in other words, ought not to be allowed to obscure the importance of the fact that embedded in that reading are significant differences in the assessments of the philosophical and historical meaning of Locke's political ideas, of the nature of political theory as viewed by contemporary political theorists, and of the practice of interpretation within the methodology of the social sciences.

Two problems associated with the *Two Treatises* have remained more or less impervious to the recent interpretative developments.

The first concerns the philosophical inconsistencies and logical flaws which, it is alleged, permeate that work. Plamenatz, for example, writes of the many 'ambiguities and false reasonings which spoil the second *Treatise*'. Locke's text, he argues, is so full of 'inconsistencies and confusions' and 'bad arguments' that 'the more carefully we attend to his arguments, the less intelligible they appear'.[3] Sabine is equally harsh in his pronouncements, condemning Locke for his lack of 'formal clarity' or analytical consistency. The consequence, Sabine maintains, is that Locke's political theory in the *Two Treatises* has 'no logical structure' which moves from the first principles of Locke's philosophy to the specific political propositions defended in that work.[4] Gough summarizes the point with the declaration that Locke's political theory 'is full of illogical flaws and inconsistencies'.[5] This criticism was of course formulated in terms of a particular conception of what a good political theory should look like and according to methodological criteria which placed great weight upon logical consistency, clear definitions and an analytically structured argument.

Advocates of a more historically grounded approach to Locke's thought, while they accorded less emphasis to these canons of philosophy as hermeneutic standards, did not so much deny the existence of philosophical inconsistencies in the *Two Treatises* as offer an explanatory account of their presence in terms of the importance Locke attached to certain religious or political beliefs. Even if one accepts this redistribution of emphasis in an interpretative account of Locke's political thought, however, any analysis of the text of the *Two Treatises* must still come to terms with the problem of delineating its internal structure. In this endeavour, the issue of whether there are logical errors in philosophical reasoning in Locke's argument cannot be put aside. Moreover, are these defects present to such a degree as to vitiate the cogency of Locke's argument? Do they, when added up, force one to accept Sabine's conclusion that the *Two Treatises* has no 'logical structure'?

The second intransigent problem concerns the importance of Sir Robert Filmer to Locke's argument in the *Two Treatises*. Although Locke describes his work as a single 'discourse concerning government', it has appeared to many readers to be two very different 'books'. The *First Treatise* is a sustained polemic directed against Filmer's *Patriarcha* and his attempt to demarcate the political rights and duties of seventeenth-century Englishmen through an interpretation of certain passages in the Bible. The *Second Treatise* sets forth 'the true original, extent, and end of civil government', as understood by Locke. The argument in this half of the discourse is not constrained by the debate concerning the meaning of a particular text – the Bible – which characterizes the *First Treatise*, but is more abstract and wide-ranging in its marshalling of evidence. Some interpreters have gone so far as to claim that the *First Treatise*, as 'a polemical tract', is devoid of any 'permanent importance', while the *Second Treatise*, as 'a work of philosophy' containing 'principles of universal validity', deserves its recognition as a classic in the history of political theory.[6] This conclusion owes much to the presupposition that Locke was – or should have been – writing against the only philosophically worthy opponent among his contemporaries: Thomas Hobbes. Whatever his other merits, Filmer is generally regarded as being a very poor philosopher. Hence the conclusion that the *First Treatise* is not really worthy of serious philosophical consideration. The *Second Treatise*, however, was presumed to contain Locke's reply to – or, in some interpretations, his subtle agreement with – Hobbes, and this fact placed that work among the other great books of political philosophy, such as *Leviathan* or *The Republic*.

Recent interpreters have challenged this linkage of the *Second Treatise* with Hobbes's political theory, arguing that Filmer was Locke's intellectual opponent throughout the *Two Treatises*. It is the political importance of Filmer's ideas in the context of the 1680s, and not the philosophical cogency of his position in *Patriarcha*, which justifies this reassessment of his relationship to Locke's work. While this viewpoint goes some way towards removing the older bifurcated classification of the *Two Treatises*, it does not dispose of the problem altogether.[7] Indeed, in some respects, the emphasis placed upon the historical significance of Filmer's argument only increases the difficulty of answering the original question: Why should we suppose that a critical compendium of Filmer's errors, as compiled by Locke, contains anything of lasting significance so far as contemporary students of political theory are concerned? To put it another way, even if we take Filmer's ideas more seriously, we are still faced with the distinction Locke draws between 'the false principles' of his opponent that occupy his attention in the *First Treatise* and the 'true' principles of government laid out in the second half of his discourse. To the degree that truth-claims are a constitutive part of one's definition of 'political theory', this dichotomy poses problems for the interpreter seeking to uncover a unified structure of 'the text' of the *Two Treatises*. Moreover, despite the increased attention given to Filmer by recent scholars, there is still no extended discussion of the

First Treatise in the secondary literature on Locke.[8] Yet, unless we can demonstrate the importance of Locke's critique of Filmer in the *First Treatise* to the understanding of the *intellectual* framework Locke employs in the *Second Treatise* – that is, for reasons other than the practical influence exercised by Filmer's ideas on Locke's contemporaries – the temptation to disregard the former's errors in order to move expeditiously to a consideration of the 'truth', as presented by Locke, remains a very powerful one.

In addition to these two problems bequeathed to contemporary interpreters of Locke's thought by the traditional orthodoxy, there is a newly uncovered problem which affects in a general way one's view of Locke's political thought and, to a lesser degree, one's reading of the *Two Treatises*. Until recently, virtually all interpreters began their discussion of Locke's political thought with an exegesis of the text of the *Two Treatises*. Leaving aside the fact that, as Laslett has shown, that work was written almost a decade earlier than had previously been assumed, the publication of some of Locke's early writings has provided a much more extended time-frame, from 1660 to 1690, within which to view his political thought. Not only does the *Two Treatises* represent the end product of a long process of political thinking by Locke, but it is also clear from these early manuscripts that his initial approach to politics began from a vantage-point very far removed from the one embodied in the later work. Such important aspects of Locke's political thought as natural rights, toleration, property, limitations on the magistrate's power, and the right to resistance are either absent from these early writings or, more often, are actually rejected by Locke, writing as the opponent of beliefs which later came to be identified as essential ingredients of his thought. To state the point crudely, these early writings show that Locke was not always a 'Lockean' with respect to his political theory. It is clear that a rather dramatic shift in political perspective occurred in Locke's life some time between 1660 and 1680, when he was at work on the *Two Treatises*. While this shift certainly affects one's conception of Locke's political thought, viewed as a whole, the extent to which it bears upon the interpretation of the *Two Treatises* is much less obvious.

If it were the case that *every* significant proposition in these early writings was subsequently rejected by Locke, it might be plausible to assume that one could simply begin an analysis of Locke's political thought with an examination of the *Two Treatises*. In fact, the issue is more complicated than this. For some of the presuppositions held by

Locke in these early writings are important to his later writings, even though the practical political commitments attached to those presuppositions are radically different. In other words, there are both continuities and discontinuities between Locke's early and later writings with respect to the structure of his political thought as a whole. Any attempt to reconstruct that framework, therefore, must adopt a developmental approach; that is, one capable of specifying the areas of stability and change in Locke's political theory. Moreover, unless this is done, any attempt to characterize the structure of Locke's political thought merely from a consideration of his arguments in the *Two Treatises* is, at best, incomplete and, at worst, subject to serious errors of interpretation.

These, then, are the three significant problems which must be addressed in a book which focuses upon the text of Locke's *Two Treatises of Government*. In any effort to explain the relationships that obtain between the various arguments employed by Locke in that work, the interpreter must decide (1) whether and to what extent one assumption or argument is inconsistent with respect to another, (2) whether the treatment of Filmer's ideas in the *First Treatise* is merely an adjunct to or is a necessary part of Locke's argument in the *Second Treatise*, and (3) how to relate the internal structure of the text of the *Two Treatises* to the structure of Locke's political thought as a whole.

Since I propose to say something, briefly, regarding Locke's early life and the historical context within which he undertook to write the *Two Treatises*, I will begin with a consideration of the third problem. The first step is to clarify the nature of the 'break' in Locke's political viewpoint, and to suggest some reasons for it. Then, beginning with Chapter 2, I will move from the more obvious political consequences attached to this shift in Locke's perspective to an attempt to delineate those general assumptions which retained an essential importance to the formulation of Locke's political theory throughout his life. My aim in this chapter is to uncover the basic dimensions of Locke's thought, as expressed in certain ontological presuppositions, religious beliefs and empirical generalizations about the nature of God, man and the conditions of social existence. These beliefs, I shall argue, constitute the foundation for Locke's discussion of politics.

In Chapter 3, I turn to Locke's critique of Filmer in the *First Treatise*. Locke's polemic, I suggest, is guided by certain hermeneutical principles that he employs against Filmer's interpretation of the Bible in order to undermine the claims advanced for absolute

monarchy by Filmer's political theory. In addition to this method-
ologically grounded attack, Locke argues that Filmer's theory cannot
be accommodated either to the Law of Nature as understood through
the use of human reason or to the precepts of the Scriptures as
delivered through revelation. The result, according to Locke, is that
Filmer enjoins absolute obedience to whatever political power exists,
thereby obviating the very undertaking of attempting to develop a
theory of obligation.

Filmer's conjunction of the transmission of property rights and
political authority is the focus for the discussion in Chapter 4. In
addition to offering an extension of Locke's critique of this area of
Filmer's thought, I argue that Locke develops a significant part of his
own position regarding the relationship between property and political
authority in the *First Treatise*. The separation of property and political
power, which is the axis from which Locke's attack on Filmer is
formulated, and his redefinition of the latter's notion of familial
obligations under natural law are two important elements of Locke's
political argument in the *Second Treatise* that are first stated and
defended in the *First Treatise*.

Chapter 5 is the first of four chapters devoted to an analysis of
Locke's argument in the *Second Treatise*. Beginning with the concept
of the state of nature, I suggest that Locke employs that term in order
to develop three distinguishable aspects of his political theory. First,
the state of nature describes the moral condition that Locke assumes
characterizes the natural life of all individuals. Second, there are some
actual instances in history in which individuals or countries can be
said to exist in a state of nature, and some understanding of the
empirical conditions as they pertain to these pre-political relationships
is therefore useful to the construction of a political theory. Third,
there is a very specific set of institutions and practices relating to the
establishment of an 'indifferent judge' to decide controversies among
individuals that permits Locke to draw a line separating the state of
nature from a political society, as he defines it. Hence I argue that
there is a political meaning to the state of nature, in the sense that
certain political actions taken by rulers that destroy the meaning of an
indifferent judge chosen by the community return the people to the
state of nature, whenever the government they originally instituted
has 'dissolved'. The first and third of these meanings of the concept of
the state of nature are discussed in Chapter 5.

In addition to considering the second or historical meaning of the
state of nature, Chapter 6 examines Locke's argument concerning the

origins and rights of property. As an institution, the latter, I maintain, is assumed to develop within the context of a historically defined natural condition, which is itself divided into two distinct stages. The simple social relationships that prevailed during the first ages of man's existence in the state of nature, Locke observes, can be described essentially as a subsistence form of society. The very limited amount of property owned by an individual arose within social conditions characterized by natural needs, labour and a general compliance with the Law of Nature. With the invention of money, however, the situation changes. Property relationships are extended beyond the boundaries of subsistence, through the linkage of the definition of 'use' of property to the activity of trade, so that the production of commodities for the exchange of money becomes the essential feature of the second form of the social relationships that Locke presents as part of his historical account of life in the state of nature. It is this second form of society, which is associated with the rise of cities, the establishment of legal limits to property claims, the increase of controversies over rights, and an increased need for government to act as umpire in settling these controversies, that provides the empirical basis for the emergence of political society. Thus, I argue that Locke's historical account of the state of nature and his theory of property are designed to lend support to his general theory of constitutional government outlined in the *Second Treatise*.

The details of this theory are elaborated in Chapter 7. Locke's discussion of paternal authority and its relationship to political authority forms a starting-point for this discussion, thus carrying forward some aspects of his argument treated in earlier chapters. Locke's willingness to make historical, but not ideological, concessions to paternal monarchy as a form of government in the early stages of the state of nature, I suggest, involves him in a theoretical dilemma with respect to his definition of political society, *unless* he can provide an account of the establishment of constitutional government that is sufficiently concrete as to its requisite institutional make-up to exclude paternal and absolute monarchies from the claim of being legitimate forms of government. This is precisely the path Locke chooses to follow. Therefore, both the dilemma and its resolution must be viewed in terms of Locke's ideological purposes in the *Second Treatise*; namely, to supply a political defence for a form of government in which the role of an elected legislative assembly assumes primary importance. Against the prevalent opinion in the secondary literature, I maintain that Locke did defend the natural right of every man to give his personal consent to the government as a condition of his definition of political society. Whether or not this universal consent is actually incorporated into a particular form of representative government is an empirical question, but, by the same token, I argue that Locke establishes a much closer empirical link between his notion of consent and the institutional practice of elections than has generally been assumed by interpreters of his political thought.

Chapter 8 addresses itself to Locke's theory of resistance and the conditions under which a legitimate form of government can be said to have dissolved. The general theme of this chapter, applied not only to Locke's concept of revolution but also to his treatment of usurpation, conquest and tyranny, is that these terms are rooted in an empirically grounded discussion of government in the context of the political life of seventeenth-century England. This means that Locke's political argument derives its radical character not merely from the moral assertions about natural law and natural rights that comprise one aspect of his political theory, but also from the more concrete references to the political activities of the 1680s which were familiar to the readers of the *Two Treatises of Government*. Besides justifying resistance on the part of the body of the people to a king who has forfeited the trust of political power the community placed in him, Locke also sanctions the act of tyrannicide. Although we have always been aware of the radical dimensions of the *Second Treatise* as an argument in defence of revolutionary activity, I believe it can be shown through an analysis of the text that Locke actually went much further in committing himself to the radical implications of his general theory of resistance than is commonly recognized.

In Chapter 9, I take up the problem of relating Locke's political theory to his general philosophical position, as well as to some of the specific arguments he expounds in his other writings on toleration, education, religion and economics. With respect to the first point, I suggest that Locke's efforts to formulate a theory of practical action provide the basis for any attempt to integrate the argument of the *Two Treatises* into the argument of the *Essay Concerning Human Understanding*, where the basic outlines of a theory of practical action are sketched by Locke. This discussion leads to a consideration of some problems, as stated in Locke's writings on religion, regarding the social roles he assigns to reason and religion in so far as they operate as constraints on the activities of the members of Locke's political society. Specifically, I reject Macpherson's assignment of a differential rationality to the working class, and his interpretation of *The*

Reasonableness of Christianity as the source of Locke's disparagement of the reasoning abilities of the members of this class. I maintain, on the contrary, that Locke's defence of his personal belief as to what is important about Christianity is dependent upon a theological egalitarianism explicitly defended in the *Reasonableness*, and grounded in the very same presuppositions that form the basis for the moral assumptions that structure Locke's political theory in the *Two Treatises*. Still, there is a legitimate question to be raised as to how Locke can reconcile certain egalitarian assertions with the defence of economic inequalities and with his conservative attitude expressed towards the economically disadvantaged members of his society as set forth in his writings on the subject of trade and the economy. I suggest that these two dimensions of Locke's thought provide the key for understanding the intellectual framework for liberalism as a political theory. That is, liberalism embodies, on the one hand, a radical moral egalitarianism rooted in the assumptions of theology and philosophy, and, on the other, a conservative defence of social–economic inequality, grounded in the presuppositions of an epistemology based upon experience, history, and the requirements of practical necessity.

Chapter 10 pursues this theme by providing a very brief sketch of the way in which Locke's ideas flowed into two distinctive expressions of eighteenth-century thought, each of which incorporated one of the two features of Locke's thought described above. This discussion is obviously not intended to displace a careful examination of the ideas of Burke, Paine, Hume and Rousseau in relation to the historical and political context within which they were formulated, nor does it present itself as a substitute for an analysis of the texts they wrote, according to the standards here applied to the *Two Treatises*. Rather, I have simply tried to offer the reader a heuristic guide to the study of eighteenth-century political thought, starting from what I have termed 'the structure of intentions' that directed and constrained Locke's political writings. The dissolution of that structure or, rather, its reconstruction, with a differential emphasis accorded to science, religion, economics, and political action and their interrelationships, not to mention a set of concrete problems different from those that preoccupied Locke, requires that eighteenth-century thinkers be understood in their own terms and not merely as adjuncts to Locke's political theory. Nevertheless, it is possible, I believe, to gain some appreciation of the gains and losses involved in the further 'development' of that political theory following Locke's death.

In the Appendix, I have assembled the evidence and arguments that seem to me to bear upon the writing and the dating of the *Two Treatises of Government*. I give my reasons for rejecting Laslett's assignment of the *Second Treatise* to 1679 and his assertion that it was written prior to the *First Treatise*.

The *Two Treatises of Government* is a complicated and important work, and the analysis of the text necessarily imposes some limits upon what can be undertaken within the confines of this volume. There is, for example, a need for a detailed examination of the relationship of Locke's ideas to those of Aristotle, Cicero, Hooker and other thinkers from whom Locke drew much of his inspiration. So little work has been done in this area, however, that I have chosen to leave the task to others rather than to offer an inadequate and schematic account of Locke's relationship to his intellectual predecessors. Nor have I sought to situate the writing of the *Two Treatises* in its specific historical and political context, except through a general description of this context and its bearing upon Locke's ideological purposes in the *Two Treatises*. On this point, at least, I can refer the interested reader to my discussion of this subject elsewhere.[9] What I have attempted to do in this book is to offer the reader an interpretation of the arguments and internal structure of the text of the *Two Treatises of Government*, proceeding in a more or less chronological fashion from the first to the last chapters of that work, as the reader encounters the text. In this endeavour, I have tried to defend an interpretation of the *Two Treatises* that not only reconstructs Locke's political theory, but also preserves the basic integrity of the formal structure of his text.

NOTES: INTRODUCTION

1 See, for example, James Tully, *A Discourse on Property: John Locke and His Adversaries* (Cambridge: Cambridge University Press, 1980); Quentin Skinner, *The Foundations of Modern Political Thought*, 2 vols (Cambridge: Cambridge University Press, 1978); John Dunn, *The Political Thought of John Locke* (Cambridge: Cambridge University Press, 1969).

2 Julian H. Franklin, *John Locke and the Theory of Sovereignty* (Cambridge: Cambridge University Press, 1978); J. P. Kenyon, *Revolution Principles: The Politics of Party, 1689–1720* (Cambridge: Cambridge University Press, 1977). Also see the work cited in note 9 below.

3 John Plamenatz, *Man and Society*, 2 vols (New York: McGraw-Hill, 1963). Vol. 1, pp. 211–13, 227, 235, 249, 251.

4 George H. Sabine, *A History of Political Theory*, 3rd edn (New York: Holt, Rinehart & Winston, 1961), pp. 517–40; esp. pp. 533, 537–8.

5   John W. Gough, *John Locke's Political Philosophy, Eight Studies* (Oxford: Clarendon Press, 1956), p. 123.

6   See, for example, Sabine, *History*, p. 523; Gough, *Locke's Political Philosophy*, p. 122; Maurice Cranston, 'The politics of a philosopher', *Listener*, 5 January 1961, p. 18.

7   This is the argument advanced by Peter Laslett in his introduction to the *Two Treatises*. For a defence of Filmer's importance as a political thinker, see W. H. Greenleaf, *Order, Empiricism and Politics* (London: Oxford University Press, 1964); Gordon J. Schochet, *Patriarchalism in Political Thought* (New York: Basic Books, 1975). For another view of Filmer critical of the position taken by these authors, see James Daly, *Sir Robert Filmer and English Political Thought* (Toronto: University of Toronto Press, 1979).

8   This point was most recently made by Charles D. Tarlton, 'Rope of sand: interpreting Locke's *First Treatise of Government*', *Historical Journal*, vol. 21, no. 1 (1978), pp. 43–73.

9   Richard Ashcraft, *Revolutionary Politics and Locke's 'Two Treatises of Government'* (Princeton, NJ: Princeton University Press, 1986). Although my reading of the text of the *Two Treatises* is obviously informed by the historical evidence relating to Locke's political activities during the period of its writing which is presented in my book, I have tried to refrain from making references to it in this examination of the text, except in those instances in which a particular argument is considered at greater length in *Revolutionary Politics*.

CHAPTER 1

The Development of Locke's Political Thought

Locke was 17 when Charles I was executed. It is unlikely that he or his fellow-students at Westminster School were witnesses to what their staunchly Royalist headmaster, Richard Busby, must have regarded as an injudicious murder. We do not know what Locke thought of that particular event, but his remarks on the Civil War, recorded a decade later in his correspondence and notebooks, are decidedly negative. According to Locke, 'those tragical revolutions', including the English Civil War, which have caused 'such havoc and destruction' in recent years, are the consequence of the 'zealous mistakes and religious furies' perpetrated upon a gullible multitude by a few 'crafty men' (FTG, 118).

We might have expected a somewhat more favourable assessment of the accomplishments of the English Revolution from the son of someone who had fought in Cromwell's army, and who owed his own place at Westminster to the influence of one of the latter's colonels. Moreover, Locke had been raised in a family in which Puritan sympathies were pronounced.[1] Yet, on reflection, it is clear that Locke's views were not so far removed from those of the majority of Presbyterians, who had seen their limited objectives of resistance overrun by Levellers, Republicans and radical sectarians who seemed to spring up like mushrooms as the revolution ran its course. And, in this period (1659–60), many of them, including Locke's future friend and patron, Anthony Ashley Cooper, definitely preferred a restoration of the monarchy to any relapse into the anarchy which, in their view, characterized the Interregnum period.

For most of that decade, Locke held a studentship at Christ Church, Oxford, which in the natural course of events should have led him, as it did the overwhelming majority of his college contemporaries, to accept a position in the Anglican Church. Locke, however, went to considerable lengths to avoid taking holy orders. Despite his enthusiastic endorsement of Charles II's restoration to the throne,

Locke appears never to have displayed any concomitant enthusiasm about becoming a clergyman in the re-established church. He declined the clerical appointments offered him, and sought instead to retain his studentship at Oxford through the pursuit of medicine.[2] Nevertheless, Locke's disaffiliation from Anglicanism did not extend to such lengths that, like some of his acquaintances – including his tutor, Thomas Cole – he was forced to leave the university and/or the Anglican Church altogether.[3]

It is difficult to form a distinct impression of Locke's political and religious views during his tenure at Oxford because, while he was in favour of the monarchy and even sanctioned the absolutist claims for the civil magistrate's power, he never pursued the standard royalist ideological justifications for the exercise of that political power. If Locke was a royalist in 1660, in other words, he certainly had not arrived at that conviction by thinking through the arguments attached to patriarchalism, to a divine right theory of government, or to an interpretation of English legal history, the three mainstays of the intellectual edifice of royalism. And, if Locke had personal and religious reasons for not wanting to accept clerical duties, these did not lead him to abandon the Anglican Church or even, in a more general sense, the basic dimensions of the theological framework that supplied the social and religious meaning for that institution.

However we choose to distribute the emphasis with respect to the various influences acting upon Locke between 1632 and 1665 – when he left Oxford to go abroad as part of a diplomatic mission to the Elector of Brandenburg – there seem to be counter-influences of sufficient strength as to render highly problematic any definitive claim on behalf of a particular influence in shaping Locke's political thought. Locke managed to assimilate the Puritan instruction of his youth, the Royalist tincture Busby passed on to his pupils, the fiercely Independent views of his Dean, John Owen, and the equally strongly held Anglican and Royalist convictions of Owen's successor, John Fell, without, it appears, devoting himself to the cultivation and care of the roots of any of these belief-structures. This is not to say that Locke did not subscribe to some deeply held religious beliefs, nor was the intermixture of enthusiasm and anxiety with respect to the re-established order a response peculiar to Locke among his contemporaries. Still, in terms of what we know of the later Locke, it does seem fair to say that his early political and religious opinions lacked those intellectual moorings which we might have expected from a thinker of his calibre. The evidence suggests that in the early 1660s Locke was not very sure of who he was or what role he could expect to play in society. As one scholar has remarked, Locke 'was casting around to discover and establish his own particular intellectual identity'.[4]

The underdevelopment of the broader dimensions of his thought did not, however, inhibit Locke in the employment of his polemical skills. His first writings were political tracts attacking the claims for religious toleration advanced by one of his fellow-students at Christ Church.[5] Locke's position in this early work is both simple and absolutist. There are, he argues, no grounds whatsoever for any dissent from or disobedience to the will of the civil magistrate on the part of the subject. The latter is obliged to obey all commands of the ruler, even those that are 'sinful' for him to enact as laws (FTG, 152; STG, 220). Neither toleration nor property, nor anything else, can be claimed as a natural right by the citizen. Though Locke has nothing specifically to say against the existence of a legislative body such as Parliament, his references to the civil magistrate are remarkably indifferent to the question of whether political power is shared or balanced between different branches of the government or whether it remains in the hands of a single executive. Indeed, the latter is most consistent with the logic and tone of Locke's argument in these tracts inasmuch as he never imagines the possibility of a division within government regarding particular policy decisions, nor does he wish to meddle with competing claims for legitimacy between a hereditary monarch and a representative legislature. In short, no one who defended the claims of political authority in seventeenth-century England argued for a more absolutist exercise of power than does Locke in these early writings.

Yet, as I have suggested, his argument in the *Two Tracts on Government* is both conventional and consequentialist. It may be, as Locke says, that our memory of the 'miseries' and 'calamities' of the English Civil War – 'the discord of the immediate past' – ought to be sufficient to prevent anyone from challenging 'the magistrate's power in respect of indifferent things'; but, whatever can be said on behalf of the prudential wisdom of approaching the issue from this standpoint, the intellectual scope and symmetry of the argument is hardly its most impressive or compelling feature (STG, 211–12). Locke accepts as a fundamental premiss of his position the divine authority of the Law of Nature, but beyond the fact that its precepts obviously establish the boundaries between morally prescribed and 'indifferent actions' – the latter being the focus of the controversy over toleration – he has almost nothing to say in these tracts concerning the epistemological foundations of our knowledge of natural law or the extent to which differing political theories might claim its sanctions on their behalf.

Locke was offered the chance to remedy this lacuna in his political thought when, in conjunction with his appointment as Censor of Moral Philosophy, he delivered a course of lectures on natural law in 1664. These writings, previously unknown except to a few auditors and friends, have also recently been published. The content of these essays on the Law of Nature will be more fully discussed in Chapter 2 since they have an important bearing upon any attempt to delineate the basic presuppositions of Locke's political thought prior to his writing of the *Two Treatises*, but what the work as a whole demonstrates is that Locke is attempting to locate his identity as an intellectual through a serious exploration of a subject that was at the heart of any seventeenth-century discussion of religion, philosophy or politics. In this respect, it is equally significant to record what is not included in these writings. There is no discussion of property rights, or of any natural rights, no consideration given to the problem of resistance to the magistrate, no attempt to relate the precepts of natural law to a theory about the legitimacy of particular forms of government, and no indication that Locke has changed his mind on the issue of toleration. There is, in short, nothing in Locke's essays on the Law of Nature that is incompatible with the political conservatism he expressed in the *Two Tracts on Government*.

It may seem peculiar to us that a lecturer on philosophy at Oxford could give a course of lectures on natural law without ever mentioning, let alone discussing, the views of Aquinas, Cicero or other traditional thinkers who wrote extensively on the subject.[6] It is true that both Aristotle and Hooker figure more prominently in these essays than they do in the *Tracts*, and there is also evidence that Locke has moved further away from Hobbes's perspective in these later writings. But, while these points are of some biographical interest with respect to Locke's intellectual development, the fact is that the *Essays on the Law of Nature*, viewed as a work of philosophy, is strikingly unoriginal in its treatment of the topic. In the context of the multifarious religious and political uses to which a natural law argument was put by seventeenth-century writers, Locke's essays flow through a very narrowly constructed channel of Anglican orthodoxy. Whatever benefits Locke derived from the intellectual atmosphere of Oxford in the 1650s and 1660s – and he later remarked that these benefits were few – a spirit of adventurous exploration of the wide-ranging political and philosophical dimensions of his contemporaries' arguments about politics and natural law was not among them.[7]

In November 1665, Locke left Oxford in order to serve as secretary to Sir Walter Vane, who was sent by Charles II on a diplomatic mission to the Elector of Brandenburg. The details of this mission, which, in any case, was unsuccessful, need not concern us. What is interesting, however, is that Locke appears to have been impressed by the practice of religious toleration in Cleves. He wrote to his friend Robert Boyle that all the churches in that city 'quietly permit one another to choose their way to heaven; and I cannot observe any quarrels or animosities amongst them on account of religion'. That individuals could 'entertain different opinions without any secret hatred or rancour' towards each other was transformed from an empirical observation into a basic presupposition in the course of Locke's development of an argument favouring religious toleration.[8] It is thus possible, though unlikely, that Locke's views on toleration had already changed by the time he returned to England the following year.

Although Locke obtained a dispensation enabling him to retain his studentship at Christ Church without taking orders, his future appears to have remained as unclear as it had been prior to his departure. In fact, Locke declined offers of both diplomatic and clerical positions in 1666. He continued to pursue his interest in experimental science and medicine, but the prospects for his official advancement within the university by this means were extremely dim, nor were they improved by Locke's refusal to attend the lectures or to submit to the examination required for the degree of Bachelor of Medicine. Much has been claimed for the experience Locke gained assisting Boyle, Thomas Willis and Robert Hooke in their laboratory experiments at Oxford, and even greater significance has been attached to his association with Thomas Sydenham and the practice of medicine. It may be, as is often asserted, that Locke's appreciation of the merits of an empirical approach to intellectual and social problems was enhanced through his contact with his scientific contemporaries, but since he himself claimed that his love of philosophy derived from his reading of Descartes one should be cautious about postulating a causal link between Locke's efforts to pursue a medical career and the restructuring of his intellectual *Weltanschauung*. Even in the case of philosophy, there is little evidence to suggest that any significant shift occurred in Locke's thinking, leading to the reversal or rejection of previously held views prior to his decision to leave Oxford in 1667. In other words, what the recently discovered writings on politics and morality demonstrate is that Locke's thinking on these subjects began well within accepted orthodoxy. How deeply committed Locke was to the beliefs and practices of Anglican royalism is open to question, but it is safe to say that he was a *de facto* supporter of the dominant political and intellectual assumptions that structured the social consciousness of the inhabitants of Restoration England.

If the older view of a continuous commitment on Locke's part to the tenets of liberalism must be rejected, we are still faced with the problem of supplying reasons for the change in his political perspective. In the absence of explicit statements by Locke, two explanatory accounts for this shift in his thought have been offered by scholars. The first portrays the liberalism of Locke's mature writings as the logical development of his interest in the new experimental science, which prompted him to examine certain traditionally held epistemological assumptions. On the basis of Locke's formulation of 'a new way of ideas', it is argued, he redefined his moral and political position. Thus, Lockean liberalism is not only compatible with, but – at least in an indirect sense – actually grows out of the progressive developments in natural science. Since seventeenth-century science was known as 'natural philosophy', any changes in Locke's political thought can be seen as the necessary by-product of his philosophical achievements.

Within this general explanatory framework, there are discernible differences between those who place great emphasis upon the historical significance of science as a social phenomenon and those who assign primary importance to Locke's personal quest for knowledge. Neither view represents, in my opinion, a persuasive interpretation of the evidence. With respect to the former, the problem is that it is extremely difficult to establish any clearly delineated linkage between the pursuit of scientific objectives and a particular political viewpoint in seventeenth-century England. Certainly, the overwhelming majority of the members of the Royal Society were decidedly traditional in their political and religious beliefs. Boyle, it is true, favoured religious toleration, but Thomas Sprat, the historian of the Royal Society, was an Anglican bishop and a solid royalist. Moreover, it is Sprat, rather than Boyle, who most closely typifies the membership of the Royal Society. But even if, on a very high plane of generality, one could discover a connection between a predisposition for the new science and a watered-down version of Whiggism this would hardly explain how or why Locke came to hold such distinctively radical political beliefs, from which not only the majority of Whigs but also the majority of scientists among his contemporaries consciously dissociated themselves. And, from the other side, the vast majority of those who shared the radical political perspective with Locke had little discernible interest in the advancement of the new science, except, perhaps, from the standpoint of its technological benefits. And, unless such a connection could be shown to exist, it is hard to see why Locke's scientific activities should have led him, but not many others, to adopt the political position he did. Indeed, the more importance we attribute to the growth of the natural sciences as a social feature of seventeenth-century England, the less adequately it functions as part of an explanation for the development of Locke's political thought.

Instead of this sociological approach to the problem through science, others have offered a more psychologically rooted explanation. Locke, it is said, was led, by imperceptible degrees, to question the foundations of the political arguments he expressed in his early tracts on toleration. Gradually, with the assistance supplied by his application of scientific methods, he explored the weaknesses of the traditional defences of the basic tenets of Christianity and of certain knowledge-claims advanced by philosophy. Since we are here dealing with a highly individualistic effort on Locke's part, this explanatory account is not subject to the criticism cited above, which challenges the historical and sociological basis for the general connection between science and politics being applied to Locke. It is, in fact, the uniqueness of Locke's endeavour that preserves the philosophical purity of his intellectual undertaking. Clearly, it cannot be denied that Locke possessed the ability to reconstruct a new political philosophy from the materials supplied by his inner doubts and anxieties concerning the status of his most deeply held theological and moral convictions. I do not see, therefore, how the plausibility of this interpretation, resting as it does upon the interior workings of Locke's mind, can be denied. And yet I have already indicated that I find this approach, in the last analysis, unconvincing.

The explanation for this lies in the fact that one must impute to Locke the existence of an interior dialogue grounded in the importance of epistemological problems to which there is no direct access in the evidence supplied by his journals, correspondence or manuscripts. If it is true that Locke displays a Puritan propensity for recording his thoughts and keeping an account of his activities, he does not reveal through this endeavour the Augustinian self-examination of his ideas that one finds in Richard Baxter's autobiography or, on another level, in John Bunyan's *Pilgrim's Progress*. Moreover, Locke's scientific activities began at Oxford in the 1650s and were thus viewed by him as being, in some sense, compatible with the political views he expressed in his early writings. At the same time, although he denies the existence of innate knowledge and defends the importance of sense-experience as the ground for our knowledge of the existence of God and the Law of Nature in his essays on that subject, there is little evidence to suggest that Locke perceived that any serious epistemological difficulties were attached to his position. When later, in 1671, he did address himself to this question he began, as he tells us, by considering an intellectual problem that was 'very remote' from the epistemological discussion that occupies so much of the *Essays Concerning Human Understanding*. This statement hardly lends credence to the supposition that Locke's mind was in a state of more or less constant turmoil produced by his uncertainties regarding the boundaries of knowledge. More important, Locke had already reversed himself on the major political issue of Restoration England – religious toleration – some years before he engaged in the process of re-examining the epistemological foundations of his thought. It is hardly convincing, therefore, to premiss this reversal upon an attempt to eliminate epistemological uncertainties, the existence of which do not surface until several years later. Indeed, the hypothetical relationship presumed to exist between Locke's philosophical and his political beliefs seems designed merely to preserve the importance of the former relative to the latter, rather than to explain the available evidence in the most cogent and consistent manner.

The second explanatory account reverses this emphasis, maintaining that it is precisely Locke's political volte-face that prompted him to rethink the intellectually supportive arguments attached to his new political perspective. In 1666, Locke met Anthony Ashley Cooper, later the Earl of Shaftesbury, for the first time. The two men formed a fast and a lasting friendship. Shaftesbury subsequently invited Locke to live with him in London – an offer that Locke accepted in 1667. For the next fifteen years, Locke resided as a member of Shaftesbury's household, though he occasionally made brief trips to Oxford. It is difficult to characterize more precisely Locke's status or the relationship between the two men. Locke was, first of all, Shaftesbury's friend; indeed, he was the latter's closest friend. But, in addition, Locke served as tutor to Shaftesbury's grandson, later the third Earl of Shaftesbury, the noted eighteenth-century writer and philosopher.

Locke also served as political secretary to Shaftesbury, who, as Chancellor of the Exchequer, and later Lord Chancellor, occupied the highest posts of government under Charles II, before becoming the leader of the political opposition to the Court. Locke vetted applications for the appointments Shaftesbury was entitled to make, kept a journal detailing the progress of bills in Parliament, helped the Earl with his speeches, conducted research, drafted memoranda and policy papers on political subjects, conducted correspondence concerning Shaftesbury's colonial and trading interests, performed personal and political errands, and accompanied Shaftesbury to numerous political meetings. In short, Locke was a trusted political adviser to one of the shrewdest and most powerful politicians of seventeenth-century England.

Shaftesbury already subscribed to most of the important tenets of liberalism prior to his association with Locke. He was a leading advocate of religious toleration, a staunch defender of legislative authority and the rights of Parliament, and, in Locke's words, 'an indefatigable champion' of the individual's civil liberties. With respect to Locke's liberalism, therefore, it appears, as Cranston has observed, that 'he learned [it] from Shaftesbury. For it is certainly not the case that Shaftesbury learned his liberalism from Locke.'[9] This states the point perhaps too crudely, since what is at issue is not so much a direct transmission of political values from Shaftesbury to Locke as the contention that Shaftesbury gave Locke the opportunity and the responsibility of thinking through the major political problems of the day. It was in conjunction with this process of rethinking, it is argued, that Locke refashioned his political perspective, the end product of which can be seen in his published writings of the 1690s. The second explanatory account for the shift in Locke's political thought thus maintains that political theory develops not out of the effort to find a solution to a set of philosophical problems but, rather, out of a confrontation with the practical issues that describe the day-to-day political lives of people.

Almost immediately upon joining Shaftesbury's household, Locke drafted an essay on toleration, in which he not only reversed his position on that question, but also advanced for the first time the theoretical proposition that individuals had 'an absolute and universal right' that could be claimed against the civil magistrate. In 1668, Locke wrote a manuscript on the question of lowering the rate of interest 'at the direction' of Shaftesbury. The following year he helped Shaftesbury draw up the *Fundamental Constitutions of Carolina* for the colony of which the Earl was one of the original proprietors. In 1673, Locke became Secretary to the Council of Trade and Plantations, of which Shaftesbury was the President. Later Locke helped Shaftesbury with the witnesses who testified to the existence of a 'popish plot', and, it was alleged by several of his close friends, 'assisted' Shaftesbury in the writing of tracts that expressed the latter's political viewpoint. According to Shaftesbury's grandson, his grandfather 'encouraged' Locke to become interested in the political issues of the day.

> He put him upon the study of the religious and civil affairs of the nation with whatsoever related to the business of a Minister of State, in which he was so successful that my grandfather began soon to use him as a friend, and consult with him on occasions of that kind. He was not only with him in his library and closet but in company with the great men of those times, the Duke of Buckingham, Lord Halifax, and others who were much taken with him.[10]

Whatever we may imagine Locke's internal intellectual struggles to have been, there is sufficient evidence in the writings he actually produced to establish the fact that, coincidentally with his association with Shaftesbury, Locke began to develop his interests in political and economic issues in a manner that identified his fundamental principles and general political perspective with Shaftesbury's publicly stated position. This was certainly the case with respect to Locke's writing of the *Two Treatises of Government* in the 1680s, as we shall see. Even in relation to the development of Locke's purely philosophical interests, it is fair to characterize Shaftesbury's role as that of a catalyst, since it appears to have been through his efforts that Locke was accepted as a member of the Royal Society in 1668, and it was at Shaftesbury's house in London that Locke met with a small group of friends to discuss the questions of theology and philosophy which led, eventually, to the writing of the *Essay Concerning Human Understanding*.

In addition to receiving Shaftesbury's encouragement for his intellectual pursuits, Locke's financial situation improved considerably following his association with the Earl. On the death of his father in 1661, Locke had inherited some small property whose rents provided him with a very modest income. Through Shaftesbury's efforts, however, Locke was able to obtain salaried political appointments, to invest his money profitably in commercial and colonial enterprises, and to exchange some of his property holdings for an annuity of £100 provided by Shaftesbury.[11] From 1667 to the end of his life, Locke's annual income probably never fell below £200, and in some years, especially those following the Glorious Revolution, it reached a figure many times that amount. Locke was thus able to live in a style suitable to that of a middle-class gentleman.

Not only did Locke and Shaftesbury agree on political matters, but they also shared the same attitude on the importance of international trade and the industrious application of labour to the cultivation of land as necessary ingredients of England's economic well-being. Shaftesbury is the typical example of a seventeenth-century capitalist landlord, colonial proprietor and commercial investor. As Cranston remarks, he might almost have been invented by Marx as part of a historical explanation for the development of capitalism in England. He was the leading spokesman for 'the trading interests' of the nation, which, through his own activities, he did so much to promote. In the 1668 manuscript on the lowering of the interest rate that he wrote for Shaftesbury, Locke argued not only that the advancement of trade would produce riches for England, but also that the economic system as a whole functioned best when its natural tendencies were allowed to operate without governmental interference. So long as artisans and manufacturers were encouraged to produce commodities for exchange, and the quantity and circulation of money remained at a level sufficient 'to drive the wheels of trade', Locke believed the economy would develop in a healthy manner. This growth was threatened by monopolies, the wasteful use of resources – especially land – idleness, and an insufficient labouring population, as well as by the exercise of arbitrary political power on the part of the government.[12]

In 1670 the Anglican Church, with some assistance from the king and Parliament, launched a renewed attack upon nonconformists in an effort to suppress, once and for all, religious dissent. The most influential defence of this policy was provided by Samuel Parker in his *A Discourse of Ecclesiastical Polity*, to which virtually all the leading dissenters, and many others, wrote replies. Locke made several pages of notes in the form of replies to specific points in Parker's book and, although these notations are caustically cryptic, what they reveal, taken together, is that Locke's views supporting religious toleration and the proposition that all political authority is grounded in the consent of the people have begun to crystallize into a political perspective at odds with the one he had previously endorsed. Locke rejects any claim by the civil magistrate or clerical authorities to a privileged or superior knowledge of the individual's religious obligations, and he dissociates himself from 'Mr. Hobbes's doctine' of absolute political power.[13] Thus, by 1670, Locke's polemical skills are being deployed – albeit in unpublished writings – on behalf of a perspective associated with a minority of religious dissenters in Restoration England.

It is in this context that Locke first began to explore the epistemological dimensions of his thought during the winter of 1670–1. In the early draft of the *Essay Concerning Human Understanding*, Locke is especially concerned to show that most of our beliefs fall under the category of 'probable knowledge' rather than of certainty. This is particularly true of the religious opinions which, from childhood, we are taught by others to 'swallow down' without subjecting these beliefs to a careful examination. The primary thrust of Locke's argument is that, in place of the 'received principles' of theology or philosophy imbibed from their parents or teachers, individuals ought to rely upon 'the clear evidence' supplied by sense-experience and their 'faculty of reasoning'. The practical consequences attached to this epistemological viewpoint are obvious; for if 'most of those propositions we think, argue, reason, discourse, nay, act upon, are not evident and certain', then they are matters about which someone may offer 'arguments to persuade us' to accept as the truth, but they cannot be transformed into enforceable decrees by the church or the state on the presupposition that either institutional authority can lay claim to the possession of 'certain knowledge' (*Early Draft*, pp. 55–6, 61–9). Moreover, since in the case of our 'assent' to statements of probable knowledge we suppose, according to Locke, that the individual engages in a 'voluntary action' of his will, this means that we must expect a diversity of viewpoints regarding the truth of various propositions as the normal result of this infinitude of free choices on the part of individuals. In other words, given the probable status of most knowledge-claims and the exercise of free will by individuals, differences of opinion, even on the most important subjects, must be looked upon as an inherent feature of human action and the pursuit of knowledge. Quite apart from the moral repulsiveness of persecuting individuals for holding certain religious beliefs, therefore, such a political policy makes no sense in terms of an understanding of the process by which human beings acquire 'knowledge'.

In addition to discussing specific points in the *Essay Concerning Human Understanding* as they illuminate particular arguments in the

Two Treatises in the chapters below that focus upon that text, I will later relate in a more general way Locke's writings on philosophy, toleration, economics and other topics to the main principles of his political thought. What I have argued thus far is that, biographically speaking, the development of Locke's political thought occurs in a context in which he is simultaneously rethinking his position regarding the fundamental problems of philosophy, economics and theology. The reformulation of Locke's political thought represents not merely a pragmatic shift of partisanship from one side to the other within the political spectrum of Restoration England; rather, it reflects Locke's effort to discover the theoretical and practical means by which the social and political existence of his contemporaries could be reconstructed according to the principles of 'Lockean' liberalism.

In 1670, Charles II negotiated a treaty of alliance with Louis XIV on the basis of which England and France launched a war against Holland. England's primary objective was to recover some of the trade it had lost to the Dutch, especially in the New World. For reasons that are still a matter of controversy among historians, however, Charles II also signed a secret treaty with the French king from whom he received subsidies in exchange for which he promised at some indeterminate time to declare publicly his conversion to Roman Catholicism. Nothing haunted the imagination of the seventeenth-century Englishman so much as the prospect that Catholicism would become the ruling ideology of the nation. Most people had little understanding of the intricacies of Catholic theology; what they feared and disliked was the theory of political and religious authority they associated with the institutionalization of Catholicism. That is, Locke's contemporaries believed that Catholics subjected their consciences to a spiritual tyranny exercised by the Pope, and that Catholic monarchs subscribed to a political theory of absolutism. Hence the return of Catholicism to England meant to them not merely the religious persecution of Protestants, but also the substitution of the king's will for parliamentary government, the confiscation of property formerly owned by the Catholic Church, and the imposition of a whole way of life that they regarded as being alien to their most fundamental beliefs.

Charles may or may not have been a secret Catholic all his life, but his brother, James, successor to the throne, was by 1673 openly worshipping as a Catholic. In that year Shaftesbury very likely learned of the secret clauses of the Treaty of Dover and, when he was relieved of his duties as Lord Chancellor by the king, he entered upon a course that during the next decade was to make him the leader of the political opposition to Charles II. Along with the Duke of Buckingham, Shaftesbury became a prominent spokesman for the interests of the dissenters and for a virulently anti-Catholic strain of Protestantism. In a notorious pamphlet published in 1675, *A Letter from a Person of Quality to His Friend in the Country*, Shaftesbury's views were succinctly summarized in the form of a critique of the political objectives of the Anglican hierarchy and some of Charles II's ministers of state. Shaftesbury asserted that individuals from these two groups had for some years been attempting to create 'a distinct party' of old cavaliers who subscribed to the view that both the monarchy and the church hierarchy exercised their authority by divine right. Since such authority could not 'be bounded or limited by any human laws', Shaftesbury declared that their intention was 'to take away the power and opportunity of parliaments to alter any thing in church or state'. If this 'party' were successful, he warned, Englishmen would find themselves living under an absolute monarchy, supported by a standing army, and the state-imposed religion of Catholicism.[14]

The *Letter* caused a sensation, and within two days of its appearance on the streets of London it was condemned to be publicly burned. An attempt was made to discover its author, who, if not Shaftesbury himself, was certainly someone very close to the Earl. Many of Locke's friends believed that he had written the *Letter* or, more probably, had a hand in its writing, and for a century and a half the tract was included in Locke's published works. It is very likely, though difficult to prove, that Locke did assist Shaftesbury in writing the *Letter*. At any rate, he hurriedly left England a few days after the House of Lords Committee was named to discover and punish its author, and for the next four years Locke travelled throughout France. During this period, Locke's journal notations reveal that he continued to think through the problems of demarcating the boundaries between faith and knowledge, reason and revelation, which were central, on the one hand, to his definition of the limits of the human understanding and, on the other, to the claims of toleration. Locke also purchased a great number of voyage or travel books, and some of his observations drawn from these works of comparative anthropology were later incorporated into both the *Essay Concerning Human Understanding* and the *Two Treatises of Government*.

Meanwhile, Shaftesbury, Buckingham and the opposition to the Court were trying to bring about the dissolution of Parliament, thereby ensuring that new elections would be held. Neither their parliamentary nor their propaganda efforts succeeded in persuading the king to take this action. But at the end of 1678 several individuals of questionable character, the most infamous of whom was Titus Oates, unleashed a state of national hysteria with the story that there was a popish plot to assassinate Charles II, the result of which would place his Catholic brother on the throne. As more and more witnesses appeared, the scope of the plot grew to truly frightening – and highly imaginative – proportions. Yet, beneath the undergrowth of perjury and fiction, a few solid pieces of disturbing evidence were discovered that lent credence to the claims of a conspiracy to restore Catholicism to England. Charles II could neither ignore nor gain control of the unfolding plot. Shaftesbury was in the forefront of those in the hunt for the popish agents and sympathizers within the government. One response to the alleged conspiracy was the introduction of a bill in the House of Commons that proposed to exclude any Catholic from succeeding to the throne. This bill of exclusion was aimed at preventing James, Duke of York, from inheriting the crown, in the event that anything did happen to Charles. The political pressure produced by the Popish Plot, coupled with a renewed series of financial intrigues with Louis XIV, eventually forced the king to dissolve Parliament in 1679.

The 'Exclusion Crisis' period (1679–81) witnessed: (1) three national elections, more than have been held in any two-year period in British history; (2) a gigantic surge in the publication of political tracts and pamphlets the volume of which, in the seventeenth century, was exceeded only during the Civil War years; and (3) the formation of distinct political party organizations, the Whigs and the Tories. The anti-Catholic propaganda prompted by the Popish Plot, the effort to exclude James from the throne, and the struggle between the House of Commons and the king all served to polarize the nation into two opposing factions, and this division was deepened by the elections, the propaganda, and the development of political parties. Using his considerable leadership skills, Shaftesbury orchestrated the opposition to Charles II and the Tories. The Whigs mounted massive petition campaigns, and they created an impressive network for distributing their political literature published in London to all parts of England in an effort to win the country gentry and yeomanry over to their side. In each of the three parliamentary elections, the Whigs elected an increasingly large number of their supporters. At each session of Parliament, the Commons passed the Exclusion Bill, refusing to grant the king any appropriation of money until he had given his assent to the legislation.

Nevertheless, Charles II refused to accede to this demand. He used his royal prerogative to prorogue or dissolve Parliament in order to interrupt the legislative progress of the Exclusion Bill. When the House of Lords demonstrated their agreement with the king by defeating the measure by sixty-three votes to thirty in November 1680, the legal efforts by the Whigs to block the succession of James, for all practical purposes, came to an end. A third elected Parliament was called to meet at Oxford in March 1681, but it was abruptly dissolved by Charles II after only five days, and for the remaining four years of his reign he ruled England without calling a legislative assembly into session.

Locke had been recalled from France by Shaftesbury in the spring of 1679 because the latter desired the advice and assistance of his most trusted friend during this political crisis. Although few letters between Locke and Shaftesbury have survived, it is clear that Locke did resume his political duties for the Earl. That is, Locke identified himself with the cause of the Whigs. And as the most radical wing of the party, led by Shaftesbury, moved towards the justification of a theory of active resistance to the government, especially after the dissolution of the Oxford Parliament, Locke's political views likewise became increasingly radical. The *Two Treatises of Government* was one of a small handful of revolutionary tracts written during the 1680s defending the right of subjects to take up arms against the government.

The issue of resistance, however, emerged only gradually out of the political controversy generated by the Exclusion Bill. Initially, the debate was much more narrowly constructed around the question of whether a law passed by Parliament could be applied to the heir apparent. Legislation already existed that barred Catholics from holding public offices in the military or the government. But could Parliament apply that law to prevent James's succession without altering the constitutional form of government? According to what claim for authority could such an action be justified? If, on the other hand, James did become king, were Protestants bound to obey the commands of a Catholic prince, whose religion pronounced them 'heretics' and fit objects for persecution? Are there any limits to the individual's obedience to the civil magistrate? These questions could not be answered without reference to a theory stating the nature and origins of political obligation. The Exclusion Crisis, therefore, posed directly the problem of formulating a theory of political authority.

The simplest response to this dilemma was, of course, a defence of the king's absolute power. According to this view, not only was the king superior to and above any legislation enacted by Parliament, but also, since the king's will was law, there could be no grounds for any individual's disobedience to his commands. Although several arguments had been developed earlier in the century to support this position, no theory was as resolute in its exclusion of exceptions as the principled defence of absolutism produced by Sir Robert Filmer. Filmer had written *Patriarcha: or, The Power of Kings* some years before his death in 1653, but the manuscript had never been published, though it had achieved wide circulation even as an unpublished work. When it did appear in print in 1680, its relevance to the Exclusion debate was immediately recognized by participants on both sides. Here was a theory that combined arguments for a hereditary monarchy (thus denying the legitimacy of Parliament's attempts to interfere with the succession) with an analogical argument linking the role of the king in society to the father's role within the family, thereby drawing support for the former's exercise of power from the everyday social practices of individuals raised in a society in which the patriarchal family was the dominant socializing institution. Both of these defences were ultimately grounded in a theory of the divine right of kings. Filmer maintained that God had granted political power to Adam by direct appointment and that this power was transmitted to posterity through Adam's heirs. Not only was Filmer's argument derived from and dependent upon an interpretation of the Scriptures, but it was also an interpretation of the Law of Nature. In other words, Filmer tried to unify several defences of absolutism into one comprehensive theoretical framework supported by theology, the Bible and a belief in natural law. Despite the extremism of certain propositions contained in Filmer's theory, therefore, it is hardly surprising that *Patriarcha* served as the focal point for the ideological defence of royalist absolutism in the 1680s.

Many Whigs besides Locke wrote replies to Filmer, defending the right of Parliament or the people to make adjustments in the political system. Precedents from English history were frequently cited to prove that Parliament had intervened in the past in order to alter the line of monarchical succession. Moreover, according to the adherents of this approach, the king could not exercise absolute authority without destroying the balance of the ancient constitution which distributed political power among king, lords and commons. While this argument was responsive to some of the defences of royal authority advanced by the Tories, it was wholly inadequate as a reply to Filmer or to any natural law theory which staked its claims for authority on higher ground than mere historical precedent.

Most Whigs accepted the proposition that political power was ultimately derived from the consent of the people, although the difficulty of specifying what this statement meant in a historical or sociological sense was often passed over in silence. A number of Whig theorists, including Locke, developed a natural law defence of the people's right to delegate political power to their representatives. Hence a freely elected Parliament had every right to act in the interest of the common good of the people by excluding a Catholic from the throne. Indeed, as the radical Whigs argued, if this parliamentary enforcement of the common good failed, the people retained the right, under natural law, to act in their own defence to prevent James from becoming king.

After the dissolution of the Oxford Parliament, Shaftesbury and a few other Whigs began to develop plans for the practical implementation of this principle; that is, through organized armed resistance to Charles II. The latter suspected as much, and had Shaftesbury arrested on 2 July 1681. However, the government had little evidence to support these suspicions of treasonable activity, and the London grand jury impanelled to hear the case refused to issue an indictment. Just prior to Shaftesbury's hearing, John Dryden's *Absalom and Achitophel*, one of the most powerful political poems ever written, was published. Though it failed to sway the jury, Dryden's work was an immediate bestseller, and probably the single most effective piece of Tory propaganda published during the Exclusion Crisis. Following Shaftesbury's acquittal, Dryden published another poem, *The Medal*, which, though less successful politically or aesthetically than his earlier work, was an even more bitter attack upon the Whigs' political objectives.

In many respects, Dryden's efforts set the tone for the political atmosphere that prevailed in England throughout 1682. Whig and Tory writers engaged in a fierce propaganda war in which 'treason', 'conspiracy' and 'rebellion' were frequently employed as characterizations of the actions of the author's opponents. In addition, Shaftesbury and Charles II battled to gain or retain control over the election of the sheriffs of London, who, through their control of the composition of juries, played a crucial role in determining the outcome of the judicial process. When the Whigs lost this battle through the election of two Tory sheriffs in July 1682, Shaftesbury's plans for a revolution assumed a new sense of urgency. With the assistance of a few prominent Whigs, including Charles II's favourite illegitimate son, the Duke of Monmouth, Shaftesbury proposed to mount a three-pronged attack on the government. Simultaneously with an uprising in London, there would be a revolt in the west of England, and also some form of internal rebellion in Scotland led by Shaftesbury's allies in that country. Since most Whigs would have nothing to do with any plan for rebellion, it represented the extreme response to the political situation by a small minority of radicals, most of whom were drawn from the ranks of artisans, tradesmen and labourers. It is, however, extremely significant for the purpose of understanding the political argument of Locke's *Second Treatise* to recognize that it was written in the language and from the standpoint of this minority of radical Whigs.

In the event, the difficulty of raising the money needed to buy arms and to underwrite the participation of the Scots in the rebellion, the hesitancy of some radicals to translate their ideological commitment into military action, and the differences of opinion among the leaders regarding the timing of such action were sufficient to prevent the realization of these revolutionary plans. When the newly elected Tory sheriffs of London assumed office in September 1682, Shaftesbury went into hiding, staying at the houses of several of his supporters in the city. When it seemed to him that his colleagues either would not or could not begin the rebellion on the day appointed (19 November), Shaftesbury left England that evening for Holland, where, a few months later, he died in exile. While Shaftesbury's death was a serious blow to the radicals' political organization, they did not abandon their plans for armed resistance. By early spring 1683 meetings were being held daily for the purpose of implementing the original three-pronged attack devised by Shaftesbury. At some point in the autumn of 1682 a scheme for assassinating both Charles II and James had been developed as an adjunct to or substitution for the general uprising. This proposal was also being seriously considered by the radicals in 1683. However, on 12 June one of the conspirators confessed the existence of these plans to a secretary of state, and through the arrests and confessions of other participants the dimensions of the entire conspiracy began to unfold. Because the assassination had been designed to take place as the king's carriage passed by a public tavern – the Rye House, owned by one of the radicals – on Charles II's return to London from the horse-races at Newmarket, all of the radicals' activities directed against the government were subsumed, rather misleadingly, under the general heading of the Rye House Plot.

Even after Shaftesbury's death, Locke continued to associate with those who were deeply involved in this conspiracy, which indicates, I believe, the strength of his own political commitment to the radical cause. With the discovery of the Rye House Plot, those conspirators who escaped arrest fled to Holland. Locke, too, became an exile. For the next six years he lived in Holland as part of a sizeable community of radical exiles and fugitives from England and Scotland. The latter continued their plotting against Charles II, and when, on his death in 1685, James II became the first Catholic king of Great Britain in over a century the exiles mounted an invasion force that sailed from Holland under the general leadership of the Duke of Monmouth. After a few skirmishes and one major battle, this abortive attempt to overthrow James II (Monmouth's Rebellion) was crushed by the king's forces. In addition to those killed or executed in the trials that followed the fighting, hundreds of Monmouth's supporters, mostly artisans and labourers, were transported to America. A few radicals managed to escape arrest and return to Holland, where they awaited a more favourable opportunity to reclaim their political rights as Englishmen.

Between 1685 and 1688, Locke wrote the *Letter Concerning Toleration*, reworked the earlier drafts of the *Essay Concerning Human Understanding* into its final form, developed through his correspondence with his friend Edward Clarke the substance of what became *Some Thoughts Concerning Education* and, of course, revised and added to his manuscript of the *Two Treatises of Government*. It was during this period, in short, that Locke's thoughts on a variety of interrelated issues and problems that had occupied his attention for a number of years came to fruition. All the above works, in addition to a revised version of a manuscript he had written for Shaftesbury in 1668, *Some Considerations on the Lowering of the Rate of Interest*, were published within two years of each other, following Locke's return to England in the wake of the Glorious Revolution of 1689, which placed William and Mary on the English throne.

Locke declined William's offer of an ambassadorial appointment and accepted instead a minor position within the new government. Some of his friends, notably John (Lord) Somers and Lord Mordaunt, now the Earl of Monmouth, were among the most powerful of William III's Whig advisers, and there was a small coterie of members of the House of Commons with whom Locke was very influential. However, at this point in his life, Locke appears to have preferred to remain largely on the sidelines politically, counselling his friends through letters and memoranda he drafted for their consideration. He did become embroiled in a controversy over whether 'clipped money' should be recalled from circulation and revalued coins should be issued by the government. Locke's *Further Considerations Concerning the Raising the Value of Money* urging the government to undertake a recoinage prompted so many letters and replies and, as he later said, cost him so much time that it probably reinforced the wisdom of his decision to withdraw from the 'bustle' of political affairs. Both the *Letter Concerning Toleration* and the *Two Treatises of Government* were published anonymously, and except for infrequent passing remarks recorded in his journals or correspondence Locke had relatively little to say about politics during the remaining fourteen years of his life.

Though he was very active in writing defences of his various publications and in making revisions for new editions of them, after 1692 Locke lived a life of semi-retirement in the countryside just outside London. His health suffered when he was in the city, especially during the winter, and he accepted the offer of a residence at the home of Sir Francis Masham at Oates in Essex. Lady Masham, formerly Damaris Cudworth, the daughter of the Cambridge Platonist philosopher Ralph Cudworth, was an extremely well read and intelligent person. She and Locke had been friends and correspondents in the 1680s before her marriage to Sir Francis, who was a Member of Parliament for the county of Essex.

It was at Oates that Locke wrote his last major – and, in many respects, his most radical – work, *The Reasonableness of Christianity*. Nothing is required of any Christian, Locke argued, but to believe that Jesus is the Messiah. Since the essence of Christianity and the requirements for the individual's salvation could be reduced to acceptance of this proposition, and since anyone could through his or her own efforts derive an understanding of this truth from reading the Bible, Locke believed he had freed religion from its dependence upon the impositions of authority and externally enforced discipline. The argument of the *Reasonableness* was both strenuously attacked by conservative critics and logically extended by admirers who were even more extreme in their religious views than was Locke.

In 1696 a new Board of Trade was created, and Locke was named one of the commissioners by the king. Though he might have declined on account of his poor health, Locke accepted the appointment and, in fact, played a leading role in the activities of the Board. The Board was responsible not only for all matters concerning Britain's trade, but also for overseeing the administration of its far-flung colonial empire.

The work made great demands on Locke's time. Despite the honour with which he viewed his appointment, Locke more than once considered resigning his place, which he finally did after four years' service. As Locke wrote to a friend, he had decided to spend the remainder of his life in rest, study and religious meditation. The last four years of Locke's life were devoted to these pursuits, and on 28 October 1704 he died quietly while Lady Masham read to him from the Bible.

NOTES: CHAPTER 1

1   Maurice Cranston, *John Locke: A Biography* (London: Longmans, Green, 1957), p. 3.
2   H. R. Fox-Bourne, *The Life of John Locke*, 2 vols (1876), Vol. 1, p. 131; *Two Tracts on Government*, ed. Philip Abrams (Cambridge: Cambridge University Press, 1967, introduction, p. 56; Cranston, *Locke*, pp. 96–7.
3   Thomas Cole became a popular Independent preacher in London in the 1670s, and later the head of a dissenting academy. Walter Wilson, *The History and Antiquity of Dissenting Churches*, 4 vols (1808–14), Vol. 3, pp. 79–80.
4   *Two Tracts*, ed. Abrams, introduction, p. 58.
5   See the work edited by Abrams cited in note 2 above.
6   It is W. von Leyden's view that Locke did read Aquinas, although there is no evidence to support this assertion in Locke's journals, notebooks or library catalogue: *Essays on the Law of Nature*, ed. W. von Leyden (Oxford: Clarendon Press, 1954), introduction, p. 36.
7   'I have often heard him say, in reference to his first years spent in the University,' Lady Masham wrote of Locke, 'that he had so small satisfaction there from his studies that he became discontented with his manner of life': cited in Cranston, *Locke*, p. 38.
8   *The Correspondence of John Locke*, ed. E. S. De Beer, 8 vols (Oxford: Clarendon Press, 1976–85), Vol. 1, p. 228.
9   Maurice Cranston, 'The politics of John Locke', *History Today*, September 1952, pp. 619–22; esp. pp. 620–1.
10 Jean LeClerc, *An Account of the Life and Writings of John Locke*, 3rd edn (1714), pp. 8, 10; *Two Treatises of Government*, ed. Peter Laslett, 2nd edn (Cambridge: Cambridge University Press, 1967), introduction, p. 26; Cranston, *Locke*, p. 159.
11 ibid., pp. 70, 114–15; Fox-Bourne, *Life of Locke*, Vol. 1, pp. 432.
12 *The Works of John Locke*, 12th edn, 9 vols (1824), Vol. 4, pp. 8–9, 15, 20, 28–9, 39. In a manuscript note, Locke argues that the exercise of 'arbitrary power' to arrest and imprison individuals is amongst the 'hindrances of trade', while 'freedom of religion' is one of the 'promoters of trade' (MS c.30, fol. 18).
13 Some of these notes are reprinted in Cranston, *Locke*, pp. 131–3.
14 This tract was included in the published works of Locke until the end of the nineteenth century. I have stated my reasons elsewhere (*Revolutionary Politics and Locke's 'Two Treatises of Government'* (Princeton, NJ: Princeton University Press, 1986), ch. 3) for assuming that, at the very least, Locke 'assisted' in the writing of *A Letter from a Person of Quality*. The views of Shaftesbury cited in the text can be found in *Works of John Locke*, Vol. 9, pp. 201–2, 226.

CHAPTER 2

The Foundations of Lockean Political Theory

'There is', Locke insists, 'one science . . . incomparably above all the rest . . . I mean theology, which, containing the knowledge of God and his creatures, our duty to him and our fellow creatures, and a view of our present and future state, is the comprehension of all other knowledge directed to its true end, i.e., the honour and veneration of the Creator, and the happiness of mankind. This is that noble study which is every man's duty, and every one that can be called a rational creature is capable of' (*Works*, 2:360). Throughout his life, Locke subscribed to this basic proposition. Some of the earliest notations recorded in his journals schematically represent the branches and sub-branches of knowledge which flow from these main divisions according to the priorities stated in the above quotation. Knowledge pertaining to the spiritual universe and its laws is of the highest order; below this level is a knowledge of the foundations of political society, the science of bodies and the physical world, and the nature of moral phenomena. The architectonic importance of theology, both for its comprehensiveness as the intellectual framework within which all knowledge is accorded its meaning, and for its existential significance as the key to an understanding of all human action, is a constant feature of Locke's thought.[1]

In the *Essay Concerning Human Understanding*, Locke informs the reader that 'the main end' of his inquiry is 'the knowledge and veneration' of God, because that is 'the chief end of all our thoughts and the proper business of all understandings' (2:7, 6; cf. 1:1, 5; 2:23, 12; 4:12, 11). Hence 'religion, law and morality . . . are matters of the highest concernment' and supply the framework for the rest of our thoughts (3:9, 22). In the *Second Treatise*, Locke premises his discussion of political theory upon the supposition that 'men being all the workmanship of one Omnipotent and infinitely wise Maker . . . [they] are sent into the world by his order and about his business' (II, 6). This hierarchical ordering of ideas and actions recurs throughout

Locke's writings. In order to appreciate what importance the argument of the *Two Treatises of Government* – indeed, *any* political argument – could have had for Locke, therefore, we need to have some idea of the criteria and presuppositions he employed in his treatment of political phenomena.

Locke was hardly alone among his contemporaries in the general viewpoint he adopted, and, were it not for our distance from the seventeenth century in temperament and philosophical outlook, the fact that the nature and role of God are essential to an understanding of his social and political ideas would scarcely be worth mentioning. We could simply assume, as Locke did, the Deity's importance and pass immediately to a consideration of the implications of that assumption as they relate to some particular topic. It is precisely Locke's conviction that no one would deny the validity of this essential presupposition that renders unnecessary, from his standpoint, a detailed elaboration of all the interrelated assumptions and arguments that he attaches to this premiss. It seems a worthwhile endeavour as a preface to our discussion of the *Two Treatises*, however, to spell out the dimensions of this network of shared beliefs, not only for the interpretative light they may later shed upon particular passages in that work, but also because, as was stated in the Introduction, in order to appreciate the continuities and discontinuities between Locke's early and later political writings we require some reference-point rooted in the basic structure of his thought. And this, as Locke indicates, entails an understanding of theology, as he has defined it.

Naturally, a belief in the existence of God constitutes the bedrock of Locke's religious perspective, but this belief is so widely shared by the audience to whom Locke's writings are addressed that it might better be characterized as a given axiom of his thought. The opening paragraph of the first essay on the Law of Nature clearly establishes the tone of Locke's viewpoint:

> Since God shows Himself to us as present everywhere and, as it were, forces Himself upon the eyes of men . . . I assume there will be no one to deny the existence of God, provided he recognizes either the necessity for some rational account of our life, or that there is a thing that deserves to be called virtue or vice. This then being taken for granted, and it would be wrong to doubt it, namely, that some divine being presides over the world. (*ELN*, 109)

Two corollary beliefs stated in this passage are so inextricably linked with Locke's affirmation of God's existence that they must also be included under the category of axioms of his thought. The first is that anyone 'who would pass for a rational creature' must believe in God. Both in the *Essay Concerning Human Understanding* and in his journals, Locke repeatedly insists upon the point that part of what it means to be a 'rational creature' involves the recognition 'that some divine being presides over the world'. Not only would it be 'wrong' to deny this truth of human existence, according to Locke, it would also be irrational.[2] The second and related assumption is that the foundation of all morality rests upon the acceptance of God as the creator of the world.

> The belief of a Deity is . . . the foundation of all morality and that which influences the whole life and actions of men, without which a man is to be counted no other than one of the most dangerous sorts of wild beasts and so incapable of all society.[3]

As soon as the existence of God is conceded, Locke maintains, 'the notion of a universal law of nature binding on all men necessarily emerges' (*ELN*, 133). In other words, in so far as individuals claim to be rational and moral beings, they must share Locke's belief in the Deity, for 'the taking away of God, though but even in thought, dissolves all' human bonds and renders them 'incapable' of society.[4] It is 'the idea of a supreme Being, infinite in power, goodness, and wisdom, whose workmanship we are, and on whom we depend; and the idea of ourselves, as . . . rational beings', according to Locke, that supplies the 'foundations of our duty and rules of action' (4:3, 18). Given this inclusive and interdependent relationship of Locke's conceptions of rationality, morality and belief in God's existence, it follows that the latter is a prerequisite for membership in political society. Any theory purporting to offer an account of the origins or nature of political society must, therefore, presuppose the existence of this religious belief *as well as the further assumptions concerning the nature of mankind that it entails* in the consciousness of the individuals who constitute that society.

That individuals cannot be rational or moral in a world without God is simply the negative phraseology of Locke's positive insistence that the capacity of human beings to be rational or moral is dependent upon their having been created in a certain way and for certain purposes by the Deity. 'According to His infinite and eternal wisdom', Locke observes, God has made man such that his moral duties 'follow from his very nature'. Hence 'natural law stands or falls together with the nature of man as it is at present' (*ELN*, 201). Locke is arguing that the mere existence of God is an insufficient ground for our understanding of morality unless we add to that fact some appreciation of His purposes or intentions. God has not only put us here; He intends us to do something (*ELN*, 157).

> It does not seem to fit in with the wisdom of the Creator to form an animal that is most perfect and ever active, and to endow it abundantly above all others with mind, intellect, reason, and all the requisites for working, and yet not assign to it any work, or again, to make man alone susceptible of law precisely in order that he may submit to none. (*ELN*, 117)

The ideas of rationality or morality that individuals hold are thus not only linked with their *idea* of God; their meaning must also derive, in part, from the nature of the specific activities in which they engage. To render a judgement on this matter, however, we need to know what God wishes us to do or not to do. It is important to recognize that, for Locke, all discussions of morality begin from some statement of the imputed intentions of God (however problematic from an epistemological standpoint these imputations subsequently turn out to be), and that these purposes have a built-in naturalistic quality to them which makes them appear to be reflections of our perception of the way things are. Thus, he writes,

> [The Law of Nature] does not depend on an unstable and changeable will, but on the eternal order of things. For it seems to me that certain essential features of things are immutable, and that certain duties arise out of necessity and cannot be other than they are. And this is not because . . . [God] could not have created man differently. Rather, the cause is that, since man has been made such as he is, equipped with reason and his other faculties . . . there necessarily result from his inborn constitution some definite duties for him, which cannot be other than they are. (*ELN*, 199)

The performance of 'certain duties', like the consciousness of certain ideas, is a prerequisite feature of the individuals who create a political society. Unless these duties are performed, politics can have no meaning for Locke.

Now, it is obviously crucial to the further development of Locke's argument that we should have a clear idea of what these duties are. And since we have already gathered from his remarks cited above that any statement of these duties will be contained in the Law of Nature this means that a knowledge of the content of that law is an essential precondition to the performance of those duties. There are, however, two fundamental problems that arguably demand attention before one proceeds to a consideration of these divinely imposed prescriptions. The first is: how do we know that the Law of Nature is a 'law'? What makes it a law, and how do we come to have obligations to obey this or any set of rules that forms part of 'the eternal order of things'? The second problem is that, even if some formal and authoritative answer is provided for the first question, how can human beings through their activities and social relationships ever hope to know, much less fulfil, in practice, the requirements of natural law? Regardless of its specific content, therefore, we need to be assured that natural law is a law, and that human beings possess the ability to perform the actions it requires of them.

According to Locke, 'certain facts . . . are necessarily presupposed in the knowledge of any and every law'; namely, that 'there is a law-maker' who is directly responsible for the existence of the law (*ELN*, 151, 173). Moreover, he insists, 'without a notion of a law-maker, it is impossible to have a notion of a law, and an obligation to observe it' (1:4, 8; cf. 1:3, 12). This voluntarist conception in which a law is defined in terms of an action taken by an existent being is consistently defended by Locke. The rule enacted may be rational – and in the case of the Law of Nature it certainly is – but whether or not it is in fact a 'law' does not depend upon anyone's definition of rationality, but simply upon a recognition of the status of the lawmaker. In his essays on natural law, Locke explained, 'That thing binds "effectively" which is the prime cause of all obligation . . . namely the will of a superior. For we are bound to something for the very reason that he, under whose rule we are, wills it' (*ELN*, 185). This 'formal cause of obligation' assumes a precedence in Locke's argument not only because it reflects the influence of scholasticism upon his own thinking, but also, more important, because, in whatever other terms we might choose to conceptualize the relationship between God and man, we must, in Locke's view, begin from a recognition that it is superior–inferior relationship.[5] Thus,

> All obligation leads back to God, and we are bound to show
> ourselves obedient to the authority of His will because both our
> being and our work depend on His will, since we have received
> these from Him, and so we are bound to observe the limits He
> prescribes. (*ELN*, 183; cf. 187)

In short, the Law of Nature is a law for Locke because it is 'the decree
of the divine will', that is, 'the will of God' as the law-maker (*ELN*,
111, 187; STG, 222; II, 135; 1:3, 6).

It is important to insist upon this point precisely because most of
Locke's discussion of natural law centres upon the evident rationality
of its substantive prescriptions and the faculty of reasoning by which
individuals gain a knowledge of these commands. From this it might
be erroneously concluded that it is the rationality of the law which
makes it a law, but this view, which does have considerable merit as
applied to civil laws, cannot supply the authoritative and hierarchical
framework that is crucial to Locke's understanding of theology. The
temptation of modern interpreters to push Locke towards the
Enlightenment is made all the greater because he is generally
impatient with those who have become embroiled in the long-standing
scholastic controversy over whether we are obliged to obey the Law of
Nature because it is 'the law of reason' and thus in conformity with
our (and God's) rational nature, or whether we are obliged to obey
because it is God's command (and the power to enforce that
command) that we should obey His will. To this question, Locke
gives a brusque but ambiguous answer. Our obligation to obey God,
Locke observes, 'seems to derive partly from the divine wisdom of the
law-maker, and partly from the right which the Creator has over His
Creation' (*ELN*, 183). In the last analysis, however, Locke never
permits *any* argument advanced by human beings to diminish 'the
right which the Creator has over His Creation', whereas he frequently
remarks upon our inability to grasp 'the divine wisdom' of the Deity's
actions or purposes.[6] Hence, while Locke's answer is ambiguous, the
preponderance of emphasis must be placed upon the voluntarist side
of his response. If we know God to be the author of the Law of
Nature, then the latter is obligatory 'of itself and by its intrinsic force'
as an expression of divine will (*ELN*, 187; cf. 113).[7]

'*That* God has given a rule whereby men should govern themselves,'
Locke declares, 'I think there is nobody so brutish as to deny' (2:28,
8). Nevertheless, the existence and obligatory force of natural law
provide no guarantee that men *can* 'govern themselves' by fulfilling its

commands. The issue here is not, in any simple sense, whether human beings are good or bad as a general moral description of human nature. Rather, the question for Locke is how can the gap between the capacity of humans to act morally and God's enforcement of His command that they do so be bridged in such a way that neither the free will of individuals nor the goodness of the Deity are sacrificed in the process. One prominent traditional answer to this question, advanced by Aristotle and adopted by many later Christian writers, including Richard Hooker, maintained that since individuals naturally desired the good they directed their actions and designed their social institutions to achieve the good. Thus, human behaviour, natural law and the purposes of God could easily be fitted into a conception of the universe as being governed by a harmonious network of laws.

This view was challenged most forcefully by Thomas Hobbes. In place of the assumption that individuals are naturally attracted towards the good, Hobbes argued that an explanation of human behaviour must begin from the presupposition that avoidance of pain is the governing principle of human action. Not only is the Aristotelian link between nature and morality broken with respect to man's actions, but also, for Hobbes, it is precisely the inability of individuals to perform their natural law duties that justifies the necessity of their membership in political society. This view granted individuals total freedom in determining their fate (though there are special difficulties attached to Hobbes's theory in relation to the traditional controversy concerning 'free will'), but it appeared to many of Hobbes's contemporaries that it did so at the expense of denying the goodness of God. To put it another way, Hobbes radically transformed the nature of the discussion by demolishing the traditional way in which the problem had been structured. There neither was nor could there be any bridge between God's purposes, whatever they were, and human action. This view undermined the status of the Law of Nature as a law and as the foundation of morality. In addition to his insistence that there could be no moral actions in the state of nature, Hobbes's description of human existence as 'nasty, brutish, and short' seriously impugned God's purposes in having placed individuals in this condition.

Despite a certain fascination with Hobbes's philosophy, which is most prominently displayed in Locke's earliest writings, he never accepted the theological implications of Hobbes's position. 'It is impossible', Locke wrote in the eighth essay on natural law, 'that the primary law of nature is such that its violation is unavoidable' (*ELN*,

211). Yet, Locke believes, this is the conclusion that necessarily follows from the assumption that 'men are . . . by the law of nature in a state of war' with each other. Besides rendering impossible 'all justice, friendship, and generosity' between human beings, this view, according to Locke, inflicts a divine punishment upon mankind that not even the doctrine of original sin can justify (*ELN*, 213; cf. 201).

> We cannot imagine [God] hath made anything with a design that it should be miserable . . . [or] put in a worse state than destruction, misery being as much worse state than annihilation as pain is than insensibility.[8]

For Locke, every individual must be assumed to be *capable* of obeying natural law because 'a manner of acting is prescribed to him that is suitable to his nature' by God, who could not be supposed to have equipped man with reason and intellect except on the assumption that he would employ these faculties in order to discover that law. Nor, Locke adds, are we entitled to assume that it 'fits in with the wisdom of the Creator' that he should 'make man alone susceptible of law precisely in order that he may submit to none' (*ELN*, 117). 'Since therefore all men are by nature rational, and since there is a harmony between this law and the rational nature, and this harmony can be known by the light of nature', Locke concludes that 'all those who are endowed with a rational nature, i.e., all men in the world, are morally bound by this law' (*ELN*, 199).

Having established what makes natural law a law and the ground of our obligation to obey it as well as our ability to do so, we can now turn to a consideration of the particular duties it imposes upon us, according to Locke. The 'precepts of the law of nature', he writes, require us to demonstrate 'sentiments of respect and love for the deity, obedience to superiors, fidelity in keeping promises and telling the truth, mildness and purity of character, a friendly disposition' and 'all the other virtues' (*ELN*, 129; cf. 1:3, 19). Parents have a natural law obligation 'to preserve, nourish, and educate' their children, while the latter are expected to show 'an inward esteem and reverence' towards their parents (II, 56, 58, 60, 63, 66, 67, 69, 170; cf. I, 64, 89; *ELN*, 197; *STCE*, §34).

The Law of Nature, then, prescribes sentiments, dispositions and actions. In the seventh essay on natural law, Locke explains the different 'degrees' of obligation attached to the various commands of that law. Certain kinds of action – murder, theft, rape – 'are altogether forbidden' by the Law of Nature at all times and under all conditions. Moreover, the positive requirement that individuals inwardly maintain 'certain sentiments' or 'mental dispositions', such as 'reverence and fear of the Deity, tender affection for parents, and love of one's neighbour', is likewise an absolute and universal duty dictated by natural law. Finally, there is a third category of natural law commands pertaining to the 'outward performance' of some of these 'mental dispositions'. These include, for example, 'the outward worship of the Deity, the consoling of a distressed neighbour, the relief of one in trouble, and the feeding of the hungry'. With respect to these actions, however, Locke argues that 'we are not under obligation continuously, but only at a particular time and in a particular manner'. That is, 'we are not obliged to provide with shelter and to refresh with food any and every man, at any time whatever, but only when a poor man's misfortune calls for alms and our property supplies means for charity' (*ELN*, 193, 195; cf. 1:3, 19). Some commands of natural law are, therefore, to be viewed as absolute, while others are merely conditional as they pertain to human action. Nevertheless, Locke does not permit any variance in circumstances to affect the absolute status of the law itself. Thus,

> the binding force of the law of nature is permanent, that is to say, there is no time when it would be lawful for a man to act against the precepts of this law . . . The bonds of this law are perpetual and coeval with the human race, beginning with it and perishing with it . . . However, this permanently binding force must not be supposed to be such that men would be bound at all times to perform everything that the law of nature commands. (*ELN*, 193, 197)[9]

Hence, while 'we can sometimes stop acting according to the law', we cannot, Locke insists, 'act against the law' (*ELN*, 193).[10]

These distinctions between 'mental dispositions' and actions, and between actions that are absolutely proscribed and actions that can only conditionally be performed, are crucial to Locke's discussion of the state of nature, property, political obligation and natural law in the *Two Treatises of Government* and to his defence of religious toleration in the *Letter*, though they have been generally ignored by interpreters of Locke's thought. It is a primary aim of education, Locke maintains, to teach individuals 'to show respect, esteem, and goodwill' towards everyone (*STCE*, §144; cf. §67, 145). He means, in the first place, that we must preserve 'a disposition of the mind not to offend others', so that 'civility is nothing but outward expressions of goodwill and esteem' towards others, which all individuals – Locke cites the example of the American Indians – are naturally capable of expressing. Even if the practice of civility is, under certain conditions, rendered difficult, we are nevertheless obliged by the Law of Nature not to entertain a disposition of 'hatred or contempt' towards others (*STCE*, §143; cf. §145; MS, c.28, fol. 140v). Thus, 'the law of nature', Locke argues, 'neither supposes nor allows men to be inflamed with hatred for one another' (*ELN*, 163). Locke insists that 'we are *bound* to maintain and promote' sentiments of 'universal charity, goodwill and love' towards others according to natural law under all conditions whatsoever.[11]

When Locke denied the validity of Hobbes's premiss that individuals were placed in a natural state of war with each other, his denial was not based upon the assumption that, in fact, individuals would always show themselves obedient to commands of natural law. Locke's position is far too realistic and informed by the empirical knowledge of human behaviour provided by comparative anthropology to sustain such a belief. Rather, his point was that human beings cannot have been *constituted* in such a manner that disorder is the natural consequential outcome of their actions. We may encounter instances of robbery, murder and war, but we are not entitled, according to Locke, to assume that such actions establish the universal and *a priori* terms in which human existence may be characterized. Yet Locke's own position is stated in the terminology of logic and mathematics. That is, God 'has made man such that these [natural law] duties of his necessarily follow from his very nature' (*ELN*, 199, 201). Or, citing Aristotle, Locke argues that 'the proper function of man is acting in conformity with reason, so much so that man must of necessity perform what reason prescribes' (*ELN*, 113). Thus, the Law of Nature must 'be described as being the decree of the divine will . . . indicating what is and what is not in conformity with rational nature' (*ELN*, 111).

Are we entitled to draw this conclusion from the evidence? The question might be better phrased if we asked to what evidence can Locke appeal in order to justify his conclusion? The discussion of this epistemological issue, which is an important aspect of the argument of the *Essay Concerning Human Understanding*, could be extended to considerable lengths through the citation of passages from Locke's writings but, in the end, I think it must be concluded that

Locke offers no satisfactory philosophical answer to the question. Locke maintains that the way in which individuals are constituted defines their 'real essence', of which, he argues, we cannot claim to have any 'knowledge' (2:31, 6; 3:6, 27; cf. 3:3, 15, 17; 3:6, 6, 9, 19, 21, 27). 'The real constitutions or essences of particular things existing do not depend on the ideas of men but on the will of the Creator' (*Works*, 3:91). Using the analogy of a watchmaker, Locke declares that only the maker of the object has a knowledge of its constitutive nature, or real essence, and in the case of human beings this means that such knowledge is part of the 'divine wisdom' to which we have no direct access (3: 6, 3; 4: 3, 25). In other words, what we believe about the real nature of man is inextricably tied to what we believe about the character of the Deity, and this, as I have argued above, subordinates the disputations of philosophy to the claims of theology. The moral characteristics of natural law are thus dependent upon an ontological assumption about the nature of the relationship between God and man. And, while we may say that Locke believes that empirical evidence can be cited in support of this assumption, he does not believe that any amount of empirical evidence can call into question the constitutive rationality of the natural world or of its human inhabitants. Thus, while Locke is too shrewd a philosopher to assume that he can *prove* that human nature is rational and good on the basis of knowledge supplied by our senses – though he does attempt to defend his position on this ground – he is also too committed a Christian to impugn the goodness or rationality of God, in whose image we are made. It is this purposive standard – the assumption that a watchmaker would not make a watch that did not work – applicable to the Creator which serves as the basis of Locke's argument.[12] If any convincing epistemological claim can be advanced on behalf of Locke's view of human nature – other than through divine revelation, which, for the moment, I have set aside – it is that individuals must grasp intuitively that this is the way in which things are in the world. The reason such knowledge-claims can be framed in the language of definitions or logic is that the formal structure of things cannot become part of our certain knowledge in any other way.[13]

I wish to draw from the preceding discussion two general points that I believe are essential to any consideration of Locke's view of the human condition. The first is a reaffirmation of the importance of having a clear understanding of the differential emphasis accorded to the various assumptions and arguments that comprise the basic structure of Locke's thought. This means not only that Locke's presupposition about human nature is dependent upon his theological conception of God, but also that, were he to change his views on the former subject, the entire structure of his world-view would be affected. We could phrase this in another way by saying that Locke's disagreements with Hobbes or Filmer are never merely political disagreements, but reflect a different conception of how things are in the universe, especially with regard to the relationship between God and man. In the end, the status of natural law, the nature of man, the definition of morality, and a hundred other particular concepts employed by Locke rest upon a recognition of this point.

The second proposition to which I wish to draw attention is, in Locke's view, entailed by the first; namely, it is 'man' as a collective noun that expresses this structuralist position. This means that individuals must be presumed to exist in a natural community, 'because according to the law of nature all men alike are friends of one another and are bound together by common interests' (*ELN*, 163). As Locke puts it in the *Second Treatise* when speaking of the condition of men in the state of nature, the individual is subject to the Law of Nature, 'by which law common to them all, he and all the rest of *mankind are one community*, make up one society distinct from all other creatures'. It is 'this great and natural community', Locke maintains, that must be taken as the moral starting-point for any consideration of political relationships (II, 128). (The question of whether this 'natural community' also has any existential or historical status will be discussed later.) Despite the impetus towards the privatization of relationships provided by the religious tenets of Protestantism, Locke's notion of morality is firmly rooted in the assumption that individuals bear a collective responsibility towards others, defined for them by the precepts of natural law. The latter provide 'the common bond whereby humankind is united into one fellowship and society' (II, 172). It is 'the preservation of all mankind', Locke insists, that constitutes 'the true principle to regulate our religion, politics, and morality by' (*STCE*, §116). We shall later have frequent recourse to this 'true principle' as a guide to the interpretation of specific aspects of Locke's argument in the *Two Treatises*, but the point I wish to make here is that whatever degree of emphasis one wishes to attribute to the individualism of Lockean thought it cannot be allowed, from the standpoint of the way in which that thought is structured, to override the importance of Locke's conception of the universe in terms of the collective and communal responsibilities of mankind. This hierarchical theory of obligation is summarized in Locke's statement of the duties that men 'owe to God, their neighbour, and themselves' (*ELN*, 159; MS f.1, fol. 431).

If political associations and political theory must be viewed within a universe structured by the presuppositions of theology and morality, it is also true that the constituent elements that make up political society – individuals – must be supposed to possess certain given characteristics. We have already alluded in passing to the faculty of reasoning which Locke assumed was part of the divine endowment of mankind in order to show that, for him, the Law of Nature served as a link between the rationality of God and the rationality of man. Now, however, it is necessary to take a closer look at the essential properties of the individual. For, viewed from the ground up, so to speak, political society is created by individuals who are assumed by Locke to be structured in a certain way in terms of their capabilities. Just as any definition of moral action in relation to natural law was dependent upon the actual existence of the human abilities necessary to fulfil its demands, so the creation of political society presupposes a particular type of individual. Although I shall focus primarily upon the formal aspects of Locke's definition of the individual, the latter easily elides into a network of substantive moral beliefs that Locke also employs as ontological presuppositions. As we have already seen, this is a characteristic feature of his discussion of God and natural law.

What are the necessary ingredients of the Lockean 'individual'? The concept of a 'person', Locke argues in the *Essay Concerning Human Understanding*, 'belongs only to intelligent agents capable of a law, and happiness and misery'. This is not his most philosophical answer to the question, but it does show very clearly that only 'a self' capable of consciously 'appropriating actions' as its own, receiving 'pleasure or pain; i.e. reward or punishment, on the account of any such action', can possibly be imagined as the 'author' of civil society. For, Locke observes, 'the personality extends itself beyond present existence to what is past, only by consciousness, whereby it becomes concerned and accountable, owns and imputes to itself past actions, just upon the same ground, and for the same reason, that it does the present' (2:27, 26; cf. 2:27, 11, 17). Without this linkage between consciousness and action by the 'person', we could never hold the individual 'accountable' for 'his' action, and thus it would be impossible to establish any standard of morality (2:27, 18; *Works*, 2:301, 303). Nor, it follows, could we enact laws that necessarily presuppose such a connection. Because the notion of 'person' stands for those aggregated qualities that allow us to treat the individual 'as an intelligent being subject to government and laws, and accountable for his actions', some understanding of 'personal identity' is absolutely essential to any political theory that explains the origins of political society in terms of the actions of 'intelligent agents' (*Works*, 2:320).[14]

According to Locke, no one 'can be capable of a law, that is not a free agent' (1:3, 14). Freedom is therefore a constitutive element of the individual.

> . . . every man is put under a necessity by his constitution, as an intelligent being, to be determined in *willing* by his own thought and judgment, what is best for him to do: else he would be under the determination of some other than himself, which is want of liberty. (2:21, 48)

Since liberty consists 'in a power to act, or not to act', an individual must be in a position to translate his preference into action through an act of will in order for 'freedom' to exist or to be associated with a particular person's actions (2:21, 23; cf. 2:21, 8, 10, 12, 15, 16, 27, 73).

So far we have concentrated upon the internal qualities – freedom, will, consciousness, and so on – that form part of Locke's definition of the individual, and provide him with a defence against that view of men that regards them as being 'bare machines' moved by the sensory effects produced by external objects in motion (1:3, 14). Nevertheless, it is necessary to Locke's conception of moral or legal accountability that the individual should be receptive to pain or pleasure. For, without the attachments of rewards or punishments defined in sensory terms, no rule, according to Locke, can be viewed as a 'law'. Moreover, the entire structure of his epistemological argument is founded upon the proposition that pleasure and pain, 'which we receive both from sensation and reflection', supply the springs of human action, including thinking (2:20, 1, 3). If, therefore, no action can be taken that is not conjoined with the perception of pleasure or pain, and if liberty is dependent upon the existence of actions, then a 'free' individual must be an entity that experiences pleasure and pain.

Yet, as Locke well knew, this capacity was shared by human beings with other sentient creatures. All animals seek to satisfy their desires or appetites, which can easily be described – as it was by Hobbes, for example – as the pursuit of pleasure and the avoidance of pain. What, then, distinguishes man from the other animals? Locke replies that it is the power an individual has to act or not to act, 'to suspend the execution and satisfaction of any of [his] desires . . . In this lies the liberty man has' (2:21, 47). So that 'all the actions' of men are reduced 'to these two, viz., thinking and motion'. Thus, 'so far as a man has a power to think, or not to think; to move, or not to move, according to the preference or direction of his own mind, so far is a man *free*' (2:21, 8). Because Locke locates this power in the mind, he maintains that 'during this suspension of any desire, before the will be determined to action, and the action . . . done, we have opportunity to examine, view, and judge, of the good or evil of what we are going to do' (2:21, 47). Against Hobbes, Locke argues that 'deliberation' cannot be equated with the pursuit of our last appetite but, rather, must be seen as a conscious act of an intelligent agent who was free to act otherwise (2:21, 50). The will, in short, 'supposes knowledge to guide its choice' (2:21, 52).

These bare outlines of Locke's argument could of course be filled in with greater detail, but it is sufficient for our purposes to note that Locke has constructed a concept of 'personal identity' that is, on the one hand, central to the epistemological argument of the *Essay Concerning Human Understanding* and, on the other, an ontological presupposition of his moral and political theory. Only a being moved by the 'natural tendencies' of appetite, pain and pleasure, but equipped with the power to suspend those desires, so that his subsequent action will result from a 'due examination' of its possible consequences, can satisfy Locke's definition of a 'person' as an intelligent free agent capable of a law. 'Rationality', 'freedom' and 'morality' are all dependent upon the existence of a sentient being with these characteristics.[15] This does not mean, as Locke is careful to point out, that one could arrive at an adequate notion of these concepts through inductive observation of human behaviour. For, though individuals are endowed with free choice, 'men may choose different things' as objects of their desires, and thus are liable to make wrong judgements. Yet, Locke insists, 'the eternal law and nature of things must not be altered to comply with [the individual's] ill-ordered choice' (2:21, 55–6). The 'true' foundation of morality and reason is established by God, and its transcendental status cannot be challenged on the basis of what men actually do.

Indeed, allowing for the anachronistic formulation of the question in Kantian terms, we might say that Locke is attempting to establish the necessary *a priori* categories of human existence that allow individuals to behave as rational and moral agents. Thus, he argues that God 'has put into [men] the uneasiness of hunger and thirst, and other natural desires' that 'move and determine their wills, for the preservation of themselves, and the continuation of their species', all of which is 'suitable to our constitution and frame' according to the wisdom of the Deity (2:21, 34; 2:31, 2; 2:32, 14). In other words, God 'has furnished man with those faculties, which will serve for the sufficient discovery of all things requisite to the end of such a being' (1:4, 12; 2:23, 12). Since God 'requires of us no more than we are able to do' (2:21, 53), it is essential for Locke to demonstrate that such capabilities must necessarily exist, and this necessity could not, according to his own theory of knowledge, be a part of that 'knowledge' we actually derive from sense-experience.

With respect to the conjunction of the divine constitution of our natures and the existential manifestation of human action, Locke's insistence upon the ontological necessity of 'free will' appears to have caused him the greatest difficulty. If it is true that God has 'given a power to our minds . . . to choose amongst its ideas' and thereby a power to determine all our actions (2:7, 3), does this not present problems for a concept of the Deity that assumes divine omnipotence and omniscience? But, as Locke confessed in a letter to a friend,

> I own freely to you the weakness of my understanding – that though it be unquestionable that there is omnipotence and omniscience in God our Maker, yet I cannot make freedom in man consistent with omnipotence or omniscience in God; – though I am as fully persuaded of *both* as of any truths I most freely assent to. And therefore I have long left off the consideration of that question, resolving all into this short conclusion – that if it be possible for God to make a free agent, then man is free, though I see not the way of it.[16]

As this passage shows, the Aristotelian link between God, morality and the exercise of man's faculty of reason is never breached by Locke, although his defence of the teleological structure of the universe is stated in theological rather than in philosophical terms.

In addition to these constitutive elements of human existence, there are several empirical generalizations which, though they stand on a different level of Locke's epistemological argument, come sufficiently close to being recognized by human beings as universal truths that they must also be taken into account as necessary preconditions for the establishment of political society. On purely philosophical grounds, this conclusion might be resisted, but politics, as Locke defines it, is in part structured by the demands of practical experience. 'True politics', Locke declared, 'I look on as a part of moral philosophy.' However, that is only one part of a political theory, for 'the study of morality should be joined . . . with the reading of history'. The purpose of gaining a knowledge through experience and history 'of the actions of men as embodied in society' is to supply the other part of 'the true foundation of politics' (*Correspondence*, 6:215). Thus, 'politics contains two parts, very different the one from the other'. The first ingredient of a political theory is a 'study of morality', and its application to 'the natural rights of men, the origins and foundations of society, and the duties resulting from thence'. The second ingredient of politics is prudence or a practical knowledge gained through the reading of history or experience in the actual governing of individuals in society. The object of prudential knowledge, Locke explains, is to avoid the 'inconveniences' that beset individuals in their social relationships. This type of knowledge requires some understanding of 'men and manners' and 'the history of matter of fact', that is, the various circumstances and conditions under which individuals have lived (*STCE*, §185–6; *Works*, 2:408–9, and 9:306–7; Journal, 5 April 1677, MS f.2, and 26 June 1681, MS f.5).

Therefore, whereas the individual's moral obligations remain constant and unchangeable, requiring only the existential possibility of being fulfilled, the actual construction of political society in terms of particular institutions is dependent upon the practical constraints placed upon the action of free agents defined in relation to the specific materials at hand. What political society looks like is determined, in part, by the actual conditions existing at the time of its creation. Given the degree to which Locke's thought was indebted to the Aristotelian tradition, this statement can hardly appear surprising to any reader of the *Politics*.[17] Nevertheless, its importance to an assessment of the meaning Locke gives to particular concepts of his political theory, such as the state of nature or civil society, needs to be emphasized. For, given Locke's understanding of politics as a bifurcated activity rooted in the transcendental principles of morality and in the practical demands of experience and prudential calculation, there is necessarily a sociologically grounded meaning attached to the central concepts of Locke's political theory.

In the fifth essay on the law of nature, Locke argues that 'the general consent of men' cannot supply the foundations 'to build up a law of nature' or any other principle of morality. In part, Locke's argument is directed towards showing that, in fact, 'no universal and general consent is found among men about morals'. But, he adds, even 'if there did exist an invariable and unanimous consent concerning dutiful actions among all men in the world, still from this the law of nature could not be inferred and known for certain' (*ELN*, 165, 167, 169). In other words, even the best empirical evidence – a universally accepted principle or practice – could not be substituted in place of the constitutive principles and tendencies placed in human beings by God. This position is reiterated by Locke in the first book of the *Essay Concerning Human Understanding*, where the denial of 'universal consent' is used to undermine the claims made for the existence of innate principles (1:2, 4, 28). Since Locke generally agreed with Hobbes's remark that 'experience concludeth nothing universally', any precept or practice that could enlist universal consent in its favour represents, for him, the extreme test case with respect to the significance that can be attached to empirical generalizations. Yet not even in this instance will Locke grant that it is a necessary truth on the same plane with those we have considered above.

When 'the general consent of all men, in all ages, as far as it can be known, concurs with a man's constant and never-failing experience in like cases . . . and the regular proceedings of causes and effects in the ordinary course of nature', Locke observes, we assign to a particular proposition within this classification the 'highest degree of probability'. We certainly possess good reasons for believing it to be true; nevertheless, such propositions, Locke insists, 'come not within the reach of our knowledge' (4:16, 6). For 'the highest probability amounts not to certainty, without which there can be no true knowledge' (4:3, 14). Since our knowledge is 'very narrow and scanty' (4:6, 13, 15), the enforcement of Locke's rigid definitions might induce in us a state of despair or scepticism, except for the fact that the kind of knowledge of which we are most in need of certainty – 'morality and divinity' – is available to us, and for the fact that in order to carry out most of the practical actions of life certain knowledge is not required. Thus, an individual 'would be often utterly in the dark, and in most of the actions of his life, perfectly at a stand, had he nothing to guide him in the absence of clear and certain knowledge' (4:14, 1). What guides him in executing these actions, Locke argues, is his judgement exercised in situations of 'probability' (4:14, 3). Hence 'most of the propositions we think, reason, discourse, nay act upon' fall under the category of probability. Yet 'some of them border so near upon certainty, that we make no doubt at all about them', but act upon them 'as resolutely, as if they were infallibly demonstrated' (4:15, 2; 4:16, 6; *Works*, 3:299; *Early Draft*, §34). Probability is an extremely important category in relation to practical action, because probable beliefs 'supply the defect of our knowledge, and . . . guide us where that fails' (4:15, 4). And, as we have seen, 'most of the actions of life' are covered by this description.

It is obvious, as a corollary to this proposition, that most political actions must be included within the framework of probability. The grounds of probability, Locke explains, are supplied either by our own observation and experience or by the testimony of others based upon their observation and experience (4:15, 4). Almost all our political knowledge, save for a few structuring propositions of morality and theology, must therefore be derived from these experiential sources. 'The conduct of our lives, and the management of our great concerns' in 'public or private affairs', according to Locke, 'depend, for the most part, on the determination of our judgment in points wherein we are not capable of certain and demonstrative knowledge'; rather, we must rely upon 'probability grounded upon experience' (4:16, 3; Journal, 26 June 1681, MS f.5).

The most useful type of probable knowledge as a supplier of benefits to mankind, Locke argues, is that knowledge from which 'we may draw advantages of ease and health, and thereby increase our stock of conveniences for this life' (4:12,10).[18] Locke draws the comparison between European civilization and the 'savage Americans', arguing that the wealth and ease of the former might be almost wholly attributable to the discovery and use of iron, without which 'we should in a few ages be unavoidably reduced to the wants and ignorance' of the Indians in America (4:12, 11; Journal, 8 February 1677, MS f.2). It is the invention of printing, the use of the compass, and other activities that have provided 'for the supplying and increase of useful commodities' and have greatly altered the character of our practical lives (4:12, 12). In the essays on natural law, Locke speaks of 'a pressing need' or 'the common interests and convenience of men' as providing the rationale for a reliance upon probable evidence (*ELN*, 161, 163). Similarly, the universal consent of men to accept money in exchange for commodities is justified by Locke in terms of the 'usefulness' and benefit to mankind through trade which is made possible by money (II, 47; *Works*, 4:22, 44). In the face of such world-historical changes that supply the basis for Locke's frequent comparisons between 'civilization' and 'savagery', it is clear that political institutions must likewise undergo radical changes over time as part of this progressive development of mankind. This point will be considered at greater length in our discussion of certain chapters of the *Second Treatise*, but I have introduced it here in order to show that, for Locke, the practical dimensions of our lives are almost wholly shaped by the probable information we derive from empirical generalizations, or from the testimony and experience of others.

I began this discussion by noting that 'the necessity of believing, without knowledge . . . in this fleeting state of action' (4:16, 4) we are in is defended by Locke chiefly on the grounds of practicality. And once we shift our perspective on 'knowledge' towards this criterion it is relevant to ask what type of knowledge do we need to have in order to carry out most of the actions of our lives? The general answer to that question is that we require some knowledge of 'useful commodities' that will secure to us the 'advantages' and 'conveniences' of wealth and civilization. Among these practical discoveries we may list the use of iron, the invention of printing, the agreement to accept money and, I shall argue, the construction of a constitutional form of government. If political institutions are, to a large extent, the product of our probable knowledge tied to the practical necessities of life, then, I am arguing, we could expect that changes in those institutions will be explainable in terms of the empirical conditions that most influence or structure our practical activities. Hence, in order to determine the specific form of the political institutions that an intelligent free agent should create, one needs to have a knowledge of the empirical conditions under which the individual lives.

> The well management of public or private affairs depending upon the various and unknown humours, interests and capacities of men we have to do with in the world, and not upon any settled ideas of things physical, polity and prudence are not capable of demonstration. But a man is principally helped in them by the history of matter of fact, and a sagacity of finding out an analogy in their operations and effects . . . But whether this course in public or private affairs will succeed well, whether rhubarb will purge or quinquina cure an ague, is only known by experience, and there is but probability grounded upon experience, or analogical reasoning, but no certain knowledge or demonstration.

In short, politics demands a knowledge of the 'humours, interests and capacities of men', which 'is only known by experience' (Journal, 26 June 1681, MS f.5).

One empirically grounded proposition crucial to Locke's argument is that 'in all collections of men' there are a 'variety of opinions and contrariety of interests'. This means that disagreement and/or conflict 'unavoidably' follows from this clash of opinions and interests (II, 98). Since 'the mind has a different relish, as well as the palate', it is hardly surprising that 'men may choose different things' as 'goods' to satisfy their desires or that they may 'pursue happiness by contrary courses' (2:21, 55–6). Hence 'there is nothing more common than contrariety of opinions' (4:20, 1; Journal, 5 April 1677, MS f.2). On the basis of this empirical observation, Locke argues that individuals are 'accustomed to the most diverse institutions, and driven by impulses in quite opposite directions' to such an extent that the 'diversity of opinions' among them 'cannot be avoided' (*ELN*, 191; *Works*, 5:53; cf. *ELN*, 129). Consequently, as a matter of practical policy, it is foolish 'to hope to cast all men's minds and manners into one mould' (FTG, 146). Rather, 'this diversity among mortals, both in their manner of life and in their opinions' was, for Locke, an existential limitation upon the kinds of political or social institution one might hope to establish (*ELN*, 203).

Not only is it true in general that government is instituted in order 'to decide all controversies' that arise among individuals (II, 124), but it is also the case that political institutions should 'be suited to the several exigencies of times and tempers of people' (FTG, 132). Moreover, even 'in civil society one man's good is involved and complicated with another's', and this, too, must be taken into account as part of the given conditions under which political society is created.[19] In other words, if there exists a 'great variety of opinions concerning moral rules' (1:3, 6) and the pursuit of happiness, and if individuals make 'various and contrary choices' about not only these great ends of human life but also about more mundane matters of taste and the 'goods' that satisfy their appetites, then, these existential conditions supply the context within which political society must arise. On the one hand, this means that political institutions must recognize and accept the naturalness of this variety of opinions and contrariety of interests, which implies a certain tolerance for the various and contrary choices individuals make concerning things that are important to them.[20] On the other hand, political institutions ought to provide a fair and impartial resolution of the 'controversies' among individuals, so far as this is possible. For Locke, a political system that succeeds in realizing both of these objectives will clearly be superior to one that does not.

The precise form of social relations produced by different individual choices is itself an empirically determinable question for Locke, since the nature and significance of the resulting conflict among individuals will vary over time. One institution that he does include among the pre-political conditions of human existence, however, is the family. Locke follows Aristotle in holding that the family is 'the first form of association naturally instituted for the satisfaction of daily recurrent needs'.[21] Thus, 'whether a family by degrees grew up into a commonwealth', or whether 'several families' united together to form a political society, the existence of familial associations are presupposed (II, 110).

One could make a case for several other empirically grounded assumptions about the conditions under which political societies are instituted (for example, the existence of property), but if this endeavour is pressed too far it would necessarily involve the reconstruction of the specific dimensions of Locke's political theory, since he naturally believes that the particular propositions he is defending are inextricably linked with what are, in his judgement, the generalizable empirical conditions of human existence. It is sufficient for my purposes here, however, simply to illustrate the general point that, in addition to the divinely established parameters of 'the human condition', there are constraints placed upon the form of political institutions by the network of social relationships in which individuals naturally find themselves prior to the creation of civil society. Locke's political thought is thus structured by a set of what *we* would regard as metapolitical beliefs and what *he* regarded as a number of pre-political empirical observations derived from his experience or from the testimony of others. Locke's definition of political theory arises within this framework, and we shall have frequent occasion in the succeeding chapters to refer back to it in order to situate the meaning and significance of the particular concepts and arguments that he employs in the *Two Treatises of Government*.

NOTES: CHAPTER 2

1 'Heaven being our great business and interest, the knowledge which may direct us thither is certainly so too; so that this is . . . the study which ought to take up the first and chiefest place in our thoughts' (Journal, 29 March 1677; cf. 8 February 1677). A few days later, Locke noted that moral philosophy, 'in my sense, comprehends religion too, or a man's whole duty' (reprinted in James L. Axtell (ed.), *The Educational Writings of John Locke* (Cambridge: Cambridge University Press, 1968), pp. 411, 420).

2 Journal, 29 July 1676, MS f.1. 'There was never any rational creature that set himself sincerely to examine the truth of these propositions' pertaining to God's existence, who 'could fail to assent to them' (1:4, 16; cf. 1:4, 9; 2:17, 17; 4:10, 8).

3 *Essay Concerning Toleration* (1667). This passage is printed in the appendix to John W. Gough, *John Locke's Political Philosophy, Eight Studies* (Oxford: Clarendon Press, 1956), p. 197. Moral virtue is dependent upon 'a true notion of God' (*STCE*, §136, 139; cf. §61).

4 It is on this ground that atheists are excluded from toleration (*The Works of John Locke*, 12th edn, 9 vols (1824), Vol. 5, p. 47.

5 'The original and foundation of all law is dependency. A dependent intelligent being is under the power and direction and dominion of him on whom he depends and must be for the ends appointed him by that superior being' ('Ethica', no date, MS c.28, fol. 141).

6 'On the evidence of the senses, reason lays down that there must be some superior power to which we are rightly subject, namely God who has a just and inevitable command over us and at His pleasure can raise us up or throw us down, and make us by the same commanding power happy or miserable.' Thus, while 'reason can lead us to the knowledge of a law-maker or of some superior power to which we are necessarily subject', God's 'pleasure' in exercising His 'commanding power' over us is not dependent upon our 'reason' for its legitimacy (*ELN*, 153, 155). God 'has a right' to punish us, simply because 'we are his creatures' (2:28, 8). Obedience to God is the 'tribute' we pay to Him for all that we have received from Him (Journal, 1 September 1676, MS f.1; cf. 3 April 1681, MS f.5).

7 Whenever we suppose a law, we must suppose that some reward or punishment is annexed to the rule which flows from the power and will of the lawmaker, and not from 'the natural product and consequence of the action itself'. Locke applies this principle to his definition of natural law (2:28, 6, 8). 'Since God is supreme over everything and has such authority and power over us . . . and since we owe our body, soul, and life . . . to Him and to Him alone, it is proper that we should live according to the precept of His will. God has created us out of nothing and, if He pleases, will reduce us again to nothing: we are, therefore, subject to Him in perfect justice and by utmost necessity' (*ELN*, 187). When a critic tried to force the issue by making Locke choose between 'reason' and 'will' as the basis of natural law, Locke replied: 'Whoever sincerely acknowledges any law to be the law of God, cannot fail to acknowledge also that it has all the reason and ground that a just and wise law can or ought to have, and will easily persuade himself to forbear raising such questions and scruples about it' (*Works*, Vol. 3, p. 188).

8 Journal, 1 August 1680, MS f.4. One might as well imagine that we are being punished by God for sins committed in a previous life as to suppose that we are 'created miserable' in this life (2:27, 26).

9 'The duties of [natural] law, arising from the constitution of his [man's] very nature are of eternal obligation; nor can it be taken away or dispensed with, without changing the nature of things, overturning the measures of right and wrong, and thereby introducing and authorizing irregularity, confusion, and disorder in the world' (*Works*, Vol. 6, p. 112). Nevertheless, 'some' of God's commands are 'suited to particular circumstances of times, places, and persons', and therefore carry with them 'a limited and only temporary obligation' (p. 13).

10 'All negative precepts' or prohibitions of natural law 'are always to be obeyed', but 'positive commands only sometimes upon occasions' when this is possible, although 'we ought to be always furnished with the habits and dispositions to [execute] those positive duties' when the occasion permits (Journal, 20 March 1678, MS f.3).

11 *The Correspondence of John Locke*, ed. E. S. De Beer, 8 vols (Oxford: Clarendon Press, 1976–85), Vol. 4, p. 758 (my italics). 'Love to God, and charity to ourselves and neighbours are no doubt at all times necessary' (Journal, 20 March 1678, MS f.3; cf. 1 September 1676, MS f.1).

12 For example, Locke maintains that 'it is impossible to have such a notion of God as to believe that he should make a creature to whom the knowledge of Himself was necessary and yet not to be discovered' through the use of human reason (Journal, 3 April 1681, MS f.5).

13 'Intuitive knowledge' is 'the highest of all human certainty', and is not dependent upon reasoning or 'use of the discursive faculty' (4:17, 14; 4:2, 1, 5).

14 'Person', according to Locke, 'is often used to signify the whole aggregate of a rational being.' It is essentially a moral term and not an attempt to embody everything that comprises 'the natural constitution' of man. The concept of 'person', in other words, 'is an artificial distinction, yet founded in the nature, but not the whole nature of man'. Moreover, since the individual's 'personality' is 'solely a creature of society, an abstract consideration of man', which is incorporated into a particular society's understanding of the kind of moral relations to which it will attach rewards and punishments, Locke is quite clear as to the functional purpose of the concept in the construction of a theory of political society (*Works*, Vol. 2, p. 309; cf. pp. 301, 305, 310).

15 This point is made repeatedly by Locke in *Some Thoughts Concerning Education* (§33, 36, 38, 45, 52, 107, 200). As many commentators have noted, chapter 21 of the *Essay Concerning Human Understanding*, from which I have cited in the text, was for Locke the most troublesome chapter in that work, and even after the publication of the first edition he made a number of revisions in his argument. Yet it is possible to make too much of this fact, for, as Locke's journal notations and other writings show, he had arrived at an intellectual standpoint between Aristotle and Hobbes many years before the appearance of the *Essay* in print. The philosophical cogency of this position may be questioned, of course, and in that respect I agree with Aarsleff's assessment of Locke's revisions that they 'tightened the argument and gave it a firmer base'. Nevertheless, as Aarsleff demonstrates quite clearly, Locke subscribed to the basic presupposition that the individual was an intelligent free agent capable of rational behaviour long before he began writing the *Two Treatises*, and that is the point I am attempting to establish here (Hans Aarsleff, 'The state of nature and the nature of man in Locke', in John W. Yolton (ed.), *John Locke: Problems and Perspectives* (Cambridge: Cambridge University Press, 1969), pp. 99–136; esp. pp. 110–26).

16 *Some Familiar Letters Between Mr. Locke and Several of His Friends* (1708), pp. 26–7; cf. Journal, 25 August 1676, MS f.1; 4:17, 10. The problematic status of free will obviously affected the meaning of the concept of 'person' as a moral agent, as Locke defined the term. Here, too, Locke maintained that since we cannot resolve certain questions relating to personal identity through any examination of 'the nature of things', these issues are 'best resolved into the goodness of God' (2:27, 13).

17 'The foundation' of a political theory 'should be laid in inquiring into the ground and nature of civil society; and how it is formed into different models of government; and what are the several species of it. Aristotle is allowed a master in this science, and few enter upon the consideration of government, without reading his *Politics*' (*Works*, Vol. 9, p. 307; cf. 4:17, 4).

18 'The discovery of some new and useful invention' or 'the knowledge of natural bodies', according to Locke, can have no other justification than the fact that they supply 'the advantages and conveniences of life' (cited in Neal Wood, *The Politics of Locke's Philosophy: A Social Study of 'An Essay Concerning Human Understanding'* (Berkeley/Los Angeles, Calif.: University of California Press, 1983), p. 73; cf. p. 128). Wood's book contains a good general discussion of this aspect of Locke's thought, and its roots in Baconian philosophy.

19 Cited in Peter King, *The Life of John Locke*, 2 vols (1830), Vol. 2, p. 114.

20 In the face of 'the diversity of opinions', it would 'become all men to maintain

peace, and the common offices of humanity, and friendship' since 'we cannot reasonably expect that anyone should readily and obsequiously quit his own opinion, and embrace ours, with a blind resignation to an authority, which the understanding of man acknowledges not' (4:16, 4).

21 Aristotle, *Politics* (London: Oxford University Press, 1948), 1, ii, 5.

CHAPTER 3

Natural Law, Reason and Hermeneutics

Locke's skill as a polemicist in the *First Treatise* has received due recognition from scholars. He is relentless in exposing to ridicule 'all the windings and obscurities' of Filmer's 'wonderful system' (*Two Treatises*, preface), and the overall effect of Locke's critique is devastating. Long before the language of unmasking and ideological conflict became fashionable, Locke provided an example of what is meant by destroying an opponent's position through challenging the world-view with which he has identified himself. Although I wish to move beyond this recognition of the effects of Locke's critique to consider its internal structure, this feature of the *First Treatise* is nevertheless very important to a general understanding of Locke's political thought. For the *First Treatise* should not be viewed as a departure from the normally philosophical bent of Locke's mind; on the contrary, much of Locke's writing is highly polemical in nature. Indeed, the attractiveness of many Lockean arguments concerning religious, philosophical, political or economic issues derives precisely from this combative feature of his thought. The *Essay Concerning Human Understanding*, the *Letter Concerning Toleration*, the *Two Tracts on Government*, the *Considerations on the Lowering of the Rate of Interest*, *The Reasonableness of Christianity* and, of course, the *Two Treatises* all display the polemical cast of Locke's mind. Since it is frequently asserted that Locke's thought is too riddled with contradictions to gain him recognition as a great philosopher or system-builder, it could be argued that Locke is at his intellectual best when he is engaged in a polemical attack upon the ideas of his opponents. Be that as it may, what is important is that in exploring Locke's confrontation with Filmer's *Patriarcha* we are not merely detailing a refutation of a particular historical tract; rather, we are also gaining an insight into the workings of Locke's mind and the process by which his own ideas emerged out of the conflict with those of his opponents.

There is a second reason for stressing the polemical character of the *First Treatise*. Locke went to considerable lengths to criticize the ideas of a thinker long since dead, which, he says, he would not have done 'had not the pulpit, of late years, publicly owned his doctrine, and made it the current divinity of the times'. The clergy have 'dangerously misled others' as to the true principles of politics by preaching Filmer's ideas for gospel. It is the existence of these 'men amongst us, who, by crying up his books, and espousing his doctrine', Locke explains, that saves 'me from the reproach of writing against a dead adversary' (*Two Treatises*, preface). Thus, while Filmer's *Patriarcha* provides the direct focus for Locke's attack, there is an indirect objective to be accomplished through exposing the weaknesses of the political theory defended by 'a generation of men . . . among us'; namely, to force the clergy to retreat from their position by showing that Filmer's political thought cannot be rendered internally consistent or intelligible according to the standards of common sense (I, 3).

Though Locke does not say so, I believe he recognizes that the clergy's use of Filmer's political theory presents them with a practical problem. That is, the clergy's ideological defence of the established order is most effective when they can elicit absolute obedience from their audience through linking deference to authority with simple and easily comprehensible truths. Filmer's aim, however, is to develop an elaborate, comprehensive and iron-clad intellectual defence of absolutism and, in the process, to refute all theories of political obligation that might challenge his own viewpoint. To be sure, Filmer's ultimate objective, like that of his clerical followers, is to secure, in practice, the obedience of all subjects to the king, but whether or not a full-scale theoretical exploration of the controversy concerning political obligation is the most efficacious means of accomplishing this end is the point at issue. In the *Essay Concerning Human Understanding* and also in *The Reasonableness of Christianity*, Locke argues that the demands of practical conduct are not aided by complicated or exaggerated intellectual claims; rather, most of the important truths of life can be stated in simple terms. Philosophers and theologians are inclined to forget this fact. Similarly, in the preface to the *Two Treatises*, Locke maintains that if one 'strips' away 'the flourish of doubtful expressions' that give the 'glib nonsense' of Filmer's ideas the appearance of a 'popular style' the barrenness of the substantive argument will be revealed (*Two Treatises*, preface). Locke's objective is to clear away the dust that has been thrown in the eyes of the people, 'the better to mislead them', by the advocates of patriarchalism (I, 1). In place of arguments, Filmer's political theory relies upon 'the intricacy of the words' he employs (I, 21). In other words, if Filmer's writings are viewed as a political form of scholasticism, Locke might well have believed that it was precisely Filmer's overarching intellectual pretensions which made him the perfect medium for undermining the practical effectiveness of the royalist political perspective. At the same time, Locke also believes that if he can demonstrate that Filmer's arguments cannot be rendered intelligible, then this would 'give the world cause to suspect, that it's not the force of reason and argument, that makes them [Filmer's followers] for absolute monarchy, but some other by interest' that relates to their own ambitions or political objectives (I, 13).

If we recall that Locke's attack upon innate knowledge in the *Essay* is simultaneously a philosophical denial that such knowledge exists and a political critique of those (mostly theologians) who defend their authority and that of Christianity through an appeal to such knowledge, we should not be surprised to discover that a large proportion of Locke's polemic against Filmer in the *First Treatise* is devoted to a critique of the epistemological foundations of Filmer's defence of political authority.[1] Why, Locke asks, does Filmer not begin *Patriarcha* with a clear definition of fatherly authority? One might have expected such a definition from Filmer because he criticizes his opponent Phillip Hunton for not beginning his *Treatise of Monarchy* with a definition of monarchy. Locke argues that a simple statement of Filmer's position would have frightened his audience, and therefore, 'like a wary physician', he must 'dilute' or conceal the 'harsh' or aversive aspects of his perspective (I, 7). However, Locke insists that intellectuals have an obligation to strive for the greatest possible clarity precisely in those circumstances where their ideas exercise the greatest practical influence with respect to the conduct of others. Applying this principle to Filmer, Locke declares,

> it is reasonable to expect, that he should have proved [his case] with arguments clear and evident, suitable to the weightiness of the cause. That since men had nothing else left them, they might in slavery have such undeniable proofs of its necessity, that their consciences might be convinced, and oblige them to submit peaceable to that absolute dominion, which their governors had a right to exercise over them. (I, 10)

Instead, Locke writes, the 'fundamental tenet' of Filmer's thought – the absolute sovereignty of Adam – is 'taken for granted without proof' (I, 11).

Neither Filmer's failure to begin with a definition nor the possible hostility of his audience to his position goes to the heart of the problem inherent in his argument. Filmer wanted to construct a political theory based upon a literal reading of the Scriptures that was as absolute with respect to all other viewpoints as Filmer's sovereign was with respect to his subjects. There is no room for interpretative ambiguities or opposing claims for validity within the framework of Filmer's thought. If, however, his opponents could demonstrate that such ambiguities did exist, and that more than one interpretation of the evidence was plausible, the whole structure of Filmer's argument would collapse.

What I shall try to show in this chapter is (1) how Locke uses the rules of textual interpretation to undermine Filmer's substantive political position; and (2) how the latter is rooted in the two forms of natural law, namely, divine positive law expressed through revelation, and the Law of Nature which is discoverable through the use of human reason – a duality that creates serious problems for Filmer's defence of absolutism. Locke wants to demonstrate that these two sources of moral and political authority cannot be merged indistinguishably, as Filmer attempts to do.

Filmer thought it necessary as a prelude to his own argument to disclaim the validity of all sources for a discussion of political obligation except the Bible. 'It is a shame and scandal for us Christians', he declared, 'to seek the original of government from the inventions or fictions of poets, orators, philosophers and heathen historians . . . and to neglect the scriptures, which have with more authority most particularly given us the true grounds and principles of government.'[2] Both as the repository of God's word and as a historical account of the creation of the world, the Bible ought to be granted precedence over any other source. Nevertheless, the surprising thing is that Filmer was not so ruthless in adhering to the terms of this pronouncement as the demands of his methodology dictated. He was well aware of the tremendous influence the writings of Aristotle and Cicero exercised upon his contemporaries' political theory, as Hobbes had noted in *Leviathan*. 'Our modern politicians, who pretend themselves Aristotelians', Filmer wrote, have derived their commitments to democracy from a reading of his writings. Moreover, it is precisely because the Scriptures do not support such a political perspective, he asserted, that 'many fly to natural reason and to the authority of Aristotle' in defence of a democratic viewpoint.[3] This might have been sufficient grounds for dismissing Aristotle as an authoritative source of political principles, but Filmer refused to follow that path.

Instead, Filmer tried to integrate Aristotle's political theory into his own political perspective, but this procrustean effort was doomed to failure, for Aristotle's mind was a great deal more flexible than Filmer's in dealing with the empirical phenomena of politics and with the possibility that there were conflicting views as to the meaning of justice. Filmer lost no opportunity to cite Aristotle on the familial origins of political power, and his preference recorded in the *Ethics* for monarchy as a particular form of government, but it was stretching Aristotle's thought to the breaking-point to see in it a commitment to absolute monarchy, such as Filmer was attempting to defend.[4] Yet, it was Filmer who created these difficulties for himself by writing in praise of 'Aristotle, whose books of "Politics", and whose natural reasons are of greatest authority and credit with all rational men, next to the sacred scripture.'[5] Thus, in addition to propounding a literal reading of the Scriptures, Filmer involved himself in an interpretative battle over the meaning of Aristotle. Even if Filmer's reading of that philosopher had gained widespread recognition as being more cogent and convincing than that offered by his opponents – which it did not – this would have represented, at best, a defensive victory for him. The real struggle would still have to take place on the ground designated by Filmer, namely, the Scriptures. On the other hand, the charge of misreading Aristotle, to the degree that his opponents could make that case, could be used to undermine the credibility of Filmer's interpretation of the Scriptures. Filmer tried to protect himself by offering an explanation for Aristotle's 'errors', insisting that it was not to be expected that a heathen should have a knowledge of 'the first grounds or principles of government' because the latter presupposed a knowledge of God's creation of the world, and 'this point can be learnt only from the scriptures', of which, he maintained, the early Greek and Roman philosophers were ignorant.[6] At the same time, Filmer argued that in so far as Plato and Aristotle had accurately accounted for the origins of government this fact evidently proved that 'Moses' history of the creation guided these two philosophers'.[7] How these two statements were to be reconciled is never explained by Filmer, nor, apparently, was he troubled by the historical implausibility of assuming that Plato and Aristotle wrote with a copy of Genesis before them.

We can appreciate that Filmer wished to defeat his opponents by turning Aristotle's writings against them, but his refusal to accept the principle of interpretative charity left his own position exposed to easy attack. Filmer's substantive argument was continuously being threatened by the weaknesses of his methodological practices. Filmer dismissed as unreliable evidence the writings of the poets and philosophers from whom the opponents of absolute monarchy drew many of their arguments. What, then, was the point of *interpreting* those writings, given Filmer's commitment to a literalist approach to the textual truth of the Scriptures? For, as Locke points out, when an author rejects Aristotle and Homer as sources because it is 'the great scandal of Christianity' to rely upon them, and then quotes from their writings 'whenever they offer anything that seems to serve his turn', this leads the reader to suspect that the individual is writing to advance the cause of a particular 'interest and party', rather than to present the truth (I, 154). On the other hand, how could Filmer employ terms such as 'absolute monarchy' that had no textual warrant in the words actually used by biblical writers? Again and again, Locke hammers away at this weakness in Filmer's argument, namely, that 'Sir Robert would persuade us against the express words of the Scripture' (I, 32). After one of many such verbal comparisons of the biblical text with Filmer's words, Locke reflects:

If this be to argue from Scripture, I know not what may not be proved by it, and I can scarce see how much this differs from that fiction and phansie, or how much a surer foundation it will prove than the opinions of philosophers and poets, which our [author] so much condemns. (I, 34)

In other words, Filmer's political theory was dependent upon his ability to establish his reading of the Scriptures as authoritative, for if he could not do so, then individuals would have to rely upon their own interpretations of the Bible, which would grant them a degree of freedom in determining the basis for their political obligation to the magistrate that was incompatible with the absoluteness of the latter's authority, as defined by Filmer. This strategy was undermined not only by Filmer's propensity to offer debatable interpretations of non-scriptural sources, but also by his reliance upon Genesis as a source for his own position. For that book contains so many ambiguities and difficult constructions that a literalist reading of the text would be extremely difficult to establish. Yet no other reading of the text was compatible with Filmer's perspective. It was hardly likely – in the context of a developing tradition of biblical scholarship in the seventeenth century – that Filmer could validate his reading of Genesis to the exclusion of all other interpretative viewpoints.[8]

Locke's hermeneutical approach to the Bible also displays a dualistic character. He defends the literalness of the Scriptures against Filmer's attempt 'to warp the sacred rule of the Word of God, to make it comply with his present occasion' (I, 60). At the same time, Locke adopts, as a general rule, the principle that God, in speaking to men, does not violate 'the rules of language in use amongst them', for, if He did so, He would 'lose his design in speaking' to them, since they would not be able to understand the communication (I, 46). Thus, God speaks to man through his reason and his senses (1, 86). This means that God's words in the Scriptures must be capable of being understood in terms of 'the rules of language in use' among a collection of rational human beings and, in practice, this involves an appeal to common sense, or the way in which 'any sober man' would understand the meaning of the text. Of course, these two interpretative standards are, in the last analysis, identical since Locke equates the literal meaning of the text with a commonsensical reading of the Scriptures, that is, one available to 'any ordinary understanding' (I, 80).

Yet it should not be forgotten that this hermeneutical challenge raised by Locke against Filmer rests upon an important philosophical assumption that is crucial to the structure of Locke's thought; namely, that in all instances in which individuals are confronted with conflicting evidence they must rely upon their use of reason in order to weigh the contending probabilities. Hence, while 'ill grounded' or 'probable' opinions cannot stand against 'the direct and plain meaning of the words' in the Bible, in those instances where one must decide what is the 'most probable' meaning of a particular passage, Locke's appeal is to the reader to judge, according to his or her own reason, which meaning has the highest degree of probability (I, 36).[9] In other words, once one accepts the existence of textual ambiguities, *all* empirical evidence, including texts as particular historical documents, must be interpreted with the aid of human reason; and, for the most part, that evidence must be judged in terms of probabilities. Hence an approach that refuses to recognize the principle of interpretative charity is, according to Locke, ignorant of the basic features of the human understanding.

It is important to recognize that Locke's attack is, overwhelmingly, an epistemological and methodological one, and that it is this fact that accounts for the seemingly scholastic concern for definitions, logic and the analysis of meanings in the *First Treatise*. Only after a formalist argument has been defeated on its own ground is it worthwhile to mount a positive argument based upon empirical evidence, history, or the individual's use of reason. It is therefore a mistake to view – as many commentators have – Locke's reliance upon the Bible in the *First Treatise* as reflecting merely a concession to Filmer's outmoded religious preoccupations, while the *Second Treatise* presents Locke's own secular view of politics.[10] The difficulty with Filmer's argument lies not in the fact that he chose the wrong place to begin his discussion of politics; rather, the problem is that even the best sources (Aristotle and the Bible) cannot be brought into conformity with his methodological approach.

Besides reflecting Locke's philosophical convictions, his argument against Filmer's scholasticism coincides with his attack on the obfuscating role of clerics, in appealing to each individual to judge for himself according to the use of his reason what the Scriptures mean (I, 49). In addition to serving as a weapon against Filmer as a particular political theorist, therefore, Locke's interpretative approach is designed to undermine the authoritative weight of an interpretation of the Bible advanced by any individual or group of individuals in favour of a general appeal to the reason of any individual as an interpretative guide to the meaning of that work. The practical consequence of this position, of course, was to challenge the claims of established authority precisely at the point where the knowledge-claims advanced by the clergy and the institutional power of the state intersect. As Locke phrased the point in the *Letter on Toleration*:

> Those things that every man ought sincerely to inquire into himself, and by meditation, study, search, and his own endeavours attain the knowledge of, cannot be looked upon as the peculiar possession of any one sort of men. (*Works*, 5:25)

From which it naturally followed that neither could anyone legitimately enforce their 'knowledge' of religion upon anyone else.

Locke, I am arguing, did not have to reject the Bible as an evidential source for a political theory. Nor did he disclaim its validity as a structural component of a proper political theory; rather, he merely had to show that more than one reasonable interpretation of the meaning of the Scriptures was possible. Hence we should not be surprised to discover that, at crucial junctures in his own argument, Locke frequently cites scriptural passages in support of his position. If we do not mistake a methodological critique for a rejection of the source in the case of the Bible, neither should we overlook the importance of Aristotle to the political debate between Filmer and his opponents. It is true, Locke does not cite Aristotle in the *Two Treatises*, though we know he had tremendous respect for both Aristotle and Cicero – the very thinkers Filmer alleged were responsible for the anti-monarchical ideas of his contemporaries. Locke does rely, however, upon the authority of Richard Hooker, from whose *Of the Laws of Ecclesiastical Polity* he often quotes passages in support of his own arguments. Hooker was unquestionably the most important Aristotelian thinker (next to Aristotle himself) for seventeenth-century English political theorists. Although Locke had good political reasons for citing the words of one of the architects of Anglican thought against his Anglican opponents, this fact should not be allowed to obscure the Aristotelian dimensions of Locke's political thought. Or, to put it another way, the passages from Hooker are only the most obvious indications of Locke's indebtedness to Aristotelianism in the *Two Treatises*. It is not an exaggeration to say that the basic structure of Locke's political theory represents an alternative reading of Aristotle to the one proposed by Filmer.

What I am arguing is that the polemical confrontation between Locke and Filmer is much more deeply rooted in the cultural consciousness of seventeenth-century Englishmen than can be appreciated if we focus simply upon the specific exchange between the two thinkers as represented by *Patriarcha* and the *First Treatise*. The point of Locke's argument, intellectually speaking, is not merely to expose the absurdity of Filmer's position, but, more important, it is to preserve the Bible and Aristotle as valuable sources for a rationally constructed political theory. What is the relationship between theology and politics, and what is the relationship between classical and modern (seventeenth-century) political theory were for Locke valid questions, and both were raised by Filmer. Unlike Hobbes, who self-consciously rejected these conventional dimensions of political theory, Locke attempts to defend a position within the traditional framework shared by the majority of his contemporaries. Hence we ought to be more than a little cautious about viewing Locke as a spokesman for a modern secular conception of political theory. Not only did he not see himself in this way, placing his own *Two Treatises* in the tradition of Aristotle, Cicero and Hooker, but also the existing social conventions to which Locke, Filmer and other political theorists – Hobbes excepted – appealed for support make such an interpretation of the *Two Treatises* highly implausible.

Another aspect of Filmer's thought that placed him within a tradition that was of great importance to Locke's own argument is the role Filmer assigns to natural law as foundation for his discussion of the problem of legitimacy. Filmer's status as a theorist of natural law is a matter of some controversy among contemporary scholars, and, as Locke shows, there is a confusion concerning the relationship between the Law of Nature and the exercise of legitimate political power that lies at the heart of Filmer's definition of the latter. Yet, as both Locke and James Tyrrell pointed out, Filmer could not rest his case for absolute monarchy upon the dictates of positive law, for any such authority could unmake a king as easily as it could make one. Filmer might reply that since the king's will is always law no one except the king is ever in a position to make anyone else a king. Hence positive law, as the king's will, was always absolute. This response had the effect of silencing any challenge to the king's will, though it created some major difficulties for Filmer in his attempt to distinguish between legitimacy and usurpation, as we shall see, but it did not adequately account for the origins of legitimate government. Moreover, Filmer's voluntarism committed him to the view that 'a law in general is the command of a superior power'. He employed this general maxim in his attempt to prove that even the common law must at some previous point in time have derived its force as law from being the expression of the king's will.[11] Somewhere at the beginning of all law and government, therefore, stood a particular individual as the determinate source of political authority. Logically, Filmer had nowhere to go but to the first individual, Adam, as the existential source of absolute political authority.

Of course, one could not simply begin with Adam without accounting for his being and powers, and these derived from God. Hence any conception of legitimate political power must be traced to the will of God, and the latter was, from the voluntarist perspective, equatable with the Law of Nature. As Filmer put it, 'for as kingly power is by the law of God, so it hath no inferior law to limit it'.[12] The natural law basis of Filmer's political theory was especially important to Locke, Tyrrell, Sidney and other Whigs during the Exclusion Crisis, who wanted to move the argument about the succession to Charles II on to a higher ground than the king's own will as the final determinative factor with respect to this problem. It is true, Locke wrote,

> the civil lawyers have pretended to determine some of these cases concerning the succession of princes; but by our [author's] principles, they have meddled in a matter that belongs not to them. For if all political power be derived only from Adam, and be to descend only to his successive heirs, by the ordinance of God and divine institution, this is a right antecedent and paramount to all government; and therefore the positive laws of men cannot determine that which is itself the foundation of all law and government, and is to receive its rule only from the law of God and nature. (I, 126)

It was up to Filmer to show how political power was 'plainly determined by the Law of Nature, or the revealed Law of God' (I, 124). This endeavour, I am arguing, necessarily placed the concept of natural law at the heart of the controversy with Filmer. In other words, as with the Bible and Aristotle, what is at issue in Locke's polemic with Filmer in the *First Treatise* is an alternative interpretation of the Law of Nature and its relationship to legitimate political power.

Filmer joined together two arguments he believed were compatible and mutually reinforcing in his defence of royal absolutism. On the one hand, he maintained that God gave Adam a specific grant of authority to rule as a monarch, and that subsequent claims for kingly authority could thus be traced through hereditary succession, following the genealogical accounts contained in the Bible. On the other hand, Filmer argued that political authority derived from the absolute power that fathers exercised over their children, and since the first kings were fathers of families this absolute authority within the political realm was traceable to the rights and powers exercised by fathers. Since Adam was also the first father, these two sources of Adam's absolute power were, in Filmer's view, perfectly compatible with each other. Locke, however, contends that both the means by which political authority is originally conveyed by God to Adam and the manner by which it is transmitted to succeeding generations are different in each case, and that these differences are not reconcilable.

According to Filmer, the first monarch of the world was established by God's appointment through a 'revealed positive grant made to Adam' (I, 16). But Filmer also defends Adam's exercise of absolute power as part of a 'right of nature' grounded in the powers attached to fatherhood (I, 17). Locke argues that 'all positive grants' can extend no further than 'the express words' in which they are made (I, 25). In order to understand this aspect of Adam's power, therefore, careful attention must be paid to the actual words (the text) spoken by God. Adam's claim to power through fatherhood, on the other hand, requires only that he exercise his right of nature through the action of being a father – through begetting offspring. To understand this part of the argument, Locke writes, we need only have some appreciation of what rights and duties are attached to fatherhood in general, and how these can be related to God's will as expressed through the Law of Nature. For this claim to authority was not given to Adam exclusively as a positive grant, but was simply incorporated into the law of reason according to which all human relationships are to be morally assessed.

In other words, Filmer has appealed both to a positive divine law and to the Law of Nature in support of his position, but whereas the first source is a specific revelation and must be literally understood as the express words of God, the second source expresses God's ordering of the world according to a rational design, and must be understood through the use of human reason as the means by which God's intentions are interpreted. If either of these claims for authority fail, if Filmer cannot prove 'by right of nature, or a clear positive law of God' that kings are entitled to exercise absolute power over their subjects, then his theory must collapse (I, 119).

In attacking the first proposition, Locke shows that God's positive grant of power 'was not [made] in particular to Adam' since, in the passages from the Bible cited by Filmer, God speaks in the plural referring to *them*, meaning both Adam and Eve, as the recipients of His blessing (I, 29, 30). Moreover, in other passages quoted by Filmer, God speaks of man in general, meaning the species – as, for example, when He grants all human beings power over other animals (I, 30, 31). Both these references to the text argue against Filmer's claim that a specific positive donation of authority was made to Adam. Since positive grants depend upon express words, Locke maintains that a theory of divine appointment cannot stand on a foundation of doubtful scriptural passages (I, 112). Locke is more brusque in his dismissal of Filmer's citation of the Fifth Commandment to 'honour thy father' as a biblical source of authority, because Filmer has so obviously omitted that part of the Commandment that would undermine the point of his argument by giving the mother an equal entitlement to authority and obedience. In this instance, Locke contends, the literalness of the text is clearly sacrificed for the sake of defending a partisan interest (I, 60).

While this aspect of Filmer's argument is relatively easy to attack, since the only evidence for a claim based on revelation is that supplied by the Bible, the natural law basis of Filmer's theory must be defeated through the deployment of a more complicated argument, relying upon plausible interpretations of the meaning and purposes of the Law of Nature. Here Locke maintains that whatever natural rights are attached to fatherhood they must be derived – as is the case for all natural right claims – from natural law. The question, therefore, is what is the relationship between fathers and children as defined by the Law of Nature (I, 64, 101). This states the point more sharply than Filmer is willing to do, but it is difficult to see how his argument can avoid this issue, since there is no other means by which he can define his reference to a 'right by nature'.

Locke accuses Filmer of asserting that fathers have an unlimited power over their children which extends as far as the right to kill them (I, 56–9).[13] This Locke denies. In fact, the claim is, in itself, a form of blasphemy; fathers neither give life to their children nor have they power to take it away.

> They who say the father gives life to his children, are so dazzled with the thoughts of monarchy, that they do not, as they ought, remember God, who is the author and giver of life. (I, 52)

A workman 'might indeed have some pretence to destroy his own workmanship' (I, 53), but since we are all God's workmanship (II, 6) the right of making life-and-death decisions can only derive from God's authorization. Locke cites the example of Noah, who was given permission by God to kill animals in order to provide for his own subsistence, as an illustration of his point (I, 86). Since no such direct authorization from God is being claimed by Filmer for the right of fathers to destroy their children, his case must rest upon an interpretation of the actions sanctioned by natural law. Locke's position is that no plausible reading of the purposes of the Law of Nature can be invoked to justify the assertion of the unlimited power of fathers.

Locke is arguing that Filmer's theory is not consonant with God's purposes in having created mankind. According to Locke, these purposes are identified with the preservation of mankind (I, 86). Filmer's claim on behalf of fathers does nothing to further this objective;

indeed, it undermines the purpose of natural law. It is not the power of fathers over their children that must be stressed but, rather, the natural law obligation parents have to care for their offspring. Locke insists that children have a natural right to subsistence, and that parents have an obligation to provide that subsistence (I, 88–91). It is only through the fulfilment of this duty that parents act in accordance with the general objective of natural law to preserve mankind.

We can rephrase Locke's argument in the more generalized form in which it appears in the *Second Treatise* by saying that no one can be supposed to have an absolute unlimited power and, at the same time, also be supposed to exist under the obligations imposed upon mankind by the Law of Nature, for it is the very purpose of that law to establish the boundaries within which human beings may act. To this general rule, fathers constitute no exception. Therefore, there *must* be limitations upon what fathers can do to their children. This means that children cannot be put to death by their fathers, for if that action were permitted it would be meaningless to identify the limitations of natural law with actions of lesser consequence.

Locke also reinstates the role of the mother as part of his argument concerning the parental obligations contained in the Law of Nature. Hence, at best, fathers can claim a joint or shared power over their children, and this is sufficient to deny the absolute sovereignty of the father, as asserted by Filmer (I, 55, 61–2). Both with respect to the theoretical source of their authority in natural law, and in terms of the actual exercise of that authority within the family, there are limits to the power of fathers over their children. What Locke has tried to prove is that Filmer's theory cannot 'be accommodated to the nature of things, and human affairs', and also that 'his principles [cannot] be made to agree with that constitution and order which God [has] settled in the world, and therefore must needs often clash with common sense and experience' (I, 137).

No less damaging than these theoretical and methodological weaknesses of Filmer's perspective is its failure to provide the necessary guidelines for practical behaviour, which is a requisite feature of a political theory. Here Locke's argument shifts from an examination of Filmer's explanation of the origins of political power to the question of how that power is transmitted through time. This question must be answered if those living in the present (1680) are to have a clear understanding of why they are obliged to obey the existing government.

The ground for this part of Locke's critique of Filmer is established in paragraph 96 of the *First Treatise*, when he maintains, as a general principle, that political power can be legitimately transferred only through the means by which it was initially rightfully created. Thus,

> Power founded on contract, can descend only to him, who has right by that contract: Power founded on begetting, he only can have that begets: And power founded on the positive grant or donation of God, he only can have by right of succession, to whom that grant directs it. (I, 96)

Locke argues that neither of the two sources of political authority upon which Filmer rests his argument can legitimize the transfer of power over time. That is, fatherhood 'can neither be transferred nor inherited', and therefore the question arises, following the death of the first father (Adam), who then has a rightful claim to Adam's political power (I, 101)? For reasons that will become increasingly obvious, Filmer's position allowed for no clear or consistent answer to this question, but the answer upon which he would have liked to have rested his case, and the one against which Locke directs most of his criticism, is that political power can be transmitted through inheritance (I, 84). But if, as Locke supposes, Filmer means that this transfer of power is in accordance with the law of primogeniture, on what grounds, he asks, does an elder brother have political authority over his other brothers, since he is not their father and it is the natural power of fatherhood that supplies the basis for Filmer's definition of legitimate political power (I, 96, 111, 139)? Locke also cites the Scriptures to show that primogeniture is not a divinely decreed custom, and so cannot be invoked as a practice legitimized by natural law to support the transfer of political power through inheritance (I, 111, 128). Filmer's attempt to evade the problems posed by this aspect of his theory through invoking a grandfather clause in his argument is ridiculed by Locke. The notion that Adam retained his absolute power of fatherhood even after he became a grandfather only reveals, but does not resolve, the contradictions inherent in Filmer's position since, as Locke remarks, he has now created 'two absolute unlimited powers existing together', in Adam and in his sons, both of whom, according to the original formulation of the right of fatherhood, are presumed to exercise this absolute power over their children (I, 68-9). If Adam retains his original power over his grandchildren, this severs the link between political power and the act of begetting. If, on the other hand, political power is consequent upon that act, Filmer's 'new politics' will 'set up as many absolute kings in every country as there are fathers of children' (I, 71). Either way, the foundation of Filmer's original assertion concerning the nature and origins of political power is destined to crumble over time.

The problems relating to the transfer of power given through a positive grant are even more insurmountable since, as Locke has shown, such a grant is a direct and personal authorization, limited by the express words which convey the authority. Locke has already denied that such a grant was made to Adam in particular, but even if it had been made, he argues, there is no textual warrant whatsoever for the notion that such power is transferable to anyone else.

> If God by his positive grant and revealed declaration, first gave rule and dominion to any man, he that will claim by that title, must have the same positive grant of God for his succession. For if that has not directed the course of its descent and conveyance down to others, nobody can succeed to this title of the first ruler. (I, 95)

Indeed, in the absence of any specific directive to the contrary, Locke maintains that a specific donation of power from God would, on the death of Adam, simply revert back to God (I, 85).

Thus, Filmer has painted himself into a corner, for neither fatherhood nor divine appointment can be utilized as the means by which political power can be transferred from Adam to his posterity. To rely upon the customary practice of inheritance when custom in itself cannot legitimate the exercise of political power would defeat the entire force of Filmer's argument since he is searching for an absolute, divinely instituted, and unchangeable natural law foundation for political authority, and not a humanly determined and variable set of practices associated with a majority of mankind. At the same time, however, if there is no means by which a subject can specifically determine 'who is the person, who has a right to exercise that power over him', then the very purpose of a political theory as a theory of obligation is obviated.

> To settle therefore men's consciences under an obligation to obedience, 'tis necessary that they know not only that there is a power somewhere in the world, but the person who by right is vested with this power over them. (I, 81)

Locke repeatedly attacks Filmer for failing to provide an answer to this question.

It could be said that Filmer is simply a poor theorist for not having thought through the problems raised by Locke. This belief appears to underly Locke's remark, cited earlier, that Filmer's theory cannot be accommodated to the reality of things. Thus, 'all his abstract notions of monarchical power will signify just nothing, when they are reduced to practice' (I, 120). The confusions and contradictions which abound in Filmer's writings, in other words, vitiate his claims to be taken seriously as a political theorist. Locke does offer this argument, and it has been taken up by later scholars to the point of making Filmer into the paradigmatic example of what it means to be a poor political theorist. But Locke advances a second and more important argument: Beneath the rhetoric of fatherhood and scriptural citations, Filmer's real purpose is to justify absolute obedience to any *de facto* government, including tyranny or power gained through usurpation. This is an incredible, though not implausible, charge, given the intricacies of Filmer's argument which appear to lead in an almost desperate fashion towards some higher sanction for the exercise of political power than mere possession. That Locke believes this is the intention of Filmer, or at least of his followers, is fully compatible with the polemical cast of his mind, and the general tone of unmasking the interested motives that account for the widespread acceptance of the poor arguments advanced by Filmer in the *First Treatise*. It is not the absurdities of Filmer's political theory that most concern Locke, despite the fact that he undertakes at great length to expose them; rather, it is the dangerous practical consequences which Filmer's theory can have, despite or because of its muddled character, if it nevertheless reinforces the view that subjects have no reason to believe that there are any grounds upon which they might legitimately withhold their obedience to the magistrate. And, whatever the internal problems of Filmer's argument, the latter is certainly able to convey to the reader of *Patriarcha* a belief in that proposition.

At the beginning of his discussion of that part of Filmer's argument which deals with the transmission of political authority (I, 78), Locke quotes a passage from *Patriarcha* in order to show that Filmer is not really concerned with finding a means to legitimize the exercise of political power or its transference over time. Filmer had written that

It skills not which way Kings come by their power, whether by election, donation, succession or by any other means, for it is still the manner of the government by supreme power that makes them properly Kings, and not the means of obtaining their crowns.[14]

Nor is this the only place in his writings where Filmer dismisses as unimportant the question of how the ruler comes to power, whether 'by usurpation, or by election of the nobles or of the people, or by any other way whatsoever'. Regardless of the means of obtaining political power, Filmer insists upon defining the latter in terms of the 'right and natural authority of a supreme father'.[15] According to this doctrine, Locke argues, there can be no distinction drawn between a lawful ruler and a usurper, or between 'pirates and lawful princes', because 'he that has force is without any more ado to be obeyed, and crowns and scepters would become the inheritance only of violence and rapine' (I, 81). The general consequence of Filmer's position, therefore, would be 'to unsettle and destroy all the lawful governments in the world, and to establish in their room disorder, tyranny, and usurpation' (I, 72, 124, 142). The more specific ideological charge levelled by Locke against Filmer is that his theory justifies Oliver Cromwell's title just as much as it does that of any ruler who exercises 'supreme power' over his subjects (I, 79, 121). Indeed, in his *Directions for Obedience to Government in Dangerous or Doubtful Times*, written during Cromwell's rule, Filmer did assert that 'the title of a usurper is before, and better than the title of any other' individual except the person who, by rightful descent, would otherwise exercise political power through the natural right of fatherhood.[16] But, as Locke and virtually all of Filmer's critics pointed out, all hope of identifying who that rightful heir was had disappeared in the mists of biblical genealogy several millenniums ago. Hence all individuals – and certainly all those living in the seventeenth century – existed in a condition in which, since the rightful ruler could never be known, Filmer's argument was, in effect, an open invitation to usurpers to gain power by any means possible. This implication of Filmer's argument, of course, made the royalists among Locke's contemporaries very uncomfortable. Filmer continued to speak of power being 'unjustly usurped', and of political power being 'either derived or usurped from the fatherly power', but he seems not to have understood that his own dismissal of the importance of the means of the transference of political power, coupled with a recognition of the empirical impossibility of identifying a specific rightful ruler, rendered meaningless the notion of 'unjustly' usurped power.[17] Although Filmer spoke of 'usurpation', his own argument made it impossible for this term to have any *practical* meaning, so far as the exercise of political authority or the requirements of political obligation were concerned.

Locke argues that if Filmer does not believe that any distinction can be made between legitimate and illegitimate rulers among those who presently exist, then it is pointless to go back to Adam, the Bible and appeals to 'history out of Scripture' (I, 128) in order to instruct the reader regarding the proper origins of government (I, 104). If all rulers, regardless of their personal qualities, the conditions that brought them to power, or their specific actions as magistrates, must be obeyed unconditionally by subjects, and no grounds whatsoever can be appealed to in order to release the latter from this obligation, then it is pointless to buttress this position with some elaborate and difficult-to-prove theoretical account of political power. *De facto* obedience requires no political theory, and certainly not one as arcane as that developed by Filmer. Indeed, a poor political theory is worse than none at all, because by raising questions about the lawfulness of government and the subject's obligation to obey the magistrate that it cannot answer it actually has the effect of calling into question all grounds of obligation, thereby laying 'a sure and lasting foundation of endless contention and disorder, instead of that peace and tranquillity, which is the business of government, and the end of human society' (I, 106, 124).

Thus, in Locke's critique of Filmer's political theory, his two lines of attack merge: on the one hand, he painstakingly exposes the inaccuracies, distortions and absurdities of Filmer's theoretical account of political power and, at the same time, Locke maintains that the very point or meaning of a political theory, viewed in terms of its practical utility, is undermined by Filmer's attempt to move beyond a simple catechismic admonition to obey all rulers unconditionally. Such an instruction – as Locke's allusions in the *Essay Concerning Human Understanding* demonstrate – is best learned by rote through socialization and not through the process of reasoning required to understand a complicated set of interrelated propositions that constitute a political theory. Substantive claims for political authority, in other words, can be criticized and undermined in so far as they can be shown to be incompatible with the ontological, epistemological and methodological presuppositions that are assumed to exist – as socially established conventions – as part of the normative relationship between a political theorist and his audience. Most clerics who borrowed from Filmer, incorporating his ideas into their sermons, were shrewd enough to reduce his 'wonderful system' to a few simple propositions that retained their social effectiveness as principles of practical action through the illocutionary force of the speaker. As a political tract launched into the market-place of ideas as it existed in the 1680s, however, *Patriarcha* had to be assessed according to the prevailing standards exercised by a person of 'ordinary understanding' who entered that market-place as a consumer of political literature. By the end of the seventeenth century the political literacy of Englishmen had grown sufficiently that Locke's argument premissed upon the rationality of his readers lent considerable persuasive force to his methodological critique of Filmer.

NOTES: CHAPTER 3

1 For a discussion of the social and political implications of Locke's epistemological argument in the *Essay Concerning Human Understanding*, see John W. Yolton, *John Locke and the Way of Ideas* (Oxford: Clarendon Press, 1956).

2 Sir Robert Filmer, *Patriarcha and Other Political Works*, ed. Peter Laslett (Oxford: Basil Blackwell, 1949), p. 278; cf. p. 188.

3 ibid., p. 197; cf. pp. 78, 244.

4 ibid., pp. 79, 85, 189, 194, 229, 304. On Filmer's twisted use of Aristotle, see James Daly, *Sir Robert Filmer and English Political Thought* (Toronto: University of Toronto Press, 1979), pp. 16–17.

5 Filmer, *Works*, p. 280.

6 ibid., pp. 187, 203–4, 262.

7 ibid., p. 80.

8 Daly, *Filmer*, pp. 80–1.

9 'The mind if it will proceed rationally, ought to examine all the grounds of probability, and see how they make more or less, for or against any probable proposition, before it assents to or dissents from it, and upon a due balancing the whole, reject, or receive it, with a more or less firm assent, proportionably to the preponderancy of the greater grounds of probability on one side or the other' (4:15, 5).

10 'Locke is, in fact, the first of English thinkers the basis of whose argument is mainly secular' (Harold J. Laski, *Political Thought in England From Locke to Bentham* (London: Oxford University Press, 1920), p. 42; cf. George H. Sabine, *A History of Political Theory*, 3rd edn (New York: Holt, Rinehart & Winston, 1961), p. 518; Sterling P. Lamprecht, *The Moral and Political Philosophy of John Locke*, (1918; reprinted New York: Russell & Russell, 1962), pp. 46, 80 ff.).

11 Filmer, *Works*, pp. 106–7.

12 ibid., p. 96.

13 Filmer does not actually say this. In fact, at one point, he attacks Hobbes's portrayal of the natural condition of man as one in which there was a presumption of 'a right for the father to destroy or eat his children', which, needless to say, is a gross mischaracterization of Hobbes's position (ibid., p. 241). Filmer does acknowledge the practice of fathers selling or castrating their children (p. 231), but he does not mention the father's right to kill them. Yet, since the exercise of political power by the sovereign requires the imposition of penalties extending to death, according to both Locke and Filmer, and since the father is the ruler over his own children as subjects, it logically follows from Filmer's argument that fathers *qua* fathers must have this 'right' to kill their children. Locke's critique, therefore, while it goes beyond Filmer's text, does not violate the intentional meaning of Filmer's argument.

14   ibid., p. 106.
15   ibid., p. 62; cf. p. 84.
16   ibid., p. 232.
17   ibid., pp. 231, 233; Daly, *Filmer*, p. 106.

CHAPTER 4

Property and Political Power

In addition to the tensions within Filmer's thought between a justification of absolute monarchy by divine appointment and a justification of absolute monarchy based on the natural right of fatherhood, and between both of those arguments as part of a natural law position and a *de facto* justification of usurpation, a third source of internal instability threatened to undermine the structure of Filmer's political theory: the relationship between the ownership of private property and the exercise of political power. Here, again, Filmer's objective can be simply stated: he wanted to give the ruler absolute authority over all property under his domain. Nevertheless, given the theoretical path he chose to follow, this conclusion assumed an elusive character, always lying just beyond the reach of Filmer's arguments. Put simply, all the difficulties endemic to Filmer's political theory discussed in the previous chapter are compounded by his treatment of property.

Most seventeenth-century royalists would have subscribed to the practical conclusion of Filmer's argument that all property within the kingdom belongs to the king and that individuals hold their lands and goods at the pleasure of their sovereign. That is, property 'rights' exist as acts of grace on the part of the monarch who has granted his subjects specific privileges entitling them to own land; on this view, property cannot be a juridical right claimed against the authority of the sovereign. In so far as the adjudication of property disputes where the issue affected the king was a matter to be resolved through law, this situation arose only because, once an individual had been granted property by the king, the owner might be supposed to have certain entitlements to his property sanctioned by custom. In some instances, customary practices might serve as a constraint even upon the king's actions. Beyond this point most conservatives were not willing to venture; and even this position, it should be clear, is much further than Filmer was willing to go since he does not sanction any limitations upon the king's authority over property upon any grounds whatsoever.

In his critique of Filmer's argument, Locke fastens upon a fundamental contradiction arising from the conditions under which the ownership of property and political power are transferred from one individual to another. What Filmer offers the reader, according to Locke, are 'two originals of government', that is, two theories of the origins of political society, one founded in property ownership and the other in the right of fatherhood. Filmer maintains that 'all the estate of the father ought to descend to the eldest son', and at the same time he insists 'every man that is born, by his very birth becomes a subject to him that begets him'. While the first statement authorizes the transference of the right of dominion founded upon property to the eldest son, the second proposition cannot justify the exercise of political authority by the eldest son over his brothers since he did not beget them. With respect to him, all the sons have an equal title to authority by right of fatherhood, while, according to the custom of primogeniture, they do not have an equal title to their father's property (I, 74). Thus, upon the death of Adam, 'the sovereignty founded upon property, and the sovereignty founded upon fatherhood, come to be divided'. Since Filmer has associated 'the rights of princes' with each of these sources of sovereignty, his theory, Locke argues, provides 'two titles of dominion, which cannot descend together' to Adam's posterity (I, 75).

Locke's critique of the internal logic of Filmer's argument as it relates to property as a source of political power is an extension of his attack upon Filmer's bifurcated appeal to natural law in order to justify his account of the origins of political authority, discussed in the previous chapter. Yet Locke's treatment of property in the *First Treatise* exhibits a distinctive character, which sets that subject apart from all the other aspects of his polemic against Filmer. By that I mean that instead of merely exposing the weaknesses of Filmer's position, Locke presents a positive statement of his own position on property. Naturally, this topic receives its fullest treatment in chapter 5 of the *Second Treatise*, but some of the propositions crucial to an understanding of that later argument are presented in the *First Treatise*. This is not the case with respect to most of the precepts of Lockean political theory contained in the *Second Treatise*. The state of nature, consent, the importance of the legislative power, the balancing of power between an executive and a legislative, and, of course, the right to resistance are not mentioned – except in passing – in the *First*

Treatise. To understand the importance of these topics to Locke's political theory, one must turn to the *Second Treatise.* It would be a serious mistake, however, to adopt this approach to the subject of property. Rather, one must pay careful attention to what Locke has to say concerning property in the *First Treatise* precisely because some presuppositions in that work are carried forward as part of his argument in the second half of his discourse. In this chapter, therefore, the discussion is more evenly divided between a continuation of the attack against Filmer's ideas and a consideration of Locke's reasons for outlining his own position on the relationship between property and political power.

Early in the *First Treatise*, Locke cites a passage from Filmer asserting that 'the father had power to dispose or sell his children' – that is, to treat them as if they were his property (I, 8). Since the proposition that 'the utmost property man is capable of, which is to have a right to destroy any thing by using it' (I, 39), can logically be applied to children, according to Filmer, this would give fathers the right to destroy their own children – an action that, Locke argues, crosses 'the main intention of nature' and violates the purposes of natural law (I, 52–3, 59). Locke proposes to draw an almost absolute line between human beings and 'things', such that only the latter can be property. The distinction is not absolute, however, because Locke is willing to justify slavery, and slaves are a form of property (II, 23–4). But if he does not challenge Filmer on metaphysical grounds he certainly does so on political grounds since there is, for Locke, a clear difference between subjects and slaves; only the former can be members of political society. Or, to phrase the point negatively, subjects cannot be viewed as being the property of their rulers. If the bulk of the argument in the *First Treatise* is preoccupied with the relationship between fathers and children, because that is the way in which the issue is framed by Filmer, nevertheless, the political implication of Locke's attack upon the notion that human beings can be treated as property is revealed in his denial that individuals 'were made as so many herds of cattle, only for the service, use, and pleasure of their princes' – a viewpoint that Locke associates with absolute monarchy (I, 156). The same natural law that protects children from the exercise of absolute authority by their fathers guarantees the rights of subjects against their rulers.

Locke advances an argument based upon an analysis of the Scriptures and an interpretation of natural law to show that there are divinely imposed limitations upon the power fathers may exercise over their children, but the larger objectives of his critique of Filmer are far more radical than this. For Locke wants to demonstrate that there is no direct relationship between the ownership of property and the exercise of political power. The fact that Filmer fails in his attempt to unify these 'two titles of dominion' is less important than the fact that, for Locke, there is no reason to suppose that political authority and property ownership *should* be united. Locke is much more responsive to the historically variable forms of property than Filmer can possibly be within his rigidly determined framework which sets the definitional boundaries of political power independently of any form of property ownership. Locke's view, in other words, is that political power may or may not be tied to the ownership of property (and property of various kinds), but this contingently historical relationship cannot be transformed into a logically necessary one. My reading of Locke's position is an essentially contestable one, and I shall later have to provide a defence for it in the context of presenting Locke's discussion of the relationship between property and the origins of political society in the *Second Treatise*. But the general importance of the argument to Locke's political thought can hardly be denied, and what I am suggesting here is that Locke's treatment of this issue is central to the structure of his polemic against Filmer in the *First Treatise*.

Apart from a direct refutation of Filmer's miscitation of scriptural texts, and the juxtaposition of contradictory statements contained in his own writings, Locke seeks to outflank his opponent either by appealing to an interpretation of God's intentions or through appeals to certain social practices under the rubric of common sense. The last two tactical weapons have an especially important place in Locke's discussion of property in the *First Treatise*. For Locke wants to undermine Filmer's conception of property ownership by placing the title to the earth in the hands of God. The Deity is the 'sole Lord and Proprietor of the whole world', while we are merely his productive or unproductive tenants (I, 39). At the same time, Locke also wants to show that, based upon the social experience with which his readers are familiar, it cannot be inferred that property-owners do in fact exercise the kind of authority over their tenants that Filmer attributes to Adam as the first property-owner in human history. This last point is more significant than it might at first appear because Filmer's argument is such that he makes no concessions to history in so far as the diminution of power over time is concerned. Thus, whatever power is originally attached to property ownership must remain intact as it is transferred from one individual to another.

It is one of Locke's two principal objectives in the *First Treatise* to prove that God did not give Adam any 'private dominion' over any object or person, and that property must therefore be conceived as a 'right in common with all mankind' (I, 24, 29). The crucial conceptual distinction upon which Locke's argument rests is that between use and ownership as applied to property. God gave the earth to mankind for its use, while retaining for Himself, in some ultimate sense, the title of ownership. Nevertheless, there is an inherent ambiguity in Locke's treatment of this topic because he maintains that users of property do not thereby become owners of property – and thus the distinction is a valid one – while later he does want to demonstrate that ownership arises out of and is in an important sense inextricably tied to the use of property. The first point is the focus of Locke's discussion of property in the *First Treatise*, while the second occupies his attention in the *Second Treatise*. We could differentiate between these two discussions by saying that the former considers property as part of the theological relationship between God and man, while the latter views property within the context of human relationships. But we might also say that there is a legalistic definition of property that requires a definite title, and a practical or customary definition of property that rests upon some set of social practices.

Filmer tried to produce a title-claim to property on behalf of Adam from the Scriptures, but if this literalist argument failed, then no one could be shown to have a privileged or exclusive right to property. One might then have to fall back upon occupancy, consent or labour as the basis for an argument justifying property ownership, but these notions all derived their meaning from some hierarchical ordering of human actions. Locke argues that God never relinquished the title to His 'workmanship', but simply gave men 'a right to make use of a part of the Earth for the support of themselves and families' (I, 37). Whatever property rights are claimed by individuals, therefore, can extend no further than 'that liberty to use [property] which God has permitted' (I, 39). This challenge to Filmer's definition of property contains some significant presuppositions that merit closer attention.

In the first place, it is reasonable to suppose, Locke argues, that an owner allows someone to use his property only if certain purposes are attached to that usage. That is, something of value must be presumed to accrue to the property-owner as the outcome of the latter's arrangement with the user. This means that human beings have a relationship to property (the earth) that is conditional, not absolute, and those conditions must be defined in terms of God's purposes in permitting the use of His property. As a general rule, but not always, Locke identifies his reading of God's intentions with the precepts and purposes embodied in the Law of Nature. Thus, individuals have a right to use property so long as their usage falls within the range of objectives that can be realized through their obedience to natural law. This is an assumption that is obviously crucial to Locke's treatment of property in the *Two Treatises*, and he employs it in his argument against Filmer to show, for example, that it would be ridiculous to suppose that Adam, as the 'proprietor of the whole world', could use his right of ownership in order to 'deny all the rest of mankind food, and so at his pleasure starve them' if they did not 'acknowledge his sovereignty, and obey his will'. Rather, 'it is more reasonable to think, that God who bid mankind increase and multiply' could best have those commands fulfilled by giving all his tenants 'a right to make use of the food and raiment, and other conveniencies of life, the materials whereof he had so plentifully provided for them'. Hence 'the great design of God' to encourage mankind to increase and multiply cannot be promoted by making individuals 'depend upon the will of [one] man for their subsistence, who should have power to destroy them all when he pleased' (I, 41). Filmer himself had invoked the divine intentionality argument in his critique of Hobbes's *Leviathan*, maintaining that God would not 'create man in a condition worse than any beasts, as if he made men to no other end by nature but to destroy one another'. He went on to ridicule Hobbes's suggestion of a natural state of war on the grounds that, while it might be a plausible supposition if there were a scarcity of food, it could not consist with the fact that God had provided plenty of sustenance for men.[1] Yet Filmer did not explain why individuals should be so willing to depend for their subsistence upon the 'permission' of one man, especially in the context of a divinely provided abundance. Why might not this situation induce in them an anxiety concerning their self-preservation that was presumed to exist in Hobbes's state of nature? Why, in other words, was a monopoly (which is an artificially created scarcity) a more stabilizing condition than a natural scarcity?

We can rephrase this part of Locke's critique of Filmer by saying that had God transferred ownership of the earth to Adam – and Filmer never provides any explanation as to why He should have done so – He would no longer be in the position to continue to issue directives regarding the use of that property. But, as Locke shows, this is patently not the case, for in addition to the command to increase and multiply God directed Adam to labour, that is, to till the earth. Locke does not miss the opportunity to point out the irony of the fact that this scriptural imperative placed Adam in the position of being simultaneously both a property-owner and a day labourer (I, 44–5). Moreover, God subsequently gave Noah the right to kill and eat animals for his subsistence, and it is difficult to see why the Deity should continue to issue such specific commands concerning the use of his property if, as Filmer maintains, Adam was at his creation the absolute and unconditional proprietor of the whole world and everything it in (I, 39). In further support of his argument, Locke cites a passage from Genesis in which God gives the earth in common to Noah and his sons (I, 32–8). Quite apart from the interpretative difficulties this scriptural text poses for Filmer's position, even if his reading of it were correct and God could be presumed to have given Noah alone absolute control over property, this would not support the once-and-for-all transfer of the title of property that Filmer assigned to Adam. For, on that view, the absoluteness of the privileges of property ownership could subsequently neither be added to nor subtracted from, but would automatically accompany the transfer of property from one owner to another. Yet, Locke argues, this is evidently not God's view of the matter, since He continues to act as if He were the proprietor of the earth, which indeed He is.

Unlike political authority, which has a dual foundation in divine appointment and the natural right of fatherhood, property is wholly derivative, according to Filmer, from the positive grant of God. There is no such thing as a claim to property ownership 'by right of nature' in Filmer's political thought. Therefore, if the exclusivity of property rights cannot be justified from the text of the Bible, they cannot be justified at all. Hence it is especially the case with respect to the definition of property in Filmer's thought that the principle of interpretative charity has no place. If Locke is successful in demonstrating the untenability of Filmer's position through his own commentary on the Scriptures, then he has achieved the purely polemical objectives of his argument. Yet Locke's discussion of property in the *First Treatise* does not end there. He goes on to present an outline of his own general position on property.

Locke's account of property and the rights attached to it rests upon the proposition that property is a right held in common by all mankind. Locke first attempts to establish this point through citation of biblical passages that support the view that the original grant of property by God was to the human species as a whole. Locke interprets the passage alluded to above, for example, as stating that the earth was given to Noah and his sons collectively and, through them, to all mankind. 'This text', Locke argues, 'is a confirmation of the original community of all things amongst the sons of men', which is reaffirmed in other scriptural texts (I, 40). The second route by which Locke seeks to justify this assertion is through his assignment of natural law obligations to parents to provide for the subsistence of their children. The Law of Nature provides for the 'natural right of children to inherit the goods of their parents', and this right, Locke argues, already presupposes their 'right to be nourished and maintained by their parents, nay a right not only to a bare subsistence but to the conveniences and comforts of life, as far as the conditions of their parents can afford it' (I, 88–9). Since all children have an equal right to their father's property – I will return to Locke's discussion of primogeniture in a moment – this means that, according to natural law, everyone has 'an equal right to the use of the inferior creatures, for the comfortable preservation of their beings, which is all the property man hath in them . . . and thus men had a right in common . . . [to] provide for their subsistence' (I, 87).

Locke was willing to justify this natural rights claim even against statutory laws or customary practices that inhibited its realization. Hence, if a son dies without issue, 'the father has a right in nature to possess his goods, and inherit his estate (whatever the municipal laws of some countries may absurdly direct otherwise)' (I, 90). And, more generally, any needy individual has 'a right to the surplusage' of another's goods, 'so that it cannot justly be denied him, when his pressing wants call for it', for it is always 'a sin in any man of estate, to let his brother perish for want of affording him relief out of his plenty'. In short, 'God requires him to afford to the wants of his brother', and adherence to this principle 'gives every man a title to so much out of another's plenty, as will keep him from extreme want, where he has no means to subsist otherwise' (I, 42).[2] Locke also observes that if an individual with no kin dies his possessions 'in the state of nature become again perfectly common, nobody having a right to inherit them', and his property therefore returns to its original state. And to this passage Locke adds a cross-reference to his discussion of property in the *Second Treatise* (I, 90).

Locke's defence in the *First Treatise* of the equal natural right to property which everyone has is significant, I am arguing, not simply because it is the ground from which he launched his attack against Filmer, but also because it is so clearly tied to a natural law position and a reading of God's intentions in terms of which any concept of property must be defined. This aspect of Locke's agument in the *Second Treatise* has frequently been overlooked by interpreters of that work, despite the fact, as I shall demonstrate later, that there is a good deal of evidence indicating that Locke has not set aside the theological framework which is unmistakably central to his argument in the *First Treatise*.

The second part of Locke's critique of Filmer's view of property operates on the level of a discussion of certain social practices. Sometimes Locke appeals to these social practices or customs in order to illustrate their incompatibility with the assumptions of Filmer's argument, but occasionally Locke attacks these social practices from the standpoint of his own presuppositions about property. The general point of Locke's argument is to show that political authority and property ownership are distinctly separable features of human existence, such that one cannot simply assume that one follows from the other. This proposition need not entail, of course, the assertion that no relationship exists between property and political authority. Rather, what Locke means is that the relationship that exists between political authority and property is a humanly constituted contingency that can be known in any particular instance only through empirical knowledge of how a specific political society is constituted.

Even if 'Adam was made sole proprietor of the whole earth', Locke asks, 'what will this be to his sovereignty'? That is, how is it 'that property in land gives a man power over the life of another' (I, 41)? In fact, Locke maintains that Filmer never provides any evidence to 'prove that propriety in land . . . gave any authority over the persons of men'. That it does so is simply one of Filmer's assertions without proof. For Locke, however, 'it is clear that . . . private dominion could give [Adam] no sovereignty' (I, 43). Since Adam is the best example one might choose to illustrate the interconnectedness or unity of property and sovereignty, Locke's rejection of Filmer's position has the effect of calling into question any general presumption that there is a necessary relationship between property in land and political authority over persons. 'The power of making laws of life and death', Locke observes, 'is indeed a mark of sovereignty' (I, 129), but the question is what does this 'political power of life and death' have to do with being a 'proprietor of the goods and lands' (I, 48) within any particular society? Locke develops his analysis of the differences between these two forms of social power as they relate to the social institution of the family.

In his treatment of the rights of children, Locke argues that while a

son has 'a right to succeed to his father's property . . . this can give
him no right to succeed also to the rule, which his father had over
other men' (I, 93). Property and political authority, in short, flow in
separable channels. Filmer had challenged this proposition, which he
associated with Aristotle and Suarez, maintaining that political and
economical power do not really and essentially differ from each other.[3]
Hence no quantitative extension of Adam's family, nor any alteration
in the means by which members of society provided for their
subsistence, nor any extent of inequality of wealth and property
ownership between members of society, according to Filmer, could
have the least effect upon the nature or amount of political power that
had been granted to Adam and which was passed on by him to other
kings. For Locke, however, and for the Whigs and Republicans who
wrote against Filmer in the 1680s, such as James Tyrrell and Algernon
Sidney, it was very important to adopt a developmental approach to
the growth of economic power, and to insist that different levels of
economic development did have a significant effect upon determining
or undermining particular forms of government. Locke provides a
preview of the importance of this general argument and its specific
political application in the *Second Treatise* when he observes in
paragraph 33 of the *First Treatise* that absolute monarchy as a form of
government cannot be reconciled with God's purposes as expressed
through natural law (I, 33, 41).

Nevertheless, the full implications of Locke's position do not
emerge until the second half of his book. In the *First Treatise*, Locke
concentrates his attention upon showing that the transmission of
political power and of property occur by different means and serve
different general purposes. This aspect of Locke's argument is focused
upon the concepts of consent and inheritance, and especially upon the
attempt to locate the meaning of these concepts in the context of
seventeenth-century social life.

We have already seen that, according to the Law of Nature, one
person cannot withhold a surplusage of goods from another who is
starving, but Locke restates this general point in a manner that
conveys a specific social resonance when he observes that 'a man can
no more justly make use of another's necessity, to force him to
become his vassal, by withholding that relief' which he could provide.
The implication that Locke draws from this injunction is that the
lord–vassal social relationship is based upon force, and represents, in
essence, a form of slavery (I, 42). To this social relation, Locke
contrasts one based upon consent. Thus,

the authority of the rich proprietor, and the subjection of the needy beggar began not from the possession of the Lord, but the consent of the poor man, who preferred being his subject to starving. And the man he thus submits to, can pretend to no more power over him, than he has consented to, upon compact. (I, 43)

We may regard this as being a small triumph for the notion of consent, since the starving beggar is forced by natural necessity to 'consent' to an arrangement which, in actual social practice, may not be so easily distinguishable from the lord–vassal relationship as Locke assumes, and of which he is critical. Indeed, viewed with the benefit of hindsight and later theories of exploitation, even this phrasing of the point is rather charitable to Locke. Yet he evidently believes the distinction to be important. Later, in the *Second Treatise*, it is reaffirmed when Locke observes that 'a freeman makes himself a servant to another, by selling him for a certain time, the service he undertakes to do, in exchange for wages he is to receive', according to 'the contract between them' (II, 85). Even if this arrangement results in a life of 'drudgery' for the worker, Locke insists that it cannot be equated with a condition of slavery (II, 24).[4] Whether or not one shares Locke's enthusiasm for this distinction, the question with respect to the text is why is this point so important to Locke's general argument. The answer, I believe, lies in the different *political* meanings that can be read into or derived from the ownership of property, when the latter is viewed in the historical context of different forms of distribution of social power. That is, against Filmer and what he takes to be the assumption underlying the lord–vassal relationship, Locke argues that 'the possession of the Lord' does not, in itself, entitle him to any authority over persons. If this were not so, it might very well be argued that political power should be seen through the definitional framework of the inheritance of property. But, then, why should 'consent' enter into the consideration of political relationships at all?

In other words, Locke is attempting to demonstrate not only that the social relations of property are, at certain historical stages, based upon consent, but also that, even if they were not, political authority must be based upon consent. Both arguments are employed by Locke in the *First Treatise* in order to undermine the social and political significance of the concept of 'inheritance', upon which he believes Filmer's political argument rests. Even if the needy beggar does not appear to us to be appreciably better off, economically speaking, Locke believes that it does make a difference whether one views the

social and political relations of property ownership from the
perspective of the poor man who consents to them or from the
perspective of the rich property-owner who simply *assumes* that the
opinions of others are irrelevant to the exercise of his power because
the latter is a function of inheritance and customary practice. For
Locke, however, political authority can be conveyed by one individual
to another only through the mechanism of consent, *no matter how rich
or poor* the two individuals in question may be. Stated in this way,
there are at least potentially radical implications attached to this
presupposition if one were to employ it as the standard of membership
for political society. I shall argue in Chapter 7 that this is precisely
what Locke does.

Moreover, as we shall see, there are corollary assumptions attached
to the notion of consent that are very important to other aspects of
Locke's political argument. In the particular example cited above, it is
Locke's defence of the individual's capacity to consent which ensures
that he cannot be treated as the 'property' of another. That is, Locke
assumes that the individual 'may be disposed to consent to nothing,
but what may be suitable to the dignity and excellency of a rational
creature' (*STCE*, § 31). And, whatever the difficulties encountered by
later liberals in the face of the allegation that the social and economic
institutions established by them did, in fact, treat human beings as
things or property, it is not impossible for us to appreciate Locke's
intentions in making this point or why he believed it could be
employed as a polemical weapon against certain forms of social–
economic relationships.

In the *First Treatise*, Locke draws a comparison between money and
consent and the ownership of land and inheritance as sources of
political power. He cites the example of a colonial planter in the West
Indies, arguing that the enlargement of families through the
acquisition of servants is a process dependent upon the accumulation
of money, and not a consequence of the inheritance of property.
Thus,

> Those who were rich in the patriarchs' days, as in the West Indies
> now, bought men and maid servants, and by their increase as well
> as purchasing of new, came to have large and numerous families,
> which though they made use of in war or peace, can it be thought
> the power they had over them was an inheritance descended from
> Adam, when 'twas the purchase of their money?

'The getting a dominion over anything by bargain and money,' Locke argues, is very different from the acquisition of dominion through 'descent and inheritance' (I, 130). This point is crucial to Locke's discussion of the transmission of political power, for, 'if the agreement and consent of men first gave a scepter into anyone's hand, or put a crown on his head, that also must direct its descent and conveyance'. And again, in this passage, he draws the contrast with the succession of power through inheritance (I, 94).

Later, Locke assimilated virtually all social relationships, not only between ruler and subject, or master and servant, but also between husband and wife, under the category of consent, despite the biting criticism from contemporaries directed against such a social perspective, as expressed in some of the political tracts read by Locke during the period he was writing the *Two Treatises*. Even later commentators have been induced to smile at what sometimes appears to be Locke's naïve reliance upon the notion of consent, which (to paraphrase Humpty-Dumpty's remark in *Alice through the Looking Glass*) is one of the hardest-working concepts in the *Two Treatises of Government*. Notwithstanding the prevalence of the patriarchal family as a social institution in seventeenth-century England, and despite the fact that lords of the manor were frequently likened to little kings with respect to their tenants, Locke evidently believed that his appeal to various actions identified with consent were sufficiently well-established social practices among his contemporaries that his attempt to situate the meaning of key concepts of his political argument in these practices would redound to his benefit in his critique of Filmer in the *First Treatise*. We are entitled to voice some scepticism regarding the accuracy of Locke's perception, especially when the meanings attached to his terminology have a definite radical tinge to them, but it is important to appreciate the extent to which Locke was willing to challenge Filmer on the very ground which many scholars have seen as being the strongest aspect of his political thought, namely, its reflection of certain experiential practices which Filmer's readers recognized as being important in shaping their own lives.

At the same time, Locke showed little hesitancy about attacking some deeply rooted social practices which were at odds with his own presuppositions about property. He sharply criticized primogeniture in the *First Treatise*, for example, and he did so in a manner that indicates that this critique was not merely an adjunct to his general polemic against Filmer. We have already noted Locke's defence of the

equal right to subsistence of all the children within a family, and his
dismissal of the claim that the eldest brother is entitled by inheritance
to exercise any fatherly or political power over his siblings. Locke,
however, presses the argument further, maintaining that certain
existing laws pertaining to inheritance ought to be repealed. Many
countries, he observes, in 'their particular municipal laws give the
whole possession of land entirely to the first born'. This has led some
people to suppose that 'there was a natural or divine right of
primogeniture', a supposition Locke is anxious to refute. It has also
misled them into believing that property and political power share a
common set of rules or purposes (I, 91). To refute this belief, Locke
briefly sketches the fundamental principles that differentiate property
from political power; namely, that the former is derived from a
divinely granted right to subsistence, and 'is for the benefit and sole
advantage of the proprietor', while the latter is instituted by human
beings and 'is for the good of the governed' (I, 92). It would be a
mistake, in my opinion, to see this as anything more than a starting-
point for the argument Locke wishes to make, because, in the end,
and certainly in chapter 5 of the *Second Treatise*, the notion that
property can be seen within a framework defined in terms of the 'sole
advantage of the proprietor' is not an accurate characterization of
Locke's position. In fact, this view of property had been attacked and
rejected by Locke in his lectures on natural law at Oxford.[5] What
Locke proposes to prove in the *First Treatise* is that, in so far as the
Law of Nature is directed towards the good of all, and the ownership
of property is directed towards purely personal or selfish needs, the
two must diverge. As Locke sees it, this is a dilemma internal to
Filmer's argument, and his statement in the *First Treatise* cited above
is therefore intended to show that adopting Filmer's position as a
starting-point for one's treatment of property would make it virtually
impossible to reconcile the existence of that institution with the
purposes of natural law.

That this is Locke's intention is clear from the application he
immediately makes of the principled distinction he has just enunciated.
In asserting that, within the family, 'the first born has not a sole or
peculiar right by any law of God and nature' to inherit his father's
property, Locke appeals to natural law on behalf of 'the younger
children' to 'an equal title' to their parents' property. In support of
this appeal, he restates the maxim that 'government being for the
benefit of the governed, and not the sole advantage of the governors',
all the members of society 'are taken care of . . . for the good of the

whole' (I, 92). In other words, the application of natural law to property must undermine Filmer's defence of primogeniture, because the latter places property in the hands of the eldest son for his sole pleasure and benefit, while, according to the Law of Nature, it ought to be used for the benefit of all – in this case, for the benefit of all the members of the family. Still, Locke's argument in this passage retains certain aspects of Filmer's position as a hypothesis, since he also concedes that even if one assumed that each of the children claimed property for his own personal advantage there would nevertheless remain an important distinction to be drawn between government for the common good and private property viewed as a realization of the selfish ends of the proprietor (I, 93).

The major thrust of Locke's argument in the *First Treatise* is focused upon this dichotomy of purposes, the object of which is to demonstrate that the concept of primogeniture (and its relationship to property) cannot be applied to political power. Yet, in the course of this argument, Locke has laid the groundwork through his natural law critique of primogeniture, even in its association with property, for a reconciliation between the purposes of property ownership and the purposes of political society, provided that both are seen as a fulfilment of the obligations imposed upon individuals by the Law of Nature to act for the common good. The means by which this reconciliation can be effected, however, are not stated by Locke until the *Second Treatise*. We can rephrase this point by saying that, while in the *First Treatise* Locke contents himself with merely drawing the contrast between the purposes of political society (common good) and the purposes of property for individual use, in the *Second Treatise* Locke's own argument requires that the former take precedence over the latter, and this claim can only be upheld and at the same time be viewed as a harmonious reconciliation of property and political power through employing a concept of property that is consonant with and derivable from the purposes of natural law.

Filmer's defence of primogeniture draws much of its force from the fact that he is appealing to a custom sanctioned by the laws of society. But, as Locke points out, 'the positive laws of men cannot determine that which is itself the foundation of all law and government . . . the law of God and nature' (I, 126). Since 'the positive laws of the society' must be 'made conformable to the Laws of Nature, for the public good' (I, 92), it is always possible to criticize the former in terms of the latter, which is the viewpoint expressed in Locke's critique of the social practice of primogeniture. This position had already been articulated by the Levellers in their attack upon primogeniture, and its reassertion in the *Two Treatises* was therefore likely to resurrect in the minds of Locke's readers at least some resonance of the radical egalitarianism with which it had earlier been associated.

If, Locke observes at the beginning of the *Second Treatise*, there is 'no Law of Nature nor positive law of God' that can be appealed to in order to justify Filmer's conception of political society, then we 'must of necessity find out another rise of government, another original of political power' (II, 1). To offer just such an alternative justification for political authority is the purpose of the *Second Treatise*, to which we must now turn our attention.

NOTES: CHAPTER 4

1   Sir Robert Filmer, *Patriarcha and Other Political Works*, ed. Peter Laslett (Oxford: Basil Blackwell, 1949), pp. 241–2.
2   Locke uses this principle to criticize a corn-dealer who withholds the sale of his corn during a famine in order to obtain a higher price than people are able to pay. Such an action 'offends against the common rule of charity'. This note, entitled 'Venditio', is reprinted in John Dunn, 'Justice and the interpretation of Locke's political theory', *Political Studies*, Vol. 16, no. 1 (February 1968), pp. 68–87; p. 86.
3   Filmer, *Works*, pp. 74–8.
4   Elsewhere Locke observes that a workman must accept the rate of wages offered by his employer 'or sit still and starve' (*The Works of John Locke*, 12th edn, 9 vols (1824), Vol. 4, p. 28).
5   The interpretation of Locke's view of property as a function of the individual's self-interest can be found in Leo Strauss, *Natural Right and History* (Chicago, Ill.: University of Chicago Press, 1953), and C. B. Macpherson, *The Political Theory of Possessive Individualism* (London: Oxford University Press, 1962). I have included a discussion of Locke's views of the relationship between self-interest and property as presented in his essays on natural law in my examination of his theory of property in the *Second Treatise* (see Chapter 6 below).

CHAPTER 5

Natural Equality and Common Good

Apart from natural law, no concept is more important to Locke's argument in the *Two Treatises* than the state of nature. The significance of the concept, however, does not ensure that the meaning Locke attaches to it can be easily understood. Indeed, it could be argued that it is precisely the ambiguity of the state of nature, its several meanings in the context of Locke's argument, that accounts for its importance to his political theory. I believe the state of nature embodies a moral, historical and political meaning. Of course, this is an analytical distinction I have made for purposes of exposition, and while I think it is defensible in terms of Locke's own methodological approach to politics it must be emphasized that these meanings frequently overlap and intersect throughout the course of his argument in the *Second Treatise*. It is also useful to recall the point made in Chapter 2 that, for Locke, a political theory is composed of two distinguishable parts, one rooted in moral principles and the other in prudential judgements based upon experience. In the discussion that follows, therefore, I propose to view Locke's usage of the state of nature within this definitional framework. In addition to the moral and historical aspects of the state of nature which incorporates this dualistic conception of political theory, however, there is a specific political meaning that Locke wishes to convey through his employment of that term which must also be taken into account.

The rather abrupt methodological switch from the examination of 'history out of Scripture' of Filmer's argument in the *First Treatise* to the definitional opening of the *Second Treatise* has led some interpreters to view the latter work as being an attempt on Locke's part to develop a political theory which is, in effect, a network of interrelated abstractions. I believe this is a mistaken and, at the very least, an exaggerated reading of Locke's intentions with respect to the argument of the *Second Treatise*. A more plausible case can be made for the argument that the moral elements of Locke's political theory, and hence the moral implications of the state of nature, can be interpreted according to a model of political theory which assigns primary importance to the analytical relationship between concepts. In this view, the state of nature is fundamentally an analytical construct employed by Locke. It is ahistorical and cannot be regarded as having any significant connection with or dependency upon any empirical references.[1]

While this interpretative viewpoint is closer to Locke's position, especially in the light of his belief that the principles of morality are capable of being stated in a form analogous to the basic axioms of mathematics, in the end even this identification of the meaning of morality with an analytical approach is not an accurate rendering of Locke's perspective. In part, this is because, for Locke, morality is too closely tied to the precepts of Christianity as revealed religion to be severed from its source, even in the interests of exposition. Or, to put it another way, the gains to be made from such an identification do not equal the costs, when both of these are assessed in terms of understanding the basic structure of Locke's thought as a whole. But, even leaving aside the sacrifice of Locke's religious convictions, I would argue against the attempt to describe the moral aspects of Locke's argument in the *Second Treatise* in terms of an analytical methodology on the grounds that such a view necessarily under-estimates the degree to which the persuasive force of Locke's specific political objectives in that work depends upon the ability of Locke's contemporary readers to recognize that 'the state all men are naturally in' is deeply rooted in the experience of their own life-world. Thus, while it might seem convenient to divide our discussion of the state of nature into a consideration of its purely analytical (moral) and its purely historical meanings, there are good reasons for not adopting this approach. Even our consideration of the definitional features of the state of nature, therefore, must presuppose that these definitions are rooted in the reality of things, from an epistemological standpoint.

One of Locke's criticisms of Filmer in the *First Treatise* is that he fails to supply the reader with a clear definition of what he means by fatherly authority (I, 7). To forestall the application of this criticism to his own position, Locke begins the *Second Treatise* with a definition of political power:

> Political power, then, I take to be a right of making laws with penalties of death, and consequently all less penalties, for the regulating and preserving of property, and of employing the force of

the community, in the execution of such laws, and in the defense of the commonwealth from foreign injury, and all this only for the public good. (II, 3)

This definition, to which frequent reference will be made in later chapters, cannot simply stand alone, however, as if its meaning were self-evidently clear, either to Locke's reader or to us. Rather, it is merely the starting-point for a discussion of the presuppositions underlying Locke's conception of political power. Thus, 'to understand political power right, and derive it from its original, we must consider what state all men are naturally in', that is, a state of nature (II, 4). In other words, the 'right of making laws with penalties of death', the existence of the property to be preserved, the notion of 'the community' and some definition of 'the public good' must all be explained in terms of Locke's characterization of the state of nature if political power, which is comprised of these elements, is to be properly understood. In this chapter I propose to discuss the moral and political meanings of the state of nature, reserving a consideration of the latter's historical dimensions until Chapter 6, where this subject can be treated in relation to Locke's views on the origin and development of property.

With respect to the moral meaning of the state of nature, Locke's argument can be divided into three parts. First, 'the state of nature has a Law of Nature to govern it, which obliges everyone' (II, 6). The state of nature must be seen in relation to the true standard of morality – natural law – and, in so far as that law does 'govern' men in this natural condition, Locke's description of the latter will necessarily incorporate the normative features he ascribes to the Law of Nature. Second, human beings must be supposed to possess certain attributes which make them capable of acting as moral agents, and these attributes must be included in any description of their natural condition. Individuals are assumed, for example, to have 'perfect freedom to order their actions, and dispose of their possessions, and persons as they think fit' (II, 4). As noted earlier in our discussion of Locke's concept of a 'person', it is impossible to provide a theory of moral action without making certain assumptions concerning the attributes and powers of the actors. As we shall see, this freedom and power of individuals over their own persons is a crucially important presupposition to a number of specific arguments Locke advances in the *Second Treatise*. Third, the moral characteristics of the state of nature must be viewed in the context of certain social relations that are presumed to exist among individuals living in that state. The view that Locke conceives of the state of nature as a natural condition of atomistic individuals who have essentially no relationship to each other has, I think, now been wholly abandoned by interpreters of his thought. There may be some dispute as to whether the social relations in the state of nature contribute to or inhibit the realization of the moral purposes of Locke's argument, but the portrayal of Lockean man's natural condition as atomistic has been thoroughly and convincingly discredited by the scholarly work on Locke produced in the last thirty years. The most generalized form of social relations in the state of nature presupposed by Locke's definition of political power sees the individual as a member of a natural community. Locke assumes that it is possible for an individual to act on behalf or in the interest of the community. Without this assumption, it is difficult to see how he could envisage any realization of the public good in the state of nature. Some interpreters of Locke's thought, it is true, have suggested that Locke subscribed to just such a negative conclusion, but this renders pointless his effort to present a 'right' view of the definition he has just offered the reader. In other words, if individuals cannot be presumed to be capable of acting for the public good in the state of nature, they cannot, in Locke's view, be presumed to act for the common good within political society. For, contrary to Hobbes's approach, Locke's definition of political power is framed in such a way as to demonstrate that all of its basic ingredients are constitutive elements of the natural condition of individuals. What I am arguing, then, is that Locke assumes that individuals are members of a natural community, and that the social relationships within this larger community are evaluated by Locke according to whether or not they further the ends of this 'community of nature' (II, 6). This means that these social relations are part of the moral meaning that Locke gives to the concept of the state of nature.

Locke's comment that 'it would be besides my present purpose, to enter here into the particulars of the Law of Nature' (II, 12) has been remarked upon by some commentators as evidence of a rather loose or disingenuous attitude towards the importance of natural law to Locke's argument in the *Second Treatise*.[2] Locke's critics have a point, especially in the light of his willingness to enter into a detailed discussion of the particulars of natural law in his Oxford lectures, which, at the time of the publication of the *Two Treatises*, were available to him and from which he could easily have drawn several statements for the purpose of clarifying his argument in the *Second*

Treatise. In my opinion, the distinction Locke draws in those lectures between dispositions and actions with respect to the obligations of the Law of Nature would have been particularly useful to his description of the moral status of the individual living in the state of nature. Be that as it may, if we try to view the issue from Locke's perspective and ask what it is about natural law that is absolutely essential to Locke's argument in the *Second Treatise*, the proposition that what he says is at least necessary, if not sufficient, for his 'present purpose' might prove to be a defensible one.

According to Locke, the Law of Nature is a rule 'of reason and common equity, which is that measure God has set to the actions of men, for their mutual security' (II, 8, 11). Natural law is therefore intrinsically linked not only with God, as the divine lawmaker, but also with the purposes for which God created individuals in the first place. Thus,

> men being all the workmanship of one omnipotent, and infinitely wise Maker; all the servants of one Sovereign Master, sent into the world by his order and about his business, they are his property, whose workmanship they are, made to last during his, not one another's pleasure.

The question is, then, what is the 'business' or purpose to be achieved through God's having created individuals in a state of nature. Locke replies that the Law of Nature 'teaches all mankind . . . that being all equal and independent, no one ought to harm another in his life, health, liberty, or possessions'. Moreover, as it is clear from natural law that 'every one as he is bound to preserve himself . . . so by the like reason when his own preservation comes not in competition, ought he, as much as he can, to preserve the rest of mankind' (II, 6). 'The Law of Nature', that is, 'willeth the peace and preservation of all mankind', which means that individuals are proscribed 'from doing hurt to one another' (II, 7; *ELN*, 163). In short, 'the peace and safety' of life in the state of nature is 'provided for by the Law of Nature' (II, 8).

This does not mean that the state of nature is, in fact, a condition of peace and safety, but that is not the subject presently being considered. Rather, what Locke is attempting to show is that there is a moral standard that God has given to individuals in their natural condition prohibiting them from taking *any action* that would harm another individual. And, positively, natural law obliges them to act in a manner that will preserve mankind in general. The outcome of complete adherence to natural law would therefore be a condition of peace and safety.[3] In so far as the moral meaning of the state of nature is rooted in an understanding of God's relationship to man expressed through natural law, Locke has described that relationship in its barest essentials, but in a manner that is necessary to his argument in the *Second Treatise*.

The degree to which individuals do fulfil the obligations of the Law of Nature depends upon what powers, desires and faculties we imagine them to have. Locke assumes that individuals possess the freedom to order their actions, because 'that freedom [is] the foundation of all the rest' (II, 17) of the moral actions they execute in the state of nature. Moreover, God's purposes in establishing natural law would be obviated if he had not endowed human beings with this freedom to direct their own actions. As Locke observes, 'God having given man an understanding to direct his actions, has allowed him a freedom of will, and liberty of acting, as properly belonging thereunto, within the bounds of that law he is under' (II, 58). But, while freedom is a necessary element of human action, Locke argues that it is not equatable with an absolute liberty to do whatever one wants. Rather, freedom presupposes 'a standing rule to live by, common to every one of that society', so that liberty in practice means 'a liberty to follow my own will in all things, where the rule prescribes not'. Hence the natural freedom of man in the state of nature 'is to be under no other restraint but the Law of Nature' (II, 22).

> For law, in its true notion, is not so much the limitation as the direction of a free and intelligent agent to his proper interest, and prescribes no farther than is for the general good of those under that law. Could they be happier without it, the law, as a useless thing, would of itself vanish . . . so that . . . the end of law is not to abolish or restrain, but to preserve and enlarge freedom: For in all the states of created beings capable of laws, where there is no law, there is no freedom. (II, 57)

This statement certainly applies to individuals living in the state of nature, for 'were there no law [of nature], there would be no moral good or evil, but man would be left to a most entire liberty in all his actions' (FTG, 124). Such a claim for liberty, Locke argues, would 'negate the law of nature'. Not only does this viewpoint sanction actions that Locke believes are immoral, but it also represents a blasphemous attack upon the Deity in its 'brutish' denial that God has given man a rule of morality to live by (*ELN*, 119, 123, 189, 201, 207, 211, 213). In short, the individual's natural freedom is 'a liberty to dispose, and order, as he lists, his person, actions, possessions, and his whole property, within the allowance of those laws under which he is; and therein not to be subject to the arbitrary will of another, but freely follow his own' (II, 57). Hence, while we are under 'the rules and restraints of reason', the individual is also presumed by Locke to have 'a mind free, and master of itself and all its actions' (*STCE*, § 36, 66).[4]

But if man's actions are, in one sense, limited by God's purposes they are also a fulfilment of those purposes, in so far as an individual uses the understanding God has given him to direct his actions. I have framed the issue in this way because, when speaking of the moral dimensions of the state of nature, the argument should remain on the same plane and not shift back and forth between levels. Therefore, if God is responsible for natural law viewed as a restraint upon human action, he is also responsible, according to Locke, for giving individuals freedom of will and the faculty of reasoning. Despite the fact that he is describing the natural human condition, these are not merely naturalistic claims to reason or liberty on the part of man but, rather, for Locke, they are divinely decreed attributes wrought into the constitution of human nature. From this standpoint, the notion that Locke is espousing some covertly Hobbesian position in the *Second Treatise*, quite apart from the absurdity of such an interpretation in view of the political objectives of that work, would require for its support not merely the manipulation of specific passages from the *Two Treatises*, but the restructuring of the whole of Locke's thought as it relates to his interpretation of God's purposes manifest through His creation of man.

If an individual cannot be supposed to possess the understanding or reason necessary to direct his will, as is the case with children, then he cannot be said 'to have any will of his own to follow' (II, 58). 'Is a man under the Law of Nature?' Locke asks. What is it that 'gave him a free disposing of his property according to his own will, within the compass of that Law? I answer: state of maturity wherein he might be supposed capable to know that law, that so he might keep his actions within the bounds of it.' Without 'such a state of reason', no individual could be assumed to be free (or moral). But 'when he has acquired that state, he is presumed to know how far that law is to be his guide, and how far he may make use of his freedom, and so comes to have it' (II, 59).

> The freedom then of man and liberty of acting according to his own will, is grounded on his having reason, which is able to instruct him in that law he is to govern himself by, and make him know how far he is left to the freedom of his own will. To turn him loose to an unrestrained liberty, before he has reason to guide him, is not the allowing him the privilege of his nature, to be free; but to thrust him out amongst the brutes, and abandon him to a state as wretched, and as much beneath that of a man, as theirs. (II, 63)

'Thus we are born free, as we are born rational; not that we have actually the exercise of either: Age that brings one, brings with it the other too' (II, 61).

In other words, what is absolutely crucial to Locke's description of the state of nature is his characterization of human nature in terms of God's workmanship and purposes which require that human beings be endowed with free will and reason, and without which 'moral action' would have no meaning whatsoever.[5] It is from this standpoint, Locke argues, that an individual can 'be supposed capable of knowing the law [of nature], and so living within the rules of it' (II, 60, 170). Individuals living in the state of nature must be 'presumed to know how far that Law is to be [their] guide'. This presumption is not always fulfilled in practice, but the very fact that it is not means that, in those specific instances, the individual has 'quit the principles of human nature' (II, 10) in so acting, and thereby merits punishment for seeking 'to live by another rule, than that of reason and common equity' (II, 8). 'For having quitted reason, which God hath given to be the rule betwixt man and man', the individual, by 'revolting from his own kind to that of beasts by making force which is theirs, to be his rule of right', has forfeited his claim to be a rational, moral human being, and he may be destroyed 'as any other wild beast, or noxious brute with whom mankind can have neither society nor security' (II, 172). But, until he does in fact demonstrate through his actions that he has adopted another 'rule' to live by, the individual must be presumed to be a rational moral person. Even children, though they are not able to act as fully rational beings, are entitled 'to be treated as rational creatures' (*STCE*, § 54, 81). There is no reason to suppose that Locke did not incorporate this same principle into his conceptualization of the natural condition of man in the *Second Treatise*.

To abandon the use of one's reason, or to trespass against the Law of Nature, according to Locke, is to place oneself in a state of war.

The difference between the state of nature and the state of war thus turns on whether or not there is a Law of Nature which 'truly governs' individuals in the state of nature, or whether they 'live by another rule', which is that of force and violence (II, 16). Locke maintains that 'men living together according to reason, without a common superior on earth, with authority to judge between them, is properly the state of nature' (II, 19). As Locke declared in his essays on the Law of Nature, the alternative to this condition is one in which individuals follow 'the urges of their base instincts rather than the dictates of reason'. We cannot suppose, Locke argues, that 'the principles of moral action' can be grounded in this description of human nature. On the contrary, beginning with this presupposition would require us to believe that individuals naturally exist 'in a state of war' with each other – an assumption that he characterizes as 'absurd' and contrary 'to reason [and] to human nature' (*ELN*, 115, 203, 211, 213, 215).

Thus far, Locke has postulated that there is a Law of Nature and that individuals are naturally capable of obeying it. But, just as the concept of a law without a lawmaker is meaningless, so is the notion of a law that is not enforced. For 'where the laws cannot be executed, it is all one as if there were no laws' (II, 219). Here Locke's argument moves on to rougher ground, for he must designate some definite means whereby natural law *is* – not merely hypothetically, but actually – enforced in the state of nature. If he does not do so, then the existential link between God and man is broken, and the entire argument becomes merely an analytical construct in Locke's mind. But if, as Locke believes, he is describing the natural condition of man as created by God and in terms of His purposes, then the reality of that description requires that human beings actually realize those purposes in the state of nature. Locke confronts the problem boldly, by placing the power of enforcement of natural law in the hands of the individual.

the execution of the Law of Nature is in that state, put into every man's hands, whereby everyone has a right to punish the transgressors of that law to such a degree, as may hinder its violation. (II, 7)

Locke recognizes that 'this will seem a very strange doctrine to some men' (II, 9) but, he asks, what are the alternatives? This is more a rhetorical than a philosophical question, for here his case is helped by the fact that he is arguing against a defence of absolute monarchy. Hence, when Locke considers the objection that individuals in general cannot be trusted with the power to execute the commands of the Law of Nature because all individuals are inclined to act in their own self-interest, he replies that 'I shall desire those who make this objection, to remember that absolute monarchs are but men' capable of employing their power for the same prejudicial purposes. This does not answer the objection against the assumed rationality of men in the state of nature, but it does bring the issue of power into the equation on Locke's side, for his point is that if individuals are as irrational as his critics claim, then it makes no sense to place the total concentration of political power in the hands of one irrational absolute monarch. 'I desire to know', he writes, 'what kind of government that is, and how much better it is than the state of nature, where one man commanding a multitude, has the liberty to be judge in his own case, and may do to all his subjects whatever he pleases, without the least liberty to anyone to question or control those who execute his pleasure' (II, 13)? In Locke's view, those who underestimate the rationality of mankind do so because they overestimate the necessity and value of absolute monarchy. 'This is to think that men are so foolish that they take care to avoid what mischiefs may be done them by polecats, or foxes, but are content, nay think it safety, to be devoured by lions' (II, 93).

Even if it were true as a general proposition that individuals invariably acted in their own self-interest – and Locke does not accept this premiss – their lack of power *vis-à-vis* other individuals would make them less of a threat to the welfare of mankind than one man capable of commanding a multitude who act in his interest. The individual is 'in a much worse condition who is exposed to the arbitrary power of one man, who has command of 100,000 [men], than he that is exposed to the arbitrary power of 100,000 single men' (II, 137). Rather than to choose to live in such a political society, it is 'much better', Locke argues, to remain 'in the state of nature wherein men are not bound to submit to the unjust will of another' (II, 13). Locke therefore defends the proposition that 'the people . . . have the sense of rational creatures' (II, 230), despite what 'some men' assert. He is able to do so, not so much because he can produce convincing philosophical proofs of the rationality of mankind, but because the contrast he draws between life in the state of nature and life under an absolute monarch is to his advantage to the degree that he can portray the latter as being more irrational and miserable than the former.

Since 'no rational creature can be supposed to change his condition with an intention to be worse' (II, 131, 164), Locke is willing to defend the rationality of mankind in the state of nature to the point of denying that they would choose to put themselves under the worse condition of absolute monarchy, where they would be 'degraded from the common state of rational creatures' (II, 91). This is one of several places in the *Two Treatises* where the ideological objectives of the work assume a primary importance in the construction of the theoretical framework Locke is defending.

Locke's royalist opponents thought of the individual as being irrational, but even more frightening to them was the prospect of a multitude of irrational individuals. Given this identification of irrationality with the multitude, the state of nature necessarily looked to them like Hobbes's war of all against all. Royalist pamphleteers repeatedly emphasized this identification in their Exclusion tracts. It was particularly important, therefore, especially for those Whigs writing against the defenders of Filmer's political position, to stress the clear distinction between the state of nature and the state of war as a starting-premiss for the defence of the political standpoint adopted by the radical Whigs. For Locke, this distinction was grounded not merely in a recognition of the status of natural law, or in the attribution of rationality to individuals living in the state of nature; he also assumed as an ingredient of his definition of that state that individuals were members of a natural community.

Referring to the individual's existence in the state of nature under natural law, Locke observes that 'by which law common to them all, he and all the rest of mankind are one community'. Later in that passage he speaks of 'this great and natural community' which exists in the state of nature (II, 128). At the beginning of the *Second Treatise*, Locke wrote of individuals 'sharing all in one community of nature' (II, 6). For, according to the Law of Nature, 'all men alike are friends of one another and are bound together by common interests' (*ELN*, 163). It is 'the common bond whereby human kind is united into one fellowship and society' (II, 172). Now, it might be argued that Locke is merely describing a hypothetical community, and not one to which he attributes any degree of reality, but I think this will not do. As we shall see, one of the specific challenges to which he must respond is precisely that the state of nature is a 'fiction', lacking in reality. The historical examples Locke provides to answer this objection will be considered later, but even in his definition of the moral characteristics of the natural condition of individuals there is a definite empirical resonance to his description. In accounting for the origins of political society, Locke suggests that individuals must already have 'liked one another so well' as to constitute themselves into a political society. Hence they must 'be supposed to have some acquaintance and friendship together and some trust in one another' while living as members of the 'great and natural community' in the state of nature (II, 107). Some such assumption is needed in order to defend the proposition, *contra* Hobbes, that it is possible to make and keep contracts in the state of nature, which, of course, presupposes some degree of acquaintance and trust among individuals (II, 14). And, in defence of his account of the establishment of civil society presented in the *Letter on Toleration*, Locke maintains that many of the benefits and advantages of society were 'attainable by men living in neighbourhood without the bounds of a commonwealth' in the state of nature (*Works*, 5:212). In his essays on natural law Locke had associated the 'rationality' of individuals with 'some sense of a common humanity, some concern for fellowship' among individuals, and a rejection of the depiction of 'the state of nature [as] a general war and perpetual and deadly hatred among men' (*ELN*, 205; cf. 163).

If Locke places the execution of the Law of Nature in the hands of every individual, therefore, this is because he assumes that individuals see themselves as members of a community in whose interest they are capable of acting. Indeed, since the general purpose of natural law is to provide for the preservation of mankind, they could hardly claim to be its executors if they did not see themselves in this way, that is, as belonging to a natural community with shared interests. In other words, Locke not only believes that 'the preservation of all mankind' is 'the true principle to regulate our religion, politics, and morality by' (*STCE*, § 116); he also presupposes that this belief is a constitutive element of human consciousness in the state of nature. It is the ability of individuals to act on the basis of such a belief that ensures that the precepts of natural law can, *in any degree*, be enforced in that state (II, 11, 134–5, 159, 171, 182–3). Clearly, this argument lacks philosophical rigour and displays circular reasoning but, in a sense, even this helps to confirm the point I am making. For, having committed himself to certain definite assertions about the natural condition of man, Locke must defend the rationality of individuals within a context of social interactions that is morally distinguishable from the actions taken by a disordered multitude.[6] He does this through the application of the concept of a natural community to life in the state of nature.

In some respects, the negative expression of this point is more clearly and frequently stated by Locke. That is, violations of the Law of Nature are not simply transgressions committed by one individual against another; rather, they are crimes committed against the entire community. The violator is someone who is 'dangerous to mankind', because he has committed 'a trespass against the whole species' (II, 8). Not only the injured party, but 'any other person who finds it just, may also join with him that is injured, and assist him in recovering from the offender, so much as may make satisfaction for the harm he has suffered' (II, 10). Locke's references to 'the right' the individual has 'to preserve mankind in general' (II, 8) – a 'common right of punishing' (II, 11) he shares with all others in the state of nature – are misleading, in the sense that any justification of this right is dependent upon and derivative from the *obligation* everyone has, under the Law of Nature, to do all that he can to preserve mankind. The Law of Nature is, for Locke, 'the law of reason, whereby every one is commissioned to do good' (*Works*, 5:213). Hence the individual's right to execute the commands of natural law might better be described as his duty to do so. The degree to which the state of nature is in fact a more or less peaceful condition depends, in part, upon the deterrent effects Locke attributes to the viewpoint that the aggressor must take into account; namely, that his action will be interpreted as an act against the community as a whole, and that some collectivity of individuals will take it upon themselves to enforce his punishment (II, 11). This may or may not happen in any particular case, but the point is that Locke assumes that the communal objectives of natural law are supported by a sense of community shared by those who enforce its commands.

This sense of community already exists on a smaller scale, within the family, which is one set of social relationships that obtain among individuals in a state of nature. 'Conjugal society', Locke writes, 'is made by a voluntary compact between man and woman.' But, in a larger sense, marriage and the family have to be viewed as a society based upon 'mutual support, and assistance, and a communion of interest' (II, 78, 83). This 'common concern' which the husband and wife share (II, 82) might extend as far as a 'community of goods' or property (II, 83). The point Locke wants to make is that not only are parents under a natural law obligation to preserve, nourish and care for their children – an argument he had already employed against Filmer in the *First Treatise* – but also there are sentiments, dispositions and feelings wrought into human nature that support the execution of this obligation. Although there are traces of this argument in the *First Treatise*, it is much more fully stated in the *Second Treatise*. After repeating the basic parental obligation several times (II, 56, 58, 60), Locke now adds that God 'hath placed in them suitable inclinations of tenderness and concern to temper this power, to apply it as his wisdom designed it, to the children's good' (II, 63, 170). And, on the other side, God 'has laid on the children a perpetual obligation of honouring their parents, which containing in it an inward esteem and reverence to be shown by all outward expressions, ties up the child from anything that may ever injure or affront, disturb, or endanger the happiness or life' of his parents. These feelings of 'honour, respect, gratitude and assistance' form an integral part of any theory of natural law obligations as these apply to the family. Locke's conception of the family assumes that all of its members will engage in 'actions of defence, relief, assistance and comfort' for the mutual benefit of each other (II, 66, 170).

The family can be viewed in these terms because God has 'made parents instruments in his great design of continuing the race of mankind', and this 'design' encompasses more than biological reproduction; as an expression of the Deity's moral intentions, it restates the purpose of natural law itself. Thus, 'God hath woven into the principles of human nature' the feelings and attitudes necessary to support this 'great design' (II, 67). If conjugal society is to be distinguished from the mating of animals because it is founded on a contract, so it is distinguished by the fact 'that society of man and wife should be more lasting, than of male and female amongst other creatures', and this fact, too, is attributable to 'the wisdom of the great Creator' who has built into human nature the means and attitudes necessary to realize this end (II, 80). What makes 'the conjugal bonds more firm and lasting in man, than the other species of animals' (II, 81) is the sense of communal concern and sharing of interests between husband and wife and all the members of the family. Locke believes that God is, ultimately, responsible for instilling in parents these 'principles of human nature' which express themselves as a concern for a common good (of the family), but he is also pointing out the importance of the *effects* of these feelings as part of his descriptive characterization of the family's existence within the state of nature. And, on that level of his argument, the fact that Locke's definition of the role of the family is so heavily framed in terms of the responsibility of parents to 'instill sentiments of humanity' (*STCE*, § 117) in their children is an important ingredient of his conception of the state of nature.

In other words, a significant aspect of Locke's political thought is missed if the role of the family as an agent of socialization – even in the state of nature – is not recognized, for the very fact that parents can educate their children to think and act with a view to the common good of all provides a realistic basis, in Locke's view, for his description of the condition of mankind in the state of nature. The socializing role of the family as a means by which children are taught to diminish the importance of self-interested motives and are instead enjoined to seek virtue, preserve mankind, display civility towards all persons and, in general, develop attitudes of other-regarding concern is elaborated at great length by Locke in his *Some Thoughts Concerning Education*. What I am suggesting is that this conception of the family as a social institution is not simply a consequential product of the establishment of political society; on the contrary, the latter is possible, in part, precisely because the attitudes and practices necessary to bring it into existence and to maintain it are assumed by Locke to be part of his definition of the natural sociability of individuals in the state of nature, as expressed through the institution of the family.[7]

We could state the point another way by saying that Locke views all social relationships in the state of nature according to the moral purposes that he identifies with God's 'design' for mankind. God is responsible for providing individuals with a standard of morality, for equipping them with the natural powers and inclinations they need to obey it, and for placing them in a condition in which their social interaction with each other reinforces both of these features of the state of nature. If political power emerges out of this situation bound to the realization of the common good, it is because Locke's conception of the state of nature, as a moral construct, allows for no other meaning.

> So that the end and measure of this power, when in every man's hands in the state of nature, being the preservation of all of his society, that is, all mankind in general, it can have no other end or measure, when in the hands of the magistrate, but to preserve the members of that society in their lives, liberties, and possessions. (II, 171)

I want now to turn from the moral to the political meaning of the state of nature. In one sense, of course, it is misleading to speak of the political meaning of the state of nature because, as a term used in contrast with political society, it might be supposed that, logically, the state of nature can have no political meaning. Nevertheless, I shall argue that there is a political meaning Locke attaches to that concept, although I will begin, as Locke does, with the contrast between the state of nature and political society. Midway through the *Second Treatise*, Locke summarizes his position, listing the three things that distinguish the state of nature from political society: 'First, there wants an established, settled, known law, received and allowed by common consent to be the standard of right and wrong, and the common measure to decide all controversies. For though the Law of Nature be plain and intelligible to all rational creatures; yet men being biased by their interest, as well as ignorant for want of study of it, are not apt to allow of it as a law binding to them in the application of it to their particular cases' (II, 124). Second 'in the state of nature there wants a known and indifferent judge, with authority to determine all differences according to the established law' (II, 125). Finally 'in the state of nature there often wants power to back and support the sentence when right, and to give it due execution' (II, 126).

Now, the first and third propositions describe the difficulties of enforcing the Law of Nature, for Locke is not suggesting that the creation of political society represents the substitution of some other standard of right and wrong for that of natural law which already exists in the state of nature. On the contrary, not only is it true that the civil laws individuals establish 'are only so far right, as they are founded on the Laws of Nature, by which they are to be regulated and interpreted' (II, 12), but also it is within civil society that the Laws of Nature 'have by human laws known penalties annexed to them, to enforce their observation' (II, 135). Indeed, that is the point, to which Locke's third statement addresses itself, since political society can be seen as the collective enforcement of natural law. While these defects of the state of nature cannot be ignored, what is crucial to Locke's account of the establishment of political society, I suggest, is the institution of an 'indifferent judge' to determine the controversies among individuals. In fact, Locke's second proposition actually incorporates the main features of the other two conditions, for the judge's authority must ultimately rest upon his acting in accordance with the Law of Nature, and he could hardly be said to determine the controversies within society unless he is assumed to possess the means to enforce his decisions. Locke's definition of political society, therefore, turns upon what he means by an indifferent judge, and how the latter comes to be instituted, for it is this action that removes individuals from the state of nature.

In a passage cited earlier, Locke characterized the state of nature as 'men living together according to reason, without a common superior on earth, with authority to judge between them'. In short, 'want of a common judge with authority, puts all men in a state of nature' (II, 19). This point is repeated in the following two paragraphs. Then, in a very brief section, 'Of Slavery' (chapter 4), Locke describes 'the liberty of man in society' as that of being 'under no other legislative power, but that established, by consent', that is, 'to have a standing rule to live by, common to every one of that society, and made by the legislative power erected in it' (II, 22). This is Locke's first attempt to provide a specific illustration of what he means by an indifferent judge and some indication as to how the latter is created. At this point, the argument shifts to a discussion of the origins of property and of paternal power but, in paragraph 87, Locke returns to the definition of political society with this declaration:

> there, and there only is political society, where every one of the members hath quitted this natural power, resigned it up into the hands of the community . . . [and] to the law established by it. And thus all private judgment of every particular member being excluded, the community comes to be umpire, by settled standing rules, indifferent, and the same to all parties; and by men having authority from the community, for the execution of those rules, decides all the differences that may happen between any members of that society, concerning any matter of right; and punishes those offences which any member hath committed against the society.

According to Locke, this makes it 'easy to discern who are, and who are not' in political society or in the state of nature, and he reinforces this point by restating his earlier definition of the latter (II, 87).

It appears, then, that it is the community as a whole which is identified with the legislative or lawmaking power, and hence with Locke's notion of an indifferent judge. All particular administrative means by which the general objectives of political society are to be realized are thus dependent upon everyone having first engaged in the action described by Locke.

> And this puts men out of a state of nature into that of a commonwealth, by setting up a judge on earth, with authority to determine all the controversies, and redress the injuries, that may happen to any member of the commonwealth; which judge is the

legislative, or magistrates appointed by it. And wherever there are any number of men, however associated, that have no such decisive power to appeal to, there they are still in the state of nature. (II, 89)

Locke's last statement might appear puzzling or redundant since it repeats for the fifth or sixth time what the reader already knows. But Locke immediately makes it clear that there is a political significance attached to the argument he is making, which, in effect, proscribes at least one particular form of government from being included under his definition of political society. 'Hence it is evident', he concludes, 'that absolute monarchy, which by some men is counted the only government in the world, is indeed inconsistent with civil society, and so can be no form of civil government at all' (II, 90, 174). The reason for this, Locke explains, is that the king 'being supposed to have all, both legislative and executive power in himself alone, there is no judge to be found, no appeal lies open to any one, who may fairly, and indifferently, and with authority decide, and from whose decision relief and redress may be expected of any injury or inconveniency, that may be suffered from the prince or by his order' (II, 91). Since Locke maintains that 'wherever any two men are, who have no standing rule, and common judge to appeal to on earth for the determination of controversies of right betwixt them, there they are still in the state of nature', his application of this principle to the relationship between 'every absolute prince' and any one of his subjects means that 'those persons are still in the state of nature' (II, 90, 91, 94). An absolute monarch, *ipso facto*, is not an indifferent judge, according to Locke's definition. This is another of those junctures at which Locke's political objectives play a key role in the structuring of his formal (definitional) argument, and this particular presupposition, as we shall see, creates certain difficulties or contradictions with respect to Locke's historical account of the origins of legitimate government. What I want to stress here, however, is that Locke's polemical intentions actually serve to clarify in an important way the meaning of an indifferent judge, for we now see that the legislative and executive power cannot remain in the same hands. Or, to put it another way, in order for political society to exist these two forms of power must be divided and allocated to different persons.

This point was not immediately obvious from Locke's earlier general discussion of the differences between the state of nature and civil society, and there is at least one important objection that might be cited against it, namely, that the community itself may retain and exercise both powers. This is true, but there are two ways of interpreting this proposition. It could be maintained that if the community does retain both powers, then it is not, properly speaking, any form of government at all. 'By commonwealth,' Locke writes, 'I must be understood all along to mean, not a democracy, or any form of government, but any independent community' (II, 133). This notion of an independently existing community that precedes the establishment of any legislative power outside of itself (and thus retains both the legislative and executive power in its own hands) is reaffirmed by Locke when he describes what he means by his assertion that 'the community perpetually retains a supreme power'.

> And thus the community may be said in this respect to be always the supreme power, but not as considered under any form of government, because this power of the people can never take place till the government be dissolved. (II, 149)

Locke's language appears to rule out any characterization of this community as a democracy – though we shall return to this issue later – since that is a definite form of government which requires, at a minimum, that the majority of the community appoint individuals to execute the laws they make, and this creates a division between the legislative and the executive powers in practice, though, of course, they are both ultimately rooted in the same source (II, 132).

The more difficult question is whether Locke means to say that this community, without any particular form, is nevertheless a political society, or whether he means that individuals, though they are part of a community, remain in the state of nature until they have established some specific form of government. In favour of the first interpretation is Locke's application of 'commonwealth' to this formless political society, and his definition of political society in terms of the act of individuals resigning their power into the hands of the community, which, in fact, means the majority or some larger number of the community (II, 95–9). Yet it is apparent from what Locke says above that merely resigning power to the community does not *in itself* establish the legislative power of that political society, for that is a decision yet to be taken by the majority, and until they do make that decision no form of government has been created. From this standpoint, individuals can be said to be in the state of nature, *however they are associated*, in the absence of some clearly designated and indifferent judge to decide the controversies among them, which is precisely what the state of nature lacks. And, on the other side, it is not true that individuals may not be members of a community in their natural condition. In support of this reading of Locke's meaning, consider the following passage:

> The constitution of the legislative is the first and fundamental act of society, whereby provision is made for the continuation of their union, under the direction of persons, and bonds of laws made by persons authorized thereunto, by the consent and appointment of the people, without which no one man, or number of men, amongst them, can have authority of making laws, that shall be binding to the rest. (II, 212; cf. 134)

In other words, unless some definite man or number of men are appointed by the community to make and execute laws, there is no judge with authority to determine the controversies, which is to say, *notwithstanding their being members of a community*, these individuals are still in the state of nature. However, the moment particular individuals are granted executive and lawmaking power, some definite form of government – democracy, monarchy and so forth – has been instituted, and they are no longer in the state of nature. For, unless 'the community put the legislative power into such hands as they think fit, with this trust, that they shall be governed by declared laws', the existence of individuals 'will still be at the same uncertainty, as it was in the state of nature' (II, 136). Not only must power be placed in the hands of particular persons, but it must also be conveyed to them with a definite understanding as to the purposes for which that power is to be employed, and both of these conditions indicate that Locke has in mind some determinate empirical action in terms of which one can speak of a transition from the state of nature to existence within a political society. Moreover, this action is *not* equatable with the establishment of the community as such, despite the fact that he sometimes calls this community a political society. 'When the people have said, we will submit to rules, and be governed by laws made by such men, and in such forms', Locke maintains that this is to be understood as 'a positive voluntary grant for institution' of the legislative power by the people, and all subsequent actions must adhere to 'what that positive grant conveyed' (II, 141).[8] As we have seen, Locke's argument against Filmer in the *First Treatise* stressed the point that a positive grant must be understood in terms of and limited by the 'express words' used (I, 25). If we apply this rule to the manner by which the legislative power is established by the people, then no transfer of power can simply be *assumed* to take place since, according to Locke, this situation cannot be equated with the conditions that define a positive grant. And, unless it can be shown that individuals have made a positive grant of power to particular persons, they remain members of a state of nature, regardless of the other types of social interaction in which they engage. To assert that individuals are members of a community – which, *de facto*, could always be said to have the supreme power in its hands – is, therefore, not sufficient to prove that they have left the state of nature.

We can approach the problem from another direction by asking, if the government is dissolved, are individuals returned to the state of nature? As Locke's theory of resistance, to be discussed in Chapter 8, depends upon an affirmative reply to this question, it must be the case that, in the absence or destruction of the government as a specific set of institutions, individuals are residents of the state of nature. And this conclusion must also be compatible with the assertion that, upon the dissolution of government, political power returns to the community as a whole, which is another key proposition of Locke's resistance theory. Thus, an individual 'can never be again in the liberty of the state of nature; unless by any calamity, the government, he was under, comes to be dissolved' (II, 121). But the converse is also true; namely, that whenever the government he is under is dissolved the individual is returned to the state of nature. Since there are numerous specific actions that cause the dissolution of government, Locke is not describing a highly improbable situation but, rather, he is making a point of considerable importance to his argument in the *Two Treatises*.

It is clear that we are at an important interpretative crossroads in the text, and much depends upon which path is taken. There are passages in which Locke says that individuals remove themselves from the state of nature through consenting 'to make one community or government', and these statements appear to support the first interpretation, although his tendency to run together 'community' and 'government' does not help to clarify his position (II, 95–9). For it is precisely in distinguishing between the community and its government that the second interpretation draws much of its persuasive force, and there are many passages, as we have noted, that indicate the importance to Locke of making such a distinction. There is one reference in the *Second Treatise* where Locke speaks of forming the community as 'one politick society', which action 'brings men out of the loose state of nature' (II, 211), and some implication might be drawn from this that there is a 'loose' and a strict sense in which the concept of the state of nature might be interpreted. This is possible, but I do not think much can be made of this one statement, other than to reinforce the point made in many other passages that life in the state of nature is socially organized in the form of a community and is not to be conceived of as a loose collection of individuals.

Although I cannot resolve the definitional difficulties raised by Locke's contrast between the state of nature and political society, I do believe it is possible to see why these difficulties should have arisen in Locke's argument. I began this discussion by noting that Locke proposed to include within his definition of the state of nature a particular form of government, absolute monarchy, which in his opinion is no form of government at all. There are two grounds upon which Locke makes this denial, and they do not flow from the same source nor do they invariably run in the same channels in so far as the positive institution of government is concerned. First, absolute monarchy is not generally, and certainly not by Filmer in particular, presented as a form of government that is dependent upon the consent of the governed. Therefore, if, as Locke believed, the two main 'originals of government' were either divine appointment or consent, then requiring the consent of every individual as a precondition for the institution of political society necessarily defeated the alternative justification (or explanation) of the origins of government. The mere creation of the community through consent in the manner described by Locke is sufficient to distinguish between 'any lawful government in the world' (II, 99) and one (absolute monarchy) created by other means. Even if we supposed that, historically, absolute monarchy was the first form of government, this would only mean that the individuals subject to such a ruler were still in the state of nature until such time as they took a definite action to remove themselves from that state. This is not an unimportant point, since it is used by Locke to deny that government by conquest is, properly speaking, a form of government at all, in just the same sense in which he applies that judgement to absolute monarchy (II, 192).

But now suppose that, having formed the political community through consent, the community decides to place all its lawmaking and executive power in the hands of one man. It might be denied that Locke's argument allows for this possibility, and in the final analysis I think this is a correct reading of his intentions. Nevertheless, strictly speaking, the objection is not true. In his account of the forms of government Locke observes that 'the whole power of the community', which is to say 'the power of making laws', may be put into the hands of a few men, and then the government is an oligarchy, 'or else into the hands of one man, and then it is a monarchy' (II, 132). On the face of it, this statement is difficult to reconcile with Locke's earlier objection to absolute monarchy, namely, that one man is 'supposed to have all, both legislative and executive power in himself alone', in which condition his subjects have no appeal against his judgement and so are still in the state of nature (II, 91). It is no help to interject into the argument some notion of tyranny or some particular set of offences committed by the monarch, because Locke is not here discussing the substantive problems that might arise within a specific political society; rather, he is simply defining the formal conditions of the exercise of political power. Even if the king were the most benevolent individual imaginable, the very fact that he is in possession of both legislative and executive powers constitutes the basis for Locke's objection. Nor can the difficulty be escaped by assuming that the majority of the community actually retains the lawmaking power, so that the monarch is merely the executive officer carrying out its will, for this is Locke's definition of democracy, which he has just given, and the point of the paragraph is to state the distinction between different forms of government.

For reasons to be considered more fully in Chapter 7, Locke wants to argue (1) that all legitimate governments are founded in consent and in the decision taken by the majority of the community, and (2) that no one, including a majority, can legitimately consent to place all political power in the hands of one individual, for to do so violates the precepts of natural law and places them in a worse condition than the state of nature. Both of these arguments can be employed, ideologically, to deny the legitimacy of absolute government, as Locke does in the *Second Treatise*, but this does not mean that from these two axes of his political argument he can construct a consistent formal definition of political society. Thus, if we define political society according to the first proposition, it can be identified with the community or formless commonwealth, but if we define political society according to the second assumption, then only certain forms of government are legitimate and, until a legitimate form of government has been instituted, individuals have not removed themselves from the state of nature. In other words, it is Locke's tendency to merge his notion of a lawful government with his formal definition of government that gives rise to the confusion and logical inconsistencies in his argument.

As a prelude to the historical discussion in the next chapter, and as a succinct statement of the theoretical dilemma described above, we could cite Locke's observation that it might be true that men in 'the first ages' of the world placed themselves 'by a tacit consent' under the rule of 'some one good and excellent man', but, he argues, these individuals 'could never be safe nor at rest, nor think themselves in civil society, till the legislature was placed in collective bodies of men, call them Senate, Parliament, or what you please'. Locke quotes a passage from Hooker at this point which maintains that 'to live by one man's will, became the cause of all men's misery', and he concludes the paragraph by referring to the contrast he has just drawn as an illustration of the difference between the state of nature and civil society (II, 94). Later, when discussing how laws are enacted and administered under particular forms of government, Locke is inclined simply to begin with the presupposition that 'in all . . . well-framed governments . . . the legislative and executive power are in distinct hands' (II, 159). He makes this assumption 'because it may be too great a temptation to human frailty apt to grasp at power, for the same persons who have the power of making laws, to have also in their hands the power to execute them . . . Therefore in well ordered commonwealths . . . the legislative power is put into the hands of divers persons' (II, 143). Thus, 'well-ordered commonwealths' and 'civil society' come to mean the same thing, and both are denials of the legitimacy of absolute monarchy, which is equated with the state of nature, which, in turn, is contrasted with civil society.

I believe that Locke's argument in the *Second Treatise* can be forced into a logically consistent usage of the definitions he provides of the state of nature and political society only by dismissing other textual passages – which might turn out to be quite numerous – that do not conform to the interpretation being offered by the commentator. Since logical inconsistencies are taken to be evidence of poor philosophizing, interpreters of the *Second Treatise* have generally opted for this approach to the text in order to preserve, as much as possible, Locke's status as a great political philosopher. My aims in this discussion of the text are rather different. First, I have tried to establish that there is a theoretical problem in Locke's argument, and to suggest that its existence is to be explained in terms of the political objectives Locke attached to the writing of the *Two Treatises of Government*. Second, I have defended my interpretation of what Locke means by 'political society' and the relationship it has to the state of nature at those junctures where interpretative choices must be made with respect to textual meanings by appealing to those political objectives and authorial intentions. The significance of this interpretative position cannot be fully defended, of course, until it has been viewed in the context of Locke's use of history, his conception of constitutional government, and his theory of resistance, to which subjects the next three chapters are devoted.

NOTES: CHAPTER 5

1 For Wilmoore Kendall, for example, Locke's state of nature is purely 'an expository device' with no relationship to any 'historical fact' (*John Locke and the Doctrine of Majority Rule* (Urbana, Ill.: University of Illinois Press, 1941), p. 75). Kendall is restating the traditional view, which has recently been reasserted by John Dunn, *The Political Thought of John Locke* (Cambridge: Cambridge University Press, 1969), pp. 96–119. See also Plamenatz, who explains the meaning of the state of nature in the *Second Treatise* in terms of his view of Locke as an abstract political philosopher (John Plamenatz, *Man and Society*, 2 vols (New York: McGraw-Hill, 1963), Vol. 1, pp. xi, 241). For a criticism of this interpretative approach to Locke, see Richard Ashcraft, 'Locke's state of nature: historical fact or moral fiction?', *American Political Science Review*, Vol. 62, no. 3 (September 1968), pp 898–915.

2 Richard Cox, *Locke on War and Peace* (Oxford: Clarendon Press, 1960), pp. 79 ff.; cf. Leo Strauss, *Natural Right and History* (Chicago, Ill.: University of Chicago Press, 1953), pp. 202–51. It should be noted that much of the disappointment concerning Locke's treatment of natural law in the *Two Treatises* is rooted in the expectation that Locke should have offered a philosophical exposition of his position, when instead his remark occurs in the course of a polemical argument. His point is simply that if we assume that most people are law-abiding individuals most of the time, then it is much easier to assume that they possess a basic knowledge of what they must do in order to obey the Law of Nature gained through natural reason than it is to assume that 'the fancies and intricate contrivances of men' that constitute 'the municipal laws of countries' are so easily known to them. Locke's opponents, of course, would have replied that the obedience of individuals is not a function of their knowledge of the law, and in other contexts Locke himself makes significant concessions to this argument. Here, however, he is attempting to establish the postulate that the individual in the state of nature is 'a rational creature' and that 'reason' in any particular social context must presuppose a general state of reason. Hence the rationality and 'rightness' of 'the positive laws of commonwealths' must necessarily be grounded in the rationality of the Law of Nature.

3 'The observance of this law gives rise to peace, harmonious relations, friendship . . . to sum it all up in one word – happiness' (*ELN*, 215).

4 Individuals who have arrived at the age of discretion, according to Locke, 'are free and at their own disposal' (*The Works of John Locke*, 12th edn, 9 vols, (1824), Vol. 5, p. 211.

5 'All people are by nature endowed with reason' (*ELN*, 115, 199). 'We would be thought rational creatures, and have our freedom' (*STCE*, § 41). A moral action is executed by the individual 'as a rational and voluntary agent' (4:21, 1).

6 The view of Locke as someone committed to the ethical principles of individual self-interest can still be found in the secondary literature on his thought. Putting aside the fact that the text of the *Two Treatises* will not bear the weight of this interpretation, it is worth emphasizing that Locke directed a sharply critical attack against this viewpoint in his essays on natural law. 'We do deny', he wrote, 'that

each person is at liberty to do what he himself, according to circumstances, judges to be of advantage to him.' Such an assumption makes 'each person's own interest' into 'the standard of what is just and right'. On the contrary, Locke maintains that the preferable standard of virtue and justice 'consist[s] only in this: that we do good to others at our own loss' (*ELN*, 207, 211; cf. 159, 181, 213, 215). In his other writings, Locke reaffirms this point. For example, in the *Conduct of the Understanding*, he suggests that the proposition, 'we should love our neighbour as ourselves', is 'such a fundamental truth for the regulating human society' that one ought to 'determine all the cases and doubts in social morality' according to that precept (*Works*, Vol. 2, p. 395; cf. *STCE*, § 139). In his notebooks, journals and correspondence – that is, in his private as well as in his public writings – there are many similar endorsements of a 'social morality' framed in terms of the common good. The latter is, for Locke, the ultimate standard that overrides any claim of self-interest – except the individual's responsibility for his personal salvation, which is not subject to a communally imposed ethical standard. 'An Hobbist with his principle of self-preservation whereof himself is to be judge', Locke declared, 'will not easily admit a great many plain duties of morality' (Journal, 5 April 1677, MS f.2). We will later consider the practical question of the degree to which individualistic rights-claims are *compatible* with the social morality and the political institutions Locke favours, but what I am arguing here is that these questions cannot be resolved through reference to a moral perspective in which priority is granted to the pursuit of individual self-interest.

7   I have no idea, therefore, what Plamenatz means when he asserts: 'For Locke, as for Hobbes, natural man is a creature loose from all social discipline; he is autonomous and self-contained, and belongs to no social order, no community. There is no sense at all in Locke that it is the pressure of society on man, his being brought up to conform with established ways, which makes him sociable and moral . . . Of social institutions prior to government he says not a word' (*Man and Society*, Vol. 1, p. 221). It is incredible that any reader of the *Essay Concerning Human Understanding* or *Some Thoughts Concerning Education*, where the importance of habits, custom and the general process of socialization into the acceptance of moral beliefs is discussed with tireless repetition by Locke, could make such a statement. Even if Plamenatz held to the strange view that Locke so compartmentalized his beliefs concerning this subject as systematically to exclude them from the *Two Treatises*, it is clear that, within that work, the beliefs individuals come to have in the state of nature they possess as members of a family. The latter may be quite large, extending over several generations and including servants. This is certainly a social institution, and if individuals in this condition are capable of acting as moral agents, as Locke believes they are, it is because they have been socialized as members of a family to act in this manner.

8   Locke speaks of the political relations which can 'be called instituted because they depend on the peaceful consent and constitutions of men'. The creation of these political institutions requires 'some act whereby anyone comes by a right power' or the legitimate possession of something. This remark is contained in a manuscript among the Shaftesbury Papers in the Public Record Office, London: PRO 30/24/47/7.

CHAPTER 6

The Virtues of Commerce

I have conjoined the discussion of the historical meaning of the concept of the state of nature with the examination of Locke's treatment of property because his account of the origins and development of property presupposes the historical existence of individuals in the state of nature. Locke's justification for the right to own property and his assertion that political society is created in order to protect that right necessarily presuppose, as he notes in paragraph 138, that individuals '*have property*', and this empirical observation requires an argument grounded in the evidence supplied by history. It is important to Locke to prove that there is a temporal precedence to the institution of private property in relation to the origins of political society during 'the first ages of the world' (II, 36). Locke therefore sets out to show how individuals come to have property in the state of nature, how their claims to that property precede the existence of political society, and how the form of the latter is shaped by the particular nature of the property they possess. Since these arguments rest upon appeals to historical, demographic and sociological evidence derived from records of voyages to the New World, this aspect of Locke's discussion of the state of nature has a distinctly empirical cast to it.[1]

It might be argued that Locke need only demonstrate the logical possibility of property ownership preceding the institution of government, but this supposition ignores both Locke's understanding of the compositional elements of a political theory and the political context within which the arguments of the *Two Treatises* were formulated.[2] It is true, Locke believes there is a definitional relationship between justice and property, and both concepts form part of the network of ideas which comprise his moral philosophy (4:3, 18; *STCE*, § 110). Yet a political theory is more than a formal statement of rights and duties; it is also an account of prudential wisdom gathered from experience which, for Locke, is linked to the judgement of individuals who make practical decisions. In other words, history is clearly part of our 'civil knowledge' (*STCE*, § 182).

If, therefore, Locke is writing with the intent of urging his readers to engage in the practical action of defending their property rights against an absolute monarch, he must show not only that it is morally right to do so, but also that there are harmful practical consequences attached to their not taking such action which can be understood, in part, through an examination of the reasons why, in a historical sense, individuals decided to place certain limitations upon the exercise of political power in the first place. How and why 'different models' of government were instituted by individuals in possession of different amounts and types of property, and why some commonwealths flourish while others decay, are questions that can only be answered on the basis of empirical evidence. When Locke observes that certain 'useful inventions' and practical actions constitute those features of our 'civilization' that separate us from the condition of 'wild Indians' in America, he means to show that, despite the fact that we take these institutions, inventions and social practices for granted, they are grounded in nothing more certain than probable judgements based on experience made by our predecessors.[3] Locke's account of the origins of property and political society in the *Two Treatises*, I am arguing, is written with the same intention, that is, of validating the practical judgements made by individuals who created a particular form of political society as the most efficacious means by which they could preserve a specific form of property. Hence, if this form of property (in a commercially developed society) is to be preserved, it cannot simply be taken for granted; rather, its continued existence and development, Locke believes, depend upon the probable judgements and practical actions taken by his readers.

In addition to Locke's belief that history and morality are the two basic elements of a political theory, an understanding of the polemical context within which his theory is advanced provides a clue as to why Locke should have felt it necessary to ground his argument in an appeal to historical evidence. Because Locke recognizes, within certain limits, the legitimacy of the historical aspects of his opponents' arguments, he must address himself to this dimension of a political theory. 'An argument from what has been, to what should of right be, has no great force' (II, 103), according to Locke, but this does not mean that historical examples have no place at all in a political argument. Probable judgements cannot establish the certainty of moral truths, but this is no argument against the proposition that 'one who hath well settled in his mind the principles of morality . . . may learn great and useful instructions of prudence' from a study of history (Journal, 6–10 April 1677, MS f.2). Instead of dismissing out of hand the 'mighty objection' that is frequently raised against a political theory that makes use of the concept of the state of nature (II, 14) – its questionable historical status – Locke specifically responds to this objection (II, 100–12). In reply to Filmer's critique of the position he adopts, Locke defends his approach by giving 'several examples out of history' (II, 103–4) and by appealing to 'records' and 'matter of fact'. Locke is willing to discuss the historical origins of government, in other words, provided one's conception of history includes some understanding as to *why* individuals in the past made the probable judgements they did (II, 101, 106). I will take up the details of Locke's argument relating to this point in a moment. What I am attempting to show here is that Locke concedes the legitimacy of incorporating historical evidence into one's political theory, and that this aspect of his argument in the *Second Treatise* assumes its most significant role in his discussion of property and the origins of political society. What I shall argue in this chapter, therefore, is (1) that Locke believes his historical account of the development of unequal property ownership is compatible with his natural law justification for the right to own property, and (2) that he incorporates both these aspects of his theory of property into his explanation for the origins of political society. In this sense, Locke's conception of a legitimate political society certainly rests, in part, upon the empirical foundations of his treatment of property.

In addition to whatever ties it may have to an intellectual tradition stretching back from Grotius and Pufendorf to Cicero and Aristotle, Locke's chapter on property in the *Second Treatise*, as Laslett observes, is firmly rooted in his polemic against Filmer. Indeed, it is Filmer's attack in *Patriarcha* upon Grotius' assertion that property was originally given by God to mankind in common that forms the starting-point for Locke's discussion. Filmer not only rejected the claim that consent could bring about a change in the distribution of property or prove itself binding upon succeeding generations, he also charged that 'upon these two propositions of natural community and voluntary propriety, depend divers dangerous and seditious conclusions'.[4] In his reply, Locke proposes to show 'how men might come to have a property in several parts of that which God gave to mankind in common, and that without any express consent of all the commoners' (II, 25). Whether one can arrive at this conclusion without subscribing to certain propositions that Filmer's followers viewed as seditious, Locke does not say.

The first sentence of chapter 5 has more importance in structuring Locke's argument than has sometimes been recognized by commentators on the text. Locke appeals both to natural reason and to revelation in support of the assertion that 'men, being once born, have a right to their preservation, and consequently to meat and drink, and such other things, as nature affords for their subsistence' (II, 25). This, I shall argue, is the only natural rights claim Locke makes for property, that is, a natural right to subsistence. It is a claim grounded in natural law, known through reason or Scripture, and not only does it lay the foundation for everything Locke has to say about property in the *Two Treatises*, but it also demarcates the boundaries between those property rights that are absolutely independent of any form of political society from those rights that are conditional upon the individual's consenting to be a member of a particular political society.

Although it takes us beyond the chapter on property into other sections of the *Second Treatise*, let me pursue this argument a bit further before returning to Locke's developmental account of property in that chapter. Locke established in the *First Treatise* that 'man had a right to a use of the creatures, by the will and grant of God', and that in 'pursuing that natural inclination he had to preserve his being, he followed the will of his Maker . . . And thus man's property in the creatures, was founded upon the right he had, to make use of those things, that were necessary or useful to his being' (I, 86–7). This 'right', it will be noticed, has the same justificatory sources, natural inclination and the will of God, as the statement from the *Second Treatise* cited above; moreover, it also has the same built-in limitations, that 'every man had a right to the creatures . . . by the right everyone had to take care of, and provide for their subsistence' (I, 87). God may have given the earth to everyone to enjoy, but He did not give them a natural right to property beyond the level of subsistence, because the Deity's purposes extend no further than what is necessary for the preservation of mankind, which is the declared general objective of natural law. For their part, men may engage in many activities, as we shall see, that are in conformity with the purposes of natural law, but that is another matter. Being compatible with natural law does not transform an action into a natural right, but all natural rights are, for Locke, traceable to some specific obligation laid upon individuals by the Law of Nature. In this instance, the obligation – and hence the basis for their rights claim – is to preserve themselves by providing for their subsistence. Even this phrasing of the point is too individualistic, for a better statement of the natural law obligation would be that everyone has a duty to provide for the subsistence of everyone else, where this does not come into competition with a person's efforts to provide for his own subsistence (II, 6, 159, 183). It is only through the fulfilment of this obligation that the preservation of mankind is assured.

The obligation of parents to provide for the subsistence of their children obviously extends the notion of subsistence beyond the individual *qua* individual, but it should also be noted that Locke reaffirms in the *Second Treatise* the principle of charity he announced in the *First Treatise*. 'He that hath, and to spare,' Locke writes, 'must remit something of his full satisfaction, and give way to the pressing and preferable title of those, who are in danger to perish without it.' This judgement is explicitly defended by Locke through an appeal to 'the Fundamental Law of Nature', which decrees 'that all, as much as may be, should be preserved' (II, 183). It is from the same perspective that Locke maintains that 'everyone must have meat, drink, clothing, and firing. So much goes out of the stock of the kingdom, whether they work or no.'[5] Therefore, not only is it true that we are each responsible for securing the right of everyone to subsistence, but it is also true that this rights claim is *not* tied to the labour of the individual or framed in terms of it. It is simply a mistake to assume that any Lockean natural right to property is derivative, in a naturalistic sense, from labour.[6] Individuals (children) are entitled to a right to subsistence even if they do not labour; other individuals who should not have to labour (widows of conquered soldiers) are entitled to subsistence; and still others (aged, ill, poor) are entitled to subsistence even if they cannot labour. The fact that their subsistence will generally be provided for through the labour of the majority of any community, or that without such labour these other rights claims will in practice not be met, describes the means by which the natural law obligations cited will be fulfilled. However, that labour, as a discrete activity by the individual or by any number of individuals, is decidedly not the source of those obligations. It therefore cannot be the source of any right to property at the level of subsistence. So much has been written about Locke's justification of the natural right to property, his labour theory of value, the individualistic claims to property ownership, and the interrelation between all of these, that it is important, at the outset, to clear away this underbrush and gain a clear view of the juridical argument Locke is actually making in the *Two Treatises*.

It is true that, according to Locke, individuals have a right to their own person to which no one else can claim a right, but this is not the same thing as a right to subsistence, though, in general, the connection between these claims will in practice be very close. 'Every man', Locke asserts, 'has a property in his own person. This nobody has any right to but himself' (II, 27). Hence every individual has 'a right of freedom to his person, which no other man has a power over, but the free disposal of it lies in himself' (II, 190). This freedom of one's person Locke describes as 'a native right' (II, 194). He also insists that the individual 'by being master of himself, and proprietor of his own person, and the actions or labour of it, had still in himself the great foundation of property' (II, 44).

> the labour of his body, and the work of his hands, we may say, are properly his. Whatsoever then he removes out of the state that nature hath provided, and left it in, he hath mixed his labour with, and joined to it something that is his own, and thereby makes it his property. (II, 27)

This is probably the most frequently cited passage from the *Two Treatises of Government*, but before we assume that this link between labour and property is conclusive evidence that the latter is founded upon the former let us pause to ask *why* we may say the labour of his body 'are properly his'?

The commonly accepted answer to this question restates the naturalistic assertion that we must be presumed to 'own' our own persons, and hence our labour.[7] Now, there is a sense in which this is both true and not true for Locke, and both responses are important to his discussion of property. As we have seen, we must presuppose some concept of a 'person' as the ground for any moral argument, and this means that individuals possess the 'freedom to order their actions, and dispose of their possessions, and persons as they think fit, within the bounds of the Law of Nature, without asking leave, or depending upon the will of any other man' (II, 4). God has given man reason and freedom of will, without which he could not act as a moral agent by obeying natural law. To this extent, it is clear that the assumption that the individual has a right to his own person is an essential element within the divinely structured universe of moral obligations. In another sense, however, it is not true that we are the owners of our persons, since Locke insists that we are God's workmanship or property; in effect, it is He who owns our persons. This is no scholastic debating point for Locke. In addition to the many references in his writings where he invokes the theory of creationism in support of this view, Locke employs the proposition as part of his argument that no individual is authorized to make himself a slave to another individual through his own consent. Nor is he entitled to destroy himself by committing suicide (II, 23,135).

> . . . it being out of a man's power so to submit himself to another, as to give him a liberty to destroy him; God and Nature never allowing a man so to abandon himself, as to neglect his own preservation: And since he cannot take away his own life, neither can he give another power to take it. (II, 168, 172)

There are some types of action that an individual does not have the right to commit against his own person because the individual's freedom over his own person is defined in terms of and limited by the precepts of the Law of Nature.[8]

In other words, if Locke's argument is stated in the language of obligations, we can see why there can be no claim by one individual to another's subsistence or to the labour necessary to provide that subsistence, whereas it is more difficult to perceive the basis for this conclusion if the discussion is formulated exclusively in the language of rights. In describing the relationship between individuals in the state of nature, Locke declares that 'there cannot be supposed any such subordination among us, that may authorize us to destroy one another, as if we were made for one another's uses, as the inferior ranks of creatures are for ours' (II, 6). No one can use another human being as his property and, Locke insists, this is precisely the relationship that would ensue if one were allowed to 'take away the freedom, that belongs to anyone in that state' (II, 17), that is, the freedom to dispose of his own actions and possessions. Every individual in the state of nature, then, has 'no arbitrary power over the life, liberty, or possession of another, but only so much as the Law of Nature gave him for the preservation of himself, and the rest of mankind' (II, 135). Since 'no man, or society of men, [have] a power to deliver up their preservation, or consequently the means of it' to another, 'they will always have a right to preserve what they have not a power to part with' against the attempt by anyone to take the means of their own preservation from them (II, 149). Moreover, anyone who makes such an attempt upon the freedom of another's person or actions thereby forfeits all of *his* rights claims and cannot possibly have 'a right and title' to the possessions of others (II, 180; cf. 172, 178).

With respect to the individual, we may say that 'the labour of his body, and the work of his hands . . . are properly his', because, given the structure of natural law obligations that define and limit the kinds of action in which individuals may engage in the state of nature, there is no possibility of anyone else being in a position to advance a superior rights-claim to the labour of that individual, while he, by labouring, is fulfilling his obligation to provide for his subsistence according to the Law of Nature. It is not the individual's labour that gives him a 'right' to the property it produces; indeed, if that labour produces a surplus, he may be obliged to sacrifice the products – and therefore the labour that produced them – to the more pressing needs and rights-claim of another. Rather, it is the fulfilment of his natural law obligations, to which freedom over his own person and actions is a necessary precondition, that 'excludes the common right of other men' so far as the individual's right to subsistence is concerned (II, 27). If we choose to employ the language of rights in order to defend 'this labour [as] being the unquestionable property of the labourer', to which 'no man but he can have a right to what that is once joined to' (II, 27), then we ought to recognize that Locke's argument depends upon two propositions: first, this right, in a positive sense, is a logical extension of the right a person has to his own actions as part of a larger context of obligations; and, second, this right, in a negative sense, belongs to the individual by default, there being no one else who has a right to claim it by appealing to the Law of Nature. *Both* arguments are deployed by Locke in his defence of the individual's natural right to property as subsistence. It is important to recognize this point before entering into a discussion of chapter 5 of the *Second Treatise* because, as we shall see, these two lines of Locke's argument are unified in an absolutist sense only at the level of subsistence; beyond that level they diverge, and the possibilities that conflicting rights-claims with respect to property will be advanced by individuals are greatly increased. Moreover, a clear understanding of the form of Locke's argument, that is, how rights are related to and derivative from obligations, will prove helpful in considering some of his specific assertions in that chapter.

In the first few paragraphs of chapter 5 Locke defends labour as the activity that supplies the link between a person and an object, because if an object did not become the property of the individual when he first picked or gathered it, how could it be said to be his property at some later moment (II, 28–30)? If we hold a person's actions to be his, in the sense that he controls them, then he must control the object that he removes out of the common state of nature by his action (labour). 'Thus this law of reason makes the deer, that Indian's who hath killed it . . . who hath bestowed his labour upon it, though before, it was the common right of everyone (II, 30).'

At this point, however, Locke's argument shifts from a defence of labour as the necessary means between the person and the object within a theory of private possessions, to a defence of labour in terms of the purposes for which the activity is carried out. Locke makes this shift because he anticipates an objection others will make to his argument, namely, that 'any one may engross as much as he will' since if the individual's right to possess an object is grounded in his action, then the most active individuals will soon amass a great quantity of objects.

> To which I answer, not so. The same Law of Nature, that does by this means give us property, does also bound that property too . . . As much as any one can make use of to any advantage of his life before it spoils; so much he may by his labour fix a property in. Whatever is beyond this, is more than his share, and belongs to others. Nothing was made by God for man to spoil or destroy (II, 31).

There are two interrelated points of considerable significance for Locke's theory of property contained in this passage: first, Locke applies a standard of use to the notion of property, which is here limited to subsistence, and he claims that the meaning of 'use' is referable to the moral boundaries established by natural law; and, second, Locke appeals to God's intentions as a ground for his argument against spoilage and waste.

In paragraph 28, Locke had denied that it was 'robbery' for an individual in providing for his subsistence 'to assume to himself what belonged to all in common'. But, a few paragraphs later, Locke maintains that if an individual in the state of nature took more goods than he could use 'he invaded his neighbour's share' (II, 37), and thereby, Locke argues, he 'robbed others' (II, 46). This act of robbery, be it noted, does not actually involve any interaction between two individuals. It is obvious to Locke that, if one person decides 'to meddle with what was already improved by another's labour . . . he desired the benefit of another's pains, which he had no right to', and this is a plain case of robbery (II, 34). But that is not the point at issue in the discussion above. Rather, it is possible for the individual to engage in a 'dishonest' action if he simply endeavours 'to hoard up more than he could make use of' (II, 46, 51). In so doing, the individual 'offended against the common Law of Nature, and was liable to be punished' (II, 37), as much as any other violator of natural law in the state of nature. The reasoning underlying this usage of moral terminology, Locke explains, is that the individual 'had no right, farther than his use called for any of [the goods]' he extracted from the state of nature. This conjunction of natural law limitations and use, I am arguing, is tied to the level of subsistence property, for on that level everyone must be presumed to have an equal 'share' with respect to the available goods. It is therefore possible for the 'common right' of mankind to be violated by the individual, in so far as he allows his actions to exceed the boundaries established by the Law of Nature, which, to emphasize the point once more, oblige him to act in such a way as to preserve all mankind. If he hoards commodities in a situation where his own subsistence is not at stake, he fails to fulfil this obligation, and becomes an offender against the Law of Nature.

It is worth noting that Locke had arrived at this moral position long before he wrote the chapter on property in the *Two Treatises*. In his lectures on natural law, Locke rejected the view that it was based upon 'the private interest of each person'. Rather, natural law is both grounded in and designed to preserve the 'common life of man with man', which is to say, it enforces the virtues of 'justice, friendship, and generosity' (*ELN*, 213). Locke applied this view of natural law to property in his eighth lecture, observing that 'victuals, clothes, adornments, riches, and all other good things of this life are provided for common use'. To this statement, he contrasts the argument of self-interest (which he generally identified with Hobbes's theory):

And so, when any man snatches for himself as much as he can, he takes away from another man's heap the amount he adds to his own, and it is impossible for anyone to grow rich except at the expense of someone else . . . if we make every man's self-interest the basis of natural law . . . everyone is obliged, as much as he can, to have regard for himself, so that the standard of rightness is private interest and all the duties of life are founded on it. From this assumption it follows . . . [that] in such a case each person is required to procure for himself and to retain in his possession the greatest possible number of useful things; and when this happens it is inevitable that the smallest possible number is left to some other person, because surely no gain falls to you which does not involve somebody else's loss. *But obviously a contrary result follows if we lay down another foundation for moral virtue.* (ELN, 211; my italics)

I have quoted this passage to show that Locke rejected the identification of natural law with self-interest, which he associated with the attempt by one individual to 'snatch for himself as much as he can' with respect to property. If, however, one began with 'another foundation for moral virtue', that is, an alternative interpretation of the Law of Nature, it was clear that the basic goods of life were provided for the 'common use' of individuals. This is the argument presented by Locke in the *Two Treatises*, and the foundation for his attack against hoarding as a form of robbery. This moral position is restated in his book on education, where Locke observes that the preservation of mankind is the true standard of morality and politics, while 'covetousness, and the desire of having in our possession, and under our dominion, more than we have need of' is 'the root of all evil' (*STCE*, § 110). There is, in other words, a general connection in Locke's mind between natural law, the common use of property, and the right individuals have to subsistence that functions as the moral framework for his discussion of property in the *Second Treatise*.

The second point in the passage from paragraph 31, cited earlier, decrees that nothing was made by God for man to spoil or destroy. Interpreters have generally referred to this as the spoilage limitation, but, in some respects, this is a misleading characterization of Locke's argument. For a better way of putting it would be to say that God does not intend that anything He has created should be wasted or uselessly destroyed; that is, this intentional objective applies to everything, human beings, animals, land and so on. If God's purposes are to be invoked as part of a natural law argument Locke is making in order to demonstrate that there are limits placed on human actions, then it ought to be recognized that these divine purposes cannot be stated in terms of some peculiar preoccupation with the spoilage of fruits and vegetables. This is obvious from Locke's immediate invocation of this reading of God's intentions which he applies to land. 'God gave the world to men in common . . . for their benefit', but, Locke argues, 'it cannot be supposed he meant it should always remain common and uncultivated' (II, 34). Since Locke refers repeatedly throughout the chapter to uncultivated land as 'waste' land (II, 36–8, 42–3, 45), we may take this as an elaboration of his point that God does not intend us to waste anything. On the contrary, he has given the earth 'to the use of the industrious and rational' individual whose 'labour was to be his title to it'.

We can restate this proposition, as Locke does many times in his discussion, in the form of an assertion that land without the application of labour to it is of little value to man; it is a wasted resource. It follows, for Locke, that God would not have given mankind the land unless he expected them to apply their labour to it, and thereby 'make use of it to the best advantage of life, and convenience' (II, 26). Moreover, it is difficult to reconcile this generous gift of a wasted resource with God's directive to provide for the subsistence of all mankind unless we assume labour to be the bridge connecting these divine actions. Thus, Locke insists that 'God, when he gave the world in common to all mankind, commanded man also to labour'. That is, God 'commanded him to subdue the earth, i.e., improve it for the benefit of life', so that through 'subduing or cultivating the earth' the individual came to have a property in it (II, 32, 35).

Now, it should be noticed that this argument radically transforms the status and meaning of 'labour'. For, instead of merely serving (as a form of action) as a logical extension of the definition of a person as a moral agent – being, so to speak, twice removed from any connection with natural law – labour has now become identified with a direct command of the Deity. In short, everyone now has an obligation to labour. Therefore, 'He that in obedience of this command of God, subdued, tilled and sowed any part of it [the earth], thereby annexed to it something that was his property, [his labour] which another had no title to, nor could without injury take from him' (II, 32). 'So that God, by commanding to subdue, gave authority so far to appropriate' the materials He had provided to mankind, and this situation 'necessarily introduces private possessions' (II, 35). Labour as an activity, and its end product, private property, have become through this shift in Locke's argument a fulfilment of man's natural law obligations, expressed as the will of God. Among other things, this gives a critical edge to Locke's discussion of property, for it is of some importance from a moral standpoint to distinguish between those who engage in productive labour in fulfilment of God's command and those who do not. As Locke wrote to a friend, 'I think everyone, according to what way providence has placed him in, is bound to labour for the public good, as far as he is able, or else he has no right to eat' (*Works*, 8:332). If one assumed that this distinction, as to who is or is not productive in labouring for the public good, could be applied to specific groups or classes of individuals in seventeenth-century English society, it would also clearly have considerable social significance.

The general point I am making is that, instead of focusing upon the declarative, naturalistic language of rights, we view Locke's discussion of property in terms of the intentional language of divinely instituted obligations. Or, rather, that we interpret the former in terms of the latter. This means that Lockean natural rights are always the active fulfilment of duties owed to God. It also means that these rights are never simply posited as logical inferences based upon any set of empirical observations concerning 'the nature of man'; rather, they are given to us in the context of a hierarchically structured universe. If, as an empirical observation, it appears odd to speak of 'wasting' the products of nature, when, as a matter of fact, the natural wastage of products in the state of nature far exceeds that produced by human action, it is nevertheless meaningful for Locke to employ morally condemnatory language when speaking of such actions precisely because his perspective is shaped by his understanding of divine intentions and is *not* grounded in an assessment of empirical human behaviour.[9]

Once Locke has brought labouring activity within the province of natural law obligations, he tries to show, by way of an empirical argument, how the development of property defined in terms of the cultivation of land is in fact consonant with the purposes of the Law of Nature. In the beginning, or 'the first ages' of the world before the invention of money, no individual could appropriate very much land for his use, because there were natural limits to his consumption, and there was plenty of land left for others to use. 'This measure did confine every man's possession, to a very moderate proportion', which could not be regarded as being an injury to anyone else (II, 36). Moreover, 'he who appropriates land to himself by his labour, does not lessen but increase[s] the common stock of mankind'. This is the crucial point Locke wants to establish. He reasons that

> the provisions serving to the support of human life, produced by one acre of enclosed and cultivated land, are (to speak much within compass) ten times more, than those, which are yielded by an acre of land, of equal richness, lying waste in common. And therefore, he that encloses land and has a greater plenty of the conveniencies of life from ten acres, than he could have from a hundred left to nature, may truly be said to give ninety acres to mankind. (II, 37)

This argument is repeated in various ways in the next several paragraphs, reinforcing the point that 'labour makes the far greatest part of the value of things we enjoy in this world'. In the state of nature, therefore, if an individual enclosed the land as his property, but allowed its products to spoil or go unused, then this land, 'notwithstanding his enclosure, was still to be looked on as waste, and might be the possession of any other' (II, 38). This radical proposition is later reaffirmed by Locke when he insists that 'anyone has liberty to make use of the waste' (II, 184). It is not the appropriation or possession of land, in other words, that Locke wishes to emphasize but, rather, the productive uses of labour. According to Locke, as a matter of social policy, 'this shows how much numbers of men are to be preferred to largeness of dominions' as the means by which nations accumulate wealth (II, 42).

Leaving aside for the moment that 'the great art of government . . . [is] to secure protection and encouragement to the honest industry of mankind', Locke returns to the argument he has been making about the value of productive labour, this time drawing the contrast between the labour of an Indian in America and the labour of an English farmer. But now, in addition to the superiority of the latter stated purely in the empirical terms of comparative productivity, Locke assesses the labour of each individual according to 'the benefit mankind receives' from each (II, 43). In other words, Locke has brought the fundamental principle of the Law of Nature into the argument on his side in defending the enclosure and productive use of land by civilized countries who, comparatively speaking, have contributed much more to the preservation of mankind than have the inhabitants of America, who still resemble what mankind was like during the first ages of the world (II, 49; cf. II, 30). Hence, when Locke writes in paragraph 32 that God commanded man to improve the earth 'for the benefit of life', he means not only that 'life' not be interpreted in a purely individualistic sense but, rather, as the common life of all, but also that this moral precept can be better fulfilled under some forms of social organization than under others. For it is Locke's objective in the *Second Treatise* not merely to justify private property, or even the 'disproportionate and unequal possession of the earth' (II, 50); he is also concerned to defend certain *kinds* of property as being more beneficial to mankind than others. Indeed, it is precisely from this evaluative standpoint that the historical account of property Locke presents in the *Second Treatise* achieves significance as part of his political argument in that work.

Before pursuing this point further, however, let us attempt to find a place for the invention of money within the moral structure of Locke's theory of property. Thus far, the discussion of property has remained on the level of 'the labour of the body' of the individual in the state of nature. Because this activity is justifiable as a specific commandment from God and, generally, as a fulfilment of the obligations of natural law, and because property ownership is bounded by the limitations of use and subsistence, Locke is entitled to conclude that in this early state of nature 'right and conveniency went together' and there was 'no room for controversy about the title' to property among individuals. Nor, he adds, was there any possibility 'for encroachment on the right of others' (II, 51). During this early stage in the state of nature, life was simple, desires were few, and disputes among individuals were almost nonexistent. But, of course, this stage of the state of nature disappeared, and the chief factor that brought about its disappearance was the invention of money. In paragraph 36, having summarized the basic features and natural law limitations of the early state of nature described above, Locke declares:

> This I dare boldly affirm, that the same rule of propriety, (viz.), that every man should have as much as he could make use of, would still hold in the world, without straitening anybody . . . had not the invention of money, and the tacit agreement of men to put a value on it, introduced (by consent) larger possessions, and a right to them.

There are three aspects of this statement that I believe merit our attention: (1) money is the product of consent amongst individuals; (2) there is a rights-claim that follows from the agreement to accept money; and (3) Locke appears to be pointing to a general change in the social relationships between individuals that is associated with the invention of money. This change is hinted at in his observation that we now live according to a different 'rule of propriety' from that which once prevailed, but even this statement does not adequately express the transformation of social life to which Locke is alluding.

That money is brought into being 'by mutual consent' of individuals (II, 47; cf. 37, 45) appears, at first sight, to be a wholly unproblematic assertion, at least so far as a reading of the text is concerned. Yet the character of this consent and the conditions under which it was given do raise certain interpretative issues that are important not only to Locke's discussion of money, but also to the general structure of his argument in the *Two Treatises*. Locke is quite clear on the point that money is the product of 'a tacit and voluntary consent', that is, a 'tacit agreement' among men. Thus, it is 'only by putting a value on gold and silver and tacitly agreeing in the use of money' that individuals have created the latter (II, 50; cf. 36). Since Locke is attempting to show how individuals came to have property without 'any express compact' or 'explicit consent' as a precondition for their ownership of that property (II, 25, 28, 29), we may suppose that this emphasis upon tacit consent is a purposeful and important part of his argument. But tacit consent may be contrasted not only with express consent, as it is when Locke is describing the establishment of political society, it may also be compared, as a source of obligations, to natural law. In his lectures on the Law of Nature, Locke drew a sharp distinction between consent and natural law, maintaining that 'it is quite evident that natural law can in no wise be inferred from the general consent to be found among men'. He cites the specific example of the value attached to gold through the consent of individuals, arguing that this consent 'is in no wise a law of nature', nor is it 'decreed by natural law' (*ELN*, 177). In the *First Treatise*, Locke wrote that 'common tacit consent', such as that which accounts for the invention of money, creates 'but a positive and not a natural right' (I, 88). Elsewhere Locke states that 'a tacit contract' is 'prompted by the common interests and convenience of men' (*ELN*, 161, 163). In the *Second Treatise*, Locke explains the origins of monarchy 'in the first ages of the world' as the product of 'a tacit and scarce avoidable consent' on the part of the children to cede all political authority to their father, but he is careful to stress that this fatherly authority cannot, therefore, be expressed in the language of 'natural rights' (II, 75–6). Similarly, in the *First Treatise*, when Locke justified 'the authority of the rich proprietor and the subjection of the needy beggar' as the product of 'the consent of the poor man, who preferred being his subject to starving' (I, 43), he thought of this relationship as the result of a 'scarce avoidable consent', but not as one referable to natural law.

What I am arguing is that the tacit agreement to accept money cannot, in Locke's view, supply a foundation for a natural rights claim to property. The latter is derivable only from the Law of Nature, and specifically from some obligation dictated by that law, and it is clear from Locke's argument that he has no intention of producing a justification for the use of money in these terms, such as he used to justify the exercise of labour as a title to property. We may state the issue simply by saying that consent, in any form, cannot be the basis for a natural rights claim, and, indeed, a Lockean natural right is something that individuals *cannot* consent to give up, precisely because it is traceable to a higher authoritative source.[10] What follows logically from this is that not only money as a particular form of property, but also all enlargement of individuals' possessions that is directly attributable to the agreement to accept money can have no justification framed in terms of a natural right to property. Of course, other rights-claims can be made for such property. Still, it is significant that all of these claims are limited by the existential conditions under which they were instituted through consent, while a natural right is absolute and unlimited, at least with respect to particular social formations. To state the point succinctly, all forms of property beyond the fulfilment of a use/subsistence function are, and can be, nothing more than conventionally held rights.[11]

Although we have already entered into the discussion of the second topic listed above, the association of a rights-claim with the agreement to accept money, let me restate the argument I have been making in another way. According to Locke, money 'has its value only from the consent of men', and by this he means that it has no intrinsic or natural value. The argument underlying this point is sufficiently important that Locke repeats it several times in the chapter on property, as well as in his other writings (II, 50; *Works*, 4:22). Thus, he draws a clear distinction between those 'things really useful to the life of man' that are associated with subsistence 'and the necessary support of life', and those things 'that fancy or agreement hath put the value on, more than real use', such as 'gold, silver, and diamonds' (II, 46). Gold and silver, Locke insists, are 'little useful to the life of man in proportion to food, raiment, and carriage' (II, 50). In other words, 'the intrinsic value of things . . . depends only on their usefulness to the life of man' (II, 37; *Works*, 4:42). Although money certainly has its uses, it is 'a barren thing' (*Works*, 4:36). For Locke, the 'necessities of life' include meat, drink, clothing and shelter, and money clearly does not fall within the purview of this definition (I, 86).[12] Money, on the other hand, is the product of our 'fancy' or 'imagination', and, accordingly, it has only an 'imaginary' and not a real value (II, 46, 184).[13] Money is one of those things 'which seem not at first sight to be of any use to us' (Journal, 8 February 1677, MS f.2).

What we have, therefore, is a natural standard of real use to which Locke contrasts an imaginary standard invented by human beings. The former supplies a definition of the necessities of life, while the latter relates to 'the conveniencies of life', which are satisfied or 'improved' through the 'invention and arts' of man (II, 44; cf. 41). Money, as Locke never fails to remind us, is an 'invention' and, like all human inventions, it has its practical uses. These are not to be scoffed at; nevertheless, throughout Locke's writings, there is a general distinction he draws between 'things of necessity' and 'things of fashion', or between 'natural wants' and 'wants of fancy' (2:21, 46; *Works*, 4:31, 58; *STCE*, § 106, 107). Creations of our 'fancy' may or may not serve useful purposes within the context of our social relationships with others. So let us ask what is the purpose for which money was invented, and what moral status, if any, can be attached to this purpose. In particular, we shall want to determine what relationship exists between those social practices and the forms of property associated with the use of money and the purposes of natural law.

Though it may eventually acquire other uses, Locke has no doubt that the primary purpose for which money was originally invented was to serve as a medium of exchange (II, 47–8, 50). He refers to money 'considered in its proper use as a commodity passing in exchange' (*Works*, 4:42; cf. 4:34, 45). That is, money makes it possible for individuals to trade with each other or, perhaps more accurately, it enables them to extend the scope of commerce beyond the simple limits of the bartering of perishable commodities (II, 48). Hence, while money may not be a necessity viewed from the standpoint of subsistence, it 'is necessary for carrying on of trade' (MS b.3; cf. *Works*, 4:7, 12–14, 16, 148). For, Locke asks, what reason could an individual have for producing commodities beyond the subsistence needs of his family, 'where he had no hopes of commerce with other parts of the world, to draw money to him by the sale of the product' (II, 48)? This rhetorical question had already been answered, in effect, in paragraph 45, when Locke compared the English farmer's 'profit' from the sale of his produce for money with the value of the goods produced by an Indian in America (II, 45; cf. 184). This contrast between a primitive lifestyle and a more civilized existence is a leitmotif that surfaces throughout the chapter on property, and a very large proportion of its significance is stated simply in terms of the invention of money and the benefits that accompany that imaginary object. In fact, if individuals 'had not found out ways to shorten the labour' of our lives through useful inventions such as money, Locke maintains that we would still be living under the 'poor' and 'scanty' conditions that describe the state of nature.[14] Since Locke believes that 'the chief end of trade is riches and power' (MS c.30, f.5; MS b.3), it is only a slight exaggeration to say that virtually all the comforts of life that one associates with European civilization are directly or indirectly traceable to the invention of money.

The invention of money, then, is one of those prudentially wise actions executed within a world of probabilities, but is there, in addition, a morally defensible case to be made for the use of money? Locke believes there is. Since there is no direct authorization by natural law or a command of God that is applicable to the invention or use of money, what Locke needs to demonstrate is that the latter is compatible with and does not violate the purposes of natural law. Apart from the few specific obligations imposed upon human beings by the Law of Nature, there is a large domain within which individuals are allowed a freedom of action that is of no direct concern to God or natural law. Seventeenth-century terminology referred to these matters as the 'indifferent' aspects of religion or morality. The use of money is one of those indifferent actions in relation to the prescribed moral duties of men, but, like all actions, it still can be assessed as being morally good or bad according to the purposes that the action fulfils.[15] Since the standard for making such an assessment is the Law of Nature, the issue reduces itself to the question of whether or not the exchange of commodities for money is a practice that is in accordance with the purposes of natural law. These questions, of course, were hardly original to Locke.

The reader familiar with Aristotle will have noticed in Locke's argument the echoes of that author's position in book 1 of the *Politics*, especially the distinction he draws between use value and exchange value as applied to objects. Aristotle also entertains some doubts as to whether the acquisition of commodities through exchange for money is a practice that can be reconciled with the principles of justice. And the Aristotelian strain in Locke's thinking will become even clearer when we attempt to relate, as Aristotle does in the *Politics*, various levels and kinds of property and wealth to the origins and structure of political society.

When Locke confronted the initial challenge to the engrossment of goods acquired through labour, he replied by pointing to the limits imposed by natural law and by showing that one man's subsistence could not be regarded as being 'to the prejudice of others' (II, 31, 37). 'Nobody could think himself injured' by such an action (II, 33). To show that an action does not 'prejudice the rest of mankind, or give them reason to complain, or think themselves injured' (II, 36) is, in

Locke's view, sufficient to prove that it is not an action that violates the Law of Nature. Locke went further than this, claiming that the industrious and frugal use of land through cultivation actually represented a gift or benefit to mankind, by leaving a greater amount of unused land for others to use. These two arguments merge in paragraph 46, where Locke explains the conditions under which money makes its appearance. There he supposes that an individual has gathered more acorns or apples than he can consume. If the individual does nothing, allowing these goods to spoil, his action must be interpreted as robbery and a violation of the Law of Nature. But, Locke observes, 'if he gave away a part to anybody else, so that it perished not uselessly in his possession', then 'he did no injury; he wasted not the common stock; [and] destroyed no part of the portion of goods that belonged to others'. Locke applies the same reasoning to the bartering of plums for nuts, for 'so long as nothing perished uselessly in his hands' he cannot be said to have done an injury to mankind. Indeed, it is clear that he has, in fact, 'made use of' his surplus in a productive manner, which is beneficial both to him and to others with whom such exchanges are carried out (II, 46). 'And thus came in the use of money, some lasting thing that men might keep without spoiling' (II, 47), which as an item of exchange makes it possible for individuals to make use of the surplus of goods they have produced through their industry (II, 48). Now, 'a man may fairly possess more land than he himself can use the product of, by receiving in exchange for the overplus, gold and silver, which may be hoarded up without injury to any one' (II, 50), because no one's subsistence, according to Locke, is threatened by such action, and because the individual has actually made use of his surplus of goods in a manner that will benefit mankind.

From both standpoints, therefore, the exchange of commodities for money must be looked upon as being consonant with the purposes of natural law. There is still no natural right attached to such property gained through consent, but neither, Locke argues, can any person claim to be injured by the consequent inequality of possessions that money and consent have established. Only the natural right to subsistence can claim precedence with respect to the surplus of goods owned by an individual. Barring this specific instance, those goods are his by right, through consent, because no one else is in a position to advance a superior rights-claim to them grounded upon an appeal to natural law. It is important to note, however, that in the state of nature, where positive constitutions have not otherwise determined the matter, the owner of a surplus can forfeit his right to ownership through neglect or waste, and then, by the Law of Nature, his property returns to its original common state 'and might be the possession of any other' individual who makes use of it through his labour (II, 38; 184).

Finally, we must address ourselves to Locke's historical account of the state of nature, the place of property and money in that account, and the general relationship he believes exists between the historical development of social relations and the institution of political society. As was hinted above, I shall argue that the invention of money, along with certain other sociological factors, brings about a dramatic transformation of life in the state of nature.

Locke first raises the question concerning the historical status of the state of nature at the end of the chapter on that subject, to which he replies by citing an example from Garcilaso de la Vega's *Commentaire royale* of two men on a desert island, or the encounter between a European and an Indian in America. 'For 'tis not every compact that puts an end to the state of nature between men . . . other promises and compacts, men may make one with another, and yet still be in the state of nature' (II, 14). The relevance of this point to the agreement to use money by individuals 'out of the bounds of society' or the 'positive constitutions' they establish should be clear (II, 50). Locke also maintains that all states and governments throughout the world, as they exist in the seventeenth century, 'are in a state of nature' with each other (II, 14, 145, 183, 184); and this is not a trivial observation, for it shows that when the emphasis is placed upon the political relationships between individuals (or countries) the concept of the state of nature is perfectly capable of accommodating various types and levels of social relations. In its historical sense, therefore, it is not associated exclusively with a particular set of primitive social conditions.

Nevertheless, we shall begin with 'the first ages of the world' as the starting-point for our discussion of the historical state of nature. References to this period of human existence are scattered throughout chapters 5–8, which deal with property, family relations and the beginning of political society, but there is a consistent and recurring picture of what life was like in the early stage of the state of nature. In fact, I believe something like an ideal type emerges from Locke's discussion, which, allowing for the anachronism of the terminology, may not be far removed from the objective he had in mind in citing historical material in support of his position.

'In the first ages of the world', there was a 'thinness of people' (II, 74) in a situation of relative abundance; that is, 'plenty of natural provisions . . . [and] few spenders' (II, 31, 105). People were nomadic; they 'wandered with their flocks and their herds . . . freely up and down', and the ownership and improvement of the land were not matters of great value to the inhabitants of the state of nature (II, 38; cf. 36–7). 'Men, at first, for the most part, contented themselves with what unassisted nature offered to their necessities' (II, 45). Individuals lived in what was essentially a subsistence economy, just as the Indians in America live at present (II, 41, 46, 49, 105, 108). Since they had little property, it follows for Locke that 'there could be then little room for quarrels or contentions about property' (II, 31, 39). It is worth emphasizing this point, since Locke believes that 'quarrelling about title' or 'about the largeness of possession' of property is the major source of those controversies that make it necessary to institute government as an umpire to resolve them (II, 51, 75, 107). The inhabitants of the first ages did not need a multiplicity of laws; 'a few established laws' were sufficient (II, 107, 162). Summarizing the characteristics of individuals in the early stage of the state of nature, Locke writes that 'the equality of a simple poor way of living confining their desires within the narrow bounds of each man's small property made few controversies, and so no need of many laws to decide them'. Because 'their possessions, or way of living . . . afforded little matter for covetousness or ambition . . . there were but few trespasses, and few offenders' against the Law of Nature (II, 107). Thus, 'want of people and money gave men no temptation to enlarge their possessions or land, or contest for wider extent of ground' (II, 108). In the absence of such controversies over property rights, there was 'no contest betwixt rulers and people about governors or government' (II, 111). Well might Locke speak of the 'innocence of the first ages' (II, 94, 110) as 'the golden age, before vain ambition . . . had corrupted men's minds' (II, 111).

In response to these simple needs and socio-economic conditions, individuals in the early state of nature created a simple form of government – monarchy – which generally began with the father of a large family assuming the role of ruler or king (II, 74–6, 110, 112).

I will not deny, that if we look back as far as history will direct us, towards the original of commonwealths, we shall generally find them under the government and administration of one man. And I am also apt to believe, that where a family was numerous enough to

subsist by itself . . . as it often happens, where there is much land
and few people, the government commonly began in the father. (II,
105; cf. 106)

'Monarchy being simple, and most obvious to men' as a form of
government was 'also best suited to their present state and condition',
since they 'stood more in need of defence against foreign invasions and
injuries, than of multiplicity of laws' (II, 107). It is clear, both from
the general description and the specific examples he offers, that Locke
envisions the early state of nature as a 'poor but virtuous age' (II, 110)
where the precepts of natural law were generally adhered to, in large
part, because a subsistence level of property gives rise to few crimes or
controversies, and because 'commonwealths differed little from
families in number of people' (II, 162), which allowed for a greater
level of friendship and trust among individuals (II, 107). All of these
characteristics are recorded in the journal notations Locke made on
the books he read about the Indians in the New World. He notes that
they live a simple life based upon hunting and fishing, and although
they have little food they are willing to share it with strangers. Locke
is impressed with their charity, hospitality, and the fact that they 'very
seldom injure one another'. They 'quarrel not with their neighbours' and
are 'friendly, liberal, and charitable to all, strangers as well as acquaintances'. They 'bargain freely' in the bartering of goods, without huck-
stering. They are governed by an elective paternal monarchy, but 'their
kings are rather obeyed by consent and persuasion than compulsion, the
public good being the measure of their authority'. In short, 'they are a
very good people, kind to strangers . . . and just in their dealings'.[16]
Since Locke specifically cites from various descriptive accounts of
Indians 'in many parts of America' (II, 102; 105) as part of his attempt
to supply 'examples out of history, of people free and in the state of
nature' (II, 103), it is rather disingenuous for some interpreters to
claim that Locke has no historical conception of the state of nature.[17]
One may disagree with his view of 'history' or his use of the evidence,
or question the significance of such evidence within the general
framework of his argument, but it makes no sense at all to claim that
Locke did not intend to provide the reader with historical examples of
life in the state of nature, when he says explicitly in the text that this
is precisely what he is doing, and when he refers throughout the
Second Treatise to the Indians in America as 'a pattern' for what life is
like in the state of nature he is describing, as it existed during 'the first
ages of the world' (II, 108).

In any event, the simple life of the inhabitants of the state of nature was dramatically transformed with the invention of money, but it would be a mistake, in my opinion, to restate the truth in this proposition in the form of a simple causal assertion. Rather, keeping to the methodology I have adopted, it is preferable to say that Locke provides another ideal type, namely, that of a commercially advanced, civilized, wealthy, commodity-exchange economy in which money and trade figure prominently. This ideal typical society is contrasted with the first stage of the state of nature throughout the *Two Treatises*.

There is a type of society – England is specifically named – in which 'there is plenty of people under government, who have money and commerce . . . whereas in the beginning and first peopling of the great common of the world, it was quite otherwise' (II, 35). In the chapter on property, Locke outlines the demographic and sociological conditions that supply the historical context for the invention of money. 'Families increased, and industry enlarged their stocks . . . till they incorporated, settled themselves together, and built cities . . . and by laws within themselves, settled the properties of those of the same society' (II, 38). A few paragraphs later, Locke restates this point, associating 'the increase of people and stock, with the use of money' and the fact that communities 'by laws within themselves, regulated the properties of the private men of their society, and so by . . . positive agreement, settled a property amongst themselves, in distinct parts and parcels of the earth' (II, 45). Given the concentration of the population, the increase of wealth, the need to establish distinct boundaries, and so on, it is not surprising that it should be 'the civilized part of mankind, who have made and multiplied positive laws to determine property' (II, 30). As was noted earlier, it is 'commerce with other parts of the world' that provides the chief impetus for the invention of money (II, 48). In other words, there is a type of simple society characterized by the 'want of people and money' (II, 108), and a much more complex society where 'there is plenty of people . . . who have money and commerce' (II, 35). The latter society is complex because there is more 'room' for controversies over property rights, more need for a multiplicity of laws and regulations, more diversity in the population, and so forth. Locke had more than a small dose of scepticism concerning the increase of human virtue 'in proportion to the increase of wealth' (*ELN*, 209).[18]

By the same reasoning Locke applied to the first case, this means that a more complex form of government than the simple one of monarchy is required to meet the demands produced by these changed socio-economic conditions. Once individuals were presented with the temptation to enlarge their possessions and to contest for more property, these traits were bound to manifest themselves politically in 'the ambition or insolence of empire' or 'the oppression of tyrannical dominion' (II, 107). Thus, 'ambition and luxury . . . taught princes to have distinct and separate interests from their people'. Under these conditions, 'men found it necessary to examine more carefully the original and rights of government; and to find out ways to restrain the exorbitances, and prevent the abuses of that power which they [had] entrusted in another's hands only for their own good' (II, 111).[19] This reconsideration of the nature and purposes of political power led them 'to think of methods of . . . balancing the power of government, by placing several parts of it in different hands' (II, 107). Simple monarchy, in short, is not an appropriate form of government for an advanced commercial society, however suited it might be to life in the first ages of the world. Rather, what individuals now require is some means by which they can institute an 'express limitation or restraint' (II, 110) upon their political leaders' exercise of power. Also, political power ought to be distributed into different hands. It would appear, therefore, that Locke is advancing an argument for constitutional government which depends, in part, upon his theory of the development of property and his historical account of the state of nature.

NOTES: CHAPTER 6

1 It should not be forgotten that for Locke, and for his seventeenth-century readers, the Bible was the primary historical source for any endeavour to supply a 'historical' account of man's existence. Locke's remark that Filmer's political theory is based upon 'history out of Scripture' (I, 128) accepts the legitimacy of the source, while criticizing Filmer's interpretation of history. Thus, the status of Locke's many biblical references in both the *First* and the *Second Treatise* can only be described, from his standpoint, as being historical evidence. In the chapter on property, for example, Locke cites the example of Abraham's family to illustrate the point that the inhabitants of the early state of nature did not value fixed property in the land, and contented themselves with an essentially subsistence standard of living (II, 38). He uses the same example in the *First Treatise* to show that the various families descended from Abraham 'lived as friends and equals' and 'there was no pretence of jurisdiction or superiority between them' (I, 135; cf. I, 118). Moreover, their estates 'were very narrow and scanty' (I, 136). Other scriptural references are cited by Locke to show that 'freemen' living in the first ages built a city for themselves 'and fixed habitations to settle [their] abodes and families' (I, 146). There are many more such references, too numerous to cite here, but the point is not only that they provide a historical dimension to Locke's argument in the *Two Treatises* generally, but also that the specific language used in

these biblical references often reappears in the *Second Treatise* in passages where Locke is giving a general description of the conditions of the state of nature.

2 Lockean scholars have never quite known what to make of Locke's historical references to a state of nature. Gough refers to a 'quasi-historical state of nature', which, in terms of Locke's intentions, seems preferable to the characterization of Locke's discussion as 'conjectural history' since, for the reasons given in the note above, Locke would not have regarded all of his historical references as being 'conjectural' (John W. Gough, *John Locke's Political Philosophy, Eight Studies* (Oxford: Clarendon Press, 1956), p. 89). The most astringent denial of the historicity of Locke's argument is advanced by Dunn, who sees the state of nature as having a purely 'analytical function' in Locke's political argument. Thus, 'it has literally no transitive empirical content whatsoever' (John Dunn, *The Political Thought of John Locke* (Cambridge: Cambridge University Press, 1969) p. 103 and passim). This formalization of the argument in the *Two Treatises* is extremely odd, since Locke certainly does not hold a conception of political theory as being a piece of analytical reasoning with no empirical content. It is not even true that the state of nature as 'an axiom of theology' (Dunn) could be described in this way since Locke also did not perceive the world from a standpoint that denied the importance of historicity to his understanding of theology. In other words, I do not see how one is at all helped in understanding Locke's political argument in the *Two Treatises* by severing the connection he believed existed between political theory and history, or between the Bible and history, in order to remove the 'empirical content' from the key concept in that political theory. Nor do I see how the point of Locke's consciously intruding anthropological references to the Indians in the New World into his argument will ever be understood by interpreters who persist in assuming the meaninglessness and insignificance of such action on Locke's part. For a serious discussion of this last point, however, see William G. Batz, 'The historical anthropology of John Locke', *Journal of the History of Ideas*, Vol. 35, no. 4 (October–December 1974), pp. 663–70.

3 Throughout Locke's journals, there are a number of notations similar to the one dated 8 February 1677, in which Locke observes that were it not for the practical knowledge of some men in the past 'we should spend all our time to make a scanty provision for a poor and miserable life', such as that of the inhabitants of the West Indies, who are 'scarce able to subsist'. It is 'only for want of knowing the use of . . . inventions . . . to shorten or ease our labours . . . whereby our stock of riches . . . may be increased or better preserved' that they have not achieved the benefits of civilization which Locke associates with his own society. It seems to have been Locke's view that history allowed one to 'see a picture of the world and the nature of mankind' (Journal, 5 April 1677, MS f.2). His references to the Indians in America in the *Two Treatises* are certainly designed to hold up a mirror to Europeans to show them a picture of themselves as they once existed in the past (II, 41, 49, 92, 102, 105, 108). Since these references relate not only to the technological benefits, but also to the political institutions of 'civilized' society, I am arguing that Locke applies the same reasoning to the latter; namely, that it is the 'invention' of certain forms of government which has helped to 'preserve our stock of riches' and has thus given us an advantage over the Indians in America. It is in this sense, therefore, that the practical knowledge of our forebears in creating these political institutions merits an evaluative endorsement from Locke.

4 Sir Robert Filmer, *Patriarcha and Other Political Works*, ed. Peter Laslett (Oxford: Basil Blackwell, 1949), p. 69.

5 Locke's memorandum to the Board of Trade on the employment of the poor, printed in H. R. Fox-Bourne, *The Life of John Locke*, 2 vols (1876), Vol. 2, p. 382.

6 As Plamenatz, for example, does (John Plamenatz, *Man and Society*, 2 vols (New

York: McGraw-Hill, 1963), Vol. 1, pp. 244 ff). Also see J. P. Day, 'Locke on property', *Philosophical Quarterly*, Vol. 16, no. 64 (July 1966), pp. 207–20.

7 Thus, Seliger: 'The right to property is anchored in the moral autonomy which attaches to the phenomenological singularity of each human being' (Martin Seliger, *The Liberal Politics of John Locke* (London: Allen & Unwin, 1968), p. 194; cf. p. 146). Less pretentiously, Sabine finds the Lockean origins of property rights in the 'attributes of the individual person born with him'. Not surprisingly, Sabine concludes that Locke's theory is 'fundamentally egoistic in its explanation of human behavior' (George H. Sabine, *A History of Political Theory*, 3rd edn (New York: Holt, Rinehart & Winston, 1961), pp. 528–9. See also Leo Strauss, *Natural Right and History* (Chicago, Ill.: University of Chicago Press, 1953), pp. 247–48; Plamenatz, *Man and Society*, Vol. 1, p. 245.

8 For some interpreters, such as Day, Locke's claim that the individual owns his own person, and that we are all owned by God, is simply a logical contradiction in Locke's thought ('Locke on property', p. 215). Dunn, however, presents a good brief summary of Locke's point (*Political Thought*, pp. 125–27). Also see James Tully, *A Discourse on Property: John Locke and His Adversaries* (Cambridge: Cambridge University Press, 1980), pp. 62–3.

9 'The injunction to let nothing spoil or go to waste, is either irrelevant or inadequate', according to Plamenatz, because he sees it simply as a maxim that is tied to some peculiar set of empirical conditions (*Man and Society*, Vol. 1, p. 242). On the same basis, Strauss arrives at the equally erroneous conclusion that 'the natural law prohibition against waste is no longer valid in society' (*Natural Right*, p. 241). Unlike some of his interpreters, Locke is not so poor a philosopher as to confuse a moral (divine) imperative with its application to specific empirical objects.

10 'We are under obligations antecedent to all human constitutions' (4:12, 4). Hence it is only 'some law of God' that 'puts it beyond [man's] power to part with' his freedom (FTG, p. 126). Kendall presents the extreme opposite case, where all property rights are reducible to the consent of individuals, going so far as to maintain that 'even the individual's right to life' in the form of subsistence is dependent upon the consent of the majority of society (Wilmoore Kendall, *John Locke and the Doctrine of Majority Rule* (Urbana, Ill.: University of Illinois Press, 1941), p. 106.

11 I have phrased the point this way because I want to retain the ethically absolute boundaries of a use/subsistence conception of property, regardless of the particular form of society. Thus, while I agree with Tully that 'it is never the case that, for Locke, property is independent of a social function', and also that fixed property in land can only be viewed as a conventional and not a natural right, what I wish to stress is that *all* forms of property beyond the level of subsistence for their owner (and his family) are held as conventional rights, dependent upon the laws of the community (II, 120, 138; Tully, *Discourse on Property*, pp. 96 ff.). In this respect, Kendall's argument is much closer to the truth, in my opinion, than the traditional individualistic interpretation of Lockean property rights.

12 Journal, 8 February 1677, MS f.2; 2 December 1678, MS f.3; 2:21, 46; *STCE*, § 106–7. See Locke's reference to the Indians who have only a 'few necessaries of a needy simple life' as a specific illustration of this point (2:16, 6).

13 'By *real ideas*, I mean such as have a foundation in nature; such as have a conformity with the real being, and existence of things . . . *Fantastical* [ideas] . . . I call such as have no foundation in nature, nor have any conformity with that reality of being to which they are tacitly referred' (2:30, 1). Whatever the philosophical difficulties of this distinction, its social implications are very clear. Thus, Locke holds a conception of real natural needs, which he calls 'the ordinary necessities of our lives . . . hunger, thirst, heat' and so forth, that is contrasted

with those 'fantastical' needs, such as an 'itch after honour, power, or riches', which, obviously, includes the 'need' to accumulate money. The first set of needs all individuals would have under any imaginable conditions, while the second set of needs are those 'which acquired habits by fashion, example, and education, have settled in us, and . . . which custom has made natural to us' (2:21, 45). This natural–social dichotomy applied to property and to the rights attached to property is a basic structural presupposition of Locke's thought. The unsettling and unanswered question of course is, what status does Locke believe should be assigned to 'the desire of having more than men needed', which 'altered the intrinsic value of things' (II, 37)?

14   Journal, 8 February 1677, MS f.2; 2:16, 6.
15   'In things not absolutely commanded nor forbidden by the law of God . . . in things in their own nature indifferent,' Locke wrote, 'there is the liberty of great choice, great variety within the bound of innocence.' Thus, 'in the ordinary actions of our lives', we are allowed 'a great latitude' so long as none of those actions 'crosses that fundamental law [of nature]' (Journal, 2 December 1678; cf. 20 March 1678, MS f.3).
16   MS c.33, fols 10–11; Journal, 13 April 1680, MS f.4; MS c.42, fol. 6.
17   According to Lamprecht, for example, Locke 'had no conception of a gradual growth from relatively simple to relatively complex forms of social organization' (Sterling P. Lamprecht, *The Moral and Political Philosophy of John Locke* (1918; reprinted New York: Russell & Russell, 1962) p. 132). This is also the view of Seliger (*Liberal Politics*, p. 98) and Dunn (*Political Thought*, p. 117). While I would agree that locating some precise point in history when a simple form of society assumed a complex form was of no real interest to Locke, the contrast between the two forms of society as ideal types was of great interest to him.
18   'Virtue and prosperity do not often accompany one another' (*The Works of John Locke*, 12th edn, 9 vols (1824), Vol. 6, p. 148).
19   In a note entitled 'Homo Ante ex Post Lapsum', Locke states some of the propositions of his two-stage conception of the state of nature in the theological terminology of the fall of Adam from grace. Thus, when man was first 'put into a possession of the whole world' and was given 'the free use of all things . . . there was scarce room for any irregular desires' such as 'covetousness or ambition'. Later, when labour and 'private possessions' brought about a change in man's condition 'by degrees . . . it gave room for covetousness, pride, and ambition' to spread (MS c.28, fol. 113v). There is certainly something of this morally condemnatory tone of these 'irregular desires' of ambition or covetousness contained in his account of the origins of political society, but I do not believe there is any simple means by which what Locke says in the *Two Treatises* can be translated into the classical Christian account of the fall of man. The whole question of Locke's integration of biblical references into his account of the state of nature as described in the *Second Treatise* (see note 1 above) is a complicated and, in my view, unexplored issue.

CHAPTER 7

The Structure of Constitutional Government

According to Locke, 'the only way whereby anyone divests himself of his natural liberty, and puts on the bonds of civil society is by agreeing with other men to join and unite into a community, for their comfortable, safe, and peaceable living one amongst another, in a secure enjoyment of their properties, and a greater security against any that are not of it' (II, 95). At first glance, this seems a straightforward statement of the process by which one moves from the state of nature to membership in political society. Yet nowhere in the *Two Treatises* are so many obvious and relevant questions left unanswered by Locke than in his discussion of consent and the establishment of a legitimate political society. What kind of consent is necessary to institute political society? What is the socio-economic status of those who give this consent? Is the consent of the people expressed institutionally through elections, or by some other means? Is an elected legislature a necessary element of a legitimate government? What does Locke mean when he asserts that no one can take my property without my consent? Who are the majority of the community who hold the supreme power? These and many other issues are either ignored or responded to by Locke in ambiguous terms. Accordingly, there is a wide range of variance among interpreters of the *Two Treatises* as to Locke's meaning in the account and defence he provides of political society.

Except for an initial consideration of one question which represents a continuation of the discussion in earlier chapters, I propose in this chapter to move from the more abstract to the more concrete problems associated with Locke's theory of legitimate government. Thus, we will examine his definition of political community, and who is a member of it, and then take up his treatment of the various forms of government. Since Locke's argument, I will suggest, focuses upon one specific form of government as his definition of a well-ordered commonwealth, we will explore the relationships within that political society between the executive and the legislative branches of government, and between both of these and the people at large. Finally, we will consider the relevance of Locke's argument to the government of seventeenth-century England, and the extent to which it conforms to his model of a well-ordered commonwealth.

The problem or, rather, cluster of problems that must be resolved as a prelude to the discussion of the topics I have listed above concerns the relationship between the monarchy that grows out of an extended family and Locke's conception of a political society. I argued in Chapter 6 that this simple monarchy originated in and was suited to the first ages of the world, and that the latter formed part of Locke's historical account of the state of nature and the development of different forms of property. And, carrying forward a point raised in Chapter 5 regarding the sharp definitional contrast Locke draws between the state of nature and political society, it would appear that this paternal monarchy, as we may call it, is not compatible with Locke's definition of political society and ought, therefore, to be considered simply as part of his descriptive account of the state of nature. Although I believe this is the most plausible reading of Locke's argument, the issue cannot be so easily disposed of, for Locke's attitude towards this primitive form of government is ambiguously stated in the text. In itself, this might be of little consequence to an examination of the *Two Treatises*, except for the fact that this ambiguity discloses the central problem with which Locke must grapple in his endeavour to present a theory of a legitimate polity. And so the relationship between paternal monarchy, the state of nature, and political society merits closer scrutiny.

Let us begin with an issue that was central to the *First Treatise* – the distinction between paternal and political authority. In his chapter (6) in the *Second Treatise* on paternal power, after showing how the latter is limited by various natural law obligations, Locke argues that a father has 'no sovereign power of commanding. He has no dominion over his son's property or actions.' The power of a father is 'very far from a power to make laws, and enforcing them with penalties that may reach estate, liberty, limbs and life' of his children (II, 69). This power of making laws with penalties of death is a crucial element in Locke's definition of political power. Having denied the exercise of this power to the father, Locke feels he is justified in concluding that 'these two powers, political and paternal, are so perfectly distinct and separate; are built upon so different foundations, and given to so different ends' (II, 71), that there should be no reason to confuse them. Yet, in paragraph 74, after again stating that a father 'has no dominion over the property or actions of his son', Locke explains how understandable it is that the father of the family became the prince or ruler in the first ages of the world. This government, Locke believes, was 'by the express or tacit consent of the children, when they were grown up', placed in the father's hands, and by their 'permission' they 'resigned' up to him 'a monarchical power'. But, he insists, 'this was not by any paternal right, but only by the consent of his children' that the father was also the king (II, 74).

This passage contains a number of difficulties, but Locke continues the argument by conceding that it is true that the children 'made no distinction betwixt minority, and full age' – which Locke takes to be 21 – 'that might make them the free disposers of themselves and fortunes' (II, 75). Thus, Locke concludes, 'the natural fathers of families, by an insensible change, became the politic monarchs of them too . . . So they laid the foundations of hereditary, or elective kingdoms, under several constitutions, and manners, according as chance, contrivance, or occasions happened to mould them.' This, however, proves nothing regarding any 'natural right' claim by 'fathers to political authority, because they commonly were those, in whose hands we find, *de facto*, the exercise of government' (II, 76).

The subject of paternal monarchy is discussed by Locke in the two succeeding chapters of the *Second Treatise*, but before turning to a consideration of those remarks let us pause to take account of a few of the problems which require some clarification if we are to understand the criteria employed by Locke in making the statements cited above. When he says that a father has no dominion over the person or property of his son, he is making a juridical pronouncement, referable to natural law as a moral standard; he is not offering an empirical description of the parent–child relationship. For it is clear that the father *does* have dominion over the son, and this would have been especially true during the first ages of the world. Locke deals with this point by declaring that the father's 'command over his children is but temporary' (II, 65); it is 'a temporary government, which terminates with the minority of the child' (II, 67). Hence, when the latter arrives at 'the years of discretion', the 'father's empire then ceases', and the son is a freeman (II, 65). What Locke means, therefore, is that, while the father does have dominion over his children while they are children, that dominion ceases when they become adults, and that, in any case, the dominion the father has cannot be called political authority both because his power is defined in terms of the natural law obligations of fatherhood, and because political power cannot be exercised over children, but only with respect to rational adults.

As to the children's property, Locke maintains that the father's power does not extend to the goods 'which either their own industry, or another's bounty has made theirs'. This seems a rather innocuous limitation, at least so long as the children are minors, since they are not likely to accumulate property outside the familial requirements for subsistence. Moreover, as Locke fully recognizes, the property children have is generally inherited by them from their father, who, he concedes, has the power to bestow his property (beyond providing for their subsistence) upon whoever pleases him best (II, 72). 'This is no small tie on the obedience of children', he admits, but, he insists, if the children 'submit to all the conditions annexed to such a possession' by the father, it still represents 'a voluntary submission' on their part to his government. This 'political power', however, does not accrue to the father 'by any peculiar right of fatherhood'; rather, it is the consequence of the consent of his children, reinforced by the power the father has over the disposal of his property (II, 73, 116).

If we start with Locke's polemical objectives in making this argument, we can see that his dissociation of fatherly authority from political power depends upon: (1) showing that there are overriding natural law obligations that limit the father's actions and which protect the children's rights; and (2) showing that the father's actual power over his children is temporary, and either terminates when they have outgrown their minority or is justifiably renewed through the tacit or explicit consent of the children. Both arguments are directed against the claim for absolute political power obtained through the 'natural right' of fatherhood advanced by Filmer. Leaving aside for the moment the natural law limitations we have already discussed, is 'a tacit and scarce avoidable consent' on the part of the children to 'the father's authority and government' (II, 75) sufficient to transform an extended family into a legitimate political society?[1]

An affirmative answer to this question places the definition of legitimacy in precariously close proximity to the scarcely avoidable tacit consent one might be forced to give to a usurper or conqueror, and it clearly does not accord with Locke's insistence that a political society is created only when individuals have resigned their natural political power into the hands of the community as a whole, so that each individual 'puts himself under an obligation to every one of that society' (II, 97). Not only does this description not conform to the one he has just provided of the origins of kingly authority in fathers, but, as was noted in Chapter 5, Locke also draws a distinction between the political community and some specific form of government which rests upon some concrete action taken by the former, and this can hardly be reconciled with the 'insensible change' (II, 76; cf. 162) which stands between a family and a commonwealth. If Locke means, as I believe he does, that there is only *one* way whereby a legitimate political society is created, in the manner to be discussed below, then all other governments, however established, which do not adhere to the precise requirements contained in Locke's definition must be adjudged to be not legitimate political societes. (We will return later to the question of the subjects' obligation to obey such governments.) This would leave individuals in the first ages under the governance of their father, but still in the state of nature until such time as they created a political community in the manner described by Locke.

On the other hand, a negative reply to the query posed above undermines the force of Locke's insistence upon grounding the father's political authority in the consent of the children. If this consent does not create a legitimate political society, why make such a point of requiring the consent of the children in the first place? Indeed, it is difficult enough to prove, in response to Filmer's attack on the historical status of consent applied to adults under any condition, that such an action has an existential reality. Why, then, press the issue into the much more difficult empirical terrain of the actions of children within families in the primitive ages of the world? This is hardly an assertion in support of which Locke is able to supply any convincing empirical evidence.[2]

We may relate this dilemma to the one posed by the status of absolute monarchies. Locke maintains that, according to natural law, no one *can* consent to the despotical, absolute or arbitrary rule of one man – which is his definition of absolute monarchy – because they cannot cede to another person a power that is not theirs to give up. Accepting this point would appear to put an end to the matter; absolute monarchy is not a form of government that human beings as rational creatures can institute. But does this mean that, in fact, there are no absolute monarchies in the world? Obviously, it does not mean that. Leaving aside the contentious issue of whether Locke means to apply the concept of absolute monarchy to the English government of the 1680s, it is clear that he does mean to apply it to the Turkish government, and several others that existed in the seventeenth century (I, 33; II, 91, 192), including France under Louis XIV, which represented the paradigm example of an absolute monarchy. What, then, is the status of these governments? They may be illegitimate, but they do exist.

If Locke were as abstract a theorist as he has sometimes been made out to be, it might be argued either that Locke has entrapped himself in a logical difficulty in holding both that absolute monarchy is a government and a state of nature, or that, in the interest of pursuing his own moral objectives, Locke chose to ignore the empirical realities of governments he believed were morally condemnable.[3] Neither of these responses, I think, will do. This is not because Locke is immune from making logically inconsistent statements; he is not. Nor do I deny that moral preoccupations weigh much more heavily in the balance in his construction of a political theory than do historical or empirical concerns. Rather, it is precisely because Locke is constructing a political theory, and because he is supremely conscious of who his opponents are and what beliefs they hold, that I believe he finds himself in a situation in which he can neither deny the existential reality of the position against which he is arguing nor admit its validity. Hence there must be a place for empirically real but morally illegitimate phenomena in the structure of Locke's political theory. In my view, this is an accurate statement of the status of absolute monarchy, which explains why it is both an existing government and no form of civil society at all. I believe paternal monarchy also falls within this range of phenomena, though it is much closer to the province of legitimacy than is absolute monarchy. Nevertheless, standing outside the framework of specific actions which create a true political community, this form of government must also be regarded as existing within the state of nature. Even a very large family, including servants, Locke maintains, comes short of being a political society (II, 77, 86; cf. I, 130–2). It may be true that we commonly find political authority in the hands of the father in the first ages, but all this shows, according to Locke, is that 'the exercise of government' *de facto* was carried out by fathers; it proves nothing regarding a natural rights claim (II, 76). What I shall argue is that Locke is willing to regard paternal monarchy as a *de facto* but not as a *de jure* government and, further, that he is willing to admit the existence of such *de facto* governments – of which absolute monarchy is one example – but he considers the subjects under such governments still to be residents of the state of nature, juridically speaking, until such time as they have formed, through collective action, a political society.

In his chapter on the beginning of political societies, Locke responds to the two objections he says will be raised against his position; namely, that there are no historical examples of individuals instituting governments through consent, and that individuals are born subject to an already existing government and thus cannot be at liberty to begin a new one, according to the conditions of the state of nature as Locke has described them. In the examples Locke gives to refute the first objection, he assumes that he need only show that governments were formed 'by the uniting together of several men free and independent one of another, amongst whom there was no natural superiority or subjection' in order to prove the existence of the state of nature. And, he adds, the fact that the individual is born subject 'to his father, or the head of his family' is no argument against his having the freedom to unite in a political society of his choosing (II, 102).

In other words, the fact that individuals were members of a family and subject to the rule of their father is no argument against their being residents of the state of nature, as Locke understands that term. Indeed, since he often speaks of the existence of large families and 'troops' or 'tribes' residing in the state of nature, and since Locke concedes that these naturalistic forms of society were generally under the dominance of one man, these features *must* be incorporated into his conception of the state of nature since there is no imaginable prior condition of man that constitutes a more 'natural' state than this one. We can state the point another way by saying that no information of any kind relating to the structure of the family has any bearing upon Locke's conception of a legitimate political society. There is one exception to this statement. Locke wants to argue, as part of *his* naturalistic conception of the family, that even the father's dominion is based on the consent of the children. This is an important point against Filmer's conception of patriarchal rule, but consent does not, in itself, change the status of the family by transforming it into a political society. This is not possible for Locke, because *there is no other form of the family than one based on consent*; hence it is impossible that 'consent' should change the family into something else, for example, a political society, for it was always an institution based on consent, so far as the father's rule is concerned. Consent does not confer legitimacy upon the family as a political society; rather, it is an integral feature of the family itself, and so part of Locke's description of 'the natural state all men are in'. Just as he wants to show that all the ingredients of his definition of political power – property, the common good, equality, freedom and so on – are already present in the state of nature, so Locke wants to show that the practice of consenting is a natural characteristic of rational individuals. Part of what it means to be 'a rational creature', according to Locke, is that the individual is 'disposed to consent to nothing but what may be suitable' to the standards of rationality, and since he is speaking of the education of children, Locke must suppose that the practice of giving one's rational consent is something that must be learned in the context of the family (*STCE*, § 31). Locke can therefore insist that consent is not some unusual or unnatural feature of human existence but, on the contrary, must be contained in the very presuppositions we make about human beings. The 'natural subjection, that they were born in' is not, Locke argues, incompatible with their having consented to this subjection (II, 114). If political society is grounded in the consent of individuals, this is because men in the state of nature are already 'disposed to consent' to rational arrangements in the context of their social relationships. Thus, Locke concludes, 'politic societies all began from a voluntary union, and the mutual agreement of men freely acting in the choice of their governours, and forms of government' (II, 102).

Having advanced this sweeping claim in favour of consent as the factual basis for the origin of all governments, Locke again returns to the subject of fathers as the first rulers of commonwealths. He admits that 'children even when they were men, and out of their pupillage . . . were very likely to submit' to their father's power, 'and so in effect make him the lawmaker, and governour over all' (II, 105). Locke uses a naturalistic and almost fatalistic language. Paternal monarchies were formed 'as chance, contrivance, or occasions happened to mould them' (II, 76). Despite this concession to monarchy as a historical form of government,

> it destroys not that, which I affirm, (viz.) that the beginning of politic society depends upon the consent of the individuals, to join and make one society; who, when they are thus incorporated, might set up what form of government they thought fit.

The reason this concession to monarchy does not undermine his argument, Locke explains, is that if we consider 'why people in the beginning generally pitched upon this form' of government we find that it was not because they subscribed to a theory of paternal authority. On the contrary, he asserts, 'almost all monarchies, near their original, have been commonly, at least upon occasion, elective' (II, 106).

The reader is entitled to feel that Locke is here reaching – and, arguably, overreaching – to make an ideological claim on behalf of consent against paternal authority which is, however, phrased as a historical statement of fact. That in assigning political power to the father individuals did not act from a belief based on the natural right of fatherhood is no proof that their action was predicated upon a commitment to the presupposition of Locke's political theory – that they consciously resigned their power into the hands of the community, who then allocated it to the father. In other words, Locke seems torn between trying, on the one hand, to accommodate his notion of consent to a naturalistic description of how 'a family by degrees grew up into a commonwealth' (II, 110) and therefore how children became 'accustomed . . . by experience' to 'the custom of obeying [their father]', which 'made it easier to submit' to the rule of their father (II, 107), and, on the other hand, taking a much harder ideological position which requires a definite conscious decision by all individuals to engage in a specific set of actions, creating a political community where before one had not existed. Indeed, in paragraph 110, it appears not to matter whether the children 'tacitly submitted' to the rule of their father and 'every one acquiesced, till time seemed to have confirmed' that form of government as being legitimate, 'or whether several families, or the descendants of several families' met together and consciously 'put the rule into one man's hand'. Since both descriptions are applied to paternal monarchy in the first ages of the world, its proximity to Locke's model of a political society tends to fluctuate, although, as was noted earlier, consent of the people in any form is sufficient to defeat the theory 'of monarchy being *Jure Divino*' (II, 112). Even monarchy established by custom was an argument capable of being used against Filmer's natural law position, as Locke realized, though he does not rely upon it, except in so far as custom can be reconciled with consent as he has defined it.

What I have presented is Locke's strongest case for the legitimacy of paternal monarchy as a form of government based upon consent. But now we must decide within what interpretative context this assertion assumes significance, so far as Locke's political theory is concerned. We have seen that, on one level, this factual claim has importance as a counter-argument to Filmer's ideological position. However, suppose we view it in relation to Locke's declaration that 'all government, whether monarchical or other, is only from the consent of the people' (MS c.39, fol. 7). This manuscript note recorded by Locke is reaffirmed in the *Second Treatise*. 'Governments', he insists, 'can originally have no other rise than . . . the consent of the people' (II, 175; cf. 102, 104–6, 112, 119, 198). The more one views this proposition as a historical declaration applicable to 'all government', the more necessary it becomes to find some *additional* criterion by which to distinguish legitimate from illegitimate forms of government.[4] Indeed, if Locke were willing to rest his own case on consent alone, he could easily have regarded the argument presented above as being sufficient. Of course, there is the natural law criterion that the ruler must act for the common good of society, but while this places tyranny out of the bounds of legitimacy – since, according to Locke's definition, a tyrant is precisely a ruler who acts for his own and not the society's good – it does not, in itself, rule out a usurper who is 'tacitly consented' to by the people and who acts for their common good.[5] In view of the deep divisions of opinion among individuals in Restoration England concerning the legitimacy and social benefits associated with the Interregnum and Cromwell's reign, this was not an issue that a political theorist justifying revolution could blithely afford to ignore (I, 79, 121). To rely upon consent as a descriptive account of the origins of government at one end of the spectrum, and a general admonition to act for the common good at the other, in other words, seems to leave the definition of legitimate government in a formless state of limbo, though within boundary markers at both ends that protect Locke's notion of political authority from Filmer's claims.

Well, almost. For, it will be recalled that, with the collapse of Filmer's justification of political authority by divine appointment or the natural right of fatherhood, Locke takes great delight in the *First Treatise* in pointing out that Filmer's theory actually turns into a justification for usurpation, which means that any *de facto* government automatically becomes legitimate. To accept tacit consent and the confirmation of time as instruments of legitimacy and, at the same time, not be concerned with some definite, concrete, empirical manifestation of consent is not a very secure or obviously superior vantage-point from which to launch an attack against Filmer's second line of defence, as we may call his justification of *de facto* government. Since Filmer specifically attacked the notion that 'tacit assent' or 'silent acceptation' could be employed as an argument that the ruler was 'elected', it is highly unlikely that Locke would have exposed his position to such an obvious counter-attack by Filmer's adherents. For, as Filmer had noted, to defend elective government on the basis of tacit consent means that any prince who 'comes to a crown, either by succession, conquest or usurpation, may be said to be elected by the people'.[6]

Moreover, in the wake of the Glorious Revolution of 1689, the issue of what actions, by rulers and subjects, are necessary to transform a *de facto* government into a *de jure* government was a hotly contested one. This debate, which was already under way during the period Locke was making the final revisions in the *Two Treatises* prior to its publication, was of considerable interest to Locke, as the record of his pamphlet-buying in 1689–90 demonstrates.[7] And, from other evidence, we know that it was not Locke's view, with respect to that debate, that tacit consent and the confirmation of time were sufficient criteria for determining the legitimacy of a government. Not only was a 'general submission' by the people to the government not the same thing as a 'general consent' given by them, but even the latter might turn out to be, by itself, an inadequate measure of legitimacy. As Locke states the point pithily: 'submission gives no right'; hence there is a difference between a king *de facto* and a king *de jure*, and the amount of time the former holds power has nothing to do with the question of his legitimacy (MS c.28, fols 92, 96).

Accordingly, in his discussion of usurpation in the *Second Treatise*, Locke shifts the emphasis away from consent as such towards 'the forms and rules of the government' (II, 197). As he remarks in the context of the debate alluded to above, 'allegiance is neither due nor paid to right or to government, which are abstract notions, but only to persons having right or government' (MS c.28, fol. 85). That is, all commonwealths that have established some 'form of government . . . have rules also of appointing those, who are to have any share in the public authority; and settled methods of conveying the right to them'. Thus, 'in all lawful governments, the designation of the persons, who are to bear rule, is as natural and necessary a part, as the form of the government itself, and is that which had its establishment originally from the people'. This means that

> Whoever gets into the exercise of any part of the power, by other ways, than what the laws of the community have prescribed, hath no right to be obeyed, though the form of the commonwealth be still preserved; since he is not the person the laws have appointed, and consequently not the person the people have consented to. Nor can such a usurper, or any deriving from him, ever have a title, till the people are both at liberty to consent, and have actually consented to allow, and confirm in him, the power he hath till then usurped. (II, 198)

This does not carry us very far from the general notion of the consent of the people, which is obviously a matter of some importance to Locke in his treatment of usurpation, but, I am arguing, every step towards concreteness, towards the rules, settled methods, laws of the community, and actual consent, that Locke believes are essential to his definition of political society moves us further away from the kind of description he gives of paternal monarchy in the first ages. There, as we have seen, individuals had little knowledge of the various forms of government, nor did they 'trouble themselves to think of methods' that might restrain the exercise of political power or establish the rules pertaining to its transmission (II, 107, 110). But such 'express conditions limiting or regulating his power' (II, 112) in order to 'prevent the abuses' of that power (II, 111) are precisely the laws designating who is rightfully entrusted with political power and what conditions the community must establish in order to constitute a particular form of political society. Elsewhere, Locke speaks of the power that was 'granted' the magistrate by 'the constitution of the government', and the fact that he was specifically 'commissioned' by the community to use that power for certain purposes. In order to distinguish a political society from an army, a family, or 'the East-India company', it is essential that one specify the limitations placed on the use of that power. Political power is thus 'put into some one or few persons' hands with direction and authority how to use it' (*Works*, 5:217–18). Can these limitations upon the exercise of political power be so easily removed from the concept of legitimacy as Locke understands it, simply because he also wants to place paternal monarchy under the umbrella of consent? I think not.

In the midst of his discussion of paternal monarchy in the first ages of the world, Locke declares that 'the kings of the Indians in America' still provide 'a pattern of the first ages in Asia and Europe' (II, 108). Yet, as Locke also reminds us, the Indians in America live in the state of nature; indeed, they are the paradigm examples of inhabitants of the state of nature, and not only for Locke, but also for Hobbes and many others in the seventeenth century who made use of that concept. If they are both in the state of nature and a pattern of what the first ages in Europe were like, then are not the inhabitants who live under a paternal monarchy during that period, logically, also living in the state of nature? In one of the many journal notes Locke made from his reading about the Indians, he writes that 'their kings are rather obliged by consent and persuasion than compulsion, the public good being the reason of their authority . . . and this seems to be the state of regal authority in its original in all that part of the world' (MS c.33, fol. 11; MS c.42, fol. 6). In other words, notwithstanding the fact that all regal authority is derived from consent and limited by the public good, the Indians may still be regarded as living in the state of nature. For, if *they* have met all the criteria of Locke's definition of legitimate political society, then his references to them as inhabitants of the state of nature truly reflect an insoluble contradiction in the structure of his political theory.[8]

One reason that Locke interjects the example of the Indians at this point in his discussion of paternal monarchy is that he describes the Indian kings as being 'little more than generals of their armies' (II, 108; cf. I, 130–2). But this is exactly the way he refers to paternal monarchs in the first ages – as rulers who provide their subjects with a 'defence against foreign invasions' and who 'conduct them in their wars' (II, 107). This point is then pursued through biblical history, which supports the view, according to Locke, that the 'first kings' in Israel were little more than 'captains in war, and leaders of their armies'. Yet subjects tended to define political power 'as if the whole kingly authority were nothing else but to be their general' (II, 109). These examples reveal what life was like in the first ages, but they cannot possibly be taken as an adequate description of what, in Locke's view, constitutes a legitimate political society.

Let me restate the point in another way. One reason that Locke lays such emphasis upon placing political power in the hands of the community is that only the latter can have the power of life and death, which is a true mark of sovereignty. Locke's position appears to be that since the Law of Nature commands the preservation of mankind this will most likely prove to be an enforceable proposition when the majority of the community are the designated custodians of this executive power of natural law, because they are, in effect, acting to preserve themselves.[9] No matter how closely a paternal monarchy resembles 'a little commonwealth', Locke maintains that the father 'has no legislative power of life and death over any' of those under his dominion, except slaves (II, 86). On the contrary, even in the situation in which children have consented to the rule of their father, Locke speaks of the arrangement as being nothing more 'than the permitting the father to exercise alone in his family that executive power of the Law of Nature, which every freeman naturally has' (II, 74, 105). So a father or a general might lead the community to war, because the latter is acting in its own defence, and still be without the power to give laws or put a member of his own society to death. 'The actual making of war or peace', Locke argues, 'is no proof of any other power . . . and this power in many cases one may have without any politic supremacy' (I, 132).

There are some very interesting remarks in the *Letter Concerning Toleration* which I believe supply a picture of the state of nature encompassing all that has been said above. Locke refers to the inhabitants in the West Indies 'to whom the rivers and woods afforded the spontaneous provisions of life, and so with no private possessions of land, had no enlarged desires after riches or power'. Nevertheless, these individuals 'live in one society, make one people of one language under one chieftain, who shall have no other power to command them in time of common war against their common enemies, without any municipal laws, judges, or any person with superiority established amongst them'. The power of the chieftain, who is 'the only man of authority amongst them', is limited to the defence of 'the common-wealth'. That is, 'their captain, or prince, is sovereign commander in time of war; but in time of peace, neither he nor anybody else has any authority over any of the society' (*Works*, 5:225; cf. 5:121). And, despite Locke's use of 'commonwealth', is this not a description of life in the state of nature and/or the first ages of the world? Later Locke observes that in 'civilized and settled nations' political power has been placed in the hands of some men 'chosen by the community to govern it' so that 'the form of the government places this power out of the community itself'. If this is not done, he adds, 'there could be no civil society' established, which is to say that power still remains in the hands of the community, but no person has 'any authority' over any other member of that society (*Works*, 5:504).

'The *only* way' one leaves the state of nature and becomes a member of political society is by uniting with others to 'make one body politic, wherein the majority have a right to act and conclude the rest' (II, 95–6). 'There, and there *only* is political society, where every one of the members' has resigned into the hands of the community his natural power, and the community 'by settled standing rules . . . and by men having authority from the community . . . decides all the differences that may happen between any members of that society, concerning any matter of right' (II, 87). Thus, '*nothing but* the consent of any number of freemen capable of a majority to unite and incorporate into such a society . . . is that, and that *only*, which did, or could give beginning to any lawful government in the world' (II, 99). I have stressed the exclusivity of Locke's language because he makes the point often enough for us to be entitled to assume that he does intend to narrow the channels of legitimacy. It could be argued that the gate through which one must pass is simply consent, and much – but, I think, not all – of the text will bear this reading. I have suggested that there is a second gate, and that the key words with respect to it are 'constitution', 'majority', 'settled standing rules', 'express restraints' on political power, and, as Locke says in paragraph 131, 'established standing laws' interpreted 'by indifferent and upright judges, who are to decide controversies by those laws'. Locke insists on this last point as a crucial aspect of his definition, for without 'promulgated standing laws, and known authorized judges . . . to determine the rights, and fence the properties of those that live' in political society individuals would still exist within the state of nature (II, 137). This assumes that there is a need for laws to determine rights and the boundaries of properties, and this 'necessarily supposes and requires, that the people should *have property*'. Locke further explains that, 'men therefore in society having property, they have such a right to the goods, which by the law of the community are theirs, that nobody hath a right to take their substance, or any part of it from them, without their own consent' (II, 138). This series of descriptive/normative statements, I submit, makes no sense if we attempt to relate them to life during the first ages, on the assumption that the latter is not to be identified with the state of nature. It was Locke's very point in describing that period to insist that there was no need for many laws, and hence no indifferent judges, because controversies over property rights did not arise, and this because life remained close to the subsistence level, and property defined in those terms not only cannot be taken from an individual without his consent but also cannot be taken from him with his consent. It is not the law of the community that assigns him subsistence property, but the Law of Nature. And whether or not the people in the first ages can be said to have property in the sense which seems to be implied in this passage is a highly debatable point. Locke's discussion in that paragraph of legislative assemblies, and the propensity of rulers 'to increase their own riches and power', further decreases its applicability to his references to the Indians in America, the first kings of Israel, or the paternal monarchies of Europe, all of which fit into the general pattern of the first ages of the world. In short, I cannot see how a society in which individuals have resigned their power into the hands of one person, be he their chieftain or their father, where there are no private possessions which it is the chief end of government to protect, where there are no settled methods, constitutional restraints or standing established laws of the community, no judges to interpret them, and where the ends of political power are effectively limited to the defence of the commonwealth against its foreign enemies can be equated with the kind of society Locke describes as a legitimate polity.

Even with the clearest understanding of the formal and empirical conditions under which the latter is created, however, it would still be difficult to determine from Locke's language in the *Two Treatises* exactly who is a member of this political society. Whether Locke assumed that the members of his political society were substantial property-owners or whether he held a more extended view of political membership is one of the most controversial questions in the secondary literature on Locke. It is only fair, therefore, to warn the reader that the interpretation I shall defend as being most plausible stands in opposition to the prevailing orthodoxy, though not against what Locke *says* in the text.

That which 'actually constitutes any political society, is nothing but the consent of any number of freemen' who decide to remove themselves 'out of a state of nature into a community' (II, 99). What is the status of these 'freemen'? First, we recall that in the state of nature Locke insists that 'all men' are freemen (II, 4, 95, 113, 119). Indeed, it would be hard to overemphasize 'this equality of men by nature' (II, 5, 7) as a fundamental tenet of Locke's political thought. Since I do not believe that it can be shown that Locke means to attach any special socio-economic conditions to these assertions about individuals in the state of nature with respect to their status as freemen, if such conditions are to be included in that concept they must originate at that moment when political society is instituted, that is, as part of the conditional meaning of political society. It is true that Locke argues for the inequality of property ownership in the state of nature – as I shall try to show, this even counts against the dominant interpretative viewpoint – but he is quite clear on the point that property ownership as such cannot create political authority. Inequality of property ownership is perfectly compatible with the nonexistence of political authority. Thus, all men in the state of nature retain their natural political power as individuals until such time as they choose to give it up. In order for 'freemen' to mean something other than all individuals, therefore, there must come some moment when those who own property also turn out to be those to whom Locke is referring when he says that freemen consent to organize a political society, for, prior to that one moment, there is nothing in the text that requires a freeman in the state of nature to own any amount of property in order to qualify for that title. He need only be capable of disposing of his person and actions, to which the only contrast Locke draws is that of slaves (II, 24). The thesis I shall defend, therefore, is that Locke does not change his definition of a freeman, so that whoever qualifies for that status in the state of nature is also qualified to be a member of political society. This means that a freeman does not have to own land, nor does he have to possess any certain amount of property whatsoever, although, unlike a slave, he does have to be *capable* of possessing property.

In chapter 6 of the *Second Treatise*, Locke writes that when he says 'that all men by nature are equal, I cannot be supposed to understand all sorts of equality: age or virtue may give men a just precedency: excellency of parts and merit may place others above the common level: birth may subject some', and so on, 'and yet all this consists with the equality, which all men are in, in respect of jurisdiction or dominion one over another, which was the equality I there spoke of' (in the chapter on the state of nature). Political equality, defined as 'that equal right that every man hath to his natural freedom', is compatible with various kinds of social inequality that might be presumed to exist in the state of nature (II, 54; cf. I, 67). What is crucial to Locke is that an individual must have the freedom 'to dispose of his person or possessions' (II, 6) 'without being subjected to the will or authority of any other man' (II, 54). Locke then applies this principle to children, maintaining that 'age and reason . . . leave a man at his own free disposal' (II, 55). Reason and understanding are the criteria that determine whether a person is free or capable of obeying the law (II, 57–8, 170). This principle, Locke observes, 'holds in all the laws a man is under, whether natural or civil'. Is a person free according to the Law of Nature? 'What gave him a free disposing of his property according to his own will, within the compass of that law? I answer: state of maturity wherein he might be supposed capable to know that law' and so 'keep his actions within the bounds of it. When he has acquired that state, he is presumed to know how far that law is to be his guide, and how far he may make use of his freedom, and so comes to have it.' Even if one interprets 'property' in this passage in the narrow sense of goods – though I believe Locke means the larger definition of life, liberty and estate – it is certainly clear from the syntax that Locke is not saying that ownership of property is what makes the individual a freeman. Rather, it is 'a state of reason, and such an age of discretion made him free' (II, 59; cf. 173; *STCE*, § 108). Even if one followed Macpherson in first equating 'reason' with property ownership and then equating both with Locke's definition of a 'freeman', this would not account for 'the age of one and twenty years', that is, the 'state of maturity' which Locke includes as an important criterion of his definition of a freeman. One might not become a property-owner, either through inheritance or through one's own labour, until many years after that age, so that, if property ownership is the key criterion, then, age is simply an extraneous factor.[10] If, however, one associates reason with the definition of an 'adult', as Locke is in fact doing in these passages in order to determine when children are free from subjection to the will of their father, then it is relevant to ask at what age does a child become an adult. Locke's answer is at the age of 21. Hence, as he says repeatedly, 'age and reason' go together to comprise his definition of a freeman. 'Thus we are born free, as we are born rational . . . age brings one, brings with it the other too' (II, 61, 75). And this definition is applicable, he insists, to individuals both in the state of nature and within political society (II, 59, 170).

The same criteria that 'made his father a freeman' make the son a freeman (II, 58). This means that all adult males are, presumptively, freemen, because they are supposed to have reason, and they are thus presumed to be capable of disposing of their own actions. 'The freedom then of man and liberty of acting according to his own will, is grounded on his having reason' (II, 63). In paragraph 61, Locke makes the interesting remark that an individual subject can be presumed capable of governing himself at exactly the same age as the ruler is presumed to be capable of governing the country, and a broad interpretation of this rule could certainly place political power in the hands of all those over 21. In fact, I take this to be Locke's meaning when he declares that 'the consent of freemen, born under government, which only makes them members of it, being given separately in their turns, as each comes to be of age' (II, 117). Locke insists, even to the point of stretching the empirical plausibility of his argument in the context of seventeenth-century laws, that an individual is 'under his father's tuition and authority', and is technically 'a subject of no country or government . . . till he comes to age of discretion; *and then he is a freeman*, at liberty what government he will put himself under; what body politic he will unite himself to' (II, 118). Now, Locke is not so often so clear or determinate in stating his definition of terms in the *Two Treatises* that we can afford to dismiss this textual insistence upon age and presumptive reason as the criteria of what he means by a freeman.

Locke cites another example to illustrate his argument, which does not at all favour the association of property ownership with reason, but which does support his advocacy of presumptive reason. He observes:

> Commonwealths themselves take notice of, and allow that there is a time when men are to begin to act like free men, and therefore till that time require not oaths of fealty, or allegiance, or other public owning of, or submission to the government of their countries. (II, 62)

In the seventeenth century, oaths were administered to various kinds of civil servant, members of the armed forces, the clergy, school-teachers, members of livery companies and corporations, and many other individuals. Oath-taking is not a criterion that can be linked in any meaningful sense to property ownership of any type or amount, but it is, again, a useful example for an argument that holds that men, whatever their social station in life, may be presumed to have sufficient reason to govern themselves in their political actions.

Let us assume, for the moment, that this is at least the definition of a freeman with which Locke begins his argument in the *Second Treatise*, and turn to the question of the relationship between property ownership and membership in political society. What we wish to know, specifically, is whether property ownership as a criterion either displaces or comes to be equated with reason and the freedom to dispose of one's actions in the course of Locke's account of the institution of political society. We ought to require, as a minimum, that Locke be at least as clear about this definitional shift in his thinking as he is in stating his initial presuppositions. In this regard, it is rather surprising that one of the major premises of Professor Macpherson's interpretation of the *Two Treatises* – namely, that there is an assumption on Locke's part of a differential rationality as between property-owners and members of the labouring class – is not derived from an analysis of that text but, rather, from certain remarks made by Locke in various contexts in his other writings. I will postpone a consideration of Macpherson's misinterpretation of these works until Chapter 9, when we have an opportunity to see how the political argument of the *Two Treatises* relates to the other works published by Locke between 1689 and 1695. Moreover, even Macpherson admits that 'there is nothing to suggest an assumption of class differentiation' in Locke's opening statements in the *Second Treatise*.[11] The shift, Macpherson believes, occurs in the chapter on property (though it should be noted that all of the citations above defining a 'freeman' are given by Locke after his discussion of property), where, according to Macpherson, Locke identifies reason with the propensity to accumulate capital, to the extent that it is now 'his assumption that unlimited accumulation is the essence of rationality'.[12] The only textual source for this definition of rationality cited by Macpherson is the reference to 'the industrious and the rational' in paragraph 34, where, it will be recalled, Locke links those terms with *labour* (as a fulfilment of God's command), and not with capitalist accumulation, nor even with the appropriation of land as such, for the reasons given in Chapter 6.[13] Nevertheless, Macpherson concludes that it is now only the property-owners who are 'fully rational', while everyone else, but especially wage-earners, have lost their rationality and hence those rights-claims that were premissed upon their having reason.

This conclusion is then incorporated into Macpherson's account of the origins of Lockean political society in which, because of this differential rationality defined in terms of social classes, only property-owners can be counted as being 'full members' of that society. There are two arguments offered by Macpherson in support of this assertion: the first maintains that since 'the chief end' of government is to provide protection for property the identification of that term with land or money gives a special or privileged status to property-owners with respect to the exercise of political power; Macpherson's second argument makes use of Locke's distinction between express and tacit consent in order to show that only property-owners give their express consent to the government, while propertyless individuals are nevertheless obliged to obey its laws because they have tacitly consented to them.[14] Even from this brief sketch of Macpherson's interpretation, I think it is clear as to what the issues and the nature of the problems are. But do Locke's description of and justification for the institution of political society support this reading of the text? I think they do not.

Following his effort to show 'how a family, or any other society of men, differ from that, which is properly political society', Locke proposes to illustrate his point 'by considering wherein political society itself consists' (II, 86). It is in the following paragraph that he presents his first definition of a political society in the *Two Treatises*. Prior to this definition, Locke recapitulates those premisses which, in his view, have already 'been proved', and which are therefore necessary to an understanding of the definition itself. These are that man is born 'with a title to perfect freedom' and natural rights 'equally with any other man, or number of men in the world', and that he has 'by nature a power . . . to preserve his property, that is, his life, liberty and estate' against the injuries of other individuals. This stated, Locke defines political society in terms of an action on the part of 'every one of the members' who unites himself to the community, and the latter then 'decides all the differences that may happen between any members of that society, concerning any matter of right' (II, 87), which, it seems reasonable to suppose, pertains to any person's life and liberty as well as to his property. Now, it seems clear that since Locke restates and incorporates into his initial definition of political society the very postulates which, as Macpherson concedes, show no evidence of an assumption of differential class rationality on Locke's part – indeed, he explicitly uses the broad definition of 'property' as the basis for his definition of membership in political society – it would appear that either Locke is self-destructively digging a hole for himself by putting forward a position from which he subsequently intends to withdraw, or that, despite what he said two chapters earlier in his discussion of property, he still holds to an essentially egalitarian view of political rationality.

At the start of the chapter on the beginning of political societies, Locke again repeats his premiss that men are 'by nature, all free, equal and independent' (II, 95), and that civil society is based upon 'the consent of every individual' (II, 96). 'By which means', Locke explains, 'every single person became subject, equally with other the meanest man, to those laws, which he himself, as part of the Legislative had established' (II, 94). As Laslett notes in a comment on this passage, this certainly seems to imply that 'the meanest man', which refers to the individual's *lack* of property, is 'part ˜ᶠ ˜ e Legislative' power of the community, which is to say that he is a member of political society as Locke defines it.[15] At the beginning of chapter 9, on the ends of political society and government, Locke once more repeats the proposition that in the state of nature every individual is 'absolute lord of his own person and possessions, equal to the greatest', by which I suppose he means both the greatest person and the greatest owner of possessions. The specific question to which Locke is addressing himself in this paragraph is, why does this individual choose to leave the state of nature? The answer he gives is that 'the enjoyment of the property he has in this state is very unsafe, very insecure', and this makes him 'willing to join in society with others'. But Locke immediately states the purpose of this action as being 'the mutual preservation of their lives, liberties and estates, which I call by the general name, property' (II, 123). It is in the immediately following sentence that Locke makes his famous pronouncement that 'the great and chief end therefore, of men's uniting into commonwealths, and putting themselves under government, is the preservation of their property' (II, 124). Locke cannot possibly mean by property in this sentence only land or goods, because he has just given his general definition of property in the preceding sentence, and, if nothing else, the 'therefore' must obviously serve to connect these remarks to his pronouncement.[16] In other words, Locke has persisted in his effort to link the basic premises of his description of the state of nature and his broad definition of property with his definition of political society, his account of its origins, and his statement of its ends (II, 171).

Locke maintains that every individual joins political society 'only with an intention in every one the better to preserve himself, his liberty and property' (II, 131). This is an inclusive presupposition, for everyone is supposed by Locke to benefit from 'the labour, assistance, and society of others in the same community' (II, 130). The fact that everyone benefits, naturally, does not mean that some might not benefit more than others, since even a 'day labourer' in seventeenth-century England is better off than an Indian king in the state of nature (II, 41). Yet, in his discussion of the limits of legislative power in civil society, these limits are defined in terms of the 'life, liberty, or possession' of an individual (II, 135). In the following paragraph, Locke refers to the need for judges 'to decide the rights of the subject' and 'to determine the rights, and fence the properties' of those in political society. This need fulfils the purpose that men had in joining that society, which was 'to secure and defend their properties' (II, 136). But, lest we imagine that here Locke means the narrow definition of property, he immediately restates the purpose of individuals in leaving the state of nature in terms of preserving 'their lives, liberties and fortunes', that is, property in the general sense (II, 137).[17]

The next paragraph, however, demands careful attention, for when Locke declares that 'the supreme power cannot take from any man any part of his property without his own consent' it certainly appears that Locke is here speaking of goods. It is in this passage that Locke says that the institution of political society presupposes that 'the people should have property', and that, once they have joined political society, 'they have such a right to the goods, which by the law of the community are theirs'. Nevertheless, 'it is a mistake to think, that the supreme or legislative power of any commonwealth, can do what it will, and dispose of the estates of the subject arbitrarily, or take any part of them at pleasure' (II, 138). Does this mean that Locke has, after all, now shifted the discussion on to the ground of the rights of property-owners, assuming an identification of them with membership in political society? Strangely enough, the example Locke gives to illustrate the argument he has just made is never examined, although the point of his giving it is unquestionably to clarify the meaning of his statements. The example states that despite the fact that a general of the army has absolute authority to command a soldier to engage in an action 'where he is almost sure to perish' the general has no authority to command the soldier 'to give him one penny of his money'. Locke denies that the general has the power to 'dispose of one farthing of that soldier's estate, or seize one jot of his goods'. Only the soldier has the freedom of 'disposing of his goods' (II, 139). Not only is it interesting that Locke chooses the example of a common soldier, rather than a large landholder, to illustrate his general point that property cannot be taken from an individual without his consent, but also the specific language used by Locke in this illustration is worth our attention. That is, the soldier has an 'estate' defined in terms of money or goods, like anyone else. Moreover, the freedom he has to dispose of his possessions cannot be waived by any other person with authority, even where that authority legitimately extends to the life or death of the individual himself. If we were to assume, therefore, that Locke means to include common soldiers within his references to 'estates' and the free disposing of goods, as this passage indicates that he does, then, even when Locke is using property as a reference to goods or money, this by no means implies that he is thinking solely of those large property-owners Macpherson has in mind. Thus, in summarizing his own position, Locke repeats his argument that political power exists 'where men have property in their own disposal' (II, 174), and 'by property I must be understood here, as in other places, to mean that property which men have in their persons as well as goods' (II, 173).

In the *Letter Concerning Toleration*, Locke defined the purpose of political society in terms of preserving the 'civil interests' of individuals, which consist of life, liberty, health 'and the possession of outward things, such as money, lands, houses, furniture, and the like' (*Works*, 5:10). It does not seem unreasonable to identify this last characterization of the 'goods' owned by the individual with Locke's references to 'estate', especially since it replaces that term in the litany used throughout the *Two Treatises* when Locke is speaking of property in general. From which it is easy to see that any individual who owns furniture, a house, money and so forth can be said to have an estate. In fact, after referring to the magistrate's obligation to secure the safety of 'the estates of the people', Locke defines the meaning of this phrase as the securing 'of every particular man's goods and person'. This point is repeated a few pages later, when the purpose of political society is identified with the protection of 'every man's possession of the things of this life' (*Works*, 5:40, 43), which hardly allows for the space separating property-owners from the propertyless which Macpherson reads into Locke's words. No one has suggested, so far as I know, that Locke means to defend only the wealthy dissenters from having their 'estates', 'civil interests', 'property' or 'goods' taken from them by the state through fines, penalties or confiscation. Yet it is obvious that he assumes in the *Letter* that 'every individual' is a possessor of property defined in these terms and, therefore, every person is a possessor of certain political rights. I do not believe Locke is so confused a thinker as to have offered two different definitions of property, the purposes of political society and their relationship to 'every person' who is a member of that society in two works – the *Letter* and the *Two Treatises* – he published simultaneously.

'Every man', Locke observes, 'is born with a double right: first, a right of freedom to his person', which means 'the free disposal of it lies in himself'. And, 'secondly, a right, before any other man, to inherit, with his brethren, his father's goods' (II, 190). 'By the first of these, a man is naturally free from subjection to any government' (II, 191), and it is only through his consent as a person that he places himself under a lawful government. If men wish to 'retain a right to the possession of their ancestors', they may have to give their consent to the government on the conditions it offers them, but their membership in political society does not depend on their ownership of these possessions; on the contrary, their ownership of property depends upon their consent to be members, and this they are free to withhold (II, 192). Surely, Locke here has the opportunity to define membership in political society as being dependent upon property ownership; instead, he insists that political jurisdiction relates *only* to the individual's free disposal of his person through consent, regardless of whether or not he owns any property in land or in any other form. Thus, referring to individuals as freemen, Locke asserts, 'their persons are free by a native right, and their properties, *be they more or less*, are their own, and at their own dispose' (II, 194).[18] I can state the point I am making sharply and ideologically by saying that all adult males have a natural right to exercise political power through consent, and a conditional right to be property-owners, according to the laws of the community. In short, this is a complete reversal of Macpherson's emphasis relating property ownership to political power.

Not only can I find no assertion of differential rationality in the text at all those crucial places where Locke is defining political society, giving an account of its origins, setting out its limits and ends, or illustrating by examples the difference between political power and property ownership, I find, on the contrary, a steadfast, even an annoyingly repetitious, insistence upon the application of the propositions stated at the outset of the *Second Treatise* to all of these topics. Reason and property in one's person are, throughout the entire argument of the *Two Treatises*, given precedence by Locke over the ownership of land or other forms of property. Nor is this surprising in view of his association of the first quality with a natural rights claim, and the second with the conditional rights conferred through consent. There is no reversal of emphasis in this relationship as one moves from the state of nature to political society, and the inference to be drawn from this is that Locke intends to link his natural rights argument with his notion of consent and membership in political society in support of the conclusion that all adult males have a presumptive claim to be 'part of the legislative power' in society. This does not mean that they do, in fact, exercise such power, and even less does it mean that Locke believes this is a description of how political power is exercised in seventeenth-century England.[19]

To this argument against Macpherson's reading of the text – which Locke, of course, did not have to take into account in writing the *Two Treatises* – we may add a few comments on Filmer's views on the suffrage, to which it is reasonable to suppose Locke did have to devote some attention in formulating his own position on this issue. Now, Filmer repeatedly links the argument for natural rights and consent with manhood suffrage precisely because he hopes to frighten his opponents with this practical consequence which, he insists, flows logically from the assumptions and language of a natural rights argument. (Ireton and Cromwell had made this same point, incidentally, in their attacks upon the Levellers' position on the franchise at the Putney debates.) 'If it be admitted that the people are or ever were free by nature, and not to be governed, but by their own consent,' Filmer observes, 'it is most unjust to exclude any one man from his right in government.' In other words, 'if we will allow every man to be naturally free till they give their consent to be bound, we must allow every particular person a negative voice . . . This is grounded upon the general reason of all' individuals, which is the only thing they are supposed to have in common; and therefore, Filmer argues, they 'all have equal power' in the institution of government.[20]

Filmer leaves no doubts in the mind of his reader as to the sociological implications of the natural rights/consent argument. Quite simply, it confers political membership upon individuals from the lowest social class in society. Not even Aristotle – whose 'democratical' notions are so frequently cited by 'our modern politicians' – went so far. On the contrary, Filmer notes, he was careful to exclude 'mechanics' and artisans from the franchise.[21] But, of course, Aristotle was not a natural rights theorist. And that is exactly the point. Filmer wants to show that no one, not even the most 'democratical' authority claimed by his opponents, has ever pressed the notion of allowing 'every man' a voice in the government so far as the exponents of a natural rights/consent argument do. The consequence of accepting the validity of this argument, Filmer maintains, would be to place political power in the hands of 'the proletarian rabble'.[22] These comments were echoed by Filmer's followers in numerous political tracts written during the 1680s, and the forcefulness of this critique is reflected in the fact that many Whigs sought to dissociate themselves from the radical implications being imputed to them by stating in their works quite explicitly the qualifications that excluded artisans and mechanics from the suffrage. Locke does not adopt this defensive posture in order to deflect Filmer's attack. On the contrary, one might say that Locke almost flaunts the language of natural rights and consent in the *Second Treatise* in the face of Filmer's challenge on the question of suffrage, and thus the 'silence' of his reply to Filmer is endowed with considerable political significance.

Against the interpretation offered above, there are several passages in the *Second Treatise* which, if they do not prove the assertion of differential class rationality, are generally thought to be disclaimers on Locke's part of any endorsement of a broad suffrage. In paragraph 140 he concedes that it is true that 'governments cannot be supported without great charge, and 'tis fit every one who enjoys his share of the protection, should pay out of his estate his proportion for the maintenance of it'. We have already seen that everyone has an 'estate' of some sort, so that this term is not being used by Locke as an exclusive reference to landowners. Indeed, all Locke means to say in paragraph 140 is that every individual, rich or poor, should pay something towards the maintenance of government, out of his estate, according to its size. Locke certainly cannot have imagined that only landed property-owners were taxpayers in his society. This is to saddle him with an absurdly unrealistic assumption. Rather, excise taxes, the chimney tax and various other taxes were paid by virtually everyone in seventeenth-century England, as Locke well knew (he had, after all, been secretary to the Chancellor of the Exchequer). The passage in question simply justifies the proposition that those who own more wealth should pay more taxes. Moreover, Locke's admonition that legislators 'must not raise taxes on the property of the people' without their consent (II, 142) says nothing at all respecting the kinds of specific taxes Locke has in mind nor does it refer to some more determinate socio-economic group than 'the people' at large.

The second passage usually cited as supporting a restricted property-owner suffrage is more ambiguous in its phraseology. Locke is speaking of how various changes affect the 'customs and privileges' pertaining to the election 'of representatives chosen by the people'. He complains that the system of representation 'becomes very unequal and disproportionate to the reasons [for which] it was at first established', because 'mighty cities come to ruin . . . whilst other unfrequented places grow into populous countries, filled with wealth and inhabitants'. This situation leads to gross absurdities, where a rotten borough whose only inhabitant may be a shepherd 'sends as many representatives to the grand assembly of lawmakers, as a whole county numerous in people, and powerful in riches' (II, 157). Locke argues that this situation must be remedied because the people have a right 'to have a fair and equal representative' (II, 158). The question is what does Locke mean by this? The usual reply is that Locke is suggesting that propertied individuals, and perhaps especially the urban bourgeoisie, ought to be more fairly represented in Parliament. I do not think this view so much mistaken as only half-right. Locke's references join together 'wealth and inhabitants', 'people, riches, trade, power' and 'flourishing cities', or areas 'numerous in people, and powerful in riches', and I do not see any warrant for subtracting the people, inhabitants or cities from these references in order to draw the inference that Locke is primarily concerned with wealth, riches and property. By the same token, one could not use this text as providing clear support of an argument for inhabitant suffrage, though it should be noted that giving more representation to cities and towns in seventeenth-century England would have had the effect of enlarging the electorate.

In suggesting a remedy to unequal representation, Locke maintains that 'true reason' rather than 'old custom' or 'fashion' ought to provide the standard of fairness. This means that representation ought to be according to 'the number of members, in all places, that have a right to be distinctly represented, which no part of the people however incorporated can pretend to, but in proportion to the assistance which it affords to the public' (II, 158). Some commentators have read this passage as saying that people have a right to be represented in proportion to the taxes or assistance they pay to the government, and hence property-owners have a greater claim to representation.[23] But that is not what Locke says. He says that the number of members or representatives chosen from distinct places, such as boroughs or corporations, ought to depend upon the extent to which that system of representation furthers the public good, and not upon the pretended incorporations or pseudo-boroughs, which are 'bare names' of places. For, as Locke goes on to say, it is just 'such cases' as unequal representation, 'which depending upon unforeseen and uncertain occurrences', the prerogative of the executive 'to provide for the public good' was designed to deal with. By reforming the system of representation, therefore, 'and the establishing the government upon its true foundations . . . the good of the people' will be provided for. 'Assistance to the public' in this paragraph thus has nothing to do with taxes or amounts of property ownership, which are not mentioned, but with the public good, the true foundation of government, and the good of the people, which are discussed. In other words, none of these passages supplies the kind of defence for property-owners as citizens in Locke's society that has been claimed for them. Nor, in my view, does any of them contradict the interpretative position I advanced above.

The most important argument used by Macpherson and others, however, is that relating to the distinction Locke draws between tacit and express consent, which, they maintain, is equated with two separable levels of membership in political society.[24] At the outset, let us note a point of some importance that is generally overlooked, but that obviously has a bearing on the context within which Locke's comments on the two forms of consent are made. The latter come at the end of chapter 8, at the beginning of which Locke has stated two objections likely to be made against his position. The first, having to do with the historical status of the state of nature, has already been discussed. The second objection is that since all men are born under already existing governments they can never 'be free, and at liberty to unite together, and begin a new one'. This objection is restated in paragraph 113, and the discussion that follows is therefore addressed to that objection. This means that the contextual framework for Locke's discussion of tacit and express consent is the question: Given that individuals already exist under government, what bearing does the form of consent they give to that government, express or tacit, have upon the issue of whether or not they are free to withdraw from that government and form a new one? As will become clear, this way of stating the issue does not result in making Locke appear to be as poor or confused a thinker as he is usually portrayed in the discussions of this subject in the secondary literature.[25]

In treating the subject 'of men withdrawing themselves, and their obedience, from the jurisdiction they were born under . . . and setting up new governments in other places' (II, 115), Locke rejects the notion that because 'our fathers' at some time past agreed to institute political society they 'thereby bound . . . their posterity to a perpetual subject to the government, which they themselves submitted to'. No father can give away the liberty of his son. 'He may indeed annex such conditions to the land . . . as may oblige his son to be of that community' of which his father is a subject (II, 116), but this simply means that conditions may be attached to consent, which the individual is free to accept or reject. But, because commonwealths do not permit any part of their territory to be dismembered, this gives rise to a 'mistake', namely, the belief that all individuals 'are naturally subjects as they are men'. Which is to say, merely being born under a government makes one a member of that political society. This proposition Locke denies, because, he insists, it is only 'the consent of freemen' that 'makes them members' of that polity (II, 117). This viewpoint leads Locke to maintain 'that a child is born a subject of no country or government', and therefore cannot become a subject 'till he come to age of discretion; and then he is a freeman, at liberty what government he will put himself under'. The natural rights and obligations of individuals, Locke asserts, 'are not bounded by the positive limits of kingdoms and commonwealths' (II, 118).

Having established that every man is naturally free, and not subject to any political power except through his own consent, Locke turns to the question, 'what shall be understood to be a sufficient declaration of a man's consent to make him subject to the laws of any government'? In his view, 'there is a common distinction of an express and a tacit consent, which will concern our present case'. No one doubts that an express consent of any man 'makes him a perfect member of that society, a subject of that government. The difficulty is, what ought to be looked upon as a tacit consent, and . . . how far anyone shall be looked on to have consented, and thereby submitted to any government, where he has made no expressions of it at all.' Locke replies that 'every man, that hath any possession or enjoyment, of any part of the dominions of any government, doth thereby give his tacit consent, and is as far forth obliged to obedience to the laws of that government . . . whether this his possession be of land . . . or a lodging only for a week; or whether it be barely travelling freely on the highway; and in effect, it reaches as far as the very being of anyone within the territories of that government' (II, 119). This definition of tacit consent may be riddled with flaws, but the one thing Locke's reply does not do is to establish a double standard of consent for property-owners and the propertyless working class. Tacit consent applies equally to those who own 'any part of the dominions' or land over which the government has jurisdiction as it does to those who travel on the highways or seek temporary lodging in the country. Since both kinds of individual and/or social class are supposed by Locke to be bound to the government through tacit consent, there is absolutely no warrant for the interpretation that assigns tacit consent to one social class and express consent to another. Hence, when Locke says tacit consent can be applied to anyone, he means just that – anyone. The reason for this, as Dunn points out, is that there is a correlative relationship between benefits and obligations, mediated through the concept of 'tacit consent', and the notion of 'benefits' is very broadly defined by Locke.[26]

The function of tacit consent can be better understood, Locke suggests, if we consider what happens when individuals first incorporate themselves into a commonwealth. By joining a political society, the individual 'submits to the community those possessions, which he has, or shall acquire'. Both the person and his possessions become subject to the government. Here Locke does use the example of land, because he wants to show why the government retains control over the land under its dominion under all circumstances. Moreover, those involved in the creation of political society are 'subject to the government . . . as long as it hath a being'. This is also true with respect to their land, over which the community now has a perpetual jurisdiction. Now, whoever 'thenceforth' inherits or 'enjoys any part of the land . . . must take it with the condition it is under; that is, of submitting to the government of the commonwealth' (II, 120).

> But since the government has a direct jurisdiction only over the land, and reaches the possessor of it, (before he has actually incorporated himself in the society) only as he dwells upon; and enjoys that: The obligation anyone is under, by virtue of such enjoyment, to submit to the government, begins and ends with the enjoyment; so that whenever the owner, who has given nothing but such tacit consent to the government, will, by donation, sale, or otherwise, quit the said possession, he is at liberty to go and incorporate himself into any other commonwealth, or to agree with others to begin a new one, *in vacuis locus*, in any part of the world, they can find free and unpossessed. (II, 121)

The interesting thing about this discussion of tacit consent is that it is here being applied by Locke *solely and exclusively to the landowner*. In other words, the problem for him is not how can propertyless individuals be brought within the framework of political obligation through tacit consent but, rather, under what conditions can the *owner* of property be said to be a member of the political society in which he is a resident? The issue of tacit or express consent pertains only to the individual as the owner of land, because Locke has already shown (II, 120) that the land itself, whatever the owner chooses to do, belongs to the political community, as a result of the first incorporation of the latter (by the landowner's father, for example) in which all property was ceded to the community.

Now we can see why the property-owner who has not yet 'incorporated himself' into the political society – which already exists and which currently exercises jurisdiction over the property-owner's land – can be said to have tacitly consented to that government, so long as he enjoys the benefits of its protection, and why, therefore, he can be placed in the same category with anyone else, of whatever social station, who has not expressly consented to be a member of that society, but who also enjoys the benefits of living under the government (II, 119). 'Whereas he, that has once, by actual agreement, and any express declaration, given his consent to be of any commonweal, is perpetually and indispensably obliged to be and remain unalterably a subject to it' (II, 121). Thus, submitting to the laws of any country, living quietly, and enjoying privileges and protection under them, makes not a man a member of that society . . . Nothing can make any man so, but his actually entering into it by positive engagement, and express promise and compact. (II, 122)

What Locke has tried to demonstrate is that express consent is the only means by which *any* individual can become a member of political society, and that tacit consent creates an obligation for property-owners in particular, but for everyone in general, so long as they enjoy the benefits of living under a government to which they have not, however, given their express consent. Those who have only tacitly consented and who are willing to give up their possessions, therefore, are free to leave the government they were born under and begin a new political society somewhere else (which is the central topic under discussion). Those who have expressly consented to be members of that political society are bound by their 'positive engagement', whether or not they own any land, because this form of consent, which is applicable to 'every man' (II, 120) or 'any man' (II, 122), pertains only to their person, over which, until they have given such consent, they retain the freedom of disposal (II, 121).

Not only does Locke's distinction between tacit and express consent not provide evidence for differential class membership or rationality, it provides, on the contrary, a defence of Locke's association of the 'native right' an individual has over his own person with an act of express consent as the exclusive condition for membership in political society, thus giving every person, without qualification, such a natural rights claim. Indeed, if every landowner were assumed to have given his 'express consent' as a definitional feature of his ownership of property, as Macpherson maintains, it is difficult to see why Locke should have believed that 'tacit consent' was a category with a special application to landowners.[27]

Turning to the institution of political society, Locke characterizes the two powers an individual has in the state of nature that he gives up in joining that society: the first is the right to do whatever he thinks fit for the preservation of himself and others within the bounds of natural law; and the second is the power to punish crimes committed against that law (II, 128). The first of these powers an individual gives up to the community, as far as is required to carry out the ends of the Law of Nature (II, 129). The second 'he wholly gives up' to the community (II, 130). This distinction concerns an important point, for the first power is in effect the power to interpret the Law of Nature as it applies to actions designed to preserve all mankind, which may be called the lawmaking power, because all laws, to be valid, must conform to the precepts of natural law (II, 135). The individual cannot 'wholly give up' this power to the community through the act of consent, because he is not entitled or empowered to give up his obligation to obey the Law of Nature, whatever anyone else does. Hence he gives this power to the community only to the extent that the community, through its laws, acts according to natural law. He does, however, give up his power, as an individual, to enforce the Law of Nature, because the collective enforcement of that law by the community is precisely the point of joining political society. The distinction is important, as we shall see in Chapter 8, because the individual retains the right to judge whether any political society is acting contrary to the Law of Nature, and, if it is, the political society is dissolved, and he is returned to the state of nature (II, 121; cf. 149). In that state, he is able to reclaim his executive power to enforce natural law, which, as should be evident, is the form in which Locke's theory justifying the right of revolution is stated.

For the moment, however, we are concerned with Locke's effort to identify 'the original right and rise of both the Legislative and Executive power' within governments (II, 127), which he locates in the two natural powers discussed above. We identified the various forms of government in Chapter 5, mentioned by Locke in paragraph 132, to which I will add only one observation here in the light of the preceding discussion; namely, that democracy is that form of government that remains closest to the institution of the political community itself, and this is because both are grounded upon adult male suffrage. This does not mean that Locke personally endorses this form of government over all others, nor does it mean that he is advocating a democracy for England, since there may be various benefits and drawbacks attached to the several forms of government not yet considered that must be taken into account. But, formally, Locke is committed to the view that the majority of the community may dispose of their political power as they see fit, and this includes, of course, their power to constitute a democracy. (It is difficult to see, by the way, either how a small oligarchy of property-holders could be supposed to institute a democracy in which the very meaning of 'majority' of the community did not become simultaneously problematic, or why, if the community already *is* an oligarchy, Locke identifies this as a separate form of government. This difficulty does not arise, however, if by 'majority' Locke means the actual numerical majority of the community.)

In the next four chapters (11–14) of the *Second Treatise*, Locke examines the nature and limits of the legislative and executive powers of government. He speaks rather generally of the legislative power being in the hands of a 'person or assembly' (II, 135), or 'the prince or senate' (II, 139), though the distinction he draws between 'standing rules' or 'declared laws' (II, 136) or 'settled standing laws' (II, 137) and 'rule by extemporary arbitrary decrees' (II, 136–7) does seem to favour the notion of an assembly, at least to the extent that it is unclear how the laws of one king in the past could claim superiority or a 'settled' status if the present king as lawmaker should decide to change them. And if he should decide to do so, as an act of his will, what exactly preserves this action from being characterized as 'arbitrary' or 'extemporaneous'? In any event, in discussing the preservation of property rights, Locke does speak in favour of those 'governments where the legislative consists, wholly or in part, in assemblies which are variable', while warning of the dangers associated with those governments 'where the legislative is in one lasting assembly always in being, or in one man'. In these latter cases, there is a definite danger that the ruler(s) 'will think themselves to have a distinct interest, from the rest of the community', and so take away the people's property (II, 138). Since this would undermine the very purpose of government, Locke's warning comes close to being a definitional requirement that the legislative power be placed in variable assemblies, which, I shall argue, is his personal political position.

This intermingling of formal and personal political requirements reappears in paragraph 142, where Locke summarizes his discussion of the boundaries of legislative power. He argues that the legislative power must not raise taxes on the property of the people without their consent, 'given by themselves, or their deputies . . . to be from time to time chosen by themselves'. There is not even a hint as to how this boundary could be observed in a government in which the legislative power is in one man's hands, since, *ipso facto*, no law made by him requires the people's consent. At the beginning of chapter 12, even the pretence of indifference to the form of government is dropped. Locke maintains that

there is no need, that the legislative should be always in being . . . And because it may be too great a temptation to human frailty apt to grasp at power, for the same persons who have the power of making laws, to have also in their hands the power to execute them, whereby they may exempt themselves from obedience to the laws they make . . . to their own private advantage, and thereby come to have a distinct interest from the rest of the community, contrary to the end of society and government: Therefore in well ordered commonwealths, where the good of the whole is considered, as it ought, the legislative power is put into the hands of divers persons who duly assembled, have by themselves, or jointly with others, a power to make laws. (II, 143; cf. 153)

This passage thus rules out both a legislature permanently in being and the legislative power in the hands of one man, leaving only a political society in which legislative power is exercised by an assembly of divers persons.

It is possible to read this as being merely a preference on Locke's part, leaving intact the formal structure of his argument and therefore other possible forms of legitimate political society.[28] Alternatively, one could take the view that Locke has actually identified his position with his definition of a legitimate political society so as to rule out other possible forms of government. There is no clear and unequivocal reading of the text that mandates one of these interpretative choices, but I am inclined to adopt the second interpretation for three reasons: (1) there are certain statements by Locke, already noted, even in his formal presentation that do not seem to be applicable to all of the possible forms of government, whereas all of his statements concerning the limits of legislative power are compatible with an elected assembly of divers persons. Hence the decision to preserve Locke's formal argument at the cost of accepting the internal inconsistencies of that argument appears to me to undermine the value of making such an interpretative decision in the first place (which, of course, does not mean that Locke may not in fact have committed such errors of reasoning); (2) from this point on in the *Second Treatise*, Locke simply assumes, and spells out in more detail, a form of government in which there is a ruler (king) and, at a minimum, an elected legislative assembly, and thus all of his discussion of what happens within a legitimate political society presupposes that the latter is so constituted (II, 213). It could be argued, therefore, that Locke's earlier hints, transformed into a declaration in paragraph 143, were merely designed to lead the reader towards accepting Locke's definition of a legitimate polity as being, effectively, the only definition; and (3) Locke's political objectives in the *Second Treatise* are designed to show what happens, and what should be done about it, when the ruler destroys by his actions *this* particular form of political society. This appears to be another of those places in Locke's political argument where the latter's theoretical structure is heavily dependent upon Locke's ideological objectives – in this case, a defence of the people's 'right to reinstate their legislative' assembly (II, 155), which naturally assumes that such an assembly exists. In other words, Locke's declaration that men 'could never be safe . . . nor think themselves in civil society, till the legislature was placed in collective bodies of men, call them Senate, Parliament, or what you please' (II, 94), coupled with his repeated endorsements of 'well-ordered commonwealths' that conform to this description (II, 143, 159), reflects such a strongly held conviction on Locke's part that it is difficult to imagine the grounds on which it might be overruled by the purely theoretical principles that sustain the structure of Locke's political thought, unless, of course, even this form of government could be shown to be incapable of carrying out the ends of natural law.

Having asserted that the legislative power should neither be always in being nor united with the executive power in the same hands, the rest of chapter 12 (paragraphs 144–8) is given over to a description of the executive power as being exercised by someone other than the legislative. In the following chapter, Locke addresses himself to the question, what is the relationship between the executive and legislative powers, and between both of these and the people, in 'a constituted commonwealth'? Since the legislative power is 'only a fiduciary power to act for certain ends, there remains still in the people a supreme power to remove or alter the legislative, when they find the legislative act contrary to the trust reposed in them'. In such a situation,

> the trust must necessarily be forfeited, and the power devolve into the hands of those that gave it, who may place it anew where they shall think best for their safety and security. And thus the community perpetually retains a supreme power of saving themselves from the attempts and designs of any body, even of their legislators, whenever they shall be so foolish, or so wicked, as to lay and carry on designs against the liberties and properties of the subject. (II, 149)

This foundation for all political power being established, it follows for

Locke that the legislative power as the direct link between the community and a specific form of government must be the supreme power within that government (II, 150). If the executive has no share in the legislative power, then he 'is visibly subordinate and accountable to it, and may be at pleasure changed and displaced'. If, however, the executive does have a role in the lawmaking process, such as a veto over legislation (II, 151), then 'he is no more subordinate [to the legislative power] than he himself shall think fit, which one may certainly conclude will be but very little' (II, 152). This increases the complexity of the problem in those instances where a conflict develops between the executive and legislative powers; but, Locke argues, quite apart from this specific situation, there is a general relationship between these two powers that takes precedence, and, within that framework, the legislative power is unquestionably supreme. That is, the executive power *as such* is subordinate to the legislative; hence, into whoever's hands the former power has been placed, the latter 'have a power still to resume it out of those hands, when they find cause, and to punish for any maladministration against the laws' (II, 153).

It is worth pausing for a moment to appreciate the political significance of this last declaration. What Locke is saying, in the language of his seventeenth-century readers, is that Parliament has the authority to remove the executive power from the king's hands whenever that legislative body determines, according to its own judgement, that the king has failed to execute or has badly executed the laws that they have enacted. This is not only a defence of parliamentary supremacy (while the government is in being), it is also a defence of the deposition of kings by that body; and, depending upon how one interprets the meaning of 'punish' in this sentence, its political implications might reach even further than this.[29]

The particular issue of greatest concern to Locke, upon which he focuses as an illustration of his general argument, is the right of the legislature to meet and to enact laws, which may be prevented by the executive's use (or misuse) of his power as executive to call the legislature into session or to recess or adjourn them whenever he, according to his own will, so decides. Here Locke issues another radical pronouncement, though it follows logically from what he has said above. Assuming the legislature 'to consist of several persons', Locke argues that the holders of this legislative power 'may assemble and exercise their legislature, at the times that either their original Constitution, or their own adjournment appoints, or when they please'. Since the people have placed the legislative power in them, the legislature 'may exercise it when they please, unless by their original Constitution they are limited to certain seasons' or have set the time for their meeting themselves (II, 153). The only obstacle standing in the way of Parliament's determining its own times of meeting and adjournment, therefore, is to be found in the 'original Constitution' which prescribes otherwise. This was the issue of an extensive and long-standing controversy, for it was the view of Shaftesbury and many others that, according to the original constitution, the people of England did have a right to annual Parliaments. This point is treated more hypothetically than declaratively in the text by Locke – Shaftesbury had been imprisoned in the Tower of London for a year for asserting this claim. He supposes that some part of the legislative power is 'made up of representatives chosen for that time by the people', and that 'this power of choosing must also be exercised by the people, either at certain appointed seasons, or else when they are summoned to it'. In the latter case, 'the power of convoking the legislative, is ordinarily placed in the executive', and that power is either limited by the original constitution which 'requires their assembling and acting at certain intervals . . . or else it is left to his prudence to call them by new elections' whenever there is a need for new laws 'or the redress or prevention of any inconveniences, that lie on, or threaten the people' (II, 154).

Does Locke believe that the meeting of the legislature should be left to the 'prudence' of the executive's decision? The answer to this question, I think, has to be no. I grant that it is possible to read the remainder of the *Second Treatise* as a defence of the executive's right to exercise his prudential judgement in this matter, and, at the same time, as an attack upon Charles II and James II as particular executives for not having exercised such judgement, but I prefer to believe that Locke assumes either that the original constitution of England already does or should give the people a 'settled law' respecting the meeting of Parliament, which no prudential judgement on the part of the king is entitled to set aside, though naturally he could employ it to call the legislature into session to meet some unexpected emergency.[30] Thus, in the following paragraph, the executive's prudence has disappeared as an independent variable in the summoning of the legislature, leaving only 'the original Constitution, or the public exigencies' as sources that 'require' its meeting. And the question is what happens under these circumstances 'if the executive power being possessed of the force of the commonwealth, shall make use of that force to hinder the meeting and acting of the legislative'? I suppose by 'force' in this sentence Locke means effective control of the executive branch, and not merely the armed forces as such, so that it includes the power to arrest and imprison individuals, as well as control over the militia and the army. To this question, Locke now brings forward and applies the apparently abstract description of the state of war he had offered in chapter 3:

> I say using force upon people without authority, and contrary to the trust put in him, that does so, is a state of war with the people, who have a right to reinstate their legislative in the exercise of their power. For having erected a legislative, with an intent they should exercise the power of making laws, either at certain set times, or when there is need of it; when they are hindered by any force from [acting] . . . the people have a right to remove it by force. In all states and conditions the true remedy of force without authority, is to oppose force to it. The use of force without authority, always puts him that uses it into a state of war, as the aggressor, and renders him liable to be treated accordingly. (II, 155; cf. 16–21)

This is Locke's first statement of the empirical conditions and theoretical justification of the right of revolution, which, as we can more properly see, is actually a right on the part of the people to exercise their natural law obligation of self-defence or self-preservation against anyone, including a king, who acts contrary to the general legislative imperative of the Law of Nature. And it is formulated, specifically, as a response to the executive's misuse of his power to prevent the legislature from meeting and acting to redress the grievances of the people.

This misuse of power, in turn, leads Locke to raise the general question as to what kind of power it is that the executive exercises – that is, 'the power of assembling and dismissing the legislative'. It is, he replies, 'a fiduciary trust, placed in him, for the safety of the people', that is, 'the public good'. Even 'supposing the regulation of times for the assembling and sitting of the legislative, not settled by the original Constitution', Locke writes, this would still not justify the executive's use of his prudential judgement 'as an arbitrary power depending on his good pleasure'. So that, 'whether settled periods of their convening, or a liberty left to the prince for convoking the legislative, or perhaps a mixture of both', represents one's view of the constitutional situation, ' 'tis not my business here to inquire' (II, 156). Thus, in a few sentences, Locke dismissively sets aside the entire legalistic historical debate concerning the respective rights of Parliament and the king according to the ancient constitution, because, he insists, on general principles, the executive (1) cannot be assumed to have 'a superiority over' the legislative power since, as an executive, he is by Locke's definition a subordinate appointee and representative of their will; and (2) he must in any case act for the public good, which always takes precedence over his personal will or viewpoint (as, for example, Charles II's refusal to bar his brother from the succession, or James II's personal preference for Catholicism). On either or both grounds, Locke maintains that the legislative and/or the people may overrule and oppose the executive if he hinders the legislature from fulfilling its function.

Locke knows that it will be claimed by his political opponents that the king is entitled to exercise his prerogative as he sees fit, and that none of his subjects has any right to interfere with this inherent power of the monarch. He therefore devotes a chapter (14) of the *Second Treatise* to answer this claim and to clarify his own position on the executive's prerogative. First, Locke brings forward his argument from chapter 9 that the executive power within political society is traceable to the natural power every individual 'has by the common Law of Nature' in the state of nature. This means that all executives must use their power 'for the good of the society', according 'to this Fundamental Law of Nature and Government', namely, the preservation of mankind. Hence an executive may take action 'in many cases, where the municipal law has given no direction, till the legislative can conveniently be assembled to provide for it'. And, 'in some cases', he may act against the existing law, where 'a strict and rigid observation of the laws may do harm', though here Locke's illustration of pulling down an innocent man's house to stop a fire appears to confine these cases to those of a clear and present danger to the community as a whole (II, 159; cf. 164).

So long as the executive acts for the public good, no one is likely to raise scrupulous questions about his exercise of prerogative (II, 161–2). The question of 'limitations of prerogative' (II, 162) only arises when there is some doubt about the executive's employment of it for the public good. Hence 'they have a very wrong notion of government, who say, that the people have encroached upon the prerogative', as if the people had taken from the prince something that 'of right belonged to him'. On the contrary, Locke argues, the prerogative always belonged to the people, so to speak, since it could only be defined in terms of their welfare. 'Those who say otherwise, speak as if the prince had a distinct and separate interest from the good of the community', and this is a viewpoint for which there is not the slightest justification, according to Locke (II, 163). In short, the prerogative cannot be a power belonging to the executive 'by right of his office, which he may exercise at his pleasure', nor because he chooses to use it to defend 'or promote an interest distinct from that of the public' (II, 164).

Having restated the general foundation of his own position, Locke returns to the specific issue – 'the power of calling Parliaments in England, as to precise time, place and duration', which, he admits, 'is certainly a prerogative of the king'. But, he adds, it is nevertheless still a 'trust' given to him on the condition that it 'be made use of for the good of the nation', which means not only the public good in general, but also that which 'best suit[s] the ends of Parliaments' (II, 167). Now, suppose there is a conflict between the king and Parliament about this matter, Locke asks, 'who shall be judge when this power is made a right use of'?

I answer: Between an executive power in being, with such a prerogative, and a legislative that depends upon his will for their convening, there can be no judge on earth: As there can be none, between the legislative and the people, should either the executive, or the legislative . . . design, or go about to enslave, or destroy them. The people have no other remedy in this, as in all other cases where they have no judge on earth, but to appeal to heaven.

Thus, the people have a right to appeal to the Law of Nature, as 'a law antecedent and paramount to all positive laws of men', in order to defend themselves against such action. The executive's use of prerogative to prevent the legislature from meeting brings the nation to the brink of revolution, and on natural law grounds may be resisted by 'any single man' or 'the body of the people' (II, 168). Through an examination of the theoretical framework constructed by Locke, we have arrived at the practical objective that supplies the intentional meaning for the writing of the *Second Treatise* – the effort to persuade his readers 'that it is lawful for the people, in some cases, to resist their king' (II, 232).

NOTES: CHAPTER 7

1   See, for example, Martin Seliger, *The Liberal Politics of John Locke* (London: Allen & Unwin, 1968), pp. 223–4. Hence, for him, 'a family with grown-up children is already a political society' (p. 88).

2   Since Dunn and Plamenatz maintain that Locke is not attempting to provide a justification for a particular legitimate society, and also that he is not giving evidence relating to empirical human behaviour, this is not a problem for them, at least not in the terms stated here. Because they assume Locke is making an abstract argument, the problem for them appears to be Locke's confusing and inconsistent employment of his definition of consent (tacit and express): John Dunn, *The Political Thought of John Locke* (Cambridge: Cambridge University Press, 1969), pp. 117, 129, 131; cf. John Dunn, 'Consent in political theory of John Locke' *Historical Journal*, Vol. 10, no. 2 (July 1967), pp. 153–82; John Plamenatz, *Man and Society*, 2 vols (New York: McGraw-Hill, 1963), Vol. 1, pp. 210, 218, 227–8, 234, 238).

3   Seliger, *Liberal Politics*, pp. 104–5, 244–5, 250 ff.

4   Plamenatz argues that Locke failed to draw any meaningful distinction between legitimate and illegitimate governments (*Man and Society*, Vol. 1, pp. 228–31, 234).

5   Seliger is consistent in holding that usurpers and absolute monarchs can be legitimated through tacit consent. Indeed, all forms of government, according to Seliger, are legitimate in the absence of active dissent. The only strange thing about these views is that he attributes them to Locke (*Liberal Politics*, pp. 253, 298).

6   Sir Robert Filmer, *Patriarcha and Other Political Works*, ed. Peter Laslett (Oxford: Basil Blackwell, 1949), p. 82.

7   *Two Treatises of Government*, ed. Peter Laslett, 2nd edn (Cambridge: Cambridge University Press, 1967), introduction, p. 52 n. Some of Locke's comments pertaining to this debate are printed in Dunn, *Political Thought*, pp. 122 n, 145–6 n, 148 n. For a general survey of this literature, see Mark Goldie, 'The Revolution of 1689 and the structure of political argument', *Bulletin of Research in the Humanities*, vol. 83 (Winter 1980), pp. 473–564.

8   The nominalist position taken by Dunn, for example, that because 'governors' or 'rulers' or 'people' are terms used by Locke to describe the Indians and others who live in the first ages the latter cannot be equated with the state of nature is very strange indeed (*Political Thought*, p. 117). Also see Sterling P. Lamprecht, *The Moral and Political Philosophy of John Locke* (1918; reprinted New York: Russell & Russell, 1962), p. 127; Seliger, *Liberal Politics*, pp. 87 ff. If absolute monarchy as a government can be equated with the state of nature, if those living under an unjust conqueror (e.g., the Greeks in the seventeenth century) or a usurper or tyrant, or if the actions of Charles II or James II can return seventeenth-century Englishmen to the state of nature, it can hardly be claimed that the existence of 'government' *in itself* necessarily precludes the existence of the state of nature, as Locke conceives it. The question is not whether a king exists, still less is it a question of whether Locke uses the word 'king'; rather, the issue is whether a legitimate political society exists or not. If not, individuals, 'however associated', are still in the state of nature.

9   In other words, I do not accept the prevalent view in the secondary literature that majority rule was, for Locke, merely a technical expedient within the framework of the necessity for practical decisions, or that it was his application of Newtonian mechanics to political power so that 'the greater force' can carry the community in some particular direction (II, 96). One need not go so far as Wilmoore Kendall, *John Locke and the Doctrine of Majority Rule* (Urbana, Ill.: University of Illinois

Press, 1941), in order to grant the validity of his point that Locke believed there was a connection between the moral imperative of natural law to preserve mankind, and the execution of that command by the majority.

10 Dunn develops this point in his critique of Macpherson (*Political Thought*, pp. 134–7).

11 C. B. Macpherson, *The Political Theory of Possessive Individualism* (London: Oxford University Press, 1962), pp. 230, 232.

12 ibid., p. 237; cf. pp. 232–8.

13 ibid., p. 233.

14 ibid., pp. 247–51.

15 *Two Treatises*, ed. Laslett, p. 348 n.

16 This point is also noted by Seliger, *Liberal Politics*, p. 166.

17 One reason that the broad definition of 'property' is needed is that the functional purpose of political society defined as 'the securing of men's rights' (II, 219) is not reducible to securing the 'right' of property. There are other rights to be secured. In the *Letter Concerning Toleration*, for example, Locke speaks of 'the civil rights *and* worldly goods' of the individual (*The Works of John Locke*, 12th edn, 9 vols (1824), Vol. 5, pp. 20, 40; my italics), and this distinction corresponds, I believe, to his many references to every man's 'goods and person' as two distinguishable categories of the rights possessed by every individual member of political society.

18 When the individual joins political society, he 'submits to the community those possessions, which he has, or shall acquire' (II, 120). The same point is made in the *Letter Concerning Toleration*, namely, that individuals become members of political society not only because they have 'already acquired' possessions, but also because 'they may acquire' possessions they do not now have (*Works*, Vol. 5, p. 42). In other words, neither the origin nor the purpose of Lockean political society is defined in terms of the narrow meaning of property, nor is there a built-in distinction to be made between members who possess property and those who do not. On the contrary, Locke consciously includes both classes of individual – those who already have property and those who do not – in his description of the institution of political society.

19 Plamenatz's statement on Locke's position on the question of the suffrage is typical of the discussion of this point in the secondary literature. Locke, Plamenatz writes, 'as we know', did not want to extend the franchise (*Man and Society*, Vol. 1, p. 234). For Seliger, Locke 'accepted the grading of suffrage according to income as a matter of course' (*Liberal Politics*, p. 177). Gough says Locke 'tacitly assumed the continuation of the narrow traditional electoral system which restricted the vote to a small class of property-owners' (John W. Gough, *John Locke's Political Philosophy, Eight Studies* (Oxford: Clarendon Press, 1956), p. 64; cf. p. 46. And so on. All these writers, including Dunn and Macpherson, simply assume the very point to be proven – that this was Locke's view. There is no evidence of which I am aware, external to the two passages in the *Second Treatise* which are discussed in the text, to support this 'tacit assumption' which is transformed into a piece of knowledge by various interpreters. The belief that Locke must have accepted such an assumption because no other belief was available to him is certainly not true. Lamprecht, though he, too, concludes that Locke was probably satisfied with a restricted suffrage, at least admits that Locke's position on the suffrage is unclear from a reading of the *Two Treatises*, and that it appears to favour 'a more broadly democratic view' of participation (*Moral and Political Philosophy*, p. 140). Indeed, based upon a literal reading of the text, Kendall argues that Locke favoured manhood suffrage (*Locke and Majority Rule*, p. 121). In my view, there is much more support for this interpretation than has generally been recognized. In fact it is a paradox that so much attention should be devoted to the consideration of *two* passages in the text that are alleged to support a property-owner franchise, when,

as Kendall demonstrates, there are many times that number of passages that explicitly endorse the right of 'every man' to give his consent, or to choose his 'deputies'. These passages are discounted by the authors named above on the grounds that we are entitled to assume, in relation to the historical context, that Locke did not hold such a view. This is in fact the weakest part of their position, for, as I have demonstrated in *Revolutionary Politics and Locke's 'Two Treatises of Government'* (Princeton, NJ: Princeton University Press, 1986), it is far more likely, given Locke's political association with Major Wildman, Robert Ferguson and the radicals, that he shared their views on this issue than it is that he was as conservative as the secondary literature has suggested. Because I am only dealing with the text in this book, I will go no further than to say that the 'restricted suffrage' attribution to Locke cannot be supported on the basis of the evidence of the text (*Second Treatise*), while the plausibility, at the very least, of adult male suffrage can be demonstrated on the basis of what Locke says. What I am arguing in the text, however, is that the 'natural rights' argument, as used by the Levellers, for example, was formulated as a defence of the presumption that all male adults had a moral right to give their consent through voting. This presumption might not in fact be realized within a particular political system, for various reasons, including the need to make practical compromises on the franchise. Hence, servants, beggars, the clergy and various other groups might be excluded from the franchise. The natural right to vote, in other words, was a rebuttable presumption, but it was up to the opponents to offer good reasons for excluding certain categories of individual from exercising this right, and defenders of the 'natural rights' argument did not accept the mere fact of the ownership of property as a 'reason' for denying the vote to those who were not property-owners. If social conventions are to be appealed to as an interpretative framework for reading the *Second Treatise*, then it should be pointed out that Locke's contemporary readers had no difficulty in associating a 'natural rights' argument, every man giving his consent, the majority of the community deciding, etc., with the language of the Levellers and manhood suffrage.

20 Filmer, *Works*, pp. 211, 217, 286.
21 ibid., pp. 197–8, 244, 252.
22 ibid., pp. 213–14.
23 See, for example, Seliger, *Liberal Politics*, pp. 285–6, and Macpherson, *Possessive Individualism*, pp. 253–5.
24 Both Wolin and Gough register their agreement with Macpherson in his application of the two forms of consent to property-owners and the propertyless (Sheldon S. Wolin, *Politics and Vision* (Boston, Mass.: Little, Brown, 1960), p. 485; Gough, *Locke's Political Philosophy*, p. 46.
25 Locke's argument on tacit consent 'is so ill thought out that it is hard to know what to make of it' (ibid., p. 65; cf. Plamenatz, *Man and Society*, Vol. 1, p. 218; Dunn, 'Consent in Locke,' passim).
26 ibid., p. 162.
27 Geraint Parry claims that 'inheritance of an estate is an act of express consent which makes a man a member of the political community' (*John Locke* (London: Allen & Unwin, 1978), p. 106). This is a mistake, and in the very passage he cites (II, 121) Locke states that the landowner 'has given nothing but such a tacit consent to the government', and his obligation 'to submit to the government, begins and ends with the enjoyment' of his property. This is what Locke means when he says that those who 'will enjoy the inheritance of their ancestors' must 'submit to all the conditions annexed to such a possession' (II, 73, 116–17). He may have to 'put himself' under the established government in order to enjoy his property, and so long as he does enjoy the benefits provided by that government he may be assumed to have tacitly consented to it. But Locke is quite clear that

'submitting to the laws of any country, living quietly, and enjoying privileges and protection under them, *makes not a man a member of that society*' (II, 122). It is precisely because landowners cannot be assumed to have expressly consented to the government that the problem of tacit consent is raised at all by Locke. It is sometimes said (Parry, *Locke*, p. 107) that Locke means to apply the concept of tacit consent to resident aliens who own land in order to distinguish them from other landowners. Certainly, Locke means to include foreigners within the scope of his general argument (II, 122), but since they are neither 'subjects [n]or members of that commonwealth' where they reside he appears to suggest that resident aliens may constitute a separate category from subjects (tacit consent) or members (express consent). In any event, Locke's argument cannot be reduced to any simple dichotomy, viz., landowners v. non-landowners, property-owners v. propertyless, native-born v. aliens. What I have stressed is the absoluteness of the association of express consent with the individual's *person* and not with property ownership of any type.

28 Plamenatz, *Man and Society*, Vol. 1, pp. 210, 231, 238.
29 Seliger is mistaken in his assertion that 'Locke did not suppose that a legislature in which the executive had no share could actually depose him without the revolutionary interference of the people' (*Liberal Politics*, p. 333). Locke specifically says (II, 153) that 'the legislative . . . have a power still to resume it [the executive power] out of those hands' into which it was put, and to punish anyone for acting against the laws. The difference Locke is pointing out is that where the executive has no share in the legislative power he 'may be at pleasure changed and displaced' whenever the legislature decides to do so (II, 152). But where the executive does have a share in the legislative process he can only be removed 'when they find cause' to do so, that is, for 'maladministration' and not simply at their pleasure. The question, therefore, is not whether the executive (king) can be deposed by the legislature but, rather, on what grounds he can be removed from office.
30 On Locke's attitude towards annual Parliaments, see Dunn, *Political Thought*, pp. 55–6.

CHAPTER 8

Resistance to Tyranny

We have seen that, according to Locke, it is possible even within a well-ordered commonwealth for there to be a conflict between the executive and legislative powers of government, or between either or both of these and the people at large, and that when this occurs there is a crisis of constitutional government. This is because there is no means for resolving this conflict within the framework of the original constitution. Locke describes this crisis in several ways, though all of his terms refer to the same political situation. In relation to the political system as a whole, the form of government has dissolved because power is no longer in the hands of those individuals or institutions to whom it was originally given by the community, or because those entrusted with that power have forfeited their trust by acting contrary to the precepts of natural law. Viewed as a conflict between the legislative and executive powers over the amount of power allotted to each or the purposes for which it is to be used, it can be said that a state of war exists between them, since there is no authority superior to both that can act as a judge to resolve their differences. Seen from the perspective of the people, what is significant is that political power has now returned into their hands, and they are free to constitute a new form of government, and to provide for their own safety and self-defence. All of these propositions are integral elements of Locke's theory of revolution.

In this chapter I will examine what Locke means by the dissolution of government and his use of the concept of the state of war as part of his theory of resistance. In addition I will elaborate upon the specific conditions, one of which was mentioned in the previous chapter, under which these theoretical concepts become operative descriptions of political relationships within Locke's civil society. Finally, some attention must be given to the question of who is entitled to make or does in fact carry out the revolution that Locke endorses.

It will prove helpful if we begin with Locke's discussion of the state of war, about which, to this point, very little has been said. The reason for choosing this term as a starting-point is that there is a logical relationship within Locke's political argument between the state of nature and the state of war that needs to be understood as a prior condition to the application of the latter concept to any specific situation within an existing political society. Stated simply, the state of war describes one particular set of circumstances that occur within the larger framework of the state of nature. As we shall see, the meaning of the state of war is a bit more complicated than this characterization implies, but as an initial point of departure for our discussion it will suffice.

'He who attempts to get another man into his absolute power', Locke declares, 'does thereby put himself into a state of war with him' (II, 17). This attempt need not be successfully executed; it may be 'but a sedate settled design, upon another man's life', expressed through a declared intention by the aggressor to use his power in a manner that threatens the life of the other person (II, 16). As was noted earlier, Locke includes within his usage of 'life' in these passages any threat to the individual's freedom, because he 'who would take away that freedom' in effect 'makes an attempt to enslave me, [and] thereby puts himself into a state of war with me'. To attack the individual's freedom is to undermine 'the foundation of all the rest' of his natural rights, which depend upon the freedom to control his own actions (II, 17). All such efforts are characterized by Locke as the use of 'force and violence', although it should be kept in mind that this includes for him the 'declaring by word or action' of an intention *to* act. In other words, the state of war is not confined to an empirical description of bodily movements or physical events, such as one human being striking another or a military battle between opposing armies. Rather, 'the state of war is a state of enmity and destruction' (II, 16; cf. I, 131), such as might exist, for example, between two long-standing enemies who are constantly plotting to do harm to each other, though they seldom engage in actual physical combat.

Naturally, this need to interpret another person's intentions, and to anticipate what kinds of action are likely to be taken, but which have not yet been executed, makes the application of the concept of the state of war a problematic undertaking. At the same time, however, Locke draws a distinction between the commission of mistakes or accidents and a 'design' by an individual to do harm. Hence one person may unintentionally do harm to another without being in a state of war with that individual. The philosophical issues associated with this distinction could be explored in greater detail, but it is sufficient for our purposes to point out that we commonly recognize a legal and moral difference between the action of a drunk driver who causes the death of another and the action of an individual who robs a bank. The first action may in fact cause a greater loss and physical damage than the second, but the attachment of intention and 'a sedate settled design' to the latter action generally results in a more severe penalty being imposed upon the bankrobber than is received by the drunk driver. In terms of this illustration, it is fair to say that, in Locke's view, there are many more drunk drivers than armed robbers in the state of nature. There is a meaningful difference, in other words, between the fact that 'the greater part' of men are not 'strict observers of equity and justice' and 'the corruption and viciousness of degenerate men', who may be few in number (II, 123, 128).

This means not only that the state of war describes an exceptional set of actions within the range of harmful actions, not to mention human actions in general, but also that the state of nature itself is not an existential condition free from dangers or harmful actions. Even if there were no individuals among its residents who have consciously 'renounced the way of peace . . . and made use of the force of war to compass [their] unjust ends upon another' (II, 172), it would nevertheless be true that there are 'trespassers' and 'offenders' against the Law of Nature in that state as described by Locke in chapter 2 of the *Second Treatise* (II, 7–13). Hence one might intend to follow the way of peace, and still commit injuries against another individual, which might be described as a state of inconvenience or uncertainty with respect to any particular individual's likelihood of experiencing some danger to his person or property. What entitles us to label a specific action an 'injury' or a 'crime' is the availability of a set of rules according to which actions can be categorized. Here, too, the subject might be explored further, and Locke does so in the *Essay Concerning Human Understanding*; but, as we already know, the rules presupposed by Locke in the *Two Treatises* relevant to the making of such determinations are the Laws of Nature.

This point can be restated in another way, by saying that the individual who places himself in a state of war with another is engaged in 'using force, where he has no right' to do so (II, 18). Obviously, there are conditions in which one has a 'right' to use force against another individual, which describes, on the one hand, Locke's 'strange doctrine' of punishment in the state of nature and, on the other, the efficient enforcement of the laws within a legitimate political system. The mere use of force, therefore, is not the point;

rather, what is important is the use 'of force without authority' (II, 155, 227). Thus,

> Whosoever uses force without right . . . puts himself into a state of war with those, against whom he so uses it, and in that state all former ties are cancelled, all other rights cease, and everyone has a right to defend himself, and to resist the aggressor. (II, 232)

The aggressor has no authority for his action because he is not authorized by the Law of Nature to do something that is harmful to others. But suppose he believes he is right, and the other party believes he is right, who is to judge between them? The fact that both individuals might concede that natural law is a common standard – although Locke usually structures the situation so that the aggressor does not accept this premiss – with reference to their respective actions is no guarantee that there will be any impartial judge to decide the controversy between them. In short, 'force between either persons, who have no known superior on earth, or which permits no appeal to a judge on earth, being properly a state of war' (II, 242), according to Locke, we may say this condition occurs, in effect, between two parties who are in a state of nature in respect to each other.

We recall that 'want of a common judge with authority, puts all men in a state of nature', but 'force, or a declared design of force upon the person of another, where there is no common superior on earth to appeal to for relief, is the state of war' (II, 19). There are some additional points to be considered that complicate this distinction which we will take up in a moment; but, stated in its barest form, it is clear that both of these definitions presuppose as a common feature the absence of a judge with authority to decide a controversy between the two individuals. To which is added, as a distinguishing ingredient of a state of war, a declared intention to threaten another individual's life, liberty or estate. It is true that Locke would like to have the Law of Nature entirely upon his side, which is why he so often insists upon the 'unjust use of force' or the aggressor's renouncement of reason or natural law when speaking of this confrontation between two individuals with no superior to judge between them. And, from a moral perspective, his argument only makes sense by assuming that he does have natural law on his side. If this were not the case, the distinction between the state of nature and the state of war would lose an essential part of its meaning; but, more than that, as I have argued, the entire structure of Locke's political argument would collapse. At the same time, however, if we view this conflict with a certain degree of realism, we see that, in the end, 'the injured party must judge for himself' (II, 242; cf. 241) both whether another person has put himself in a state of war with him and what to do about it. From this standpoint – that is, from the standpoint of actually judging – the situation is not so clear-cut. If it were, the injured party might have less difficulty in finding others to join with him in taking action against the aggressor than Locke implies is actually the case in the state of nature (II, 126). So, if we place the emphasis upon the nature of the rules, 'force' and 'reason', as standards of morality, we will perceive 'the plain difference between the state of nature, and the state of war' (II, 19); but, if we shift our perspective and consider the actual conflict between two individuals as a judgement about practical action to be taken, we may feel, as Locke does in the passages cited above, that the crucial point is that there is no impartial judge to decide the controversy, and that the party who feels himself injured is, in the last analysis, thrown back upon his own judgement as to what action to take. This, I am arguing, is the practical starting-point (the state of nature) for Locke's argument in the *Second Treatise*. Thus, an individual, 'by actually putting himself into a state of war' with others, 'leave[s] them to that defence, which belongs to every one in the state of nature' (II, 205).

'He that in the state of nature' attempts to harm me, Locke maintains, puts himself into a state of war with me (II, 17). But he must first be 'in' the state of nature in order for our interaction, as a generalized description of social relationships, to be, definitionally speaking, a state of war. This point, which, as we shall see, is of some importance to Locke's discussion of political revolution, is not immediately obvious, and it may even appear to be contradicted by what Locke says in the text. For, he explains, a state of war may also arise within society. A thief may set upon me on the highway, and, Locke argues, since he has put himself into a state of war with me, I have 'a liberty to kill the aggressor, because the aggressor allows not time to appeal to our common judge, nor the decision of the law, for remedy in a case, where the mischief may be irreparable'. Although, under other circumstances, I might appeal to the law and the existing judicial system to take action against a thief who breaks into my house when I am not there, in this case, where my person is threatened, I have a right to take action myself, even though there is in fact a common judge over us. Hence, Locke concludes, 'force without right, upon a man's person, makes a state of war, both where there is, and is not, a common judge' (II, 19).

Does this, then, refute what I have just said? I think not. This is because there are two levels of discourse in terms of which the example above may be described. I could say, as Locke does here, that the thief has put himself in a state of war with me as an individual, although both of us are subjects within the same political system; and, from this standpoint, the 'state of war' has meaning only as a particular incident or encounter between two individuals within a larger context that is described in other terms (as a political society). But are we both subjects of the same political system? There is good reason to answer this question in the negative because the thief is not simply doing me a specific injury; nor, if he is caught and punished, will his punishment be justified purely in terms of the harm done to me. Rather, by choosing to be a thief, he has placed himself in a state of war with all the members of my society, and the latter will punish him both for the wrong done and as a deterrent to others not to follow his example (II, 8, 11). Viewed in these terms, there is not a common judge between the thief and society, and the point must be expressed in this way because Locke can hardly maintain that an individual acting against the Law of Nature has 'quit the principles of human nature' (II, 10) or 'the common bond whereby human kind is united into one fellowship and society' (II, 172), and not also insist that he has, in effect, resigned or forfeited his status as a member of political society in so acting. And, indeed, Locke does say this, when he asserts that 'all former ties are cancelled, all other rights cease' (II, 232) between two individuals in a state of war. Thus, 'if anyone presume to violate the laws of public justice and equity established' by society, he is punished by suffering 'the deprivation or diminution of those civil interests, or goods' that he would otherwise enjoy as a member of that society (*Works*, 5:10).[1]

Since the innocent party has not given up his membership in civil society, whereas the thief has, it cannot be said that they are truly members of the same society; rather, one individual is a member of political society and the other is no longer a member of that society. And men 'when they perceive, that any man, in what station soever, is out of the bounds of the civil society which they are of; and that they have no appeal on earth against any harm they may receive from him, they are apt to think themselves in the state of nature, in respect of him, whom they find to be so' (II, 94). Therefore, 'those, whoever they be, who by force break through' the laws, 'and by force justify their violation of them, are truly and properly rebels . . . those who set up force again in opposition to the laws, do *rebellare*, that is, bring back again the state of war' (II, 226).

In other words, by acting against the laws of society, the individual has in effect placed himself outside society, and individuals outside that society are in a state of nature in respect to members of that society. He has, however, in addition, resorted to the use of force against that society, and the latter is justified in punishing him for this action. But, in so acting, he has forfeited his status as a member of that society, and not only may he be imprisoned (or executed), but also his property may be confiscated, and so on. It is true that if society apprehends him he will be tried in its courts, sentenced by its judges, and have its laws applied to him, as if he were a member of that society, which, from a certain standpoint, he is. But it is also the case, to use an illustration of some practical concern to seventeenth-century England, that he is like a pirate on the high seas, and must be viewed as not being a member of any civil society. Later Locke specifically lumps together the actions of a thief, a pirate, a conqueror, a usurper, a tyrant and so forth, none of whom can be counted as members of a political society, even if, like the thief or usurper, they began as members of that society and may still, empirically speaking, exist within its territorial boundaries. Moreover, as his discussion of conquest makes plain, the meaning of the state of war (of which conquest is one example) is assessed in terms of the 'damage . . . that men in the state of nature (as all princes and governments are in reference to one another) suffer from one another' (II, 184; cf. 183). Indeed, speaking in international terms, the state of war can *only* be discussed as an incident occurring within the framework of the state of nature.

I have dwelt on this point at some length for two reasons. First, it is important to see that the individual, by acting in a certain way, forfeits his membership in civil society and places himself outside it. He might have done this by voluntarily withdrawing from society, in which case he would be returned to the state of nature. But he may also withdraw from that society by using force against it, in which case he is returned to the state of nature in the sense that there now exists no authorized common judge recognized by both parties in dispute, and in addition the individual is in a state of war with that society because he has resorted to force. If we substitute a king for a thief or a pirate, the issue of forfeiting his membership in civil society, and not merely the specific office he holds, becomes a matter of some importance to Locke's argument. And, to understand this point, we cannot view the state of war as being merely a specific incident between two individuals who exist within the same society, as Locke's example of the highwayman seems to suggest; rather, we require the generalized notion of the state of war which places the individual outside the boundaries of political society, as a 'rebel'. And since *everyone* outside that society is in a state of nature in relation to it – though only a *few* individuals (or nations) are actually in a state of war with it – the logic of Locke's argument requires that the meaning of the state of war be treated as a special case within his general description of the state of nature. That a specific incident may occur as an empirical phenomenon within the boundaries of a particular society does not alter this theoretical relationship between the two concepts.

This point will become clearer if we consider the second reason for my putting the case in this way. Suppose we now think of the state of war not in terms of two particular individuals, but as a conflict between two political institutions, king and Parliament. What happens in this instance? The answer, according to Locke, is that since there is no authorized judge on earth to decide the controversy between these two institutions the form of government has now dissolved, and the people are returned to the state of nature until such time as they have established a new judge, that is, a new form of government. The case must be put this way because the people cannot both have and not have an authorized judge, for Locke's definitions of political society and the state of nature are mutually exclusive precisely in relation to this point (cf. II, 94). So when he asserts that in this conflict between the executive and the legislative power 'there can be no judge on earth' (II, 168) he means that they are in a state of nature in relation to each other, because 'wherever any two men are, who have no standing rule, and common judge to appeal to on earth for the determination of controversies of right betwixt them, there they are still in the state of nature' (II, 91). It surely cannot be claimed that this situation, applied to the conflict between king and Parliament, falls outside the purview of this declaration by Locke, since the latter is merely the most generalized statement of his definition of the state of nature, and the former, in any event, involves more than 'two men' who are, descriptively speaking, in this condition in relation to each other.[2]

Let us further suppose there are two possible alternatives in this situation. First, a stalemate may develop in which, because of the conflict, no legislation can be enacted; and, if the conflict drags on inconclusively, people may come to feel that a government that is incapable of action or of fulfilling its purpose is no government at all. For, as Locke rightly observes, 'it is not names, that constitute governments, but the use and exercise of those powers that were intended to accompany them' (II, 215). We could speak of this as a collapse or dissolution of the government, in which case people would be returned to the situation in which they had no government at all – the state of nature. And we might even classify this example under the general category of 'any calamity', whereby 'the government [the individual] was under, comes to be dissolved' and the subjects of that society are 'again in the liberty of the state of nature' (II, 121). But a second possibility is that one side in this dispute will decide to enforce his position as *the* position for society as a whole, even though, according to the original constitution, he is not authorized to do so. And, if he uses force without authority, he thereby places himself in a state of war with the rest of society (II, 155). In this situation, too, of course, the original form of government is dissolved, and the people have a right to provide for their own defence, as they had in the state of nature. Now, it should be clear from this illustration that the state of nature is the most generalized description of the situation, since there are a large number of ways – the executive may voluntarily abandon his position, to give one of Locke's examples (II, 219) – by which the people may be returned to this state, only one of which, involving the use of force, can be described as a state of war.

In other words, precisely because the state of war is a consciously declared intention to act in a certain way, it must be distinguished from other kinds of action, even when the effects of these actions bring about identical consequences. We have already noted this point, to extend the example cited earlier, in comparing the actions of a drunk driver with those of a bankrobber, but this distinction must also be maintained on the level of the conflict between two political institutions. That is, we may imagine a constitutional crisis in which neither party has attempted to use force against the other, but the government is nevertheless incapable of functioning and has, therefore, dissolved, returning the people to the state of nature. But, in a few cases, the conscious decision by one side to use force without authority against the other adds a new ingredient to this crisis. For example, in the midst of his discussion of conquest, which is one form of the state of war, Locke offers an illustration which supposes that 'I in the state of nature . . . have injured another man, *and refusing to give satisfaction, it comes to a state of war,* wherein my defending by force, what I had gotten unjustly, makes me the aggressor' (II, 183; my italics). First, I am in the state of nature, then I commit an injury, then I consciously refuse to make reparation and resort to force. That, I am arguing, is the logical ordering of Locke's thought, though, of course, in reality, all of these sequential steps may be telescoped into virtually the same temporal moment.

Nevertheless, the logic of Locke's argument which defines the state of war as a moment within the state of nature requires that such a distinction be made, and the latter is a basic presupposition of his political theory in the *Second Treatise*. It is much easier to grasp this point from his initial description of both states than it is from his discussion in the second half of that work. The reason for this, I suggest, is that the last half of the *Second Treatise* assumes the form of an increasingly direct political attack upon the king's actions. From Locke's point of view, the king (both Charles II and James II) has put himself into a state of war with the legislature and/or the people, and the government has been dissolved. Because he is concerned to justify armed resistance by the people against their king in *that* situation, Locke does not always bother to make the logical distinction required by his definitions between the two-step process by which the individual (thief or king) first places himself outside society in a state of nature, and then in a state of war through his employment of force without authority. Yet it is clear, as we saw in Chapter 7, that the king's prevention of Parliament from meeting places individuals in a political society where they have no elections or legislative assemblies. But this is not the form of government the people established in their original constitution. Hence that form of government has dissolved, and this is the case *regardless* of the king's motives or intentions in acting as he has with respect to the meeting of Parliament. In the absence of a functioning legislative power as their impartial judge, the people are in a state of nature with respect to the king. If the latter continues to rule and employs the force of the community to enforce his own will as the law of society, he does so 'without authority'. In short, he has placed himself in a state of war with the people. It is especially important for Locke's political argument, in other words, to recognize that a state of war can only take place where 'the want of a common judge' is a crucially defining characteristic of the situation itself, and this means that the individuals involved are necessarily in a state of nature.

In turning to Locke's discussion of the dissolution of government, the argument I shall pursue, again, runs counter to the interpretative consensus in the secondary literature. Generally, the discussion of Locke's theory of revolution remains on a rather abstract level and never attempts to forge a link with a specifically defined political perspective. I want to suggest, however, that Locke's defence of revolutionary action in the *Second Treatise* is dependent upon the specific assertion that the people have a right to a freely elected legislature of their choosing, and that any attempt to deny them this right is, *ipso facto*, grounds for revolution. This means that Locke's conception of a legitimate polity now takes on the added feature of having, as an institutionalized social practice, the holding of national elections.

In a sense, we have begun our discussion of this point in the middle of Locke's argument. That is, we have seen that a division of political power between the executive and an elected legislative assembly is what Locke means by a 'well-ordered commonwealth', which supplies the empirically defined – and, most plausibly, the theoretical – framework for his discussion of the legitimate political society. But, of course, this logically presupposes the holding of elections, without which the legislature could not be described as being the 'deputies' of the people, 'to be from time to time chosen by themselves'. And this act of choosing is specifically related by Locke to his general notion of 'the consent of the people, given by themselves, or their deputies' (II, 142). What I propose to argue, therefore, is that there is a much more integrated and concretely formulated political perspective expressed in the *Two Treatises of Government* than has generally been assumed to be the case, whereby Locke draws together the terminology he employs with reference to 'the consent of the people', the holding of elections, and a freely elected legislative assembly who act for the majority of the political community.[3]

Let us begin with a situation in which the consent of the people is not or cannot be obtained, namely, a foreign conquest of the society. Many people, Locke asserts, 'have mistaken the force of arms, for the consent of the people', and this mistake manifests itself in the belief that the 'setting up any government' in the wake of a conquest establishes an obligation on the part of the subjects of that government to obey it. It is this proposition that Locke, in his chapter 'Of Conquest', sets out to demolish, maintaining that 'polities' can never 'be founded on anything but the consent of the people' (II, 175, 186–7). Because Locke deploys several general assumptions that are by now familiar to the reader, he is able to state his theoretical argument succinctly and proceed immediately to the proposition he wants to defend. First, a conqueror is no different from any other 'aggressor, who puts himself into the state of war with another, and unjustly invades another man's right'. Since the aggressor thereby forfeits all of his rights, he 'can, by such an unjust war, never come to have a right over the conquered' individual. This proposition, Locke declares, 'will be easily agreed [to] by all men, who will not think, that robbers and pirates have a right of empire over whomsoever they have force enough to master'. The only difference between a common thief and a conqueror, Locke insists, is that the latter is a 'great robber' and the former a petty one. Nevertheless, 'the injury and the crime is equal, whether committed by the wearer of a crown, or some petty villain'. Hence, no action that precipitates a state of war can possibly create a structure of rights and obligations, not even if 'promises' of obedience are extracted by force from those conquered by the aggressor (II, 176, 186–7).

But let us suppose that the conqueror is successful, and the conquered individual has exhausted all possible attempts to bring about a reversal of this situation. What then? Locke now brings forward another proposition stated earlier in the *Second Treatise*, namely, that a father cannot give away or dispose of the liberty of his son (II, 65). This means that a father 'cannot by any compact whatsoever, bind his children or posterity' (II, 116). This prohibition clearly applies to a father living under a conqueror, for, even if we assumed – which Locke does not – that the father's promise to the conqueror to be a dutiful subject represented a valid compact under the circumstances described above, his son would have no such obligation to obey the conqueror. This is precisely the point Locke makes in paragraph 176, with the added observation that not only can the son not be assumed to have consented to the existing government, but he also has the 'right' 'to appeal to heaven' until such time as his father's original right, taken away by the conqueror, has been recovered. Because 'the conquered, or their children, have no court, no arbitrator on earth to appeal to', they are still in the state of war with the conqueror (II, 176, 189, 196). Since no structure of rights and obligations can be created through conquest, these individuals obviously do not exist within a political society, as Locke defines the term, whatever the *de facto* government of the conqueror may do (II, 187, 189, 196). (This is one of those instances in which Locke's phrase that individuals 'however associated' (II, 89) who have not followed the prescribed course of actions necessary to institute a political society are still in the state of nature (war) assumes a specific referential meaning.)

Locke justifies the right to resistance or revolution on the part of the children against their father's conqueror and the existing government, and his grounds for doing so are an amalgamation of his argument concerning the violation of the Law of Nature and his defence of the proposition that legitimate political societies are founded in the consent of the people. But Locke is more specific than this, for, by recovering through revolution the father's original right, what he means is that the children may engage in revolution 'till they have recovered the native right of their ancestors, which was to have such a legislative over them, as the majority should approve, and freely acquiesce in' (II, 176). Thus,

> the people who are the descendants of . . . those who were forced to submit to the yoke of a government by constraint, have always a right to shake it off, and free themselves from the usurpation, or tyranny, which the sword hath brought in upon them, till their rulers put them under such a frame of government, as they willingly, and of choice consent to . . . For no government can have a right to obedience from a people who have not freely consented to it: which they can never be supposed to do, till either they are put in a full state of liberty to choose their government and governors, or at least till they have such standing laws, to which they have by themselves or their representatives, given their free consent. (II, 192; cf. 196)

If one chooses to view this discussion in abstract terms, as is generally done, it is not clear what Locke means by the people having the opportunity to consent to their government or by giving their 'free consent' to their 'representatives' to make the laws for them. If, on the other hand, we suppose that he means by consent in both instances some form of election, this passage (and many others in the text) is very clear and unequivocal in its meaning: only governments elected by the majority of the community are legitimate.

Locke pursues this argument in the following chapter (17) on usurpation, which he refers to as 'a kind of domestic conquest', although, unlike a conqueror in a just war, the 'usurper can never have right on his side' because he 'is got into the possession of what another has right to' (II, 197). The usurper remains an illegitimate ruler even 'though the form of the commonwealth be still preserved' after he has gained power. The usurper may preserve the rule of the previous oligarchy, with himself as their leader, and the government remains in its form an oligarchy. He may also proclaim himself king, and the monarchy remains a monarchy, and so forth. There is, however, one obvious exception to this argument. If the usurper were to hold *free elections*, and subsequently be elected by the people, he would immediately lose the label of being a usurper and become the rightful ruler within the form of a commonwealth that was previously defined in terms of free elections. Locke initially began this chapter, which consists of only two paragraphs, by asserting that a 'usurper can *never* have right on his side', but now, he concludes, 'nor can such a usurper . . . ever have a title, till the people are both at liberty to consent, and have actually consented to allow, and confirm in him, the power he hath till then usurped' (II, 198). Locke must mean, therefore, that there is some specific action which *could* be taken by a usurper to legitimize his heretofore illegal actions, for if his initial act of usurpation permanently debarred him from legitimacy his mere existence as ruler is, in itself, the problem, and this last sentence would make little sense. And, by the same token, the mere duration of his regime cannot confer legitimacy upon the usurper, for then the 'never' in the first sentence would not make sense. The intervening factor between the statement in paragraph 197 and the one in paragraph 198 is, of course, the consent of the people. But, as we have already seen, consent extracted by force or extortion is no consent at all, according to Locke. A ruler 'has no lawful authority, whilst force, and not choice, compels them [the people] to submission' (II, 189). The issue is not the empirical fact of obedience, which, Locke concedes, 'the preservation of human society does of necessity force us' to accept, 'even of usurped powers'. But this obedience, extracted from people for reasons of self-preservation, is decidedly not the same as 'putting [the people] under an obligation' to obey a rightful ruler. There is a clear distinction to be maintained, Locke insists, between these two 'grounds' of obedience, even where the practical results are the same.[4] Therefore, the problem becomes what action could a usurper in power take in order to gain the consent of the people where the latter would not and could not be interpreted as a form of coercive consent? The answer, I submit, lies in the restoration of free elections, which puts the people 'at liberty to consent' and which provides a definite means of determining that they 'have actually consented' to the usurper's rule. This action, and only this action, would *ipso facto* confer legitimacy upon a usurper.

In the following chapter (18), 'Of Tyranny', Locke defines tyranny as 'the exercise of power beyond right', that is, the exercise of power 'which nobody can have a right to' (II, 199). Locke associates the ruler's use of power for his private advantage rather than for the public good with tyranny (II, 200), but this might lead some to think that tyranny applies only to monarchies, which is not the case. 'Other forms of government are liable' to become tyrannical as well (II, 201). The general proposition Locke uses to describe a tyranny is that 'whosoever in authority exceeds the power given him by the law, and makes use of the force he has under his command' to enforce his will against others is a tyrant. 'For the exceeding the bounds of authority is no more a right in great, than a petty officer; no more justifiable in a king, than a constable.' This phraseology, it will be noticed, links the concept of tyranny with Locke's definition of a state of war. In other words, a tyrant is someone 'acting without authority . . . who by force invades the right of another' (II, 202). Among other things, this way of putting the issue provides a clear answer to the question raised in the following paragraph: 'May the commands then of a prince be opposed?' (II, 203). Since the tyrant is no different from 'any other man' who puts himself into a state of war with others (II, 202), and since the only remedy against the use of force without authority is to oppose it by force (II, 204), the answer is obviously yes. It only remains for Locke to show under what circumstances a prince becomes a tyrant in order to justify resistance to the latter as an act of self-defence.

If we recall from Chapter 7 that Locke illustrated what he meant by 'using force upon the people without authority' by citing the example of an executive who uses his power 'to hinder the meeting and acting of the legislative', we can see that if he, and those associated with Shaftesbury, meant to apply these remarks to the actions of Charles II, as they did, then Charles was a tyrant, as Locke defines that term in the *Second Treatise*. Nor can there be any mistake about the connection between inhibiting the legislature from fulfilling its purposes and tyranny, for Locke specifically says that this action puts the executive in 'a state of war with the people', and that they have a right to use force to oppose the executive (II, 155; cf. 215). This is, then, one example of a prince becoming a tyrant, and its political applicability to Charles II's constant prorogation and dissolution of Parliament, and his rule for the last four years of his reign without Parliament, was starkly clear to Locke's readers.

Suppose, however, one were to ask why one cannot view this

conflict between the king and Parliament simply as an unfortunate impasse caused by both sides acting in good faith, but unwilling to compromise to bring about a solution. Why, in other words, must it be described in terms of 'tyranny' or a state of war, which is clearly an ideologically weighted characterization of the situation? In answering this question, I want to reverse the procedure I have adopted previously; that is, in this instance, let us bracket Locke's personal political commitment and his opposition, shared with Shaftesbury, to Charles II as a possible explanation, and look instead for a basis for this conclusion embedded in the logical structure of Locke's political thought.

Locke describes tyranny in the same terms – unbounded arbitrary power, whose employment against them transforms men into slaves (II, 199, 201–2, 210) – that he uses to define 'despotical power'. The latter 'is an absolute, arbitrary power one man has over another' that creates or arises out of a state of war. It is, however, 'a power, which nature neither gives . . . nor compact can convey', because no individual can give another this power over his life. Not only is no one authorized by natural law to consent to these conditions, but also 'despotical power . . . arises not from compact, so neither is it capable of any, but is the state of war continued' (II, 172). These statements apply even if there is a functioning government in existence, as in the case of a conquest. The key phrase here is that despotical power is not 'capable' of being gained or sanctioned through consent. This is what Locke means when he declares that tyranny is the exercise of power 'which nobody *can* have a right to', because it is not a form of power (or government) to which individuals are capable of consenting. The same argument was employed by Locke to deny that absolute monarchy was a form of political society, because rational individuals could not possibly consent to it (II, 90–4) – a point Locke repeats in his discussion of despotical power (II, 174). As we have noted, Locke applies the same terminology and arguments in his chapter on conquest. It is true that tyranny or absolute monarchy unites the legislative and executive power in the ruler's hands, that the latter acts for his private advantage rather than for the public good, that he acts by arbitrary decrees rather than by standing laws, and so on; but over and above all of these regrettable characteristics stands the Lockean proposition that tyranny is a form of political power which there is no possibility of legitimizing through consent.

What I want to suggest is that, in addition to this moral language, which contrasts despotism and slavery with freedom and consent, there is an empirical dimension to Locke's argument in which not having the possibility of consenting to tyranny means not having free elections whereby the people can consent to the exercise of political power through voting. Tyranny, that is, places people in a situation in which they have no possibility of consenting to legitimate political power because the government does not permit any elections to be held. In the *First Treatise*, Locke had juxtaposed 'tyranny and usurpation' to 'election and consent' as alternative perspectives (between Filmer and Locke) as to the origins and authority of government (I, 148). I believe the theoretical structure of Locke's political thought is built around the opposing practices, concepts and arguments associated with this juxtaposition, and that 'election', as an institutionalized form of consent, occupies a crucial place in Locke's political theory.[5] Although I have already offered some suggestions as to why I believe this to be the case, and have cited some passages from the text in support of this view, in many respects it is easier to demonstrate the significance of free elections to Locke's argument in the *Two Treatises* by examining the negative side of the question. By that I mean that when Locke states those specific actions that cause the dissolution of a legitimate government he is most concerned with those actions that subvert the holding of free elections to choose a legislative assembly. There are other actions that lead to the dissolution of government; nevertheless, the core of Locke's indictment against the king and the major premiss of his justification of revolution concerns the ruler's efforts to abolish the consent of the people through his interference with the electoral system.

Apart from the single instance of a foreign conquest (II, 211), Locke's discussion of the dissolution of government is concerned with the question of how 'governments are dissolved from within'. The first and most important general case is 'when the legislative is altered', because ' 'tis in their legislative, that the members of a commonwealth are united and combined together into one coherent living body. This is the soul that gives form, life and unity to the commonwealth . . . And therefore when the legislative is broken, or dissolved, dissolution and death follows.' Hence not only are the people not obliged to obey anyone who attempts to 'make laws without authority', in the absence of a legislative power chosen by the people, but also the latter always retain the right to 'constitute to themselves a new legislative, as they think best, being in full liberty to resist the force of those, who without authority would impose anything upon them' (II, 212). This declaration clearly sets the tone for the entire chapter (19), in that alteration of the legislative power is the major cause of the dissolution of government and an unequivocal ground for revolution on the part of the people.

This general pronouncement, however, is not likely to prove of much practical value, Locke concedes, 'without knowing the form of government in which it happens' that the legislative is altered. He therefore 'supposes' a government consisting of a single hereditary executive, an assembly of hereditary nobility, and 'an assembly of representatives chosen *pro tempore*, by the people' (II, 213). Locke focuses upon the conflict between the executive and the legislative as this relates to the practice of elections, through which the latter is constituted, in four respects: suppose (1) elections are held, but the executive refuses to accept their results as the public will; (2) the executive prevents elections from being held; (3) elections are held, but the manner of holding them, that is, the rules, are changed by the executive; and (4) elections are held, but the electors and/or the representatives are corrupted by bribes or threats from the executive.

In his earlier remarks on the relationship between the executive and the legislative powers, Locke identified 'the public will of the society' with its laws, to which he contrasted the executive who 'acts by his own private will', and who thereby loses his claim to obedience by members of society (II, 151). This point is repeated in paragraph 214 as an example of how the legislative is altered, for 'when other laws are set up, and other rules pretended, and enforced, than what the legislative, constituted by the society, have enacted, 'tis plain, that the legislative is changed' (II, 214). This charge appears to be directed primarily against James II, who used his prerogative to suspend the application of the Test Acts and penal laws against Catholics. There is no doubt that this anti-Catholic viewpoint reflected the 'public will' of seventeenth-century English society, and not only as declared in its laws. In each of the three national elections held between 1679 and 1681, the people declared their overwhelming support for the principle that Catholics should be excluded from holding public office – a principle that was endorsed by their elected legislative assembly, the House of Commons. True, the Exclusion Bill never became a 'declared law', but Locke appears to have believed that it nevertheless represented the public will of society which Charles II disregarded by refusing to allow the electoral expression of this will to be translated into law, and which James II disregarded by refusing to enforce those laws that Parliament had enacted.

The second indictment listed by Locke is the previously discussed instance of when 'the prince hinders the legislative from assembling in its due time' or from taking action (II, 215). Aside from postponements through prorogations, the hindering of the legislature from meeting means the failure to call for national elections so that the people can choose their representatives. Hence the people are not in a position to give their consent to the making of laws for society. Third, 'when by the arbitrary power of the prince, the electors, or ways of election are altered, without the consent, and contrary to the common interest of the people, there also the legislative is altered' (II, 216). This refers to the efforts of both Charles II and James II during the 1680s to restructure the electoral system by rewriting the corporation and borough charters with the object of restricting the franchise to fewer electors who might be more easily controlled by the king. Finally, the executive

> acts also contrary to his trust, when he either employs the force, treasure, and offices of the society, to corrupt the representatives, and gain them to his purposes: or openly pre-engages the electors, and prescribes to their choice, such, whom he has by solicitations, threats, promises, or otherwise won to his designs; and employs them to bring in such, who have promised beforehand, what to vote, and what to enact. Thus to regulate candidates and electors, and new model the ways of election, what is it but to cut up the government by the roots, and poison the very fountain of public security? (II, 222)

Locke's use of the phrase, 'to cut up the government by the roots', is interesting in view of the fact that he uses the identical expression to describe a 'conquest' of society (II, 211), which is an act of war. Locke goes on to assert that the people have 'reserved to themselves the choice of their representatives', and that the latter must be 'freely chosen', which, under the circumstances described above, is impossible. To undermine, alter or abolish the elections through which the people 'choose and authorize a legislative' is 'as perfect a declaration of a design to subvert the government, as is possible to be met with' (II, 222).

To this might be added the historical observation that the primary stated purpose for William of Orange's invasion of England – and the only justificatory reason that he publicly defended in the propaganda directed towards other European nations – was to ensure that a free Parliament would be called into session. When, therefore, Locke writes in the preface to the *Two Treatises* of William as 'our Great Restorer' of those 'just and natural rights' which the people of England had lost, and associates his own argument with a defence of these actions, I believe he is referring, as he is in paragraph 176, to 'the native right' of the English people to have a freely elected Parliament. It also seems to me that when Locke speaks of William's title being made good 'in the consent of the people', which is the only foundation for 'all lawful governments' (*Two Treatises*, preface), he is not employing abstract rhetoric, but is referring to the actual decision of the Convention Parliament to offer William the crown.

What I am arguing is that just as Locke had in mind a particular form of government as a well-ordered commonwealth when he was presenting his general theory of a legitimate political society, so he associated a specific set of political practices – national elections of representatives – with his general references to 'the consent of the people' as an operative action within political society. Both aspects of Locke's thought become very clear when he is presenting his justification for revolution, because, as he notes, this justification must be specific and concrete, and that requires some statement of the particular form of the government. It is precisely because Locke is not interested simply in advancing a general theory of revolution, but is, rather, writing a work (the *Second Treatise*) that urges his readers to *make* a revolution against *their* existing government, that in presenting this part of his argument he must necessarily speak directly to them. Yet since the entire work, and not merely its last chapter, is addressed to this audience we are entitled in my opinion to assign an importance to this practical objective that is not limited to the mechanical application of general principles to a specific case but, rather, has the effect of structuring the theoretical argument itself. In this sense, there are good reasons for not reading the text of the *Two Treatises* on a level that views the terminology employed by Locke, such as consent, state of nature, civil society and so forth, in its most abstract form. There is even less justification for adopting this approach to the text, and then criticizing Locke for being vague, ambiguous, or for not specifying the meaning of his terms.

There are other means by which the legislative is altered and the government dissolved cited by Locke. For example, 'the delivery . . . of the people into the subjection of a foreign power' (II, 217) has this consequence. This was the expression used by Locke's contemporaries in referring to the fact that Catholic rulers owed their first allegiance to the Pope (and the papacy in the seventeenth century could legitimately be characterized as 'a foreign power'). Therefore, any attempt to transform England into a Catholic nation was viewed by English Protestants – including Locke – in these terms. The last case is when the executive abandons his post or fails to execute the laws (II, 219), which is applicable to James II's flight from England following the arrival of William's forces in late 1688. These instances, along with foreign conquest, are not unimportant elements of Locke's theory of the dissolution of government, but it is obvious that neither do they constitute the central core of that theory, which is focused upon the relationship between the people and their legislative power. And that relationship is, in turn, tied to the holding of free elections to choose those representatives. In the end, the foundation, not only for Locke's defence of revolutionary action, but also for the entire framework of his political theory, is the right of the people 'to constitute' (II, 212; cf. 220, 222, 243) or 'to reinstate' (II, 155) a legislature that they choose through free elections. If they have no possibility of acting in this manner, they may be said to exist under a tyranny. The latter represents the exercise of power or force without authority, which is a state of war, and in those circumstances the people are obliged by the Law of Nature to preserve themselves, which they can only do by opposing their force to those who threaten their lives, liberties or estates. That, in a nutshell, is the political theory of the *Second Treatise*.

Finally, I want to turn to the question of who, in fact, is supposed to translate this political theory into action. Who are 'the people' who Locke expects to make a revolution against their king? Since the answer I will suggest is linked with our earlier discussion of the state of nature and the formation of political society, there is an aspect of Locke's theory of the dissolution of government that must first be considered in order to lay the groundwork for this discussion. That is, what in fact happens when a government is dissolved? The most direct answer to this question in the *Second Treatise* is that power 'devolves to the people' who are its original source and who may employ that power 'as they shall think fit [to] provide for their own safety and security' (II, 222; cf. 149, 243). But what is the condition of the people to whom such power has devolved? Here, too, Locke's answer seems rather clear. It returns to the people constituted as a community. Since any government is 'only a fiduciary power to act for certain ends' on behalf of the community, the latter 'perpetually retains a supreme power of saving themselves from the attempts and designs of anybody, even of their legislators', when they set about to bring the people into 'a slavish condition'.

> And thus the community may be said in this respect to be always the supreme power, but not as considered under any form of government, because this power of the people can never take place till the government be dissolved. (II, 149; cf. 243)

Now, are individuals, as members of this community, once again in the state of nature? Recent interpreters have denied that Locke suggests that individuals are returned to the state of nature when the government is dissolved, but, as I argued in Chapter 5, I do not believe the weight of evidence can sustain this viewpoint. This is not to deny that there is some support for this position in the text, but it seems to require a reading that defines 'community' and 'state of nature' as mutually exclusive concepts. However, in those passages generally cited, where Locke describes the formation of the political community, he invariably runs together the establishment of the community with the setting up of the legislative as an authoritative judge (II, 89; cf. 87), and these are both logically and temporally distinct actions. Until a specific form of government is established that defines the nature of the legislative power, an authoritative law-making judge is lacking, and it is precisely *this* element upon which the formal definitions of political society and the state of nature depend for their exclusivity. Since there is no doubt that Locke conceives of the community as existing without a form of government, as the passage above and others previously cited make clear, the real question is whether it makes more sense to speak of the community as a political society without the elements that actually constitute a political society or to speak of the community as existing in the state of nature, despite the fact that individuals have consented to be members of the community?

I have opted for the latter alternative because, not only have individuals not left the state of nature until they have definitely assigned the legislative power to someone (II, 132), but also there is no way of determining what 'tyranny' or 'usurpation' means in the absence of a specific form of government. In other words, the very meaning of legitimacy, and, *ceteris paribis*, a political argument justifying revolution, presupposes a definite structuring of political power, and not simply the amorphous reservoir of power in the community where no form of government exists (II, 133). In short, it seems to me that 'political society' loses most of its meaning in the absence of a form of government, whereas the 'state of nature' retains most of its meaning even in the situation in which individuals are members of a community without government.[6]

If the issue were merely one of semantics, the point would not be worth pursuing, but, as we now see with the scope of Locke's theory of revolution before us, it is a matter of some importance to assert that individuals are returned to their original natural condition with the authority of natural law to sanction their actions because there are no other operative rules of legitimacy. Moreover, if the efforts of Charles II to hinder the meeting of the legislature changed the form of government, thereby dissolving it, as Locke asserts, then it is possible for individuals to exist without a form of government for a relatively long time; in this case, during the period 1681–5, it would appear that no 'common judge with authority' (II, 19) to redress the people's grievances existed. Since the king became, in effect, an absolute monarch during these four years, Locke's remarks on absolute monarchy as no form of government, and the people existing in the state of nature in relation to their ruler, would also appear to be applicable. Finally, I cannot see why this situation should not be classified under 'any calamity' whereby 'the government . . . comes to be dissolved' and subjects are 'again in the liberty of the state of nature' (II, 121).

If we return to the example of conquest, we can see that at the outset the two commonwealths 'are in the state of nature one with another' (II, 183). One country conquers the other, destroying its existing form of government, leaving the latter's subjects 'at liberty to begin and erect another to themselves' (II, 185), that is, the liberty they had as individuals in the state of nature. The conqueror is in a state of war with these subjects, but this does not affect the fact that they are in a state of nature in respect to each other. Hence it is perfectly possible, according to Locke, for a ruler to put 'himself into a state of war with his people, dissolve the government, and leave them to that defence, which belongs to every one in the state of nature' (II, 205). The example of conquest, however, might be considered a special case because Locke maintains in paragraph 211 that it is the union of the commonwealth itself that is dissolved in a foreign conquest, so that its existence as an independent entity can no longer be recognized. It is the formation of this community that 'brings men out of the loose state of nature, into one politic society', although this further requires that they be able to 'act as one body' (II, 211). But what if the people cannot so act? That they cannot do so as a defeated nation at the hands of a foreign conqueror is obvious enough; but it seems equally clear that there are conditions under a tyrant or usurper – and 'usurpation is a kind of domestic conquest' (II, 197) – when they also cannot act as a body. Without any action by the majority of the community, do they in fact still constitute an independent community? When, in referring to the dissolution of government, Locke speaks of the collapse of 'the essence and union of the society . . . the soul that gives form, life, and unity to the commonwealth', the very thing according to which 'the members of a commonwealth are united and combined together into one coherent living body', is it little wonder that he calls this 'dissolution and death' (II, 212)? How different, in fact, is this condition from the one described in the previous paragraph where 'every one return[s] to the state he was in before'? It is not that one cannot perceive that Locke wishes to retain some sense of identity for the commonwealth independent of its form of government, but only that, in terms of the exercise of real political power, something more than mere names, such as 'commonwealth', is necessary to persuade us that the people do have power. Indeed, under some conditions, when the government has dissolved, the community can assert its existence as a political reality *only* through the organized act of revolution. If it fails to do this, what reason is there to refer to individuals living under a tyranny as members of a political community?[7]

But whether or not the community of individuals is in a state of nature we still want to know who will make the revolution Locke envisages. If, as I have argued, Locke means to require the consent of every free man as a condition of membership in political society, I see no reason to suppose that when he speaks of the people as the actors in resisting 'manifest acts of tyranny' (II, 208) he means some entity other than the majority of freemen. On the contrary, what is puzzling is the orthodoxy that has developed among interpreters asserting that Locke supposed that only the aristocracy or large property-owners were the conduits of the revolutionary activity he advocates in the *Second Treatise*. Leaving aside the historical implausibility of this suggestion, there is not the slightest warrant for this viewpoint in the text.[8] Locke's work positively bristles with the suggestion that he is appealing to the people at large, down to 'every individual', to take up arms against the government – an implication that did not go unnoticed among the seventeenth-century readers of the *Second*

Treatise. No wonder the Whig magnates and their conservative spokesmen sought to dissociate themselves from the radical tenets contained in Locke's *Two Treatises* at the time of its publication, following the Glorious Revolution.[9]

In order to appreciate some of these radical implications, let me summarize Locke's argument without reciting passages from the text that have already been discussed. We know that both the state of nature and the state of war are conditions of equality, where 'there is no superiority or jurisdiction' (II, 7) between the two parties. We know that every individual has the right to enforce the Law of Nature against any violator, and to punish the aggressor, even to the point of killing him. We have seen that a ruler may put himself into a state of war with his people if he attempts, by using force, to exceed his lawful authority. Such action may also be identified with tyranny. Interference with free elections or the meeting of the legislature are concrete examples of actions that Locke's audience would recognize as being applicable to Charles II and James II. These individuals were tyrannical rulers in a state of war with their people. And in this condition *every man* not only has, but must have, according to natural law, the right to punish the aggressor – the ruler. The formulation of Locke's argument demands such a conclusion, and there is no space between its premises and conclusions for the insertion of some privileged revolutionary group defined in terms of their socio-economic status.[10]

This means not only that by 'the majority of the people' Locke intends the actual numerical majority, which places revolutionary action in the hands of the members of the lowest social classes, but it may also indicate Locke's sanction of tyrannicide. I have phrased this proposition more cautiously because, while there are reasons external to the text of the *Two Treatises* for attributing this view to Locke, the text itself is understandably more ambiguous concerning this form of resistance to tyranny. Still, I believe the preponderance of evidence supports the position that any individual is entitled to take action against a tyrant, provided that he is acting with the approval and in the interest of 'the body of the people'. How one determines this is, of course, a rather large problem.

In his discussion of the state of nature and the state of war, Locke employs a colourful language, according to which he characterizes the aggressor. The latter, he says, has become 'a noxious creature' (II, 10) or 'one of those wild savage beasts' (II, 11), who 'may be treated as beasts of prey, those dangerous and noxious creatures' (II, 16), which any individual, according to the Law of Nature, has a right to kill or destroy. Now, this terminology has an ancient and classical heritage in its applicability to tyrants, who have degenerated from the status of men to beasts. And if Locke intends to invoke this identification through his usage of this bestial terminology there can be little doubt that the text of the *Second Treatise* sanctions the right of any individual to destroy such a 'noxious creature' (tyrant). Moreover, if we recall that the state of war is used by Locke to describe the relationship between a ruler and his people, this language takes on a significant political meaning. Thus, in the chapter on the state of war, Locke argues, 'he that in the state of society, would take away the freedom belonging to those of that society or commonwealth, must be . . . looked on as in a state of war' with the members of that society (II, 17). He refers to a situation in which, formally, a system of laws and judges exist within society, but there is 'a manifest perverting of justice, and a barefaced wresting of the laws, to protect or indemnify the violence or injuries of some men, or party of men', and this must be described as 'a state of war'. Hence the fact that the 'forms of law' exist is no guarantee that individuals may not be residents of a state of war (II, 20). Even in its initial theoretical formulation, therefore, it is evident that Locke means to apply the state of war to those conditions under which persons responsible for administering justice in political society fail to do so. And, if this is true, why should one not suppose that the other aspects of that concept, including the right to kill an aggressor, apply under these conditions as well?

That Locke does mean to apply this terminology to political rulers becomes increasingly obvious as the argument of the *Second Treatise* proceeds. He uses it, for example, in his reference to the absolute monarch (II, 93), and, after applying the concept of a state of war to the executive's action in preventing the meeting of the legislature, Locke warns the executive that, as the aggressor, this action 'renders him liable to be treated accordingly' (II, 155). What this means becomes clear with Locke's definition of despotical power, which is meant to apply to just such an action by a ruler. As an aggressor who has degenerated to the level of beasts, the despot 'renders himself liable to be destroyed by the injured person and the rest of mankind, that will join with him in the execution of justice, as any other wild beast, or noxious brute with whom mankind can have neither society nor security' (II, 172). Locke makes the same point with respect to a conqueror, who is liable to be destroyed by *anyone* he has injured (II, 181, 196).

It is in the chapter on tyranny that Locke faces most directly the question of what action may be taken against the king by a subject. 'In some countries', he observes, 'the person of the prince by the law is sacred; and so whatever he commands, or does, his person is still free from all question or violence, not liable to force, or any judicial censure or condemnation.' Some commentators have taken this as an assertion by Locke that the king ought not to be harmed, even in the case of a revolution against his government.[11] But Locke goes on to say that the above situation applies 'unless he will by actually putting himself into a state of war with his people, dissolve the government, and leave them to that defence which belongs to every one in the state of nature. For of such things who can tell what the end will be' (II, 205)? In other words, if the king's person is sacred by law, this precept can only apply where the laws themselves still apply. In a state of war, however, the government is dissolved and the previous laws no longer apply, because 'all former ties are cancelled' (II, 232, 235), and no one can tell what might happen to the king. That the state of war renders the king's life as forfeitable as that of 'any other man, who by force invades the right of another' (II, 202) is evident from Locke's concession that '*in all other cases* the sacredness of the person exempts him from all inconveniences, whereby he is secure, whilst the government stands, from all violence and harm whatsoever' (II, 205; my italics). In the state of war, however, the king's person can claim no privileged status both because 'there is no superiority or jurisdiction' between individuals in that state, and because the government is no longer 'standing', but has dissolved. Since Locke's general point in this chapter is to defend the proposition that 'the king's authority [is] given him only by the law' (II, 206), whereas the tyrant is defined as one who acts against or without authority from the law, a king who becomes a tyrant cannot then claim the benefit of the law that protected him when he acted as a legitimate ruler.

Still, even if there are 'manifest acts of tyranny', Locke argues, this will not necessarily lead to a disturbance of the government, because, although one or a few individuals 'have a right to defend themselves . . . by force', they are unlikely to take action against the government, 'where the body of the people do not think themselves concerned in it'. Locke is saying not only that resistance to the government requires the support of the body of the people, but also that, even if 'one or a few oppressed men' acted upon their 'right' to kill an aggressor (the tyrant), the assassins are likely to suffer death themselves, unless the body of the people supports their cause. In the absence of such support, the assassin would be viewed as 'a raving madman, or heady malcontent . . . the people being as little apt to follow the one, as the other' (II, 208), and the consequence for the assassins will be 'their own just ruin and perdition' (II, 230). Locke's argument in the following paragraph appears to be that if rulers come 'to be generally suspected of their people' this is 'the most dangerous state which they can possibly put themselves in'. According to Locke, the rulers have put their own lives in jeopardy. And because they have put themselves in a situation in which they may be killed 'they are the less to be pitied, because it is so easy to be avoided' (II, 209). In other words, just as it is the tyrant who is the 'rebel' or the aggressor, initiating the state of war with his people, so the tyrant brings upon himself his death at the hands of an assassin; therefore, he is not to be 'pitied' for his fate which could have been otherwise if he had acted for the good of his people. For whoever uses force without authority,

> and lays the foundation for overturning the constitution and frame of any just government, is guilty of the greatest crime, I think, a man is capable of . . . And he who does it, is justly to be esteemed the common enemy and pest of mankind; and is to be treated accordingly. (II, 230)

In support of his argument, Locke cites several passages from the writings of William Barclay, 'that great assertor of the power and sacredness of kings' (II, 232). Barclay concedes the community has the right of self-defence against a king who becomes a tyrant, but he still seeks to protect the king's person as that of a 'superior' who deserves the 'due reverence and respect' of his subjects (II, 233). Locke ridicules this position – how one can 'strike with reverence, will need some skill to make intelligible' – reaffirming his own view that he 'who may resist, must be allowed to strike'. He also denies that any 'reverence, respect, and superiority' is due the king in a state of war, since all former social and political relations between subject and king have been cancelled (II, 235). Locke then quotes from Barclay to show that, by committing certain actions, the king, *ipso facto*, 'cease[s] to be a king . . . and returns to the state of a private man' (II, 237). Hence, Locke declares, even 'Barclay, the great champion of absolute monarchy, is forced to allow, that a king may be resisted, and ceases to be a king'. And when his authority is forfeited he 'becomes like other men who have no authority'. Therefore, Locke asks, 'when a king has dethroned himself, and put himself in a state of war with his people, what shall hinder them from prosecuting him who is no king, as they would any other man, who has put himself into a state of war with them' (II, 239)? Locke has used these passages from Barclay to illustrate two points: first, that a king may be lawfully resisted by the people; and, second, that when he ceases to be a king the ruler becomes subject to the force or prosecution liable to befall any other person in a state of war. Barclay, however, would only agree with the first proposition, since he wishes to protect the sacred person of even a bad king. Locke not only rejects this viewpoint, he also uses these passages from Barclay to support his own case against that of Barclay. Moreover, the clear implication of the passage quoted above is that, for example, the people were justified in prosecuting Charles I and in executing him as they would any other man who engaged in a war against them.[12]

These are indeed radical implications, but that they are deeply embedded in Locke's basic concepts and terminology which he employs throughout the *Second Treatise* can hardly be denied. Nor are we entitled to suppose that he is guilty of a rhetorical flourish here and there, or a slip of the pen in a moment of zealous partisanship. Rather, the argument is quite carefully constructed; Locke consciously intends to apply his definitions to the actions of the king; and he specifically denies that the latter's person is sacred or privileged in a state of war. Whether this argument amounts to a positive endorsement of tyrannicide is admittedly less clear, for reasons that, given the general political context of seventeenth-century England, must be rather obvious. Nevertheless, so far as I can see, there is no obstacle standing in the way of such an endorsement, save the requirement that popular support is a prudential precondition for tyrannicide. And, on the other side, there is much to support the view that, since tyranny is the greatest crime imaginable, the tyrant may not only be destroyed as a pest and enemy of mankind, but also he deserves and has brought upon himself this fate.[13]

Finally, there is Locke's justification for what is, in some respects, a less radical proposition; namely, that the people acting as a body may employ force against a tyrant. So much has already been said concerning the arguments that support this conclusion, and the *Second Treatise* is so unequivocal on this point, that I will forgo an extensive discussion of it. Suffice it to say that if what is, in fact, a complexly structured work could be reduced to a single simple sentence it would be that the people always have an absolute right to defend themselves by force against the actions of a tyrant. The right is 'absolute' not only because its source is traceable to the Law of Nature, such that this action, 'though it hath the name of rebellion, yet [it] is no offence before God, but is that, which he allows and countenances' (II, 196), but it is also absolute in the sense that 'every man', of whatever social or economic condition whatsoever, is entitled to exercise this right against a tyrant (II, 241). This last point has often been denied in order to make Locke appear more politically conservative than he actually was. Yet, if Locke is willing to invoke the egalitarian conditions of the state of war in order to deny the social and political status of the king, reducing him to the level of 'a private man' (II, 237), it is difficult to see why he should involve himself in a needless contradiction by supposing that other individuals, as property-owners or members of the aristocracy, should retain *their* privileges, status and jurisdiction when faced with a state of war. And, if Locke had made such a supposition, it is absurd to imagine that he was so careless a thinker as not to have attempted to supply some defence for the proposition. Interpretative positions that not only find no support in the text, but which also actually depend for their plausibility upon the attribution of such simple logical contradictions to the thinker should, in general, be avoided. If, nevertheless, this approach is to be adopted – and I do not deny that in some rare instances it may be justified – the evidential demands must correspondingly be great in order to override the stated position of the text. In this case, however, that would involve the construction of a plausible argument relating Locke's political conservatism to his own political actions, to the context with which he and those allied with him associated with such actions, and to the audience that read Locke's arguments in the *Second Treatise* from such a vantage-point. In the absence of such extra-textual evidence, the assertion that by 'the people' Locke has in mind as revolutionary political actors primarily the propertied classes loses even its historical plausibility, and it is precisely on *that* ground that interpreters have chosen to set aside the words used in the text in the first place. As I have argued at length elsewhere, Locke's involvement in Shaftesbury's radical political movement, the Rye House Plot and Monmouth's Rebellion forecloses the possibility of relying upon this interpretative strategy to diminish the force of the radical political implications contained in the *Second Treatise*.

What Locke is concerned to defend is the assertion that the people are rational individuals who, despite holding the awesome power and right to revolt in their hands, are responsible beings. Locke does not treat this as an innocuous debate about whether human nature, in general, is rational; rather, he is arguing against political opponents – for example, the clergy – who, while they do not doubt their own rationality, do mean to impugn the rationality of those who are 'inferior' to themselves. Much of the social force of Filmer's political argument depended upon an acceptance of this hierarchical distribution of values and rationality within seventeenth-century English life. The 'multitude' and 'the people' were frequently employed as sarcastic terms in political debate, on the assumption that conventional meaning denied rationality or responsible political action to such entities. Used in this way and from this political perspective, 'the people' was not a term designed to impugn the rationality of the upper classes. They might be guilty of committing serious mistakes, but no defender of social hierarchy equated their actions with those of 'the people'. No defence of the rationality of the upper classes was necessary; it was simply assumed.

Locke's endeavour to defend the rationality of the people would therefore obviously have been made much easier if he had simply indicated that he meant to place the power of judging and acting against the king in the hands of some group of individuals whose socio-economic position within the hierarchy of English life offered some guarantee that they would use this power responsibly. And since there was a well-known doctrine of resistance against the king by 'inferior magistrates' available to Locke it would not have been difficult for him to have relied upon such a theory in order to insulate his general argument in the *Second Treatise* from the criticism attached to an endorsement of the most extreme and radical defence of resistance. He chose instead to accept the people at large as the repositories of revolutionary power, and to defend them as 'rational creatures' (II, 91, 98, 230; cf. 12, 124, 164).

Against the spokesmen for absolute monarchy who regard the people as a 'herd of inferiour creatures', Locke portrays the people as 'a society of rational creatures entered into a community for their mutual good' (II, 163). He knows that 'it will be said, that the people being ignorant, and always discontented' and subject to 'unsteady opinion, and uncertain humour', are incapable of acting responsibly in the political arena. Locke replies that people are more creatures of custom than this allegation assumes. There is a 'slowness and aversion in the people to quit their old Constitutions', despite 'the many revolutions which have been seen in this kingdom' (II, 223). Besides, Locke argues, if the people are 'generally ill treated', what does it matter what *theory* one holds about divine right or their rationality? 'For when the people are made miserable' experience alone shows that they will 'ease themselves of a burden that sits heavy upon them', whether you (Locke's opponents) believe they are rational creatures or not (II, 224). In fact, when one does consider the record of experience, Locke argues, it is obvious that 'revolutions happen not upon every little mismanagement in public affairs'. On the contrary, 'great mistakes' and 'many wrong and inconvenient laws . . . will be born by the people, without mutiny or murmur'. It is only 'a long train of abuses . . . all tending the same way' that 'make the design [of tyranny] visible to the people' and that spurs them to take action against their government (II, 225). The people, in short, 'are more disposed to suffer, than right themselves by resistance', except in those instances in which there is 'manifest evidence that designs are carrying on against their liberties, and the general course and tendency of things cannot but give them strong suspicions of the evil intention of their governors' (II, 230). In the end, Locke is arguing, everyone is forced to rely upon the evidence of their senses, what 'they cannot but feel . . . and see' (II, 225) and what is 'visible or . . . sensible to the greater part, the people'. Therefore, he asks, 'are the people to be blamed, if they have the sense of rational creatures, and can think of things no otherwise than as they find and feel them'? It is not 'the people's wantonness' but, rather, 'the ruler's insolence' that gives rise to rebellion, as a reading of 'impartial history' will prove, according to Locke (II, 230).

No one worries about the rationality of the common soldier, Locke argues, when the latter is armed and called upon to resist by force a foreign invasion of the country. 'But that magistrates doing the same thing', namely, placing themselves in a state of war with the people, 'may be resisted, hath of late been denied' (II, 231). This double standard makes no sense, because 'the people's right is equally invaded, and their liberty lost, whether they are made slaves to any of their own, or a foreign nation'. Hence the same people – meaning everyone at large – who have a right of armed defence in the one case have an equal right to that defence in the other (II, 239). Locke does not recoil from the defence of the right of 'every man' (II, 241) or 'every individual' (II, 243) to exercise his own reason, and therefore his judgement, in determining when to take revolutionary action against the government. He adds, once more, the stipulation that 'the body of the people' are not only the proper judges as to whether such rights-claims and actions are justified, but also they will, in fact, determine whether the resistance is successful (II, 242). Thus, if, on general grounds of rationality, supreme political power must reside somewhere and in some person or persons, it must be supposed to reside in the people at large because the Law of Nature that dictates the preservation of mankind in general allows for no conditional stipulations that restrict the egalitarianism of God's workmanship and confine the exercise of the natural right to enforce the obligations of natural law to a privileged few. Resistance to tyranny is everyone's business.

NOTES: CHAPTER 8

1 The 'right' of a citizen 'to certain privileges' depends upon the consent of the community, expressed in their laws, which are alterable. Such 'privileges', however, also depend upon the good behaviour of the citizen, and hence are forfeited or may be taken away from disobedient persons (2:28, 3, 9).

2 Nevertheless, Martin Seliger (*The Liberal Politics of John Locke* (London: Allen & Unwin, 1968), p. 127) and Julian H. Franklin (*John Locke and the Theory of Sovereignty* (Cambridge: Cambridge University Press, 1978), p. 107) do maintain that there is no return to the state of nature with the dissolution of government. Laslett's confusion on this question states the problem well. Locke, he writes, 'often seems to talk as if the dissolution of government brings about a state of nature'. Despite this, Laslett holds that the dissolution of government 'does not itself bring back the state of nature' (*Two Treatises of Government*, ed. Peter Laslett, 2nd edn (Cambridge: Cambridge University Press, 1967), introduction, p. 114). Earlier, however, Laslett maintained that the dissolution of government 'does not necessarily' place individuals in the state of nature. Whether or not they are returned to the state of nature depends, in his view, upon whether the existing rulers 'resist' the community's effort to replace them with new rulers. If they do, 'then the state of nature is at hand, with all its disadvantages' (pp. 107–8). But, as Laslett himself points out, this would mean that the state of nature could only return in the form of the state of war, so that the two terms become, in effect, identical (p. 114). Unless one is inclined, *pace* Strauss, to read Locke as a Hobbesian from the outset, I can see no basis for this interpretation. For the political meaning of the state of war, as Locke employs the term, *always* involves the absence of an authoritative judge to decide the controversy, and this is the key feature of the state of nature. The form of the government is not dissolved just because the people hold new elections, and thus replace their existing rulers, or appoint a new king, if that is the form of their government. These are the normal transitions of power within the form of government; it is only when the latter itself is changed that the government is dissolved, and this event does not depend exclusively upon the rulers placing themselves in a state of war with the people.

3 According to Plamenatz, 'Locke thought it best that legislative power should be vested in an assembly' and he 'greatly preferred' a system of elected representative government very close to the one that existed in England at the time he wrote the *Two Treatises*. Nevertheless, Plamenatz warns, 'we must not allow this strong preference to mislead us' into believing that Locke is in fact making an argument that political power is only legitimate where there is representative government. On the contrary, 'he does not use the notion of consent to make a case for representative government' (John Plamenatz, *Man and Society*, 2 vols (New York: McGraw-Hill, 1963), Vol. 1, p. 231). It is never clear why, except in terms of *his*

(Plamenatz's) own preference for keeping 'preferences' out of the realm of logic, which he imputes to Locke, we should not suppose that it is precisely Locke's 'strong preference' for a particular form of government that impelled him to write the *Two Treatises* in the first place, so that the 'logic' of the work is fundamentally dependent upon understanding the point or meaning of the action, and not transcendentally independent of that action, as Plamenatz and Dunn assume (cf. John Dunn, *The Political Thought of John Locke* (Cambridge: Cambridge University Press, 1969), pp. 120–7, 143–7).

4   MS c.28, fols 93–4. 'Rulers can perhaps by force and with the aid of arms compel the multitude to obedience, but put them under an obligation they cannot.' Thus, anyone, according to Locke, knows there is 'one ground of obedience' with respect to obeying 'the orders of a pirate or robber' and 'another ground' of obedience to a lawful ruler (*ELN*, 119, 185). For the opposite view, see Seliger (*Liberal Politics*, p. 253), who interprets this passage (II, 198) as saying that the 'legitimation of conquest, usurpation . . . consists in tacit acquiescence. For Locke . . . no more is implied by the willing consent of the people to a usurper or conqueror than that the majority refrain from revolt against him.' Not only does this confer legitimacy on all *de facto* conquerors or usurpers – something that, in the *First Treatise*, Locke accuses Filmer of doing, and which, in the *Second Treatise*, is the position he is attempting to refute – but Seliger's statement is also flatly contradicted by Locke's comments on the 1689 debate on this issue. 'People submit where they do not resist,' Locke observes, so that 'when there is no resistance, there is a general submission. But there may be a general submission without a general consent, which is another thing' (MS c.28, fol. 96).

5   See also Locke's contrast between 'just and moderate' governments and oppression and tyranny in the *Letter Concerning Toleration*. I believe Locke's reference to 'civil society' and 'civilized and settled nations' where there are 'some chosen by the community to govern it' has a more concrete reference to electoral and representative institutions precisely because Locke's thought is focused upon this ideological division (*The Works of John Locke*, 12th edn, 9 vols (1824), Vol. 5, pp. 49–50, 504).

6   Locke's position, I believe, is very close to that of George Lawson in his *Politica sacra et civilis*, a work that Locke owned. Lawson argues that there is a natural moral community comprised of families and neighbourhoods of free and equal individuals who constitute *in potentia* a political community. This natural community has a corporate identity and is capable of making collective decisions through a qualified democratic suffrage, but it is not a distinctly political society until it institutes a particular form of government (1689 edn, pp. 16–25). For a discussion of Lawson and his influence upon Locke, see Franklin, *Locke and Sovereignty*, pp. 69–74.

7   For Seliger, the only action a majority of the community *can* take is to make a revolution, during which society governs itself as a direct democracy, while at all other times 'majority' as used by Locke refers to an oligarchy of property-holders (*Liberal Politics of Locke*, pp. 128, 296).

8   John Dunn writes that Locke could not have imagined anyone 'but the members of the aristocracy' carrying out the revolution he justifies ('The politics of Locke in England and America in the eighteenth century', in John W. Yolton (ed.), *John Locke: Problems and Perspectives* (Cambridge: Cambridge University Press, 1969), pp. 45–80; pp. 54, 59. This view is shared by Plamenatz (*Man and Society*, vol. 1, p. 250). Sabine portrays Locke as 'a conservative' advocate of revolution who was not really committed to revolution at all, notwithstanding 'his insistence on the right of revolution' (George H. Sabine, *A History of Political Theory*, 3rd edn (New York: Holt, Rinehart & Winston, 1961), pp. 535 ff.; cf. Sterling P. Lamprecht, *The Moral and Political Philosophy of John Locke* (1918; reprinted New York: Russell & Russell, 1962), pp. 149–50.

9 For a discussion of this point, see: J. P. Kenyon, *Revolution Principles: The Politics of Party, 1689–1720* (Cambridge: Cambridge University Press, 1977); Franklin, *Locke and Sovereignty*; and my *Revolutionary Politics and Locke's 'Two Treatises of Government'* (Princeton, NJ: Princeton University Press, 1986).

10 Here, again, it may be helpful to note that Filmer deliberately drew a line separating the 'rude multitude' from the freeholders or Members of Parliament in his discussion of 'the people', which, I am arguing, Locke, with equal deliberation, chose to ignore (Sir Robert Filmer, *Patriarcha and Other Political Works* (ed.) Peter Laslett (Oxford: Basil Blackwell, 1949), pp. 170–1; cf. pp. 198, 213–14).

11 For example, Franklin, *Locke and Sovereignty*, p. 95.

12 I emphasize this is only an implication that follows from Locke's argument, and not necessarily Locke's own belief. We do not know what he thought about the execution of Charles I during the period he was writing the *Two Treatises*. In paragraph 205, after noting that the king is only liable to prosecution or acts of violence if he puts himself in a state of war with the people, and then his personal fate is uncertain, Locke remarks that England 'has showed the world an odd example' of what he means. Laslett thinks this refers to James II, but the 'odd example' of a king suffering 'judicial censure' and 'force' against his person – which James II did not – just may be Charles I.

13 It certainly was Locke's general theory of revolution that it was a response to 'mismanaged government' and the 'maladministration' of the rulers, a view he had formulated as early as the 1667 essay on toleration (*Works*, Vol. 4, p. 71; H. R. Fox-Bourne, *The Life of John Locke*, 2 vols (1876), Vol. 1, pp. 192–3).

CHAPTER 9

The Coherence of Locke's Thought

Within a few years following the publication of the *Two Treatises of Government*, Locke had published works on toleration, education, religion, philosophy and economics. By the end of the seventeenth century, Lockean ideas had infiltrated nearly every aspect of English cultural life, and were rapidly gaining widespread acceptance within Europe as well. In many respects, it is easier to appreciate the cumulative effect Locke's ideas have had upon the development of Western European culture than it is to sort out the relative influence of his particular works or to state precisely their relationship to each other within the general framework of Lockean thought.

With respect to the argument of the *Two Treatises*, however, it is possible to extract from the secondary literature on Locke three problem areas that arise from the endeavour to establish such connections between that work and Locke's other writings. In the first place, it has proven to be a surprisingly difficult task to state in specific terms what the relationship is between the *Essay Concerning Human Understanding* and the *Two Treatises of Government* and, in a larger sense, between Locke's philosophy and his political theory.[1] Second, *The Reasonableness of Christianity* has been read as supplying evidence for Locke's denial of rationality to the majority of individuals, whose moral and political discipline thus rests upon their belief in Christianity. The latter's function, it is argued, is to serve as the ideological cement reinforcing the exploitative class structure for which Locke's argument in the *Two Treatises* is said to provide a defence.[2] The third problem area is represented by a general feeling that Locke's political views, as a member of the establishment, in the period following the Glorious Revolution are difficult to reconcile with the radical revolutionary position espoused in the *Two Treatises*. The particular work that is usually singled out as an illustration of this turn towards conservatism is his *Considerations on the Lowering of the Rate of Interest*. In attempting to relate the political argument of the *Two*

Treatises to Locke's other writings in this chapter, therefore, I want to focus on these three problem areas.

That some relationship exists between the *Two Treatises* and the *Essay Concerning Human Understanding* seems a reasonable supposition, but part of the difficulty in clarifying the nature of that relationship derives from the presuppositions subscribed to by interpreters of Locke's thought that state, in general, what interdependency ought to obtain between philosophy and political theory. If it is assumed, for example, that the latter can, in some fashion, be deduced from the former, it is a relatively easy matter to demonstrate that this kind of relationship cannot be shown to exist between Locke's two works. Even in the case of Hobbes, who, much more clearly than Locke, evidently wished that his political theory might be viewed in such terms, it is far from clear that this kind of relationship can in fact be established between Hobbes's philosophy and his political theory. On the other hand, that an individual thinks in such a compartmentalized manner that what he writes on philosophy is wholly separable from what he affirms in his political writings is an extremely implausible assumption for an interpreter of the *Two Treatises* to make. And since Locke spent at least a decade of his life working simultaneously on the *Essay* and the *Two Treatises*, often recording notes he used in both works in the same journal on the same day, it does not seem worthwhile in his case even to pursue the theoretical plausibility of such a viewpoint. We are therefore brought back to the original starting-point: that some relationship, though not one that can be formulated according to an analytical model of reasoning, links the *Essay Concerning Human Understanding* with the *Two Treatises of Government*.

Drawing from the discussion in Chapter 2 the assertion that Lockean political theory combines moral philosophy with prudential judgements, let us consider how this definition of political theory relates to Locke's philosophical writings. The first question to be raised concerning the *Essay Concerning Human Understanding* is: what kind of work is it? It may seem odd to begin our discussion in this manner, since we know very well that it is a work of philosophy. Yet that characterization conceals as much as it reveals, especially if we are inclined to identify what we mean by philosophy with what we suppose Locke meant by that term. That is, if we emphasize the importance of epistemology, the use of definitions and a certain mode of reasoning as the crucial elements of our conception of philosophy, in the sense that philosophers address themselves to such matters, we can certainly justify our classification of the *Essay* as a classic work in the history of philosophy on the grounds that these subjects are discussed by Locke in that book. Nevertheless, many of the problems involved in relating the *Essay* to the *Two Treatises* have their origins in the adoption of this definition of philosophy and its applicability to the argument of the *Two Treatises*.[3] I want to approach the problem from another direction: by historicizing the notion of philosophy so that Locke's understanding of philosophy can be incorporated into the framework according to which the arguments of the *Essay* and the *Two Treatises* are comparatively assessed. Unless this is done, I shall argue, the construction of a bridge between the two works will prove to be exceedingly difficult.

Fortunately, Locke provides a clear statement of what in his view constitutes the subject-matter of philosophy. In the final chapter of the *Essay*, he declares, 'all that can fall within the compass of human understanding' can be grouped under three headings. First, there is natural philosophy, which is a 'knowledge of things as they are' in the world, and which leads to 'speculative truth'. Second, there is 'the skill of right applying our own powers and actions, for the attainment of things good and useful', which is best described as ethics. Here our objective 'is not bare speculation, and the knowledge of truth; but right, and a conduct suitable to it'. Locke refers to the third category as 'the nature of signs the mind makes use of for the understanding of things, or conveying its knowledge to others'; that is, the rules of logic applicable to our use of ideas and words. Thus, 'the three great provinces of the intellectual world' are 'the contemplation of things', the individual's use of 'power' and 'actions for the attainment of his own ends', and the rules of language and logic that must be followed in pursuing both of the above objectives (4:21, 1–5). Whatever we may think of this 'division of the sciences', it clearly expresses Locke's view of the boundaries of philosophy as stated in the *Essay Concerning Human Understanding*.

Even accepting this definition of philosophy, however, we are still faced with the question of how to distribute the emphasis among its three 'separate and distinct' provinces. And, whereas our interest in philosophy generally accords primary significance to either the first or the third of Locke's provinces, he assigned the place of first importance to the moral aspects of philosophy and, more generally, to a view of the latter as a theory of practical action. It is this emphasis, I shall argue, which must first be restored as a hermeneutic guide to the reading of the *Essay* as a precondition for any meaningful comparison to be drawn between that work and the *Two Treatises of Government*. This means that the *Essay Concerning Human Understanding*, though it obviously deals with all of the subjects that fall within the compass of philosophy, is primarily a work of moral philosophy and is intended to provide its reader with the principles appropriate to 'right conduct'. If we begin from this vantage-point, we can see that a political theory represents a guide to practical action within a larger definition of 'right conduct' which not only establishes the moral rules governing the meaning of such action, but also provides an account of the natural powers possessed by individuals that enable them to execute such actions. In other words, what we should expect to find in the *Essay* is a statement of the basic presuppositions that are essential to the moral dimensions of the practical action being urged by Locke in the *Two Treatises*, as well as some description of the powers of human beings that enable them to perform the recommended actions.

In Chapter 2 we established the general importance to Locke's thought of a belief in God and adherence to the rules of morality prescribed by Him. We were there concerned to identify those fundamental assumptions that were necessary to an understanding of Locke's political theory. Without recounting all the points made in that discussion, I want to relate some of these assumptions to the *Essay Concerning Human Understanding* in particular, in order to defend my description of it as a work of moral philosophy. According to Locke, 'the main end' of the *Essay* is to promote 'the knowledge and veneration' of God (2:7, 6), for 'the knowledge of their Maker, and . . . their own duties' (1:1, 5) is the type of knowledge with which individuals' understandings, and hence philosophy, ought to be most concerned. 'Morality and divinity', Locke advises the reader of the *Essay*, are 'those parts of knowledge that men are most concerned to be clear in', precisely because, substantively, they 'are matters of the highest concernment' to us (Epistle to the Reader, p. 11; 3:9, 22). 'Our business here is not to know all things, but those which concern our conduct' (1:1, 6; cf. 1:3, 12; 2:23, 12). This represents the 'proper employment' of our faculties. 'Hence I think I may conclude', Locke writes, 'that morality is the proper science, and business of mankind in general' (4:12, 11). The question of how to determine what is necessary to the realization of this objective, Locke tells us, 'was that which gave the first rise to this essay concerning the understanding' (1:1, 7). And, in reply to his critics, Locke insisted that 'all the great ends of religion and morality' were secured and defended in the *Essay* (*Works*, 3:34).

Nevertheless, how we may realize these ends through practical action cannot be answered without a survey of 'the powers of our own minds, and . . . some estimate what we may expect from them' (1:1, 6). 'I doubt not but to show', Locke declares, 'that a man, by the right use of his natural abilities, may . . . attain a knowledge of a God, and other things that concern him' (1:4, 12). Any estimation of our natural abilities, however, requires that we establish some relationship between the powers of our minds and those external objects which, collectively, we refer to as Nature. This means that a 'little excursion into natural philosophy' is a necessary, though subsidiary, feature of the attempt to delineate those things 'which concern our conduct' (2:8, 10–23). Moreover, the internal relationship that exists among our various natural powers and the rules that govern their employment as modes of action is also a part of 'the right use' of our natural abilities. These rules of the understanding must therefore receive some consideration in the course of realizing 'the main end' of the *Essay*. Even this phrasing of the distribution of emphasis among the three provinces of philosophy is misleading in so far as it conveys a naturalistic tone with respect to the powers of the understanding. What Locke stresses, however, is that God 'hath fitted our senses, faculties, and organs, to the conveniences of life, and the business we have to do here' (2:23, 12). In other words, that we possess the ability to act morally is not a proposition to be subjected to doubt, but is, rather, an assumption built into our recognition of our being God's 'workmanship' and a reading of His intentions in having created us. In the *Essay Concerning Human Understanding*, as some of his critics noted, Locke is concerned to show *how* we can realize an end that is not, strictly speaking, given to us by philosophy.

In addition to the emphasis Locke places upon morality in the *Essay*, he grants considerable importance to action directed towards providing for the 'conveniences' of life. These practical concerns may appear alien to some current definitions of philosophy, but there is no doubt that Locke ranks them just below the level of ethical behaviour. The use of our faculties to achieve 'ease and health, and thereby increase our stock of conveniences for this life' is to be encouraged. 'The supply and increase of useful commodities' is an objective to be pursued not for the benefits it brings to the individual but, rather, because they are 'for the common use of human life' and contribute to the advancement of mankind in general (4:12, 10–12). Locke argues that in employing 'our abilities to provide for the conveniences of living' we are fulfilling God's purposes in having furnished us with the powers and faculties necessary for such action (2:23, 12). Since acting for the preservation of mankind is the moral principle against which all actions are to be measured, it is not difficult to understand why Locke should have classified all practical action under the heading of ethics. Not only would we 'be unavoidably reduced to the wants and ignorance of the ancient savage Americans' without those 'useful arts' that supply 'the conveniences of life' (4:12, 11), but such inventions are an indirect form of ethical behaviour, when viewed as actions that contribute to the common good. That is the framework for Locke's theory of practical action in the *Essay Concerning Human Understanding*.

Enough has already been said concerning the importance of natural law as the ground for moral judgements that it should be sufficient to point out that Locke states this proposition several times in the *Essay* (Epistle to the Reader, Fraser edn, p. 19; 1:3, 6, 18; 2:21, 70; 2:28, 8). While it is true that 'all men are liable to error, and most men are in many points, by passion or interest, under temptation to it' (4:20, 17), it is also the case, according to Locke, that human behaviour does generally remain within the boundaries of natural law (2:28, 11–12). If most individuals are not 'strict observers of equity and justice' (II, 123), nevertheless, 'envy and anger', which are the chief spurs to action in a state of war, 'are not therefore to be found in all men' (2:20, 14). In other words, Locke reproduces in the *Essay* the general characterization of individuals in their natural condition as described in the *Two Treatises*. Because they are fallible rather than wicked, there are reasonable grounds for believing that most individuals can employ their natural abilities in a manner that is in conformity with the requirements of the Law of Nature.[4]

The similarity of Locke's ethical position in the *Essay* and the *Two Treatises* can also be perceived if we consider his general theory of practical action. As is well known, Locke rejected the traditional Aristotelian view that individuals are moved to action by their attraction to some good they wish to obtain. Neither did he accept Hobbes's reversal of this assumption: that we are repelled by the fears and evils that threaten our well-being. Instead, Locke postulates that human action is to be explained in terms of a morally neutral state of uneasiness. 'The chief if not only spur to human industry and action', he asserts, 'is uneasiness' (2:20, 6). Locke accepts that there are 'natural tendencies' in man in that he has 'a desire of happiness and an aversion to misery'. Thus, pleasure and pain are 'the constant springs and motives of all our actions' (1:3, 3). We cannot suppose as a general rule, therefore, that we are moved to action simply by 'the greater good in view'; rather, it is some 'uneasiness a man is at present under' that 'sets us upon those actions we perform'. This uneasiness

> is desire . . . for want of some absent good. All pain of the body, of what sort soever, and disquiet of the mind, is uneasiness: and with this is always joined desire, equal to the pain or uneasiness felt . . . Besides this desire of ease from pain, there is another of absent positive good. (2:21, 31)

For Locke, then, desire for an absent good can mean both the easement of pain or the attainment of some positive good. A state of uneasiness describes a situation in which there is something lacking, for if one were 'perfectly content with the state he is in', Locke asks, what would ever move him to action or 'industry'? He cites 'the uneasiness of hunger and thirst' as examples of natural desires that reveal the wisdom of our Maker, since it is in acting to remove the uneasiness associated with such desires that mankind preserves itself (2:21, 34). As a general description of the human condition, Locke maintains that we are 'in this world beset with sundry uneasinesses', so that 'we are seldom at ease' and subject to 'a constant succession of uneasiness' (2:21, 40, 45–6).[5]

The various ways in which Locke develops this argument in the *Essay* could be elaborated, but I think enough has been said to provide a basis for comparing this account of human action in general with the description Locke presents of the state of nature in the *Two Treatises*. Just as he rejects the notion that man's natural condition is one of perfect contentment – why, then, would he ever leave such a state (II, 123)? – so he does not accept its identification with the state of war, as a condition of constant misery, fear and pain. Rather, 'our state here in this world', Locke reflected, 'is a state of mediocrity', wherein 'we are not capable of living altogether exactly by a strict rule, nor altogether without one'.[6] Locke's characterization of the state of nature as a state of 'uncertainty' or 'inconvenience', marked by the absent good of an impartial judge, reproduces in a specific form the basic features of the general conditions under which he assumes that human beings are moved to action. Even if the greater good of the true political society were presented to men in the state of nature, they would not act to institute it until they had actually felt the inconveniences which made them feel uneasy about their present state (II, 107, 111). And, to cite another example, Locke's confidence in the stability of 'the body of the people' rests upon his general supposition that they will not act to make a revolution except in those instances in which the 'present uneasiness' they experience under the existing government reaches a level of oppression and misery in which they must act to ease themselves of the pain. It is easy to see why Locke holds rulers responsible for popular rebellions, for it is they who have created the conditions under which the uneasiness of the people has become so great as to prompt such action. Other examples could be extracted from the *Essay Concerning Human Understanding* and viewed in relation to the argument of the *Two Treatises* to provide support for the argument that there is a congruency between the two works concerning the nature of practical action as a form of ethical conduct and as a means to provide for the conveniences of life. This is a subject worthy of further exploration, which I shall leave to the interested reader.

The theory of motivation Locke advances is not, by itself, a sufficient framework for a theory of action since, as he observes, if human beings were imprisoned by their desires or appetites and the constant succession of pains and pleasures to which they are subject, they would be little better than animals. More significantly, they would, according to Locke, lack both freedom of will and reason, the definitions of which are rooted in the ability of human beings 'to suspend the execution and satisfaction of any of [their] desires'. Hence 'the liberty man has' consists in his ability 'to consider' the various desires he has, and to 'examine them on all sides, and weigh them with others' (2:21, 47). 'The great privilege of finite intellectual beings' is that they can set aside 'a too hasty compliance' with their desires through a 'mature examination' of the consequences of their actions (2:21, 52–3). Locke goes on to stipulate that 'as an intelligent being' the individual must 'be determined in willing by his own thought and judgment what is best for him to do'; otherwise he would be subject to the will of someone else, and so not free (2:21, 48). This linkage of freedom and rationality was discussed in Chapter 2 but, as is apparent, it constitutes the definition of a 'freeman' that Locke utilizes in the *Two Treatises*. Not only is the individual free to dispose of his own actions and possessions as he thinks best, without being subjected to the will of another, but he is also capable of making and obeying laws, and of suspending the gratification of his immediate self-interest in order to realize a greater good (such as the preservation of mankind). There is no need to dwell on this point, but since the rationality, equality, freedom and moral capacity of man, as a general statement of human nature, has sometimes been denied as being

Locke's view of man in the *Two Treatises* it is worth emphasizing how essential this conception of human nature is to the argument of the *Essay Concerning Human Understanding*. Either Locke was more schizophrenic with respect to his fundamental assumptions than even some interpreters have implied, or the relationship between the *Essay* and the *Two Treatises* is much closer than the compartmentalization of our discussions of philosophy and political theory has allowed us to recognize.

Locke not only presupposes man to be a free rational being, he also offers an account of 'reason' as an *activity*. He still uses the traditional language of the faculty of reason as a possession or property of the individual, but what Locke is really interested in showing is how, in practice, this property comes about. That is, how reason is produced through activity. 'All reasoning', Locke insists, is simply 'the labour of our thoughts', which 'requires pains and application' (1:2, 10; 3:6, 30). God has only furnished us with the natural materials, and, just as we must employ our 'faculties and powers industriously' in building houses or bridges, so, Locke argues, the employment of those powers of the mind (reason) is the only means by which we come to have knowledge (1:4, 12). 'We are born ignorant of everything', and therefore whatever we acquire as knowledge is the product of our 'labour, attention, and industry'. Indeed, in this passage from the *Conduct of the Understanding*, Locke employs the simile of someone who is content with a subsistence state of knowledge wherein he lives off 'the spontaneous product' that nature supplies to his senses, who he compares to the 'skilful' person who 'set[s] the mind to work' and through industry and 'labour in tillage' produces knowledge (*Works*, 2:384–5). It is true, there are some things of which we shall never have knowledge, no matter how diligently we reason but, Locke insists, if we 'employ all that industry and labour of thought' of which we are capable, 'all the great ends of morality and religion' will be 'well enough secured' to us to realize the purposes for which we were created (4:3, 6). Again, the discussion could be extended through references drawn from the *Essay*, but Locke's analogy between the labour, productivity and industrious employment of the individual's faculties in the *Two Treatises* and the terminology he uses to describe reason as an activity of the mind in the *Essay* is clear. In both works, those who labour industriously are the rational and productive members of society who contribute to the common good of all. Hence, as with labour, there is an ethical meaning attached to the concept of 'reason' as part of a theory of practical action.[7]

The question might be raised, how far can an individual be expected to go in acquiring such knowledge relying entirely upon his own labour? To what extent is he dependent upon the labour or knowledge of others? At this point I shall give a provisional answer to these questions, and return to them later as part of a more extended discussion of Locke's views on the relationship between religion and philosophy. The answer I propose to defend is that Locke believes every individual capable of employing his or her reason with sufficient industry to gain a knowledge of God and their moral duties, which describes 'the main end' of the argument of the *Essay*. The reasoning that underlies this belief is the same as that used by Locke in the *Two Treatises*, namely, that the egalitarianism of the obligations imposed upon mankind by God through natural law requires the presupposition that all individuals are capable of fulfilling these obligations through their own efforts without depending upon the will of any other individual. This does not, of course, rule out the possibility that individuals may help each other, and when he describes the institution of political society Locke speaks of the 'many conveniences' each individual enjoys in society that derive from 'the labour' and 'assistance' of other members of the society (II, 130). Is there a similar analogy to be drawn with respect to knowledge as the consequence of the social interdependency with others? The answer to this question, I am afraid, has to be yes and no. That is, there are some areas of knowledge – and here I am confining the discussion to the realm of practical action – in which we are unquestionably aided by the efforts of others, through the inventions and useful arts they supply to make our lives more comfortable. At the same time, however, the socialization process that accompanies life in society – the individual's education, formation of habits, trust in the opinions of others, and so forth – may and, Locke believes, generally do act as obstacles to the individual's reliance upon the industrious employment of his own reason, and hence to the fulfilment of *his* moral obligation as an individual.

In order to provide the foundation for a consideration of this point, let us recall two important Lockean assumptions from the discussion in Chapter 2. First, almost all the matters about which we think, speak and act lie outside the category of certain knowledge and within the realm of probabilities. Even if we were able to secure for ourselves through our own labour those few truths that do lie within the domain of knowledge, we should still be faced with an endless succession of probable judgements based on experience. If we did not rely upon the judgements and experiences of others to expand the scope of our actions, the latter would lie within a very narrow compass. Thus, within the world of probable knowledge, we have little choice but to depend upon the judgements of others. The result, according to Locke, is that these cumulative experiences and judgements exercise a significant influence upon the practical actions we take. In short, the individual's thinking is shaped by the particular configuration of collective experiences, manifest in the cultural and social practices of other members of his society, that constitute the social structure of that society.

The second assumption that plays an important role in the argument of the *Essay Concerning Human Understanding* is that there is a wide variety of opinions and behaviour among individuals, which, from the epistemological standpoint, may be viewed as the outcome of an almost infinite number of probable judgements made by individuals under different circumstances. These 'various and contrary choices that men make' do not supplant or alter in any respect 'the eternal law and nature of things' or our obligation to obey it, but they do render it difficult, practically speaking, for an individual to make his way through the myriad of opinions with which he is bombarded in order to discover the few truths of natural law (1:3, 6, 8–10, 12; 2:21, 54–7, 69; 4:4, 10). This is becuase these 'choices' made by others are attached to various practical interests, so that we encounter opinions in a context in which some particular opinions have a great deal of collective social force supporting their validity. Hence, in addition to the general fact of social life that 'custom settles habits of thinking in the understanding' and determines the will (2:33, 6), the individual must confront the opinions held by 'different sects of philosophy and religion' and political parties in his society (2:33, 18). If 'a covetous man's reasoning' so easily sets aside strong probabilities that cross his objective of obtaining money (4:20, 12), we can hardly be surprised if he and others who share his pursuit use their power and wealth to enforce those opinions that support and justify their actions, and to suppress those opinions that do not. It is always possible for an individual to 'favour the opinion that suits with his inclination or interest, and so stop from farther search' (4:20, 15), but it is also possible for others to encourage him to stop his search for knowledge because it may not agree with 'the common received opinions' of their party or sect. A survey of 'the partisans of most of the sects in the world', Locke argues, would show that most of them adhere to those opinions that give them 'credit, preferment, or protection in that society' (4:20, 17–18; cf. *ELN*, 127, 129, 135, 141). This is partly due to their laziness or to their economically constrained circumstances, but it is also the result of the fact that 'parties of men cram their tenets down all men's throats, whom they can get into their power, without permitting them to examine their truth or falsehood' (4:3, 20). Most of our opinions, according to Locke, we accept as being true 'because they assert their authority by the general consent and approval of men with whom we have social intercourse' (*ELN*, 143).

What the individual must confront in society, in other words, is the use of 'force without authority' which makes certain opinions appear to be knowledge. Whatever serves as the accepted orthodoxy, Locke notes, is merely 'the consent of private men' exhibited as the 'law of fashion'. These views are transmitted to children, and later they are reinforced by interests and inclinations. In this way, custom becomes the common judge, and it is extremely rare for an individual to choose to sacrifice the practical benefits attached to sociability in order to pursue his own reason in solitude or 'in constant disgrace and disrepute with his own particular society' (2:28, 12). As Locke repeatedly warns in his work on education, the tutor or parent must be constantly vigilant in protecting the child from developing bad habits, because habits and customs are the means by which ideas are cemented into an individual's mind. 'You cannot imagine of what force custom is', Locke declares; it 'prevails over everything' (*STCE*, § 14, 18, 38, 66). What this means, when applied to opinions, is that in adopting the commonly received truths of our society we are, in effect, 'putting our minds into the disposal of others' (4:12, 6). We have sacrificed our judgement to that of others, thereby forfeiting the very freedom and reason that define our being as intelligent agents.

It would be unrealistic for Locke to press this point to include all opinions, since he insists upon the interdependency of individuals and their natural need for social interaction. Thus, while it might always be preferable for an individual to rely upon his own reason, as a practical matter this will prove to be impossible. 'There are millions of truths that a man is not, or may not think himself concerned to know', and therefore 'it is not strange that the mind should give itself up to the common opinion' with respect to these matters. This is especially true when no important action follows from the individual's giving his assent to these opinions (4:20, 16). A distinction must be made between the action an individual takes in regard to those opinions and actions that are of relatively little concern, and what he does in relation to the matters of highest concernment to him. Since we know that religion and morality fall under the latter category, it follows that 'nothing can be so dangerous as principles thus taken up without questioning or examination; especially if they be such as concern morality' (4:12, 4; cf. 1:3, 22). We can now see clearly the strategic outlines of the *Essay Concerning Human Understanding*; for it is Locke's aim to demonstrate how, in general, but especially with respect to a knowledge of God and our moral duties, individuals can and must reason for themselves, without depending upon the opinions of others. I will take up in a moment the question of whether individuals can realize in practice the precepts Locke advances in the *Essay*; but, first, let me conclude this comparative discussion of that work and the *Two Treatises*.

I have argued that the fundamental assumptions that comprise Locke's theory of practical action, his assessment of the ends of that action in terms of morality and convenience, his definition of the natural powers of man that make such action possible, and his conception of the realization of both of these aspects of his theory within the existential boundaries of a society characterized by a plurality of interests and opinions, institutions that treat human beings as free rational agents, and so forth, provide the most important linkage between the arguments of the *Two Treatises of Government* and the *Essay Concerning Human Understanding*. Nevertheless, there is a difference in Locke's attitude towards society in these two works. Whereas the institution of political society represents a progressive step forward from the state of nature for Locke, he is much more ambivalent as to the positive virtues of society in the *Essay*. The reason for this ambivalence lies in the tremendous influence that custom, parties, sects and social groups exercise over the individual's thinking and his life. Much of this influence may be positive, but at least some of it, as it relates to a knowledge of religion and morality, is quite often negative and harmful. Practical action within the sphere of politics, if it secures the collective enforcement of natural law and the protection of the individual's temporal interests of life, liberty and property, has achieved all that can be expected of political action. But practical action within the larger sphere of morality, which for Locke includes certain basic precepts of religion (such as the worship of God, acts of charity and so forth), cannot be identified with or secured through collective action or the institution of society; rather, there are some matters of 'eternal concernment above the reach and extent of

politics and governments, which are . . . wholly between God and
me'. Thus, 'my private interest in another world' has no 'reference at
all to my governor or to my neighbour', and so cannot fall under the
authority of society's laws or opinions.[8] Notwithstanding the fact that
the care of every man's soul belongs exclusively to himself, and he
cannot allow another individual to serve as a representative for him in
matters of religion, we have seen that society does, in reality, step over
these boundaries and seek to impose upon individuals various beliefs
and practices pertaining to religion. Even when this imposition
involves no direct use of force or the instrument of government, the
socialization process to which everyone is subjected acts as a powerful
constraint upon the individual's thinking and action. In this respect, the
individual's membership in society is not an unalloyed good, because
there is no guarantee that social institutions will encourage the kinds
of practical action that are necessary for an individual to fulfil his
moral and religious obligations in those areas in which he has,
nevertheless, a purely personal responsibility. To put it simply,
society does not always feel itself compelled to promote those activities
that lead to virtue rather than to, say, the accumulation of wealth and
power, and when it does take a direct interest in securing 'the great
ends of religion and morality' it inescapably intrudes into a sphere in
which it has, and can have, no authority. In other words, because
Locke accepts as a general proposition that 'virtue and prosperity do
not often accompany one another' (*Works*, 6:148; cf. *STCE*, § 70, 94),
there is an inherent tension between the moral and religious
obligations laid upon the individual and the securement of temporal
advantages as the functional purpose of society at the heart of Locke's
theory of practical action.

The political theory in the *Two Treatises*, then, fits as a part into the
whole of 'moral philosophy which . . . comprehends religion too, or a
man's whole duty' (Journal, 6–10 April 1677, MS f.2). Since the *Essay*
is concerned with a knowledge of 'a man's whole duty', it, too, must
supply some guidelines with respect to religion. But how far can
philosophy go towards comprehending religion within its own
framework? It may be that society rarely encourages an individual to
use his own reason but, even supposing it did, what would be the non-
social or intrinsic limits of his employment of reason with respect to
his natural law obligations? There are a number of reasons why Locke
must supply an answer to this question in the *Essay*, not the least of
which is the need he feels to demarcate the boundaries between faith
and reason. I have discussed elsewhere some of the epistemological

dimensions of this problem; here I wish to focus upon the implications of Locke's answer as it relates to his theory of practical action.[9] This will lead us to a consideration of such issues as the ideological role of Christianity, the social meaning of the epistemological distinction between reason and revelation, and the importance of religion to Locke's political thought.

Let us begin by casting doubt upon the realization of the ideal of reason or the empirical existence of rational man as described by Locke in the *Essay*. This is not an unfair tactic, for two reasons. First, because Locke himself emphasizes the vast ocean of doubts and uncertainties that surround our lives and the very small province within which reason is able to supply us with certain knowledge. In the best of circumstances, reason cannot, as a general rule, free itself from probable judgements, and the latter are, under a wide variety of conditions, liable to error. Even as an activity of the mind, therefore, reason is not quite the ideal it sometimes appears to be in the *Essay* when its definitional properties are being discussed. This point is still more obvious when reason is considered as a practical activity within a social context, for even when reason is properly employed in weighing contending probabilities the actual outcome may nevertheless be determined by interest, inclination, and the pressure exerted by various social forces. Locke, therefore, can hardly be accused of failing to recognize the practical difficulties attached to the realization of the model of reasoning he describes in the *Essay*. This fact, in turn, might prompt *us* to ask what kind of ideal Locke is presenting in that work. The answer, I suggest, is that while Locke believes that all individuals can use their reason in the manner he outlines, in the sense that they possess the capacity to do so, he is fully aware of the fact that only a few individuals actually do so. This is not an unimportant point since it supplies some empirical grounding for his epistemological argument. What is crucial, however, is that everyone sees that there is a moral ideal of reason according to which they ought to govern their lives, and in terms of which their own ontological status as free rational individuals is defined. It makes a considerable difference, whether we assume, as most commentators on the *Essay* have done, that Locke is primarily interested in supplying us with an empirical description of how the mind actually works, or whether we assume that he is offering us a moral portrait of ourselves which, though empirically grounded, is justified in terms of the way in which God has created us and the external world around us. If reason is viewed from the first perspective, we are inevitably led, in part, by the realism of Locke's own remarks in the *Essay*, to the conclusion that it is a flawed ideal, and that Locke must have intended his work as a defence and vindication of those few individuals who realize or come close to realizing it in practice. From here it is a relatively small step to the employment of 'reason' as an ideological weapon in defence of the activities of a particular social élite. If, on the other hand, reason signifies moral capacity, the fact that individuals are misled by passion or interest is no more an argument against the ideal of reason in the *Essay* than it is an argument against the description of man in the state of nature in the *Two Treatises*, where the same inclinations and interests are operative features of human existence. In short, the principle of moral egalitarianism is essential to Locke's argument in both works.

The second reason we may be permitted to doubt the existence of rational man is that Locke is at some pains to list in the *Essay* all those factors that inhibit the social appearance of such an individual. We need not rely upon either the epistemological or the general social constraints upon reason in order to see why reason is seriously limited in practice; Locke offers specific examples of persons and social groups who fail to put into practice the moral ideal of reason. If, therefore, we are going to move from the plane of moral argument to empirical description with respect to reason, these examples have to be examined more carefully than they generally have been. What one finds in these examples is not a simple identification of reason with a particular social class. On the contrary, Locke is egalitarian in his critical remarks, citing instances that cut across the class lines of his society. Moreover, it is precisely Locke's recognition of the limited social applicability of reason as a philosophical ideal that reinforces his own personal and intellectual commitment to the importance of religion as 'that noble study which is every man's duty'.

In the chapter on wrong assent, or error, Locke refers to those

who have not the convenience or opportunity to make experiments and observations themselves, tending to the proof of any proposition; nor likewise the convenience to inquire into, and collect the testimonies of others: and in this state are the greatest part of mankind, who are given up to labour, and enslaved to the necessity of their mean condition, whose lives are worn out only in the provisions for living. These men's opportunity of knowledge and inquiry are commonly as narrow as their fortunes . . . It is not to be expected that a man who drudges on, all his life, in a laborious trade, should be more knowing in the variety of things done in the world than a packhorse, who is driven constantly forwards and backwards in a narrow lane and dirty road, only to market, should be skilled in the geography of the country. (4:20, 2)

In addition to those who, according to this graphic description, can be considered to be members of the labouring class, 'there are others whose largeness of fortune would plentifully enough supply books, and other requisites for clearing of doubts, and discovering of truth: but they are cooped in close, by the laws of their countries'. Although 'they may seem high and great' when compared to the 'poor and wretched labourers', in fact their understandings are as 'enslaved' and 'confined to narrowness of thought' as are those of members of the working class (4:20, 4; cf. 1:4, 12).

Still others, engaged in the 'hot pursuit of pleasure, or constant drudgery in business,' though 'they have riches and leisure enough' to pursue knowledge, choose not to use their natural abilities to reason. 'How men, whose plentiful fortunes allow them leisure to improve their understandings, can satisfy themselves with a lazy ignorance', Locke exclaims, 'I cannot tell: but methinks they have a low opinion of their souls, who lay out all their incomes in provisions for the body, and employ none of it to procure the means and helps of knowledge.' The fact that by 'birth and fortune' these individuals 'call themselves gentlemen' does not entitle them to be thought rational men, when it is plain that they are 'ignorant in things they are concerned to know'. Thus, Locke concludes, 'most men, even of those that might do otherwise, pass their lives without an acquaintance with, much less a rational assent to, probabilities they are concerned to know' (4:20, 6).

In other words, it is not simply the members of one particular social class – the working class – who fail to live up to Locke's model of the rational man, but 'most men' of *all* social classes in seventeenth-century England. It is true that Locke wrote the *Essay* for an educated audience, most members of which we can assume were gentlemen; yet he tells us that he has taken great pains to make his work 'intelligible to all sorts of readers'. Locke's metaphors in the Epistle to the Reader confirm this appeal, on the one hand, to the country gentleman engaged in 'hawking and hunting' and, on the other, to the individual 'who has raised himself above the alms-basket' (Epistle to the Reader, pp. 7–12). However, the problem is not that of determining who the majority of the readers of the *Essay* were but, rather, of deciding what meaning ought to be attributed to the fact that Locke has suggested a pattern of life and reasoning that he knows most individuals in his society do not live up to. The transformation of a moral critique of everyone who fails to conform to the model of rational man into a defence of a particular social class, of country gentlemen, and an attack upon the rationality of another social class, the labourers, is not only a misreading of Locke's intentions; it also represents a fundamental misunderstanding of the kind of book the *Essay Concerning Human Understanding* is. Obviously, Locke was no more free of certain prejudices and class attitudes than any of us is and I am not suggesting that we substitute a conception of him as a classless intellectual for an empirically definite location of his position within the class-structured society of seventeenth-century England. The assertion of moral or political egalitarianism is patently no guarantee whatsoever that social institutions do or will attempt to realize the presuppositions upon which such an assertion rests. But my point is precisely that Locke understood this. He clearly saw the disparities between the position he wished to defend in the *Essay* and what individuals in his society did. This recognition, I am arguing, provides, in itself, no warrant for dismissing the importance of his assertion of moral egalitarianism as the axis from which the argument of the *Essay* is to be interpreted, merely because, on the basis of empirical knowledge of Locke's society, we can see, as he could, that the programmatic recommendations of the *Essay* were not translated into actual practice.

The second point to be noted with regard to the passages cited above is that ignorance is not all of one kind. It may be that 'the greatest part of men, having much to do to get the means of living, are not in a condition' to discover those opinions that depend upon 'learned and laborious inquiries'. To be sure, this reflects a certain kind of ignorance, especially of those 'propositions that, in the societies of men, are judged of the greatest moment' (4:20, 2). But are these propositions of 'the greatest moment'? Locke does not think so, nor does he believe that those matters that are of greatest concern depend upon 'learned and laborious inquiries'. The working class is clearly the victim of ignorance by virtue of its economic condition, but it matters to Locke that it is ignorance of some but not of all subjects. When Locke criticizes those of leisure and wealth, the point he emphasizes is not the amount of their knowledge about the affairs of society relative to that of labourers, but the fact that they do not have any regard for their souls, nor do they 'ever think of a future state, and their concernment in it'. A man may be rational in handling his business affairs, Locke argues, without having the slightest idea of what he should do about the much more important matters of religion and morality. Hence 'men of lower condition, who surpass them in knowledge' concerning these questions have a better claim to be considered 'rational' beings (4:20, 6). 'Everyone,' Locke writes, 'in his private affairs, uses some sort of reasoning . . . enough to denominate him reasonable. But the mistake is, that he that is found reasonable in one thing, is concluded to be so in' everything, and this is patently not true (*Works*, 2:337).

In other words, if we define rationality formally as the capacity to reason, Locke defends the egalitarian position as part of his moral conception of the individual. If, on the other hand, we attempt a definition of substantive rationality, for Locke most of this substantive content is comprised of moral or religious beliefs, and these, too, are to be found in all types of individual, irrespective of social status. The kind of knowledge possessed by members of the upper social classes which is useful in the acquisition of 'a stock of riches' not only stands on the lowest plane within Locke's conception of ethical behaviour, but it may also actually inhibit these individuals from gaining the kind of knowledge they ought to possess. If there is a model of differential reason in Locke's writings, therefore, it does not reflect a division between social classes as Macpherson suggests but, rather, a distinction relating to the type of knowledge a rational individual is most concerned to have. Locke's position on the relative importance of these two aspects of a substantive definition of rationality is very clear, and it does not translate into a direct correspondence to the class divisions as they existed in his society.

But, if Locke does not deal with the flawed ideal of rational man as a defence of a particular social élite's claim to rationality, how does he respond to the fact that most individuals do not follow his prescribed course of reasoning? For, if there were no means of salvaging his assertion of moral egalitarianism from the realism of the critique he provides in the *Essay*, the latter might very well be read as a work of moral despair. Yet Locke did not choose the path of scepticism as a way out of the situation he described. Instead, he reasserts the importance of religion and reminds the reader of the main end of the *Essay*. 'What shall we say, then?' he asks, following his description of the labouring class. 'Are the greatest part of mankind, by the necessity of their condition, subjected to unavoidable ignorance in those things which are of greatest importance to them?' Locke replies that 'no man is so wholly taken up with the attendance on the means of living, as to have no spare time at all to think of his soul, and inform himself in matters of religion' (4:20, 3). Locke refuses to accept that anyone is 'so enslaved to the necessities of life' as to be unable to employ their faculties in the pursuit of that knowledge they are most concerned to have.

> Everyone has a concern in a future life, which he is bound to look after. This engages his thoughts in religion . . . men, therefore, cannot be excused from understanding the words, and framing the general notions relating to religion, right.

Locke goes on in this passage to speak of 'very mean people, who have raised their minds to a great sense and understanding of religion', and have thereby become 'rational creatures and christians'. For, Locke argues, no one who is ignorant of the fundamental principles of religion can truly be thought a rational person. 'I see no reason', he declares, why it should be 'concluded that the meaner sort of people must give themselves up to brutish stupidity in the things of their nearest concernment' – their moral duties and the salvation of their souls. If this precept applies to them, Locke argues, it obviously must apply with greater force to those who possess more leisure time than do members of the working class (*Works*, 2:342–3).

This assertion of moral egalitarianism as an aspect of Locke's theory of knowledge, where the latter is defined in relation to religion and morality, thus places all individuals in an epistemological state of nature, where differences of birth, fortune, occupation, political power and even education do not matter. What is important is the right use an individual makes of his natural abilities to discover those few essential truths of religion that he is capable of knowing. Those who do so are 'rational creatures', while those who do not are not 'rational' in the most meaningful sense, whatever their social condition. Not only is this view consistent with and supportive of Locke's assertion of moral egalitarianism in the *Two Treatises*, but it is also restated as a basic feature of Locke's argument in the *Letter Concerning Toleration*. There he insists that the care of every man's soul is wholly his own responsibility, that he has an indispensable obligation to exercise his judgement with respect to matters of religion, and that his association with others in a particular church depends entirely upon his own personal consent. (There has never been any doubt that, so far as joining a church is concerned, Locke means to give *every* individual the power to consent as a conscious act of membership, but he employs exactly the same phraseology in the *Two Treatises* with respect to joining civil society.)

This epistemological/moral presupposition is absolutely necessary to the structure of Locke's argument because (1) he insists that God has laid upon every individual a natural law obligation to worship Him, and this duty could only be fulfilled if human beings possess the capacity to fulfil it. No contingent social circumstances or accidents of birth can be permitted to set aside or suspend this natural law obligation (4:20, 3). Indeed, it is precisely in terms of this obligation that it can be claimed that each individual has a natural right to toleration. (2) If it were once conceded that *any* individual could claim superiority or jurisdiction over another by virtue of his knowledge and/or social position, this would allow some individuals to shift the responsibility for their eternal fate into the hands of other men. Locke refuses to sanction such an action. No one can authorize another person to act for him in matters of religion. On the contrary, he steadfastly insists that

> Those things that every man ought sincerely to inquire into himself, and by meditation, study, search, and his own endeavours, attain the knowledge of, cannot be looked upon as the peculiar profession of any one sort of men. (*Works*, 5:25)[10]

And (3) it cannot be supposed that God created the world in such a way that the majority of human beings would be disadvantaged through no fault of their own in their efforts to obey His commandments. God, Locke argues, would not do anything to subvert His own workmanship (4:18, 5). 'I cannot imagine', Locke wrote, 'that God . . . would put poor men . . . under almost an absolute necessity of sinning perpetually against Him' (Journal, 20 March 1678, MS f.3; *Works*, 6:6). On the contrary, 'God, who knows our frailty . . . requires of us no more than we are able to do' (2:21, 53). For Locke, 'ought' always implies 'can', in reference to our natural duties of religion or morality. In other words, the working class cannot be supposed to exist in a state of ignorance of their moral and religious duties simply as a consequence of their economic condition because, in the last analysis, this fact would reflect negatively upon the character of an omniscient Deity.

A very different view is put forward by Macpherson. According to him, Locke believed that 'the members of the labouring class are in too low a position to be capable of a rational life – that is, capable of regulating their lives by those moral principles Locke supposed were given by reason'. Since 'the greatest part of mankind, Locke concludes, cannot be left to the guidance of the law of nature or law of reason, they are not capable of drawing rules of conduct from it'. Quite obviously, this fact, if true, would constitute a very wide breach in Locke's theory of practical action. And, in order to shore up that theory, Macpherson asserts, Locke wrote *The Reasonableness of Christianity*, with the object of defending 'a few simple articles of belief "that the labouring and illiterate man may comprehend"'. In this way, religion could be employed as the instrument of social cohesion, securing obedience from individuals who were 'incapable of following a rationalist ethic . . . without supernatural sanctions'.[11] On the basis of this distinction between 'a rationalist ethic' and a belief in a 'supernatural' religion, Macpherson argues that Locke assumed the existence of a differential rationality in individuals such that when he 'looked at his own society he saw two classes with different rights and different rationality'.[12]

Macpherson appears to believe that Locke unquestionably accepted for himself the 'rationalist ethic' while recommending supernatural religion as a sop to lesser minds. In the light of all that Locke says concerning his own religious convictions, this is a patently ridiculous assumption.[13] But, if Locke himself subscribes to the few simple articles of faith he outlines in *The Reasonableness of Christianity*, and, moreover, if he does so because he knows that, regardless of the amount of knowledge a rational individual might accumulate, his fate rests, ultimately, upon that simple faith, what grounds have we for attributing to Locke a condescending attitude towards others who are in the same condition with respect to their salvation as he is? Or we could reverse the question. Suppose *no one* is able to provide for himself by means of a rationalist ethic, what, then, becomes of Macpherson's differential rationality? In other words, Locke not only argues that everyone needs faith, revelation and Christianity, whatever their social position or claims to rationality, he also argues that no amount of reason can supply an adequate standard of 'ethics'.

Yet Locke did not write *The Reasonableness of Christianity* simply to affirm his personal faith in Christianity, nor to give a pious endorsement to the moral equality of individuals. His aims are much more polemical and specific. Macpherson maintains that the *Reasonableness* is not 'a plea for a simple rationalist ethical religion to replace the disputations of the theologians'.[14] Since Locke is not arguing for a 'rationalist religion' at all, but one derived from revelation, we may set aside the first part of Macpherson's statement. That Locke was writing against the disputations of theologians, however, there can be no doubt. Yet they constitute only half of his opponents in the *Reasonableness*; Locke is also concerned to dismiss the efforts of philosophers – and, indeed, of all wise and learned men whatsoever – who have in any way supposed that their 'unassisted reason' could supply an ethical standard for mankind. *The Reasonableness of Christianity*, in short, is a sustained polemical attack upon the presumptuousness of philosophy and a priest-dominated theology for having arrogated to themselves the authority to instruct mankind in matters for which they have neither the authority nor the adequate knowledge. Far from providing a socially defensible assignment of a rationalistic ethic to the upper class, Locke's work is a relentless critique of the clergy, the universities, and any social group in his society who would advance such claims on their own behalf. Against such high-handed endeavours, Locke defends, as his own position, the simplicity of Christianity, and the intentions of God in having addressed its basic teachings to the poor rather than to any other group of human beings.

It should be noted at the outset that, unlike many of Locke's other works, *The Reasonableness* is set within the basic framework of historical time. That is, Locke's purpose is to show why individuals, despite having been created by God, need the doctrine of Christianity. Of course, in the theological sense, this need is traceable to the fall of Adam from a state of grace. But for several thousand years mankind lived under the Law of Moses and the Old Testament. So the more specific question, raised by Locke, is how Jesus' mission is to be viewed in its historical sense. That is, in relation to the actual life of man prior to his coming to earth as the messenger of God. Locke first establishes that God created man as 'a rational creature' and 'required him to [live] by the law of reason . . . or as it is called, of nature'. This law 'was suitable to his nature', but, even so, he did not always follow it. And, Locke asks, 'if rational creatures will not live up to the rule of their reason, who shall excuse them'? The law of reason cannot simply be set aside on one point and not on another, for 'where will you stop' in obviating the fulfilment of its obligations? On the other hand, if obedience is commanded, and these demands are not met, then are not the trangressors doomed to death by their sin? Locke answers that God recognizes the frailty of human reason, and therefore has allowed us to substitute faith for complete obedience to His commands. This does not mean that we are relieved from our obligations of reason and obedience; we still must seek to perform good works. But it does mean that faith and sincere belief are the instruments whereby we overcome the defects of reason and action in God's eyes. It was to deliver this message to mankind that He sent His son into the world (*Works*, 6:11–16, 110–13).

Much of the *Reasonableness* is, of course, taken up with presenting the scriptural passages that support this theological position. However, Locke also turns to the historical record of mankind prior to Christ's appearance in order to drive home the polemical implications of his reading of the Bible. What he is especially interested in showing is the desperate and miserable state human beings were in during that period as a consequence of their dependence upon either priests or philosophers for their moral guidance. The former filled men's heads 'with false notions of the Deity, and their worship with foolish rites', so that, 'in this state of darkness and ignorance of the true God, vice and superstition held the world'. These theologians, in effect, banished reason from religion, and exercised their political and religious authority over the masses to further their own ambitious and greedy ends. It is true that philosophers, as 'the rational and thinking part of mankind', when they directed their inquiries towards God could discover His existence, 'but if they acknowledged and worshipped him, it was only in their own minds'. Because they 'kept this truth locked up in their own breasts as a secret . . . [reason] had never authority enough to prevail on the multitude' (*Works*, 6:135–6). Locke makes two arguments against the rule of philosophy: first, philosophers never discovered all the necessary precepts of morality; and, even if they had done so, they had no authority to compel belief in such truths.

'Unassisted reason', Locke declares, never established 'morality in all its parts, upon its true foundation, with a clear and convincing light . . . We see how unsuccessful in this the attempts of philosophers were before our Saviour's time.' It is 'very visible . . . how short their several systems came of the perfection of a true and complete morality' (*Works*, 6:139). Hence

> it is plain, in fact, that human reason unassisted failed men in its great and proper business of morality . . . And he that shall collect all the moral rules of the philosophers, and compare them with those contained in the New Testament, will find them to come short of the morality delivered by our Saviour, and taught by his apostles;

a college made up, for the most part, of ignorant, but inspired fishermen. (*Works*, 6:140)

It is evident from these remarks that Locke associates the failure of human reason with the unsuccessful attempts of philosophers to develop a rationalist ethic. These attempts, however, represent the *best* effort of man to realize this objective and, if the most educated and learned individuals failed in this respect, what warrant is there for Macpherson to assume that members of the propertied classes in seventeenth-century England, merely by virtue of their ownership of property, were supposed by Locke to be in possession of something that his reading of history demonstrated that no one ever possessed? To imagine that Locke preferred the efforts of country gentlemen – who are subjected to a sharp critique in the *Essay Concerning Human Understanding* – to those of 'the studious and thinking philosophers' of whom he is speaking in the *Reasonableness* is ludicrous (*Works*, 6:143).

Even if we supposed that someone 'had gathered the moral sayings from all the sages in the world', Locke asks, what authority would such a moral system have? 'The opinion of this or that philosopher was of no authority.' In order to attain 'the force of a law' morality must be transmitted, according to Locke, through someone who 'comes with authority from God, to deliver his will and commands to the world . . . Such a law of morality Jesus Christ hath given us in the New Testament . . . by revelation.' Moreover, this revealed morality is 'conformable to that of reason, but the truth and obligation of its precepts have their force, and are put past doubt to us, by the evidence of his mission'. This is, of course, the central point of the *Reasonableness* – 'morality has a sure standard, that revelation vouches, and reason cannot gainsay, nor question', provided we place our reliance upon the New Testament Scriptures, *and nowhere else* (*Works*, 6:141–3). Locke's argument is not merely that we all are, in some sense, better off adhering to the precepts of Christianity than to anything else, as Macpherson would have us believe.[15] Rather, Locke's point is that all of mankind needed this revelation in order for morality to assume the force of a *law* to which we are all equally subject.[16] Since this could be achieved by no other means than through the historical mission of Jesus, the ability of 'fundamental Christian doctrine to satisfy men of higher capacities' can hardly be regarded by Locke as being 'only a secondary advantage' in respect of their knowledge, as Macpherson suggests.

That Christianity is 'a religion suited to vulgar capacities', and is, therefore, addressed to the greatest part of mankind who are poor or illiterate is not the issue in dispute. The question is, what does this fact mean to Locke? Macpherson reads Locke's statement as a negative reflection upon the rationality of the labouring class. But this is not the point of Locke's argument in *The Reasonableness*. It is, rather, that the ability of Christianity to appeal to all understandings, even the lowest, is a positive feature of Christianity compared to other systems of morality. Not only is this appeal part of its 'reasonableness' but, Locke argues, it also reflects the wisdom and mercy of God that He should have designed human beings – even members of the working class – with those capacities sufficient to know and follow His dictates. Locke is not complaining because the labouring class is unable to follow long trains of reasoning; he is defending Christianity because it has made a rational system of morality available to everyone through revelation, and this is one of its primary virtues.

When Locke first raises the issue of the comparative advantage of an approach to morality that depends upon 'the long and sometimes intricate deductions of reason' versus 'one manifestly sent from God, and coming with visible authority from him', it is, as we have already seen, within the general context of his argument for the superiority of the latter over the former. That is, revelation over reason, the Bible over philosophy, and so on. Hence, when Locke writes that 'the greatest part of mankind have neither leisure to weigh; nor, for want of education and use, skill to judge of . . . such trains of reasoning' as might be required by the rationalist approach to morality, this statement is followed by Locke's remark about 'how unsuccessful in this the attempts of philosophers were' (*Works*, 6:139). In other words, Locke is neither singling out the mass of mankind with respect to their inability to follow the intricate deductions of reason, since even philosophers have failed in this enterprise, nor is Locke recommending a morality based upon such an approach, so that he can hardly be condemning the mass of mankind for not possessing it. Later, after again remarking upon the failure of philosophy, Locke writes that even if we supposed that philosophy could supply a system of 'ethics in a science like mathematics, in every part demonstrable', still this would not be suitable 'to man in this imperfect state'. This is because 'the greatest part of mankind want leisure or capacity for demonstration' which involves 'a train of proofs'. Thus, 'you may as soon hope to have all the day-labourers and tradesmen, the spinsters and dairy-maids, perfect mathematicians, as to have them perfect in ethics this way'. Before we conclude that this represents a derogatory reflection upon labourers and tradesmen, we should put into the equation the fact that Locke did not want them to become mathematicians, nor did he hold the latter in high regard, any more than philosophers, with respect to the question of ethics.

We can see what Locke is getting at when he reflects – still hypothetically, since he is not, as Macpherson assumes, referring to an actually existing system of rationalist ethics – that 'were all the duties of human life clearly demonstrated . . . that method of teaching would be thought proper only for a few, who had much leisure, improved understandings, and were used to abstract reasonings' (*Works*, 6:146). Now, the question is, why would God have created individuals lacking the abilities to follow the long trains of reasoning demanded by such an ethics? What is the point of commanding obedience from everyone when only a few with leisure are able to gain a knowledge of these commands? Locke replies that this is not the image of God to which he subscribes. Rather, the Deity, considering the frailty of man's reason, designed His religion to suit the 'vulgar capacities, and the state of mankind in this world, destined to labour'. Hence the basic tenets of belief required by Christianity, as defined by Locke, 'are articles that the labouring and illiterate man may comprehend'. So that, in effecting a harmonious relationship between the workmanship of His creation, the rules of ethical conduct, and the specific requirements attached to the worship of God, it appears to Locke that 'God seems herein to have consulted the poor of this world, and the bulk of mankind'. If we are to read Locke's comments as a negative reflection upon those 'destined to labour', we might as well read them as a negative reflection upon God in addressing himself primarily to these individuals.

Locke, however, is defending both his conception of God and the simplicity of his definition of Christianity in relation to the mass of mankind against 'the writers and wranglers in religion' who 'fill it with niceties, and dress it up with notions . . . as if there were no way into the church, but through the academy or lyceum'. If 'the greatest part of mankind have not leisure for learning and logic, and superfine distinctions of the schools', so much the better for them! This is not, *pace* Macpherson, a critique of the rationality of the masses, but an attack on the 'superfine distinctions of the schools' which are both unnecessary and detrimental to the advancement of Christianity, from Locke's standpoint (*Works*, 6:157). Locke had made the same point in the *Essay*, condemning the 'logical niceties' and 'empty speculations' of the learned commentators on the Bible to the extent of having 'destroyed' or 'rendered useless' the simple truths contained in that work. And, he asks, 'doth it not often happen, that a man of an ordinary capacity, very well understands a text . . . that he reads, till he consults an expositor' (3:10, 12)? If the labourer does not deal in 'sublime notions' or 'mysterious reasoning' such 'as the notions and language that the books and disputes of religion are filled with', this can hardly be counted a damaging indictment of the labourer. It is the 'mysterious reasoning' of theologians and schoolmen Locke is condemning in this comparison, not the reason or lack of it in the labourer. He remarks, rather caustically, that 'had God intended that none but the learned scribe, the disputer, or wise of this world, should be christians, or be saved', then He would have promulgated a religion 'filled with speculations and niceties, obscure terms, and abstract notions', such as those individuals who depend upon trains of reasoning are used to. Instead, those men 'are rather shut out from the simplicity of the gospel, to make way for those poor, ignorant, illiterate' persons to whom Christ preached. In fact, it was precisely the 'business of his mission' to preach to the poor (*Works*, 6:157–8). Not surprisingly, he chose 'a company of illiterate men' to be his Apostles. Locke's point is that Christianity 'suits the lowest capacities of reasonable creatures' (NB: they *are* 'reasonable') and this is one of its best features (*Works*, 6:147). Moreover, 'it is plain that the teaching of men philosophy was no part of the design of divine revelation' (*Works*, 7:xx).[17]

In other words, it is not merely the fact that God consulted the poor, that he sent His son to preach to the poor, and that Jesus chose poor fishermen to be his chief spokesmen, but the implication of this entire argument is that these actions reflect the wisdom of God and the goodness of His intentions, the superiority of Christianity to rational approaches to ethics, the purpose of Christ's historical mission, and the sincerity and truth of the testimony of the Apostles as the authors of the New Testament. There is simply no room in the structure of this argument for Locke suddenly to insert into it the kind of wholesale condemnation of the poor labouring class that Macpherson suggests. On the contrary, their existential condition is actually a very important part of Locke's *positive* defence of Christianity in the *Reasonableness*. Macpherson's twisting of Locke's meaning in the text is so patently obvious that the infrequency of comments upon it in the secondary literature can only be taken as an indication of how rarely interpreters of Locke's political thought pay any attention at all to *The*

Reasonableness of Christianity. Moreover, from a purely political standpoint, it is obvious that neither the *Two Treatises* nor *The Reasonableness of Christianity* was written to express the ideas or the interests of a propertied oligarchy in Locke's society. On the contrary, both works – and, one may add, the *Letter Concerning Toleration* – express the beliefs and political perspective of a minority of political and religious dissidents in Restoration England.

On a more general level I have tried to demonstrate that there is a consistently expressed set of presuppositions that comprise Locke's theory of practical action, and that these are to be found not only in the *Two Treatises*, but also in the *Essay Concerning Human Understanding*, the *Letter Concerning Toleration*, the *Reasonableness of Christianity*, and in *Some Thoughts Concerning Education*. The most important of these presuppositions is that all individuals possess the capacity and the knowledge to engage in the practical action necessary to lead moral lives and to fulfil their religious obligations, and they must, therefore, be provided with the social institutions that make it possible for them to execute these actions.

Finally, let us turn to the third problem area – Locke's apparent drift towards political conservatism following the Glorious Revolution. Did Locke grow more politically conservative during the last fifteen years of his life? I think the answer to this question has to be a qualified yes. It makes some difference how the question is phrased, because there is no warrant for concluding that Locke repudiated the political views expressed in the *Two Treatises*. On the contrary, he devoted some effort to revising that text for publication in two further editions during that period, and none of these revisions involves any modification of the radical political ideas contained in that work. At the same time, however, Locke was not anxious to have these political ideas applied to the case of Ireland in its struggle with the English government, as his friend William Molyneaux suggested they might be.[18] It seems clear that the revolution Shaftesbury planned, and for which the *Two Treatises* provided the justification, would have developed along more radical lines, had it been successful, than the one which, in 1689, allowed Locke to return to England. The Glorious Revolution did not achieve all the political objectives Locke might have hoped for, but he was generally satisfied with its outcome, and he certainly abandoned the activity of plotting a new revolution, which had occupied much of his life during the previous decade. In relation to that standard, it is impossible not to conclude that Locke became more politically conservative after 1690.

The real issue, however, seems to lie on the plane of the agreement of ideas as they appear in various works written by Locke. Even if, as I have argued, there is a set of consistently held moral assumptions expressed in these writings, still Locke's policy recommendations as a Commissioner on the Board of Trade and his economic writings evince a rather callous attitude towards the plight of the economically disadvantaged members of his society. While I do not think Locke's viewpoint is quite as extreme as it has sometimes been portrayed in the secondary literature, there is, nevertheless, a substantial core of truth to the accusation of his conservatism as applied to matters of economic policy. In one sense, this fact is not so surprising, for the radical dimensions of Locke's thought are rooted in the areas of religion and morality. Locke's statements about equality, natural rights, freedom and rationality are uncompromising and absolute when they flow directly from his religious beliefs. These propositions inform his political theory in so far as political life must be structured according to the boundaries established by the Law of Nature. Because political theory rests in part upon the assumptions of moral philosophy, this connection with the radicalism of Locke's thought as an interpretation of natural law cannot be severed. Only one part of political theory, however, deals with natural rights, the origins of political power, and the Law of Nature. The other part of politics concerns prudential matters, such as the skill of administering government, reconciling the various interests of individuals, and making decisions that contribute to the prosperity and security of one's country. But, as Locke observes,

> the ways of attaining . . . the management of trade, the employment of the poor, and all the other things that belong to the administration of the public . . . are so many, so various, and so changeable, according to the mutable state of men and things in this world, that it is not strange if a very small part of this consists in book-learning. (*Works*, 9:308–9)

Rather, these subjects are best learned from experience, and reflect judgements of probability based upon that experience.

In other words, the further one moves away from the province of natural law towards the realm of prudential action, which deals with 'conveniences' rather than with rights, the further away one moves from the radical dimensions of Locke's thought. And, except for 'true notions of . . . property', which fall within the moral parameters of political philosophy, virtually *all* matters of economic policy are, for Locke, questions of prudential judgement. As the citation above indicates, this was certainly his attitude towards the management of trade and the employment of the poor, which are the main subjects discussed in Locke's economic writings.

In his *Some Considerations of the Consequences of Lowering the Rate of Interest, and Raising the Value of Money*, Locke's primary concern is to relate these 'consequences' to the subject of trade; that is, whether the advancement of trade would be helped or hindered by a revaluation of the pound and/or a lower rate of interest. The question is, what is the relationship between the value of money and its circulation and trade? There is no need to summarize here Locke's argument in the *Considerations*. Suffice it to say that the amount of money in circulation and the speed with which it circulates throughout the economy are the crucial factors, according to Locke, that determine how 'the wheels of trade' are driven by money. Within this framework, there is no place for any extended discussion of the labouring class, because 'the labourer's share, being seldom more than a bare subsistence' (*Works*, 4:71), they can be said to live generally 'from hand to mouth' (*Works*, 4:23–4). That is, the working class spends the money it receives as wages to buy subsistence goods; their money is in constant circulation within the economy. What Locke is interested in uncovering, however, are the factors that drain off money from this process of circulation into 'standing pools', where it can no longer operate to the advantage of trade and hence to the increase of the nation's wealth (*Works*, 4:21). It is obvious that the labouring class can be omitted from this discussion since nothing they do in the normal course of economic activity creates any disruption with respect to the amount or rapidity of circulation of money. Indeed, the labourer is not even a participant in 'the usual struggle and contest . . . between the landed man and the merchant'. Only in the exceptional circumstance in which 'the mal-administration' of government causes 'some common and great distress' that threatens the labourer's subsistence will members of this class resort to armed force and jeopardize the economic well-being of the other classes in society (*Works*, 4:71). Barring that occurrence, the labouring class does not enter directly into a discussion of the prudential matters of economic policy Locke is considering in his work.

We may feel that a defence of the moral, religious and political rights of the greatest part of mankind or the majority within society, on the one hand, and their exclusion from the discussion of economic policy as administered by the government, on the other, reflects, if not a direct contradiction, at least a tenuous compartmentalization of attitudes towards the same set of individuals. We may even decide, on the basis of the hierarchical ordering of values that inform our political perspective, to interpret the former set of propositions as providing an ideological defence for the refusal by Locke and those who shared his viewpoint in seventeenth-century English society to take political action that would have improved or recast the role of the labourer in that society. I will return to this point in a moment, but if this argument is to be made it should be made in such a way that it does not depend upon a total disregard for Locke's intentions and *his* ordering of values, the meaning of the text, or upon a reductionist levelling of the structure of his thought to the single-minded defence of capitalist exploitation. It is possible to heed these interpretative admonitions, and also to criticize the ideological limitations of Locke's political theory.

Perhaps the single piece of writing in Locke's corpus that presents the most serious challenge to the separability of the moral and prudential aspects of his political thought is the policy memorandum Locke wrote as a member of the Board of Trade discussing what to do about the employment of the poor in England. Again, I shall not attempt a summary of the argument of that document here, but it suggests, among other things, that beggars be seized and sent to seaports 'to be kept at hard labour' until such time as they can be impressed into the navy where they will serve as seamen for three years 'under strict discipline'. Indigent females would be put to work in a house of correction, as would vagabond children. The unemployed poor who refuse to accept work at wages below the prevailing standard would either be impressed into the navy or sent to a house of correction. Children from the ages of 3 to 14 would be placed in a working school, allowing mothers to leave home to find work. The children would subsist on bread and 'a little warm water-gruel', and could be put to work in the manufacture of woollens. At the age of 14 the boys could serve as apprentices in various trades. The discipline – including punishment by whipping – the food, housing conditions, working conditions and health considerations are described in Locke's policy recommendation in terms that are, to put it mildly, grim. Indeed, that is too mild a word, for even after allowances have been made for the historical context it is still an oppressive and depressing atmosphere that pervades his memorandum.

The causes of poverty, according to Locke, are not to be found in the scarcity of provisions or the want of employment but, rather, in 'the relaxation of discipline and corruption of manners' that especially afflict the poor. Idleness, debauchery in alehouses, resistance in the form of a refusal of the poor to work under virtually any conditions offered them are qualities that must be ruthlessly stamped out. The coercive social force underlying Locke's observation that an individual must accept whatever rate of wages is offered him by an employer, 'or sit still and starve' (*Works*, 4:28), is nowhere more strongly felt than in his memorandum on the poor. Of course, Locke does not intend that the poor should starve, and he even recommends that those responsible for the welfare of the poor be charged with a 'crime' if the indigent under their custody do die of starvation.[19] Nevertheless, it is clear that moral depravity and economic hardship are interconnected in Locke's mind, and that very few qualities that define a human being in Locke's other writings manage to shine through the harshness of tone exhibited by this document. Rather, the poor are simply bodies to be set to work so that others may be 'eased' of the burden of having to pay taxes to provide for their subsistence. They are, in short, commodities, like money, to be put back into circulation in the economic market-place. It is true, Locke is speaking only of the idle poor and not of the employed members of the working class, for whom he has much more respect as rational creatures; even so, the question is, could we not expect more from a thinker such as Locke?[20]

It is difficult to see how this question could be answered in the affirmative without doing violence to the historical record, except to note that some of Locke's contemporaries displayed a more compassionate attitude towards the poor than he did. These individuals constituted a small minority, and they were not responsible, as Locke was, for formulating a state policy with respect to the poor and unemployed. This response, however, does not go to the heart of the matter, nor does it seem likely to assuage the uneasiness that one feels in attempting to integrate Locke's attitude towards the economic hardships of the poor with the rest of his thought. It is precisely this endeavour, it appears, that produces in interpreters a consciousness of the ideological frontiers patrolled by Locke's mind. For Dunn, Locke's position serves as a reminder of the limitations exercised by Calvinist theology upon even so liberal a thinker as Locke. From the standpoint of a devout Christian with lingering Puritan influences, the options were rather limited. If such suffering was not personally deserved, it was at least about the trivial concerns of material well-being, compared to eternal salvation of one's soul. If these justificatory beliefs were pushed to their limits, it was more likely that Locke would turn to the Book of Job for solace than that he would extend the meaning of his moral argument to include the right to restructure the economic order along the lines of a more equitable distribution of wealth. For Seliger, Locke's indifference to the economic sphere of life reflects the moral superiority he attributes to politics, which, in Seliger's interpretation, is itself severely restricted with respect to practical arrangements. Not only the positive face of constitutionalism resting upon a propertied oligarchy, but also the darker shadows of authoritarianism stemming from the executive's exercise of power represents the legacy of Lockean liberalism. To recognize these harsher aspects of liberalism, already present in Locke's political thought, lessens the level of disappointment one might otherwise experience in confronting Locke's attitudes towards the propertyless masses. For Wolin, on the contrary, Locke is chiefly responsible for undermining the importance of the political realm. In place of a moral community that gives meaning to political interaction, Locke substitutes a society held together by nothing more than a clash of socio-economic interests. As a consequence, the values of social life were vulgarized and reduced almost exclusively to the endless quest for wealth and worldly goods. Locke was, perhaps, the last resident of Eden, not so much malevolent as mistaken, leaving for posterity the well-intentioned but confused directives as to how liberty is to be obtained for all individuals within a social environment of hostile interests. For Parry, Locke is a rather classical liberal, for, once one has championed the virtues of self-reliance and the rule of law, one has done everything for the individual that might reasonably be expected of a liberal. Beyond providing a minimal state of security, government has no social responsibilities. Rather, the burdens of social life rest squarely upon the shoulders of the individual. For some, these will prove too heavy, but others will succeed; and, whatever the outcome, the results must be accepted. Locke's intentions, good or bad, in launching this idealized structure into the stream of history do not enter into the picture. It is the only ship we have, and there is no reason for liberals, or anyone else, to abandon it. For Macpherson, Locke was an apologist for a capitalist system of exploitation of the worker and the unlimited accumulation of wealth. Since that is what liberalism is all about, Locke is merely one of the company players – though an important one – who re-enact this socio-economic drama on the level of ideas. Given that this is a command performance of a work commissioned by the bourgeoisie, we in the audience must not be surprised by anything we witness on the stage; the playwright knew what he was doing.[21]

Doubtless the reader will not like to hear it said that there is a kernel of truth in all of these characterizations of Locke but, on reflection, it will be seen that it could hardly be otherwise. For it is like trying to describe the elephant, though the differences among interpreters concerning the nature of liberalism and Locke's relationship to that belief-system are not due to their blindness so much as to their conception of contemporary liberalism. It is this ideological perspective that ultimately closes the circle of one's interpretation of Locke's political thought. Because the question of what to do with the poor as a matter of social and political policy has become an increasingly prominent aspect of the social consciousness of liberals since the nineteenth century, it is precisely when we, as modern readers of Locke, encounter this question in his writings that we are most susceptible to a self-reflective awareness of the ideological implications of liberalism as a political theory.

It seems appropriate, therefore, to close the circle of my interpretation of Locke's *Two Treatises of Government* with some reflections on its place in the tradition of liberalism. I believe Locke's thought expresses the tension within liberalism as a social theory between its universalistic claims to moral and religious equality – liberty, equality and fraternity – and its instrumentalist treatment of human beings as part of the process of capital accumulation. The same individual with rights in one sphere of social life may function merely as a commodity in another sphere. The bifurcation between the radical assertions of moral worth and the indifference to the socio-economic suffering of the individual that characterizes Locke's political thought reappears as a constant tension within the political theories of liberals since the seventeenth century. The distribution of emphasis between these two dimensions, the specific concerns of the theorist and his ordering of value preferences and methodological assumptions, and the empirical social problems to which the political theory is addressed vary from one liberal thinker to another, but there is, I believe, a radical–conservative dichotomy at the heart of liberal political theory. In supplying the first comprehensive statement of this social, economic and political perspective, Locke may truly be said to be the father of liberalism.

NOTES: CHAPTER 9

1 See, for example, George H. Sabine, *A History of Political Theory*, 3rd edn (New York: Holt, Rinehart & Winston, 1961), pp. 530 ff. The *Essay* and the *Two Treatises*, according to Laslett, 'differ remarkably' in almost every respect, and Locke wrote each of them 'in an entirely different state of mind' (*Two Treatises of Government*, ed. Peter Laslett, 2nd edn (Cambridge: Cambridge University Press, 1967), introduction, pp. 82–4).

2 This is primarily the view of Macpherson and Strauss, but see also Sheldon S. Wolin, *Politics and Vision* (Boston, Mass.: Little, Brown, 1960), pp. 337–42.

3 For two different but not necessarily incompatible departures from this tendency to view the *Essay Concerning Human Understanding* as a quarry to be mined by contemporary philosophers engaged in debates over the fine points of metaphysics or epistemology, see John W. Yolton, *John Locke and the Way of Ideas* (Oxford: Clarendon Press, 1956), and Neal Wood, *The Politics of Locke's Philosophy: A Social Study of 'An Essay Concerning Human Understanding'* (Berkeley/Los Angeles, Calif.: University of California Press, 1983).

4 In a journal note discussing the Indians in the New World, Locke adds a general reflection about man in his natural condition: 'Another use of his knowledge is to live in peace with his fellow men, and this also he is capable of' (Journal, 8 February 1677, MS f.2).

5 An interesting discussion of this viewpoint as expressing the social psychology of liberalism can be found in Wolin, *Politics and Vision*, pp. 286–351.

6 *The Correspondence of John Locke*, ed. E. S. De Beer, 8 vols (Oxford: Clarendon Press, 1976–85), Vol. 1, p. 559. This point is repeated often enough by Locke that it qualifies as an expression of his general attitude; cf. Journal, 5 April 1677, MS f.2; 20 March 1678, MS f.3. The application of this belief to the argument of *The Reasonableness of Christianity* is discussed in the text below.

7 For an elaboration of this point, see Geraint Parry, *John Locke* (London: Allen & Unwin, 1978), pp. 42–3, and Wood, *Politics of Locke's Philosophy*, pp. 141–2. Both place too much emphasis on the individualistic conception of labour and industry, which in my view leaves this activity devoid of its ethical meaning, since Locke subscribes to a communal ethical standard on the level of practical action.

8 *Essay Concerning Toleration* (1667), H. R. Fox-Bourne, *The Life of John Locke*, 2 vols (1876), Vol. 1, pp. 176–7; cf. Peter King, *The Life of John Locke*, 2 vols (1830), Vol. 2, p. 109.

9 'Faith and knowledge in Locke's philosophy' in John W. Yolton (ed.) *John Locke: Problems and Perspectives* (Cambridge: Cambridge University Press, 1969), pp. 194–223.

10 'I affirm that it is out of the power of any man to make another a representative for himself in matters of religion . . . since nobody can give another man authority to determine in what way he should worship God' (MS c.34, fol. 122). This is from an unpublished manuscript defending the rights of dissenters written jointly by Locke and his friend James Tyrrell in 1681. The passage cited is in Locke's handwriting.

11 C. B. Macpherson, *The Political Theory of Possessive Individualism* (London: Oxford University Press, 1962), pp. 224–6.

12 ibid., p. 229.

13 'The holy scripture is to me, and always will be, the constant guide of my assent; and I shall always hearken to it, as containing infallible truth, relating to things of the highest concernment . . . and I shall presently condemn and quit any opinion of mine, as soon as I am shown that it is contrary to any revelation in the holy scripture' (*The Works of John Locke*, 12th edn, 9 vols (1824), Vol. 3, p. 96). 'A

Christian I am sure I am, because I believe "Jesus to be the Messiah" . . . and, as a subject of his kingdom, I take the rule of my faith and life from his will, declared and left upon record in the inspired writings of the apostles and evangelists in the New Testament' (ibid., Vol. 6, p. 359; cf. pp. 289, 357).

14 Macpherson, *Possessive Individualism*, p. 225.

15 ibid., p. 226.

16 Locke never at any time in his life subscribed to a 'rationalist ethic', in the sense that morality could be established through the exercise of human reason alone. Rather, he held a strictly legalist and theologically voluntarist notion that required the action of God as lawmaker. Thus, even 'honesty', 'temperance' or the rest of the 'virtues' would not have the status of morally good actions if God had not 'ordained' them to be so, according to Locke (Journal, 16 July 1676, MS f.1). There is a question to be raised as to whether human reason can discover the Law of God, and whether Locke's confidence in an affirmative answer to this question waned during the later years of his life. This is possible, but it could also be argued that Locke's position was that it was possible for all men to gain a knowledge of natural law through the use of their reason, though in fact they have not done so. Yet they may have a sufficient knowledge of the most important precepts of natural law to lead moral lives. In the *Essays on the Law of Nature*, Locke maintained that as soon as one achieved a knowledge of God a knowledge of the Law of Nature necessarily 'followed' as an inference from this fact. By the time he wrote *The Reasonableness of Christianity*, Locke has widened the gap between a knowledge of the lawmaker and a knowledge of the content of the law. In that work, this gap is described historically as a commentary on the religious consciousness of individuals who existed prior to the coming of Christ. What was needed, therefore, was a reaffirmation of the 'authority' of God as lawmaker, since reason was not able to provide this for religion merely through its proof of the existence of God. At one point Locke reflects that there are 'a great many things' that 'we take for unquestionable obvious truths, and easily demonstrable', but of which we would be ignorant 'had revelation been silent' about such matters. Thus, 'many are beholden to revelation, who do not acknowledge it . . . But it is our mistake to think, that because reason confirms [these truths] to us, we had the first certain knowledge of them from thence'. The contrary, Locke argues, is the case (*Works*, Vol. 6, p. 145). It could be argued that Locke is here expressing his view that it was his 'mistake' to believe that the truths of morality were 'easily demonstrable' through reason, when he should have recognized, as he does in *The Reasonableness*, that we actually 'know' the moral precepts of the Law of Nature through revelation and the Scriptures, the truth of which reason only 'confirms' for us.

17 A friend wrote to Locke that the Apostles and authors of the Scriptures 'used such words as the common sort of people did ordinarily use and in the sense they generally understood them, and did not send their hearers to . . . philosophers to learn the meaning of the words'. In fact it is the intrusion of 'philosophical notions' and the ideas of 'philosophers' or 'learned men' into Christianity that is responsible for the confusion and 'wrangling' among various interpreters of the Bible. Locke replied that he agreed with this assessment of 'learned commentators' on the Bible – a book that, 'as you rightly observe', was written for 'and adapted to the people' and meant to be understood 'in the ordinary vulgar sense' in which words were used by them (*Correspondence*, Vol. 6, pp. 595–6, 629). Locke applied this principle in his *A Paraphrase and Notes on the Epistles of St Paul* (*Works*, Vol. 7). Locke decided to publish this work, he tells us, 'principally for the help of ordinary illiterate readers of the scripture' (MS c.27, fol. 217).

18 See, on this point, *Two Treatises*, ed. Laslett, introduction, p. 14; John Dunn, *The Political Thought of Locke* (Cambridge: Cambridge University Press, 1969), pp. 6–7.

19 Fox-Bourne, *Life of Locke*, Vol. 2, p. 390.

20 Macpherson lumps together the idle poor and the working class, which is only one of the many liberties taken with Locke's text, for which he has been soundly criticized by Dunn and others (*Possessive Individualism*, pp. 222 ff.).

21 Dunn, *Political Thought of Locke*, pp. 264–5; Martin Seliger, *The Liberal Politics of John Locke* (London: Allen & Unwin, 1968), pp. 171–9; Wolin, *Politics and Vision*, pp. 305–51; Parry, *Locke*, pp. 86–9; Macpherson, *Possessive Individualism*, pp. 194–262.

CHAPTER 10

Locke and the Tensions of Liberalism

A discussion of the influence Locke's ideas exercised upon later political thinkers would involve nothing less than a history of political thought since the seventeenth century. Even if the subject were limited to the eighteenth century, the names of Burke, Hume, Adam Smith, Bentham, Paine, Jefferson, Montesquieu, Voltaire and Rousseau indicate the scope of the problem. Besides these well-known political thinkers, there were countless journalists, academics, clerics and other members of the intellectual strata who helped to shape the political consciousness of eighteenth-century France, England and America. Their writings are filled with references to Locke. Indeed, Daniel Defoe's writings alone extend to more than 500 titles, and Locke's arguments, often reproduced verbatim, figure prominently in these books, pamphlets and novels. Mention of Defoe, to whose name others could be added, opens up the broad area of literature and reminds us that Lockean ideas also flowed through this cultural medium. Locke was not merely an important political theorist; his writings on philosophy, religion, economics and education made him a cultural force to be reckoned with for virtually every thinker in the eighteenth century. It can be argued that Lockean thought supplied the intellectual framework for an emerging bourgeois society. Be that as it may, what is clear is that a historical account of the development of Lockean ideas during the three centuries following the publication of Locke's writings is beyond the scope of this book.

Rather, this chapter is best viewed as a brief epilogue to the discussion of the major themes contained in Locke's *Two Treatises of Government* and an elaboration of the concluding remarks of Chapter 9. That is, I will offer a few illustrations of the way in which Locke's ideas flowed into the channels of both radical and conservative political theories during the eighteenth century. My general argument will be that radical political theorists focused their attention upon the moral presuppositions of Locke's political theory, while conservative political theorists stressed the prudential aspects of that theory. Thus, the two parts of a political theory, 'very different the one from the other', that were united in Locke's approach to politics tended to dissolve in the eighteenth century, allowing thinkers across the political spectrum to claim Locke as one of their intellectual mentors, according to which aspect of his political thought they emphasized.

In rejecting the Law of Nature as the standard for assessing political action, David Hume also excluded from his political perspective virtually all the assumptions and arguments that Locke had linked with a belief in natural law. Not only natural rights, but also God, the dependence of morality upon reason or revelation, the primary importance of reason as a natural faculty of man, the political significance of the individual – and many other concepts – are either absent from or assume a radically different role within Hume's political thought. To Hume, the state of nature was a poetic or 'philosophical fiction'; it was a wholly 'imaginary state' without justice or injustice, property or any of the other qualities embodied in Locke's definition.[1] Therefore, Hume argued, it was 'fruitless' to 'seek in the laws of nature a stronger foundation for our political duties than interest and human conventions'.[2] On the contrary, 'those rules by which properties, rights, and obligations are determined' are matters 'of artifice and contrivance'; and, as conventions instituted by human beings, the 'laws of justice are so far to be considered as artificial'.[3] This does not mean that justice is reducible to conventional agreement. Hume maintains that there is a naturalistic basis in the sentiment of sympathy for 'a sense of common interest' among individuals that underlies their social relationships.[4] At the same time, however, he argues that 'the rules of equity or justice depend entirely on . . . and owe their origin and existence to that utility which results to the public from their strict and regular observance'.[5] But, for both reasons, there is no need for a doctrine of natural law, because 'the general obligation which binds us to government is the interest and necessities of society'.[6]

It would be unfair to say that Hume's argument reduces morality to prudential action, although certain versions of utilitarianism come very close to doing just that. However, viewed purely in relation to Locke's thought, what is clear is that the concept of 'the interest and necessities of society' tends to merge those things that, according to Locke, are 'useful' inventions or actions that promote the general well-being of individuals in society – such as money, science and commerce – with those actions for which there exists a direct natural law command. Since this is not a meaningful distinction for Hume, justice as social utility must be identified with actions that advance the general interests of society. Hume's statement that 'justice takes its rise from human conventions' as the 'remedy to some inconveniences' that beset individuals, for example, blurs the very distinction between right and convenience upon which Locke insisted.[7]

For Hume, 'no maxim is more conformable, both to prudence and morals, than to submit quietly to the government which we find established in the country where we happen to live, without inquiring too curiously into its origin and first establishment'.[8] The question of the origins of government will bear little examination, Hume argues, because 'almost all the governments which exist at present, or of which there remains any record in story, have been founded originally either on usurpation or conquest or both, without any pretence of a fair consent or voluntary subjection of the people'. Not consent but force and violence supply the historical explanation for the institution of political society.[9] Locke, of course, could not have accepted this divorcement between consent and political legitimacy. But to the question, how can one distinguish between legitimate and illegitimate governments, Hume offers a disarmingly simple reply: political legitimacy is a function of time. 'Time alone . . . operating gradually on the minds of men, reconciles them to any authority, and makes it seem just and reasonable.' And, as a general proposition, Hume maintains that 'nothing causes any sentiment to have a greater influence upon us than custom, or turns our imagination more strongly to any object'.[10] In short, 'Time and custom give authority to all forms of government and all successions of princes; and that power which at first was founded only on injustice and violence, becomes in time legal and obligatory.'[11]

Hume applies the same reasoning to his defence of property as an institution. Hence 'possession during a long tract of time conveys a title to any object'. 'Constant possession' and custom establish the claims to property in society, and not any supposed system of natural rights or any formal theory concerning the origins of property.[12] In fact, as in the case of government, it is imprudent, in Hume's view, to attempt to determine the historical origins of property, for the historian 'may find, as commonly happens, that its first authority was derived from usurpation and violence'.[13] Hence, with respect to property, it is best 'that every one continue to enjoy what he is at present possessed of'.[14] Political theory is thus grounded wholly in experience, custom and prudential action, and not in universalist moral claims regarding rights or laws of nature.

Hume's methodological critique of Locke for being too preoccupied with philosophical fictions forms a central part of his discussion of the theory of the social contract. Thinkers such as Locke who develop 'so refined and philosophical a system' in their political theories would discover if they 'look abroad into the world', Hume asserts, that there is 'nothing that in the least corresponds to their ideas'. 'So little correspondent is fact and reality to those philosophical notions' that they may justly be labelled 'absurdities'.[15] The fact that a political theory 'which founds all lawful government on an original contract, or consent of the people . . . leads to paradoxes repugnant to the common sentiments of mankind, and to the practice and opinion of all nations and all ages' is, for Hume, a sufficient reason to reject it as being erroneous. To illustrate his point, Hume cites the passage from the *Second Treatise* which declares that absolute monarchy is inconsistent with civil society (II, 90) – an opinion 'so wide of the general practice of mankind in every place but this single kingdom' as to subvert the force of the 'moral reasoning' that underlies such an assertion.[16]

Naturally, much more could be said, but even this schematic presentation of Hume's position reveals the depth of his attack on Locke, jettisoning natural law, natural rights, theories of the origins of property or government, and certain other elements of Lockean political theory that belong to the province of moral philosophy. It might be claimed that the juxtaposition is unfair, and hardly surprising, given that Hume was a Tory and Locke was a Whig. The truth contained in this objection cannot be overlooked, but as a general explanation of the relationship between Locke's ideas and those of Hume it will not do. Hume supported the same mixed form of government Locke had defended; he acknowledged that political power resides in the hands of the people and that governments rest upon popular opinion as a determinant of their legitimacy; Hume even endorsed the right of the people to engage in resistance, though in such general terms as to make it all but impossible to apply the right in the context of eighteenth-century politics. There is some evidence that Hume's sympathies lay with a republican form of government, though he believed the empirical constraints of custom and tradition were too great in Britain to allow republicanism to take root in that country.[17] Even with these allowances, Hume may still be characterized as a conservative thinker, but if his differences with Locke are to be understood in terms of this characterization, then conservatism must be taken in the broadest sense; that is, as an attack upon the substantive Lockean assertions of equality and individual rationality as well as upon Locke's methodological preference for philosophical reasoning as a foundation for political action rather than custom or tradition, and not merely as an expression of the party differences between eighteenth-century Whigs and Tories.

This point can be further illustrated if we consider Burke's relationship to Lockean political thought. Burke was both a Whig and, from our perspective, a leading figure within the tradition of conservatism. Unlike Hume, he thus retained a link with Locke through the medium of party principles; yet Burke's conception of politics and political theory was much closer to the view advanced by Hume than it was to the position defended in the *Two Treatises of Government*. According to Burke, 'no lines can be laid down for civil or political wisdom. They are a matter incapable of exact definition.'[18]

Nothing universal can be rationally affirmed on any moral or any political subject. Pure metaphysical abstraction does not belong to these matters. The lines of morality are not like the ideal lines of mathematics. They are broad and deep as well as long. They admit of exceptions; they demand modifications. These exceptions and modifications are not made by the process of logic, but by the rules of prudence. Prudence is not only the first in rank of the virtues political and moral, but she is the director, the regulator, the standard of them all.[19]

It is 'speculative philosophers' and 'visionary politicians' who have 'anatomized the doctrine of free government, as if it were an abstract question', rather than treating the issue as a matter of prudence and in relation to the concrete circumstances. These thinkers, Burke argues, have concerned themselves with questions such as 'whether man has any rights by nature', what is the origin of property, and other 'speculations . . . destructive to all authority'.[20] These questions are dangerous because 'the foundations on which obedience to governments is founded are not to be constantly discussed.'[21] Politicians know this, but political philosophers thrive on such speculations.

For Burke, politics is not an 'abstruse science', analogous to geometry, but an activity that is 'variously mixed and modified, enjoyed in very different degrees, and shaped into an infinite diversity of forms, according to the temper and circumstances of every community'.[22] Hence 'every age has its own manners, and its politics dependent upon them'.[23] In order to grasp the meaning of politics, what is needed is 'not any abstract theory of right' but an appreciation of the habits, prejudices and the peculiar circumstances of the people.[24] Moreover, since 'the internal causes which necessarily affect the fortune of a state' cannot be known, we must rely on 'the rules of prudence' in guiding political affairs. And, Burke adds, 'the rules and definitions of prudence can rarely be exact'; they are 'never universal'.[25] Politics, Burke argues, is a matter of balancing the 'inconveniences'. In understanding any political action, 'we consider what we are to lose, as well as what we are to gain' by it, and attempt to achieve a balancing of interests.[26] 'The world of contingency and political combination', Burke observes, 'is much larger than we are apt to imagine. We never can say what may or may not happen, without a view to all the actual circumstances.'[27] Although this places a premium upon prudential judgement, there is a sense in which politics always eludes both theoretical systematization *and* the practical experience of the politician.

> The science of government, being therefore so practical in itself, and intended for such practical purposes, is a matter which requires experience, and even more experience than any person can gain in his whole life, however sagacious and observant he may be.[28]

In a sense, Burke applies Locke's epistemological scepticism about our knowledge of the experiential world to our knowledge of the political realm. Because there are no universal certainties upon which one can rely, one is forced, as Locke put it in the *Essay*, to 'compound and divide' the materials given to us by nature according to the demands of the situation. 'A true politician', Burke writes, 'always considers how he shall make the most of the existing materials of his country.'[29] Burke employs the metaphor of a player in a game, maintaining that 'no politician can make a situation. His skill consists in his well-playing the game dealt to him by fortune, and following the indications given by nature, time, and circumstances.'[30] Politics is simply an activity that uses the materials available in the most prudential and profitable manner, according to the interests and necessities of society. The politician succeeds in realizing this objective, Burke argues, when he discovers 'by cautious experiments' and the trials and errors of experience what actions are suitable to 'the exigencies of the time, and the temper and character of the people'.[31] Such rules of prudence, however, cannot be stated in a systematic form; in practice, the meaning of any political theory must depend upon and be identified with the judgement and practical decisions taken by politicians. 'Constitute government how you please,' Burke declares, 'infinitely the greater part of it must depend upon the exercise of the powers which are left at large to the prudence and uprightness of ministers of state.'[32]

Burke also illustrates his point by drawing a comparison between the philosopher and the politician. 'It is the business of the speculative philosopher', he argues, 'to mark the proper ends of government. It is the business of the politician, who is the philosopher in action, to find out the proper means toward those ends, and to employ them with effect.'[33] Whereas the university professor 'has only the general view of society', the politician must consider circumstances that 'are infinite . . . variable and transient' in making a practical decision. Hence 'it is a very great mistake', Burke warns, 'to imagine that mankind follow up practically any speculative principle, either of government or freedom, as far as it will go in argument' and logic. This does not mean there is no place for political principles in Burke's conception of politics. 'Without the guide and light of sound, well-understood principles', he insisted, 'all reasonings in politics . . . would be only a confused jumble of particular facts and details.'[34] 'I do not villify theory,' Burke explains, 'because that would be to villify reason itself.'[35] It is not that the politician has no principles; rather, in Burke's view, the politician simply assumes that these principles are already settled because they have been agreed to by the community. Applying this point to England, it is fair to say that, for Burke, Locke is the speculative philosopher who has 'marked out the proper ends of government', while Burke is the politician who must reconcile these general ideas with the variable circumstances. Thus, as Hume maintained, Locke is too abstract a thinker; nevertheless, Burke believes that he has at least outlined the true principles of government and morality.[36] The point is that both Burke and Hume place an emphasis upon prudential judgement, circumstances, experience and history that changes the definition and purposes of a political theory as set forth by Locke, and this restructuring of political theory is not dependent upon their agreement with Locke on specific substantive issues.

Like Hume, Burke also supplies an epistemological foundation for his position which shifts the emphasis away from what he considers to be the hyper-rationalism of Locke. Politics, Burke declared, 'ought to be adjusted, not to human reasonings, but to human nature; of which the reason is but a part, and by no means the greatest part'.[37] Thus, individuals are led to associate with each other, according to Burke, not because they are guided by reason and are attempting to enforce the Law of Nature as a law of reason, but because their actions are directed by shared sympathies and feelings. As Hume argued, sympathy, compassion and sentiment supply the foundation for political society: 'Nothing is so strong a tie . . . as correspondence in laws, customs, manners, and habits of life . . . They are obligations written in the heart.'[38] Although Burke, unlike Hume, was a believer in natural law, neither the origins of political society nor the motives of political actors are to be explained with reference to its existence. Rather, these and many other aspects of a Lockean natural law approach to politics can be better understood in terms of the significance of custom, habit and tradition. Burke's defence of the American revolutionaries, for example, was formulated from this standpoint. He did not cite Locke's *Two Treatises of Government* as many of his contemporaries, including the Americans, did. For Burke, it was sufficient to point out that the Americans were simply claiming for themselves the right to enjoy those settled principles of the English political tradition to which all British subjects were entitled.

The fact that Lockean political ideas provided a substantial part of any definition of British liberty tended to obscure the differences between the political theories of Burke and Paine, who, until a few months prior to the publication of Burke's *Reflections on the Revolution in France*, maintained a friendship that had grown out of their common defence of the American Revolution. The events in France, and Burke's violent reaction to them, however, forever placed the names of Paine and Burke in polar opposition to each other. In *Common Sense*, Paine had spoken of 'mankind being originally equals in the order of creation' as the ground for his assertion that 'the equal rights of nature' applied to every individual.[39] This presupposition receives an extended defence in his *Rights of Man*, written in reply to Burke's *Reflections*. Since 'all men are born equal, and with equal natural rights', it follows for Paine that 'every generation is equal in rights to the generation which preceded it', and thus no generation is capable of consenting to a set of political institutions that effectively give away the right of a future generation to defend its natural rights as it thinks best.[40] This Lockean precept is supported by another, namely, that 'man did not enter into society to become *worse* than he was before, nor to have fewer rights than he had before, but to have those rights better secured. His natural rights are the foundation of all his civil rights.'[41] Moreover, Paine argues, 'to possess ourselves of a clear idea of what government is, or ought to be, we must trace it to its origin'. If we do so, it is clear that 'individuals themselves, each in his own personal and sovereign right, entered into a compact with each other to produce a government: and this is the only mode in which governments have a right to arise, and the only principle on which they have a right to exist'.[42]

Government, according to Paine, 'is nothing more than a national association' whose object 'is the good of all'. In joining political society, 'every man wishes to pursue his occupation, and enjoy the fruits of his labours, and the produce of his property, in peace and safety . . . When these things are accomplished, all the objects for which government ought to be established are answered.'[43] The ends of that society are limited by 'the original inherent Rights of Man'.[44] Because 'a man, by natural right, has a right to judge in his own cause', Paine argues, political society should be viewed as a depository of rights; that is, an individual 'deposits [his] right in the common stock of society' as an investor would deposit his money in a bank for safekeeping. 'Society', Paine insists, '*grants* him nothing.' Rather, 'every man is [a] proprietor in society, and draws on the capital as a matter of right'.[45] For Paine, therefore, politics must be defined in relation to the 'immutable laws of nature', the moral principles of equality and liberty that express the inherent natural rights of man, a clear understanding of the origins of political society, and the ends for which it is instituted through the consent of rational individuals.[46] It is obvious that, even when Paine is in agreement with Hume or Burke on particular political issues or institutions, the former's conception of political theory places a much greater emphasis upon situating that theory within the framework of moral philosophy, as viewed by Locke, than is the case for either of Paine's contemporaries.

Though Paine supplies no epistemological defence of his position, it is evident even from his polemical use of the concept of 'reason' that he reinstates the emancipatory claim of that ability over the power of the passions, custom and habit. As Paine sees it, the world is divided according to the influence exercised over 'the great bulk of mankind' by reason or ignorance. Whereas 'reason obeys itself . . . ignorance submits to whatever is dictated to it'. This dichotomy is reflected in 'the two modes of government which prevail in the world', namely, 'government by election and representation' and some form of monarchy or aristocracy based upon the principle of hereditary succession. In other words, 'those two distinct and opposite forms, erect themselves on the two distinct and opposite bases of reason and ignorance'.[47] From this starting-point, Paine has little difficulty in identifying Burke's political theory as an argument emphasizing the importance of custom and tradition with a political perspective whose object is 'to keep a man in a state of ignorance'. This 'political popery', as Paine refers to it, is nothing more than 'a superstitious reverence for ancient things, as monks show relics and call them holy'.[48] On the other hand, 'the representative system' of government, Paine argues, 'is always parallel with the order and immutable laws of nature, and meets the reason of man in every part'.[49] In addition to the consonance of this form of government with the moral presuppositions described above, it is founded upon reason because the exercise of political power in a representative democracy necessarily depends upon and develops the active exercise of 'the human faculties' – especially those associated with reason.[50] Only a political system that encourages individuals to develop their powers of reasoning can provide an adequate defence of their natural rights, and thus establish its own claim to legitimacy according to certain immutable moral principles.

Although he arrived at this conclusion by a slightly different route, this summary statement of Paine's position might serve equally well to describe the basic dimensions of Rousseau's political theory. There is, for Rousseau, a 'moral and legitimate' equality of all individuals that must be incorporated into the notion of the social contract that establishes political society.[51] Strictly speaking, there are no standards of morality recognized by individuals in the state of nature, since it is only within the context of society that moral actions can be taken, according to Rousseau. Nevertheless, since 'there is hardly any inequality in the state of nature' the distance between Rousseau's descriptive and evaluative account of the natural equality of individuals is very small.[52] Indeed, the very construction of the political community, as described by Rousseau, both presupposes and 'proves that equality of rights and the idea of justice which such equality creates originate in the preference each man gives to himself, and accordingly in the very nature of man'. This attributive importance to self-interest does not lead Rousseau, as it led Bernard Mandeville, for example, to identify the common good with the collective pursuit by individuals of their self-interests; on the contrary, what it means to Rousseau is that the common good can only be identified with the 'true principle of equity'.[53] Thus, 'if we ask in what precisely consists the greatest good of all, which should be the end of every system of legislation', Rousseau writes, 'we shall find it reduce[s] itself to two main objects, liberty and equality'.[54] 'The state is a moral person' which, while it rightfully establishes the duties individuals must fulfil as subjects, must also secure 'the natural rights they should enjoy as men'.[55] 'Every man being born free and his own master,' Rousseau asserts, 'no one, under any pretext whatsoever, can make any man subject without his consent.' The social contract is therefore brought into existence through the unanimous consent of individuals, and thereafter, as Locke had maintained, 'the vote of the majority always binds all the rest'.[56]

Like Paine, Rousseau believes a political perspective predicated upon a defence of the natural rights of individuals can only be understood in terms of a clear distinction between 'what is original and what is artificial in the actual nature of man'. Hence, despite whatever philosophical objections might be raised against such a methodological approach (by Hume, for example), Rousseau insists that it is only through the use of concepts such as the state of nature, and through the efforts to determine the origins of government, that the natural rights of individuals can, in practice, be defended. A 'knowledge of the real foundations of human society' is absolutely essential because, in Rousseau's view, 'it is this ignorance of the nature of man which casts so much uncertainty and obscurity on the true definition of natural right'.[57]

This discussion of origins, however, is not intended to produce 'historical truths'; rather, it is predicated upon 'mere conditional and hypothetical reasonings' that are 'calculated to explain the nature of things' and not 'their actual origin'.[58] Rousseau's identification of this procedure with the methods employed by eighteenth-century physicists raises some questions regarding the status of his own political theory as he viewed it. This is too large and complicated an issue to be dealt with here, but with respect to the specific status of the Law of Nature, for example, what is clear is that Rousseau intends to defend a position that is somewhere between an abstract conceptualization of natural law and an equation of the latter with some utilitarian definition of interests. Like almost everyone else in the eighteenth century – including, as I have argued, Locke himself – Rousseau attacks the association of the Law of Nature with certain 'metaphysical principles' of a character that 'there are very few persons among us capable of comprehending them, much less of discovering them for themselves'. Such a viewpoint effectively consigns natural law to the scholastic discussions of 'learned men'. On the other hand, Rousseau does not accept the view of some 'modern writers' who identify the Law of Nature with those 'rules it would be expedient for men to agree on for their common interest'. This way 'of explaining the nature of things' makes the definition of natural law depend upon 'almost arbitrary conveniences'.[59] 'The politicians of the ancient world', Rousseau remarks, 'were always talking of morals and virtue; ours speak of nothing but commerce and money.'[60] The moral precepts of natural law, therefore, must be defended but, for Rousseau, they are rooted in neither a metaphysical notion of reason nor the utilitarian concept of interest.

The natural foundation for morality, according to Rousseau, lies in the feeling of compassion that humans exhibit towards all other sentient beings.[61] This places Rousseau with Hume so far as the starting-point for their respective social theories is concerned. Nevertheless, no one can read the writings of both thinkers without seeing not only that Rousseau allocates, in general, a much larger and more important role to reason than Hume does, but also that there is a social development of human reason in Rousseau's political theory that is wholly absent in Hume's thought. For all of Rousseau's critical remarks directed against the perversions of reason, both historically and in the form of metaphysical philosophy, Rousseau is not inclined to follow Burke or Hume down the path of custom and tradition, nor does he stress the close proximity of political activity to the individual's exercise of prudential judgement. There are for Rousseau – as the subtitle of the *Social Contract* indicates – certain absolute 'principles of political right' that stand above history, tradition and the practical wisdom of experience. Though it would be a mistake to discount the many differences that separate Locke's political theory from that of Rousseau, still it is true that Rousseau discusses these principles of political morality within a theory that depends upon natural law, natural rights, the natural equality and freedom of individuals, the origins of political society in the consent of all individuals, a theory about the origins of property, and other elements of moral philosophy that, as Locke argued, are crucial to any theory of political action.

What I have tried to suggest – and, in view of the complicated interrelationships that existed among various eighteenth-century political thinkers, it can hardly be more than a suggestion – is that Lockean political thought tended to flow into two distinctive tributaries with respect to a theoretical definition of politics, one of which retained its connection with the elements of moral philosophy as viewed by Locke, and the other of which developed Locke's notion of practical action as the effort to remove the 'inconveniences' of social life through prudential judgement, so far as this was possible. As a generalization, to which particular exceptions might be noted, I would further argue that this division corresponded roughly to a radical–conservative dichotomy with respect to political action. It is difficult to proceed beyond this point because the specific differences between various eighteenth-century thinkers and Locke invariably tend to obscure a clearly demarcated line that divides a 'Lockean' position from a non-Lockean one. Locke's political theory was not the exclusive property of eighteenth-century radicals like Paine, Jefferson and Rousseau, but neither was it wholly assimilated into the kind of defence of property, commerce and common interests of society that one finds in Hume, Smith, Burke and Bentham. That Locke's political theory, with some adjustments, *could* be incorporated into both perspectives, however, is the point I have tried to illustrate. This is a simple but historically important point to make about Locke's political thought, and if an attempt were made to identify the kind of socio-economic interests and classes that tended to identify themselves with either of these two strains of Lockean thought, we might then, on the basis of a richly textured and empirically grounded reconstruction of the interrelationship between cultural ideas and social structure, be in a position to assess the value of the characterization of Lockean political theory as a theoretical expression of the social and political practices of bourgeois society.

Of course, there are other ways of viewing the posthumous development of Lockean ideas. In his *History of English Thought in the Eighteenth Century*, Leslie Stephen focused upon a dichotomy between utilitarianism and the philosophical or legal fictions of abstract rationalism. Thus, Stephen observes, Locke 'is forced to alternate between simple utilitarianism and an odd system of legal fictions'.[62] Or, from the other side, 'Locke's metaphysical spirit is limited by his utilitarianism'.[63] What Stephen has in mind is the assignment of any theory of the social contract to 'the sphere of speculation . . . [and a] system of legal fictions'.[64] In his opinion, this theory 'has long been obsolete', even among the Whigs, whose true doctrine, he remarks caustically, is to allow individuals to dispute as they please about words, so long as they support the police.[65] Obviously, within such a limited sphere of political action, utilitarian doctrines will suffice, and the other elements of Locke's thought appear to be very 'odd' indeed.

This observation applies with even greater force to a thinker like Rousseau, who was 'a metaphysician pure and simple', without the saving grace of the seeds of utilitarianism Stephen finds in Locke's thought.[66] In the choice between 'historical inquiries into the origin of a nation' and 'abstract theories about states of nature and social contracts' Stephen is very clear as to where his own allegiances lie.[67] Yet, as with Hume, Burke and Bentham, Stephen's objective is not to dismiss Locke as he or they would set aside the ideas of Paine or Rousseau but, rather, to save Locke for liberalism defined from the vantage-point of utilitarianism.

Nevertheless, writing as a historian, Stephen is also acutely aware of the claims made upon Locke by revolutionary thinkers in the eighteenth century. 'The revolutionary party', he writes, 'found their account in the doctrine [of the social contract] as expanded for a very different purpose by Rousseau; and they could quote from Locke very sweeping assertions as to the natural equality and liberty of mankind.' At the same time, Stephen argues, the utilitarians also quoted from Locke in support of their political position.[68]

Clearly, there are some affinities between Stephen's account and the one I have offered, but I have resisted the temptation to draw so sharp a line between utilitarianism and abstract rationalism as Stephen does, because such doctrinal characterizations are too sweeping for the limited purposes of my argument. That is, the very effort to reconstruct as ideal types two doctrinal systems or methodological approaches to politics – utilitarianism and metaphysical rationalism – leads to a factoring out of dissident elements in a particular thinker's thought so that he can then be assigned to one or the other of these traditions of thought. It is neither necessary nor useful to deny the utilitarian elements that appear in the thought of Paine or Rousseau, or to discount Burke's appeal to natural law; rather, the question, as with Locke's thought itself, is not whether utilitarian assumptions co-exist with rationalist principles, but what kind of structural relationship can be established that links these elements in a theory of practical action. Of course, I have not attempted to answer this question in general for the four thinkers discussed above. I have simply tried to indicate the degree to which the theories of practical action that an interpreter of their writings could elucidate reflects the relationship between moral principles and prudential judgement as it exists within Locke's theory of practical action. In other words, in my discussion of eighteenth-century political thought, I have sought to preserve the intentional emphasis that individual thinkers gave to these two elements of their theories of politics.

If there is a tendency for an ideal typical approach to political theories to set aside this subjectively intended meaning of the theorist, there is even less recognition of this aspect of theorizing attached to a methodological approach that decomposes political theories into an atomistic set of concepts – natural rights, reason, consent, contract, natural law – and then attempts to compare political theorists in terms of specific concepts. This interpretative approach to political theory is incapable of understanding political theorizing as an activity undertaken within definite spatial and temporal limits. Even Stephen, in his use of ideal types, at least tried to preserve the meaningfulness of distinctive traditions of political thought by viewing them within a historical context.

In short, it does not seem reasonable to argue for the importance of an interpretative approach that focuses upon the structure of intentionality that is expressed through the organization of the arguments advanced by Locke in the *Two Treatises of Government*, and then set that interpretative framework aside when considering the meaning of Locke's political theory in its historical and social context.[69] In this book, I have extended the analysis of the text of the *Two Treatises* to the point of indicating the place of the specific arguments of that work within a theory of practical action Locke develops in his other writings. I have also tried to indicate the extent to which the political theories of certain eighteenth-century thinkers viewed political action from a perspective that could be said to reflect in a general way the intentional structure of Locke's political theory in the *Two Treatises*. To venture beyond this point, and, indeed, even to supply an adequate defence of the hypothesis suggested in this chapter, would require another and a different kind of book from the one that I have written.

NOTES: CHAPTER 10

1 *Hume's Moral and Political Philosophy*, ed. Henry D. Aiken (New York: Hafner, 1972), p. 189; cf. ibid. pp. 62–3, 69.
2 ibid., p. 104.
3 ibid., pp. 92–3, 96.
4 ibid., p. 278.
5 ibid., pp. 188–9.
6 ibid., p. 371; cf. ibid, p. 368.
7 ibid., p. 63.

8   ibid., p. 117.
9   ibid., pp. 360–2.
10 ibid., p. 116.
11 ibid., pp. 124, 363.
12 ibid., p. 75; cf. ibid, pp. 71 ff.
13 ibid., p. 368.
14 ibid., p. 71.
15 ibid., pp. 359, 361.
16 ibid., pp. 371–2.
17 ibid., pp. 121–2; cf. Duncan Forbes, *Hume's Philosophical Politics* (Cambridge: Cambridge University Press, 1975), pp. 182–3.
18 *The Works and Correspondence of the Right Honourable Edmund Burke*, 8 vols (1852), Vol. 3, p. 137.
19 ibid., Vol. 4, p. 407; cf. Vol. 5, p. 258.
20 ibid., Vol. 3, p. 321.
21 *The Works of the Right Honourable Edmund Burke* (1812–15), Vol. 10, p. 51.
22 Burke, *Works and Correspondence*, Vol. 3, p. 322; cf. Vol. 2, p. 288.
23 ibid., Vol. 3, p. 116; cf. Vol. 4, p. 591.
24 ibid., Vol. 3, p. 246. 'Circumstances . . . give in reality to every political principle its distinguishing colour and discriminating effect. The circumstances are what render every civil and political scheme beneficial or noxious to mankind. Abstractedly speaking, government, as well as liberty, is good' (Vol. 4, p. 156; cf. Vol. 4, pp. 424–5; Vol. 3, p. 85).
25 ibid., Vol. 5, pp. 254, 258; cf. Vol. 4, p. 407.
26 ibid., Vol. 3, p. 284. Hence prudence is the primary political virtue (Vol. 1, p. 564; Vol. 4, pp. 201, 407).
27 ibid., Vol. 4, p. 574.
28 ibid., Vol. 4, p. 200.
29 ibid., Vol. 4, p. 280.
30 ibid., Vol. 2, p. 213.
31 ibid., Vol. 3, p. 322; cf. Vol. 4, p. 200.
32 ibid., Vol. 3, p. 133.
33 ibid., Vol. 3, p. 170.
34 Cited in R. R. Fennessy, *Burke, Paine and the Rights of Man* (The Hague: Martinus Nijhoff, 1963), p. 136; cf. Burke, *Works and Correspondence*, Vol. 3, p. 283.
35 Cited in Fennessy, *Burke, Paine*, p. 67. On the other hand, Burke declared: 'I do not pretend to be . . . qualified for the chair of professor in metaphysics' (*Works and Correspondence*, Vol. 3, p. 318).
36 Burke's political theory is an expression of 'the principles of a constitution already made. It is a theory drawn from the *fact* of our government' (ibid., Vol. 4, p. 486: italics in original). It should be noted, however, that in those places where Burke might have cited from Locke's works (for example, in his *Appeal from the Old to the New Whigs*) he chose instead to identify his views with those of Whig politicians such as Lord Somers.
37 Burke, *Works and Correspondence*, Vol. 3, p. 87.
38 ibid., Vol. 5, p. 305.
39 *The Political Writings of Thomas Paine*, 2 vols (1830), Vol. 1, pp. 24–5.
40 ibid., Vol. 2, p. 71.
41 ibid., Vol. 2, p. 72.
42 ibid., Vol. 2, p. 75.
43 ibid., Vol. 2, p. 191.
44 ibid., Vol. 2, p. 166.
45 ibid., Vol. 2, p. 73.

46 ibid., Vol. 2, p. 176.
47 ibid., Vol. 2, pp. 137–8.
48 ibid., Vol. 2, p. 189.
49 ibid., Vol. 2, p. 176.
50 ibid., Vol. 2, pp. 138 ff.
51 Jean-Jacques Rousseau, *The Social Contract and Discourses* (London: Dent, 1913), p. 22.
52 ibid., p. 238.
53 ibid., pp. 27–8.
54 ibid., p. 45.
55 ibid., pp. 26–7.
56 ibid., p. 93.
57 ibid., pp. 170 ff.
58 ibid., pp. 175–6.
59 ibid., p. 171.
60 ibid., p. 143.
61 ibid., pp. 197–8.
62 Leslie Stephen, *History of English Thought in the Eighteenth Century*, 2 vols (New York: Harcourt, Brace, and World, 1962), Vol. 2, p. 117.
63 ibid., Vol. 2, p. 163.
64 ibid., Vol. 2, p. 120.
65 ibid., Vol. 2, pp. 126–7.
66 ibid., Vol. 2, p. 163.
67 ibid., Vol. 2, p. 159.
68 ibid., Vol. 2, p. 121.
69 In this work, I have maintained that the intellectual origins of Locke's radicalism – as expressed in the political theory of the *Two Treatises of Government* – lay in certain religious and moral presuppositions associated with the Protestantism of the religious dissenters in Restoration England. This political radicalism was expressed (in its extreme form) through a specific political language employing the terminology of natural rights, state of nature, and an interpretation of natural law stressing the rights and authority of the community. Locke's politically radical intentions, I maintain, can be inferred from the way in which the text of the *Second Treatise* is structured, that is, the way in which the arguments in that work depend upon these presuppositions and terminology. In my *Revolutionary Politics and Locke's 'Two Treatises of Government'* (Princeton, NJ: Princeton University Press, 1986) I have attempted to view Locke's intentions in writing the *Two Treatises* in relation to the political activities in which he and those associated with him in the radical political movement of the 1680s engaged. I am persuaded that these are complementary and interdependent approaches to the study of political theory.

APPENDIX

The Composition and Structure of the *Two Treatises of Government*

In discussing the arguments advanced by Locke in the *Two Treatises of Government*, I have assumed that work to possess an internal structure that reflects my presentation of Locke's ideas in this book. I believe, that is, that the *First Treatise* was written before the *Second Treatise* and that it is therefore reasonable to assume that Locke's construction of the latter work is dependent, in part, upon his having already formulated certain arguments in the *First Treatise* which he developed at greater length in the *Second Treatise*. As this view contravenes the dominant orthodoxy concerning the writing of the *Two Treatises* as set forth by Peter Laslett, I shall briefly summarize my reasons for not accepting Laslett's opinion as to the dating of the *Two Treatises* or his suggestion that the *Second Treatise* was written first, and that Locke later added the *First Treatise* to it.[1]

Laslett observes that all of Locke's references to Robert Filmer in the *Two Treatises* except one direct the reader to the 1680 edition of Filmer's works. The single exception to this practice appears in paragraph 22 of the *Second Treatise* where the reference is to the 1679 edition of Filmer's writings. In one of Locke's notebooks, there is also a reference to the 1679 collection of Filmer's political tracts. Thus, Laslett concludes, 'it looks as if Locke must have been using the 1679 volume when he wrote § 22 of the *Second Treatise* . . . And it looks as if he had reached that paragraph before even reading *Patriarcha*; indeed the text of the *Second Treatise*, although written against patriarchalism, could have been originally composed without his having seen *Patriarcha* at all.'[2] This is an overhasty surmise as to how Locke went about writing the *Two Treatises*. Locke's notebooks are filled with extracts from the writings of various authors and with notes he made on his reading between 1679 and 1683 that were subsequently incorporated into the text of the *Two Treatises*, and it is extremely risky to conclude from a single reference how the rather complicated structure of that work was put together. Laslett's assertion is especially curious in view of the fact that he maintained that *all* of these notes, the vast majority of which belong to the period 1680–2, were inserted by Locke into an already written text, whereas he deduces from this one reference to Filmer that it establishes that Locke was in the process of writing the *Second Treatise* in 1679. Purely in terms of the structural dependence of Locke's argument upon the notes he made during 1680–2 relative to the sentence from Filmer, Laslett's hypothesis concerning the composition of the *Second Treatise* is implausible.[3] Indeed, there are good reasons for reversing Laslett's assumption; that is, it is the extract from Filmer that was added to the text of a nearly completed *Second Treatise*, the *First Treatise* having been written.

Laslett's description of the 'tablet' containing the reference to Filmer's 1679 tracts is rather misleading. It is not a notebook in the normal sense, that is, a repository of extracts and notes drawn from Locke's reading, such as characterize his journals and large tablets. In fact, it is very small – the size of an appointment-book – and easily carried in the hand or concealed in a waistcoat pocket. From its contents, it is evident that Locke used it to record names, places, meetings and brief notations of special interest to him. It was certainly not used for the general purpose of recording notes on the books Locke read.[4]

Laslett assumed that the '1679' above the reference to Filmer meant that Locke *made* the entry in 1679, but this reflects a misreading of the data. Locke purchased the appointment-book (MS f.28) in 1678 and he used it at least until 1686.[5] There are, therefore, numerous instances in which Locke has recorded notes made in different years on the same page.[6] Sometimes he adds the year beside the later note, but very often he does not. The year at the top of a page, however, always refers to the *first* note on that page, and when Locke records other notes on that page he generally puts a cross through the first note. Now, the sentence from Filmer is not the first note on the page on which it appears; rather, it appears under several notes which Locke has crossed through.[7] There is no date appended to the Filmer citation, so all we really know, according to Locke's note-taking practices, is that the first notation above the reference to Filmer was made in 1679. The most accurate observation one can make about the sentence from Filmer, therefore, is that Locke could have written it any time between 1679 and 1686. On the page preceding the reference to Filmer, for example, there is a '79' at the top of the page; and then, in different ink, 'Benjamin Furley, Rotterdam', with no date assigned to this entry, appears midway down the page. Yet it is virtually certain that the latter was recorded during the period Locke resided in Holland. Similarly, on the page following the reference to Filmer, '81' appears at the top of a page that includes a note concerning Jacob Vandervelde, Locke's friend and an Amsterdam bookseller with whom he had political and financial dealings.[8] It was never anything more than a guess on Laslett's part that the reference to Filmer's tracts was made by Locke in 1679, and, for the several reasons listed below, this was not a very good guess. Moreover, it should be clear that since no definite date can be assigned to the sentence from Filmer it cannot possibly constitute 'evidence' of anything with respect to the writing of the *Two Treatises*.

Laslett seems not to have appreciated the significance of the size of the appointment-book (3″ × 5″), the fact that Locke used it over a period of eight years, and that he carried it with him on his person. The first two points, even allowing for the smallness of Locke's handwriting, make it impossible for this tablet to have served as a repository for Locke's reading notes, and the third point indicates that Locke used it to record spontaneously bits of information – most frequently, meeting-places – given to him by friends when he was out and about. In other words, it is very likely that Locke was somewhere other than in his library in Oxford or London where he would have had access to the notebooks in which he regularly recorded his reading notes – most probably he was in Holland – at the time when he wrote the single sentence from Filmer cited by Laslett. If Locke made extensive notes from Filmer, as he did from Hooker, Grotius, Pufendorf, and from the literature describing voyages to the New World that he used while writing the *Second Treatise*, that notebook was destroyed or lost. Whatever Locke's note-taking practices as they relate to Filmer, they certainly cannot be reduced to this one reference in his appointment-book.

Moreover, Locke did not own the 1679 edition of Filmer's tracts. Are we to assume that he set out to write a major work of political theory directed against the ideas of a thinker whose writings he did not possess, and to which, therefore, he may have had limited access? As a description of Locke's approach to writing, and considering the detailed attention he gives to those whose ideas he criticizes, this, too, is a highly implausible suggestion, one that would make Locke's treatment of Filmer in the *Second Treatise* unique within the general pattern of Locke's writing practices.

Laslett believes his hypothesis about the dating of the *Second Treatise* is strengthened through an appeal to the analogous circumstances in which another critic of Filmer, James Tyrrell, found himself at the same time Locke was at work on the *Two Treatises*. According to Laslett, Tyrrell wrote 'the first form' of his *Patriarcha non Monarcha* during the winter of 1679–80 and sent it to the Whig historian, William Petyt. However, in view of the fact that 'a new treatise of Sir Robert Filmer's called *Patriarcha*' had lately been published, Tyrrell, Laslett alleges, had to change his plans, adding a critique of that work to his already written 'First Treatise'. Locke was thus able to recognize the effects of *Patriarcha* in shaping a critique of Filmer when he bought Tyrrell's *Patriarcha non Monarcha* on 2 June 1680. Accordingly, Locke followed Tyrrell in altering his manuscript by adding the *First Treatise* to it. Thus, Laslett concludes, 'their writing plans followed a remarkably similar pattern'.[9]

Unfortunately, this attempt to place Locke in close intellectual proximity to Tyrrell is a compound of error and supposition. Tyrrell's letter to Petyt indicates only that he is sending the latter a few papers that might prove useful to Petyt in his dispute with Robert Brady and others concerning the legal and historical precedents relating to the power of Parliament. Tyrrell's papers are more in the nature of legal research notes or commentaries on certain passages in *The Freeholder's Grand Inquest*.[10] In other words, they are in a form that has no parallel whatsoever with Locke's approach to Filmer in either the *First* or *Second Treatise*. Moreover, in his eagerness to establish a link between Locke and Tyrrell, Laslett misdates both the publication of *Patriarcha non Monarcha* and Locke's purchase of that work. Tyrrell's book was not published before June 1680, and Locke did not buy a copy until 2 June 1681, a year and a half after Tyrrell's correspondence with Petyt, and too late to affect Locke's approach to Filmer with respect to the *First Treatise*, which was certainly written prior to that date.[11]

The fact is we have no reason to assume that Tyrrell – or any other political writer – recognized the necessity of formulating a general critique of Filmer's political theory until *after* the appearance of *Patriarcha*. Prior to 1680, the Exclusion Crisis debate was focused almost exclusively upon the legal and historical precedents relating to the respective powers of Parliament and the king.[12] *The Freeholder's Grand Inquest* was relevant to this debate but, as Laslett himself notes, a refutation of this work did not require the critic to enter into a general discussion of patriarchalism or the origins of government.[13] This seems confirmed by Tyrrell's letter to Petyt in which he characterizes the papers he is sending the latter as having 'the same design' as Petyt's legalistic approach to the Exclusion controversy, for Petyt certainly was *not* engaged in writing a 'First Treatise' or general refutation of Filmer's political theory. When Tyrrell began his 'First Treatise' in the form of *Patriarcha non Monarcha*, therefore, it was some time early in 1680 following his purchase of *Patriarcha*. Tyrrell's manuscript was completed and ready for publication in the spring of 1681, and *in this respect* it seems valid to conclude that Locke and Tyrrell did follow 'a remarkably similar pattern' in their respective decisions to author a detailed critique of *Patriarcha*.[14] Locke purchased that work at the end of January 1680. Since he embarked on an extended and continuous journey a few days later, Locke had neither the time nor the opportunity to write a serious reply to *Patriarcha* until mid-April 1680, when he remained in London for six weeks.[15] The *First Treatise* thus belongs to the period 1680–1, as does Tyrrell's *Patriarcha non Monarcha*, as part of the Whig campaign to discredit Filmer's patriarchal theory, which was then being used by the Tories in their justificatory defence of the king's inherent power and his refusal to accede to the wishes of Parliament.[16]

But, Laslett insists, Locke wrote the *Second Treatise* before he wrote the *First Treatise*, and the former was 'substantially complete' prior to January 1680.[17] We have seen that neither the sentence cited from Filmer's 1679 political tracts nor the inferences concerning Tyrrell's writing of *Patriarcha non Monarcha* substantiate this conclusion. Let us turn to the third – and, in my view, the most important – line of argument developed by Laslett to support his thesis. 'The evidence suggests', he writes, that Locke 'actually wrote the [*Two Treatises*] for Shaftesbury's purposes'.[18] This premiss is only helpful with respect to the dating of Locke's work, however, in so far as one can state fairly precisely what Shaftesbury's political 'purposes' were.

If we begin with the most obvious feature of the *Second Treatise* as a work of political theory, namely, that it provides a justification for armed popular resistance to the exercise of illegitimate authority, the question can be simply stated: Did Shaftesbury's purposes include the advocacy of such a policy?[19] The answer to this question is yes, but all the evidence indicates that Shaftesbury did not arrive at the conclusion that the exclusion of the Duke of York from succession to the English throne necessitated the adoption of a policy of armed resistance until 1681 or 1682.[20] He certainly held no such opinion in 1679 when Locke is supposed to have been writing the *Second Treatise* as part of an effort to advance the political objectives of Shaftesbury and the Whig party. On the contrary, as President of the King's Privy Council until mid-October 1679, Shaftesbury directed a parliamentary and electoral campaign designed to secure passage of the Exclusion Bill. He also supported the Privy Council's decision to send troops led by the Duke of Monmouth to Scotland in order to *put down* a rebellious uprising in that country.

On 14 October 1679, Charles II dismissed Shaftesbury from the Privy Council and prorogued Parliament until 26 January 1680. Laslett maintains that it was during this period that Locke began writing the *Second Treatise*, but there is simply no evidence that Shaftesbury – or anyone else – had in fact at this time formulated a political strategy based on a defence of armed resistance or a view that the existing government had 'dissolved' into a state of nature. I do not see how the political message of the *Second Treatise* or Locke's intentions in writing it can be explained in terms of a political policy which cannot be shown to have existed. What the Whigs as a political party were actually engaged in was a massive campaign of gathering petitions addressed to the king, asking that Parliament be called into session.[21] Shaftesbury's policy during the winter of 1679–80 was to persuade Charles II to call a Parliament 'since it was taken for granted the King would yield to what everybody desired' if that body were allowed to meet.[22] This campaign of petitioning 'going forward in the city and country' was specifically Shaftesbury's 'new project' to increase the pressure on Charles for the exclusion of his brother.[23] At the beginning of December 1679, Shaftesbury and a number of other lords personally presented a petition to the king, while, in the country at large, blank petition-forms 'were put into the hands of agitants and . . . these agitators, being choice party-men, and well-instructed, went to every voter' to secure 'the hand or mark of every voting freeholder, citizen, and burgher in England'.[24]

Since it was part of the radical Whig argument that, in the absence of a sitting Parliament, subjects possessed but two means for 'redressing their grievances', namely, by petitioning or through resistance, it is clear that the party had committed itself in 1679–80 to the former policy.[25] As late as August 1680, Locke is reporting to Shaftesbury on the gathering of petitions and the expectations that Parliament will soon meet.[26] Since the Exclusion Crisis in 1679–80 was perceived by the Whigs, by Shaftesbury and by Locke as a matter to be resolved through parliamentary debate, elections, petitions – in short, through constitutional means – the problem of explaining Locke's intentions in setting out to write a revolutionary tract becomes a formidable one. In other words, the political intentions of Shaftesbury or Locke cannot be appealed to in support of an argument dating the *Second Treatise* in 'the autumn and winter of 1679–80' unless an evidential foundation can be provided for the existence of those intentions during this period, and this Laslett failed to do, for the very good reason that no one – including Locke and Shaftesbury – had adopted a policy of advocating armed resistance against Charles II in 1679.

If we pursue the implications of Laslett's sensible suggestion that the *Two Treatises* represents a defence of the Whig political position and that Locke wrote it within the context and to secure the advancement of Shaftesbury's political purposes, then we must reject as implausible Laslett's conclusions that the *Second Treatise* was written in 1679–80 and that it was written prior to the *First Treatise*. The latter work belongs to the political debate of 1680–1, when the central question was that of determining the succession, and the relative authority of the king or Parliament to render a binding decision on this issue. Locke's argument in the *First Treatise* poses the choice between the view that political power flows from the will of one man, leading towards tyranny, and the view that political power arises from the people and is expressed through consent and elections.[27] As a political tract, therefore, the *First Treatise* was written as part of Shaftesbury's electoral and parliamentary campaign to win support for the passage of the Exclusion Bill during the elections and parliamentary sessions of 1680–1, and to achieve this objective, in part, through attacking and countering the clergy's electoral influence over the country gentry.[28]

It was also part of the Whig strategy, however, to raise the threat of civil war if a Catholic (James) should succeed to the throne, that is, if the constitutional attempts to exclude him should ultimately fail. As Henry Booth put it, 'the case in short is this: Whether we shall sit still and put it to the venture of having a popish successor, then we must either submit our heads to the block, or fight and be rebels'.[29] Similarly, on the theoretical level, this charge was levelled against Filmer's thought; that is, acceptance of Filmer's political theory would lead the country into a civil war. If 'the old way' of instituting government through 'the consent of men making use of their reason to unite together into society' is abandoned for a reliance upon the divine right theory of government as the means of resolving the problem of succession, Locke warns, the consequence will be 'endless contention and disorder', that is, civil war.[30] Filmer's political theory 'dissolves the bonds of government and obedience', and its acceptance, according to Locke, would 'lay a foundation for perpetual disorder and mischief, tumult, sedition, and rebellion'.[31] This not-so-veiled threat was frequently made by the Whigs in the parliamentary debates and in their pamphlets throughout 1680, and it was intended to give force to the Whig argument that parliamentary passage to the Exclusion Bill was the only *alternative* to a civil war. Without a sitting Parliament, this argument and the political strategy that informed it collapsed. Therefore, when the king dissolved the third elected Parliament in two years, and moved in the direction of ruling without one, a new political strategy and a new political argument were required for those who, like Shaftesbury, were determined not to give up in their opposition to the Duke of York's succession to the crown.

The new political strategy was premissed upon the assumption that the Duke of York could not be excluded from the throne through constitutional or parliamentary means; thus, serious consideration would have to be given to an association of Protestants who would undertake armed resistance in order to defend their lives, liberties, properties and religion against the threat of a Catholic king. Moreover, Shaftesbury perceived an even more immediate political threat, namely, that Charles II intended to rule England without calling another Parliament into session. In a strategy meeting with other leaders of the Whig party held at his house around the time (March 1681) of the dissolution of the Oxford Parliament, Shaftesbury redirected the political argument away from the future dangers of a tyranny under James towards a more frontal attack upon Charles II and the danger that his refusal to accede to the wishes of the people's elected representatives in the House of Commons had effectively transformed the constitutional government of England into an absolute monarchy.[32] This policy shift is quite important as part of any argument pertaining to the dating of the *Second Treatise*. For the primary target of Locke's attack in that work is not Filmer, but Charles II. The absurdity or foolishness of Filmer's political ideas as a theoretical framework for understanding political life is not the main issue; rather, the problem addressed by Locke in the *Second Treatise* is a very practical one, namely, under what circumstances can it be said that a previously legitimate government has dissolved and the people are therefore justified in instituting a new government, even if this entails their use of force in self-defence against the threats posed by a reigning monarch? *This* formulation of the political problem facing the Whigs, most of whom did not subscribe to a theory of popular resistance, only gained recognition as a descriptive account of the political situation in England – and even then only among the radical Whigs led by Shaftesbury – some time between the late spring of 1681 and the end of 1682.

'It was after the dissolution of the Parliament at Oxford', according to Nathaniel Wade, 'that I first heard of any discourse about having recourse to arms.'[33] Wade was one of the radicals involved in the Rye House Plot and, later, in Monmouth's Rebellion. Robert Ferguson also maintained that prior to the dissolution of the Oxford Parliament 'there was not the least conspiracy set on foot against the King's person nor the government'.[34] Many other radicals said the same thing, and in fact the testimony on this point is overwhelming.[35] In other words, if we are to view the *Second Treatise* as having been written by Locke in accordance with Shaftesbury's political purposes, then, based upon what we know about Shaftesbury and the testimony of those associated with him who were prepared to engage in resistance to Charles II, Locke's work as a justificatory defence of popular resistance must have been written in 1681–2, and not in 1679, as claimed by Laslett. Shaftesbury understood very clearly the difference between a political strategy oriented towards electoral success and one designed to promote revolution. The paper recommending an association of Protestants to oppose James, which was found in Shaftesbury's house when he was arrested on 2 July 1681, begins with the observation that we have 'endeavoured in a parliamentary way by a bill for the purpose to bar and exclude the said Duke [of York] from the succession to the Crown', but these efforts have been 'utterly rejected'. Hence, in order to defend 'our laws, liberties, and properties', subscribing members of the association through a 'solemn and sacred promise of mutual defence and assistance' agreed to defend themselves 'by force of arms' if necessary 'against all encroachments and usurpations of arbitrary power whatsoever' which threatened 'the power and privilege of parliaments [or] the lawful rights and liberties of the subject'.[36] What I am arguing is that this shift from an electoral to a revolutionary strategy is reflected in the types of argument Locke employed and the specific focus of his critical attack (Filmer/Charles II) in the *First* and *Second Treatises* respectively.

In this regard, it is worthwhile paying careful attention to the language the radicals actually used to describe their situation in 1681–2. The 'exercise of absolute power', Ferguson declared, 'dissolves the government, and brings us all into a state of nature, by discharging us from the ties . . . we formerly lay under'. Thus, 'all the obligations they stood under to the King were become dissolved', and subjects were now free to appeal to the Law of Nature in order to defend themselves against the actions of a king seeking to rule as an absolute monarch.[37] Moreover, the radicals insisted, 'it is every man's duty' under natural law to use defensive force to prevent any 'invasion of other men's rights'. If the monarch is exercising force without authority, as the radicals believed Charles II was, then he may be resisted as any other person or 'beast' might be resisted who violated the Law of Nature; in short, under all conditions, 'illegal force may be repelled by force'.[38] From the testimony of various radical Whigs, we know that this was precisely the way in which Shaftesbury viewed the political situation in 1681–2.[39]

When Locke writes in the *Second Treatise* that whenever anyone seeks to make their arbitrary will 'the law of the society, they put themselves into a state of war with the people', who 'are thereupon absolved from any farther obedience' to the ruler, or, again, 'when illegal attempts are made upon their liberties or properties' by 'their magistrates, the people . . . are absolved from obedience' to those magistrates, and 'all former ties are cancelled . . . and every one has a right to defend himself, and to resist the aggressor', he is presenting both the argument and the specific language that Shaftesbury and the radical Whigs used to characterize the political situation following the dissolution of the Oxford Parliament.[40] In order to defend such a position, the radicals obviously required a theory premissed upon what 'rights' and 'duties' individuals could claim under natural law if their obligations to the existing government came to an end and they were returned to a state of nature. It is just such a foundation for a theory of resistance that Locke establishes in the early chapters of the *Second Treatise*.

Locke not only constructs his argument out of the terminology used by the radicals, he also restates the specific grounds for resistance to Charles II, as developed by Shaftesbury; that is, the king's refusal to call Parliament or to allow it to redress the grievances of the people. If 'the executive power' employs 'the force of the Commonwealth' to 'hinder the *meeting* and *acting* of the Legislative' power, contrary to both the public welfare and 'the original Constitution', Locke argues, this is an instance of 'exercising force without authority'. 'I say using force upon the people without authority and contrary to the trust put in him, that does so, is a state of war with the people, who have a right to *reinstate* their legislative in the exercise of their power'. Charles II's refusal to summon Parliament represents, for Locke, a threat to 'the safety and preservation of the people', and they 'have a right to remove it by force'. For, 'in all states and conditions, the true remedy of force without authority, is to oppose force to it. The use of force without authority, always puts him that uses it into a state of war, as the aggressor, and renders him liable to be treated accordingly'.[41] Thus, Locke concludes, 'he who takes away the freedom, or hinders the acting of the Legislative in its due seasons, in effect takes away the Legislative, and puts an end to the government'. The result is that the latter is now 'dissolved' and 'the people are not therefore bound to obey' the king's commands. In this situation, the people are free to 'constitute to themselves a *new Legislative*, as they think best, being in full liberty to resist the force of those, who without authority would impose anything upon them'.[42]

I have elaborated at greater length elsewhere upon the contextual character of the political language employed by Locke in the *Second Treatise*, but enough has been said, I believe, to indicate the close relationship between the ideas, arguments and political perspective espoused by Shaftesbury and the radical Whigs in 1681–2 and the political argument of the *Second Treatise* to establish the case for its having been written in 1681–2 *after* Locke had essentially completed the *First Treatise*.

On the basis of Laslett's observation that 'between 1679 and 1682 Locke was more interested in publications on political theory and natural law than ever before or after', I examined Locke's library catalogue and the book-purchases recorded in his journals. I will not reproduce the details of that analysis here, but the conclusions may be summarized as follows: Of the sixty-six titles in Locke's library that appear to have any bearing upon the Exclusion Crisis political debate, only three date from 1679, and all three works are in French. Seventy-seven percent of Locke's Exclusion Crisis holdings – fifty-one titles – were published in 1681 or later. Virtually *all* (95 per cent) the political works that 'interested' Locke during the period 1679–82 were purchased by him *after* he had acquired his copy of Filmer's *Patriarcha* in 1680. In other words, what we cannot establish from Locke's reading or book-buying interests before 1680 is precisely what Laslett hoped to demonstrate, namely, Locke's serious interest in politics, political theory, and his desire to refute Filmer as part of a contribution to his understanding of the Exclusion Crisis. It becomes rather easy to substantiate all of these assertions, however, from the evidence available relating to the period following his purchase of *Patriarcha* (1680–2). When we add to this the fact that none of the authors or notes he extracted from travel literature cited by Locke in the *Second Treatise* can be shown to have been in his possession during the autumn and winter of 1679–80, and all of them can be accounted for in relation to a later date, it really becomes quite implausible to insist upon a 1679 date for the authorship of that work.[43] In short, there is no evidence, and there never has been any evidence, that Locke was engaged in writing the *Two Treatises of Government* in 1679.

NOTES: APPENDIX

1 In addition to presenting new evidence, I have tried to collate and summarize in this appendix arguments that have appeared in print elsewhere. For an elaboration on many of the points only briefly stated here, the reader should consult my article, 'Revolutionary politics and Locke's *Two Treatises of Government*', *Political Theory*, Vol. 8, no. 4 (November 1980), pp. 429–86, and my book, *Revolutionary Politics and Locke's 'Two Treatises of Government'* (Princeton, NJ: Princeton University Press, 1986).

2 *Two Treatises of Government*, ed. Peter Laslett (Cambridge: Cambridge University Press, 1967), introduction, p. 58.

3 ibid., pp. 61, 65.

4 Laslett refers to it as a 'tablet' or a 'scribbling pad' (ibid., pp. 58–9), but it is much more accurately described as an appointment-book or a very personal (and secretive) notebook. For example, Locke notes meetings on MS f.28, fols 65, 87, 97, 98, 115, 118, 119, 140, 141, 154, 177, 178, 182. He records money transactions (fols 13, 119, 140) and ciphers relating to his correspondence from Holland (fols 139, 141, 155). There are also references to individuals or places associated with the Rye House Plot (fols 141, 154, 177). In other words, MS f.28 is the kind of notebook that, for good reasons, Locke would have carried on his person and which he took with him to Holland; it was not a 'scribbling pad' to be left in his library or in the custody of friends with his other notebooks and journals.

5 The earliest date inscribed on the inside cover is 1 July 1678, and the latest dates are for 1686 (MS f.28, fols 95–6, 119).

6 For example, ibid., fols 31, 38, 96–7, 115, 119, 140, 155.

7   ibid., fol. 118.
8   ibid., fols 117, 119. For other examples of pages with '79' at the top that contain notes made in later years, see fols 31, 96, 115, 140.
9   Laslett, introduction, pp. 59–60.
10 Petyt MS 538, Vol. 17, fol. 302 (Inner Temple). For a discussion of the Brady–Petyt controversy, see J. G. A. Pocock, *The Ancient Constitution and the Feudal Law* (Cambridge: Cambridge University Press, 1957).
11 For Laslett's confusion of the dates, see his introduction and notes, pp. 60, 145, 249. The discrepancy has been noted by John W. Gough, 'James Tyrrell, Whig historian and friend of John Locke', *Historical Journal*, Vol. 19, no. 3 (1976), pp. 581–610, and George T. Menake, 'Research note and query on the dating of Locke's *Two Treatises*', *Political Theory*, Vol. 10, no. 4 (November 1982), pp. 609–12.
12 Gilbert Burnet, *History of My Own Time*, 2 vols (Oxford, 1900), Vol. 2, p. 216; J. R. Jones, *The First Whigs: The Politics of the Exclusion Crisis, 1678–1683* (London: Oxford University Press, 1961), p. 67.
13 Laslett, introduction, p. 61.
14 Menake, 'Research note'.
15 Ashcraft, 'Revolutionary politics', p. 447. Locke's movements in 1680 are recorded in MS f.4.
16 In November 1680, Leoline Jenkins, a 'great asserter of monarchy' according to the theory of divine right, delivered two speeches in Parliament to the effect that the Exclusion Bill was 'contrary to natural justice . . . and tends to the overthrow of the very being and constitution of our government' (Burnet, *History*, Vol. 2, p. 257; Anchitell Grey, *Debates of the House of Commons from the Year 1667 to the Year 1694*, 10 vols (1763), Vol. 7, pp. 418–20, 447).
17 Laslett, introduction, p. 61.
18 ibid., p. 27.
19 The whole point of the *Second Treatise* is to demonstrate that 'it is lawful for the people . . . to *resist* the king' (para. 232: italics in original).
20 For a discussion of the reasons and circumstances that led Shaftesbury to draw this conclusion, see K. H. D. Haley, *The First Earl of Shaftesbury* (Oxford: Clarendon Press, 1968), and my *Revolutionary Politics*, esp. chs 7 and 8.
21 Jones, *First Whigs*, pp. 115ff.; Ashcraft, 'Revolutionary politics', pp. 437–8.
22 Leopold von Ranke, *The History of England*, 6 vols (1875), Vol. 4, p. 95; Roger North, *Examen* (1740), p. 541.
23 Burnet, *History*, Vol. 2, p. 248, and see the works cited in my 'Revolutionary politics', p. 478, n. 27.
24 Ranke, *History*, Vol. 4, p. 97; North, *Examen*, p. 542, and the works cited in my 'Revolutionary politics', p. 478, n. 28.
25 Jones, *First Whigs*, pp. 118–19; Ashcraft, 'Revolutionary politics', pp. 438, 478.
26 *The Correspondence of John Locke*, ed. E. S. De Beer, 8 vols (Oxford: Clarendon Press, 1976–85), Vol. 2, pp. 226–7.
27 The choice, as posed by Locke in the *First Treatise*, is between a politics based upon 'election and consent' and a politics characterized by 'tyranny and usurpation' (para. 148).
28 For a further discussion of this point, see my *Revolutionary Politics*, chs 5 and 6.
29 Henry Booth, Lord Delamere, *Works*, (1694), p. 95; Grey, *Debates*, Vol. 7, p. 426.
30 *First Treatise*, para. 106; cf. para. 72.
31 ibid., para. 105. Filmer's theory 'subvert[s] the very foundations of human society' (para. 3); cf. *Second Treatise*, para. 1.
32 Ford Lord Grey, *The Secret History of the Rye House Plot*, 2nd edn (1754), pp. 9–11; Ashcraft, *Revolutionary Politics*, ch. 7.
33 Harleian MS 6845, fol. 266.

34   James Ferguson, *Robert Ferguson the Plotter* (1887), p. 412.
35   For the evidence relating to numerous other participants in the resistance
     movement who, in their confessions or memoirs, place the time of their learning of
     the intentions of others to take up arms some time between the dissolution of the
     Oxford Parliament and the summer of 1682, see my *Revolutionary Politics*, ch. 8.
36   The text of the paper of association was printed by Roger L'Estrange, *A Brief
     History of the Times* (1687), and I have discussed it in detail in my *Revolutionary
     Politics*, ch. 7.
37   Robert Ferguson, *A Representation of the Threatening Dangers* (1688), p. 31; and his
     No Protestant Plot, Part Two (1682), pp. 1–2; James Ferguson, *Ferguson*, pp. 67,
     164, 414.
38   Samuel Johnson, *Julian the Apostate* (1682), pp. 71–7, 86, 92; William Denton, *Jus
     Regiminis: Being a Justification of Defensive Arms in General* (1689), p. 55 (a note
     indicates that this work was written several years before it was published in 1689).
     Other examples of this language are discussed in my *Revolutionary Politics*, ch. 7.
39   Grey, *Secret History*, p. 23. Other references are given in my *Revolutionary Politics*,
     ch. 7.
40   *Second Treatise*, paras 151, 155, 214, 222, 228, 232.
41   ibid., para. 155.
42   ibid., paras 215, 212; cf. para. 168.
43   Laslett, introduction, p. 56; Ashcraft, 'Revolutionary politics', pp. 439–41, 478–9.
     On pages 443–6 of the latter work, I provide some examples from some of the
     political tracts published after the appearance of Filmer's *Patriarcha* – many of
     which Locke owned – of arguments, concepts and terminology that are remarkably
     close to those used by Locke in the *Second Treatise*. There is also an attempt to
     show how the Tories tried to equate all references to the state of nature with
     Thomas Hobbes's description of it as a state of war, in order to deny the validity of
     the concept. The Whigs responded to this ideological attack by insisting upon a
     clear distinction between the state of nature and the state of war, as Locke does at
     the outset of the *Second Treatise*. A more extended discussion of both these points
     can be found in my *Revolutionary Politics*, ch. 7.

A CRITICAL NOTE ON LOCKE SCHOLARSHIP

In one sense, a critical appreciation of the *Two Treatises of Government* developed within a very short time following its publication, and Lockean political ideas form one of the undercurrents of political discussion in the early eighteenth century in the writings of individuals as diverse as Addison, Defoe, Bolingbroke or Mandeville. But while it is true to say that 'interpretations' of Locke's political thought can be found in the works of eighteenth-century thinkers such as Rousseau, Burke and Hume, for reasons suggested in Chapter 10, it seems preferable to view Locke's ideas as an integral element of political theories which retain their distinctive identities rather than as an elucidation of his political theory. Not until the twentieth century was there a sufficient distanciation from Lockean arguments to allow for the growth of what we would recognize as a body of secondary literature structured around various interpretations of Locke's *Two Treatises*. Nevertheless, the foundations of modern Lockean scholarship were laid in Victorian England; that is, in the view that developed as to what kind of person Locke was and how his ideas might be related to this conception of Locke the individual. Briefly stated, the essence of this perspective is that Locke the philosopher provided the general principles for Whig political theory and the *Two Treatises* – but especially the *Second Treatise* – ought therefore to be read as a compendium of those commonsensical beliefs which comprise the political doctrine of liberalism.

Of course, on some level, this is still the dominant interpretative framework with respect to any discussion of Locke's political ideas. Yet the particular emphasis accorded to the philosophical dimensions of Locke's political thought and to the *Two Treatises* as a source of Whig orthodoxy by Fox-Bourne, Macaulay and Leslie Stephen has in recent years lost its appeal. This decline is largely due to the same factors that supplied the basis for the Victorian view of Locke, namely, the appearance of previously unknown manuscripts by Locke, along with new biographical information concerning his activities and a general reassessment of the historical period in which Locke lived. Thus, certain religious and political beliefs have displaced philosophical concepts as the interpretative prism through which the arguments of the *Two Treatises* are seen to be significant. These are rather broad strokes in the characterization of the literature on Locke, but I shall indicate in my remarks below how this general shift away from a philosophical/analytical to a more historicist approach to a reading of the *Two Treatises of Government* bears upon the major specific interpretations of that work advanced by twentieth-century scholars.

In reply to Stephen's attempt (*History of English Thought in the Eighteenth Century*, 1876) to bring Locke within the purview of utilitarianism and empiricism, notwithstanding certain concessions made to 'metaphysical' rationalism that weakened his overall position, Sterling Lamprecht (*The Moral and Political Philosophy of John Locke*, 1918) presented Locke as a resolute defender of rationalism. Locke's 'supreme trust in reason', Lamprecht maintained (80–1), was nowhere better displayed than in the *Two Treatises*. Lamprecht recognized Locke's failure to develop 'a purely rationalistic ethics' (85–7), and he conceded that Locke's treatment of natural law displayed an unresolved tension between a rationalistic and a hedonistic ethic (105), but in the end Lamprecht situated Locke squarely within the rationalist camp. This interpretative battle, however, was fought over the status of Locke's moral philosophy, for Lamprecht showed no interest in challenging Stephen's identification of Locke with Whig political orthodoxies or the interests of the aristocratic landed class in seventeenth-century England. So long as one was clear as to Locke's philosophical purposes, the fact that he served as a spokesman for the economic interests of the ruling class (125), had no interest in challenging the position or the leaders of the established church (130, 160), and did not really believe in the right of revolution (146–50) mattered little to Lamprecht.

Like Lamprecht, Harold Laski (*Political Thought in England from Locke to Bentham*, 1920) portrayed Locke as an exponent of a 'thoroughgoing rationalism' (55). Locke's political argument, Laski asserted, was structured around a secular view of life (48), a mechanistic conception of the state (54), and an economic philosophy of 'narrow individualism' (60). As previous commentators had done, Laski identified Locke as 'the theorist' of the Glorious Revolution and the Whig party (26).

George Sabine (*A History of Political Theory*, 1937) incorporated all the major points made by his predecessors, but he was much less sympathetic towards Locke's efforts to formulate a consistent political philosophy than they had been. Sabine sharpened the philosophical conflict in Locke's thought between rationalism and empiricism, maintaining that it was virtually impossible to reconcile Locke's political theory with his general philosophical position (529). At its core, therefore, Locke's political thought, as expressed in the *Two Treatises*, was vitiated by logical difficulties (537–8). Sabine, as he acknowledged in the preface to the first edition of *History*, identified his own approach to political theory with Humean scepticism, as displayed in Hume's critique of the natural law tradition. Not surprisingly, Sabine adopted a critical attitude towards the abstractions which he believed were prevalent in Locke's political thought. Thus, Locke's endorsement of the fiction of a social contract, his atomistic portrayal of the state of nature, and, in general, his ahistorical and asocial approach to politics, his defence of egoistic individualism and the economic interests of the ruling class (525 ff.) were ultimately traceable to his philosophical confusion, which left Locke's political theory without any 'logical structure' (537–8). Of course, Locke's political ideas were immensely influential – in part, precisely *because* of their commonsensical appeal and absence of analytical rigour – but there had never been any serious doubt expressed in the secondary literature regarding that point. If Locke was 'the ideal spokesman of a middle-class revolution' (741), not the least reason for this was the fact that he 'was the most conservative of revolutionists' (535 ff.).

The standard view of Locke prior to the 1950s – with one exception, mentioned below – was that of a confused philosopher with a (perhaps misplaced) confidence in rationalism, the individual, and a selfish pursuit of material interests. While this perspective had much to recommend it, practically speaking, to the Whig party politicians and the landed property-holders whose political revolution the *Two Treatises* dutifully defended, the philosophical approach to Locke certainly did not present him as being a profound or compellingly attractive thinker. The most interesting, and almost the only departure from this interpretative orthodoxy, was Wilmoore Kendall's *John Locke and the Doctrine of Majority Rule* (1941). According to Kendall, Locke was really a democrat, advocating manhood suffrage and popular sovereignty (121). Hence the collective consent of the community is not only paramount with respect to any determination of property rights (72, 84, 104), but Kendall went so far as to identify the Law of Nature with majority consent (82 ff.). For Kendall, Locke appeared to be more like Rousseau and much less like Hooker or Hobbes than previous Locke scholars had supposed. Certainly, this made Locke a more interesting intellectual and political figure – at least, relative to the context within which his ideas were generally discussed – but it did so by taking great liberties with Locke's pronouncements on the origins and status of natural law, while ignoring altogether any contextual evidence that would either support or modify Kendall's rather sweeping claims on Locke's behalf. In short, although he laid considerable stress on certain passages in the *Second Treatise* which had heretofore received little attention from previous commentators, Kendall advanced an interpretation of Locke that went far beyond – and sometimes contradicted – the text without, however, offering any new evidence to support his reading of that work.

Purely from the standpoint of diversity of views, the 1950s were clearly a high-water mark of Lockean scholarship. Leo Strauss (*Natural Right and History*, 1953) revived an earlier theme in the secondary literature associating Locke with Hobbes, but Strauss pressed the issue beyond mere association; for him, Locke's teachings were those of Hobbes, though disguised in order to appear more palatable to a seventeenth-century audience. Like Kendall, Strauss took considerable liberties with the text, chopping it up into snippets of quotations from disparate places run together in a manner that made it difficult for the reader to follow Locke's argument in the text (for which Strauss was soundly criticized by, among others, Yolton in his 1958 article on natural law). Strauss maintained that Locke concealed his real 'philosophic' views from his readers since these, if known, would have incurred their wrath, and Locke was a far more cautious man than Hobbes. It has always been difficult to understand the esoteric reasoning underlying this claim, since it never attempts to account for the fact that Locke's *political* views, as expressed in the *Two Treatises*, were far more dangerous to his well-being than anything he *could* have said as a philosopher; it pays no attention to the fact that Locke said in his journals, unpublished manuscripts, and private correspondence – where, according to this view, he should have had no publicly oriented reason for concealing his true position – what he said in his published works; it reverses the intellectual thrust of much of Locke's writing (in the *Essay Concerning Human Understanding* and *The Reasonableness of Christianity*, for example) where he is highly critical of philosophers and the claims of philosophy by identifying his 'true' aims with those he is criticizing, thus posing insurmountable difficulties for the interpreter in assessing the credibility of Locke's statements in various published texts; and, finally, it never investigates whether, in fact, Locke's contemporaries *were* making the arguments in their printed works which it is assumed it was unsafe for Locke to make.

If Strauss approached the *Two Treatises* guided by an unsubstantiated claim about Locke's purposes in writing that work, Macpherson (*The Political Theory of Possessive Individualism*, 1962) also followed this interpretative path, though it led him not towards the mysteries of philosophy and Locke's personality but, rather, towards a view of Locke as the more or less conscious defender of exploitative capitalistic relations. This, too, was an old theme in the secondary literature, but Macpherson – as Strauss had done with Locke's intellectual association with Hobbes – transformed a passing allusion into a major interpretative axis, according to which Locke's thought could be entirely revaluated. In other words, it was not only that the appearance in print of the *Two Treatises* was a convenient circumstance so far as the Whig property-holders of the Glorious Revolution were concerned, but, Macpherson argued, Locke consciously structured the arguments in that work in such a manner that any recovery of their meaning required a reading of the *Two Treatises* in which this imputed intention is given a central place of importance. Macpherson identified Locke as an exponent of the unlimited appropriation of property and of the view that members of the labouring class were sub-rational individuals. Locke's rationalism is thus employed in defence of the political and economic relations of capitalist society, while his writings on religion serve ideologically to secure the compliant obedience of non-rational individuals to a system that exploits their labour. The ownership and rights of property, taken in its narrowest sense, are what Locke's political theory – and the *Two Treatises* – is all about. Macpherson paid as little attention as Strauss did to the fact that no one among Locke's contemporaries read or understood his argument from their postulated standpoints, or to the fact that Locke personally subscribed to and identified his own position with those religious beliefs he was presumably advancing as a sop to lesser minds, or that he was writing in defence of revolutionary political action and religious dissent – positions adhered to by a very small minority of his contemporaries – which did not appeal to the established property-owners whose interests he was supposed to be looking after. Equally damaging to Macpherson's case was his failure to provide the historical and sociological evidence necessary to establish his claims regarding the kind of society seventeenth-century England was, since the more inappropriate the 'model' of society formulated by Macpherson is as a descriptive characterization of Locke's environment, the more difficult it becomes to associate that model with Locke's intentional purposes in writing the *Two Treatises*.

Since the older approaches to Locke had concentrated upon ascertaining the correctness of his philosophical position, based upon some reordering of concepts drawn from his writings, neither Locke's intentions nor the social context within which he wrote had counted for much in these interpretations. The shift in perspective – that is, the effort to establish the relationship between Locke and his audience as a precondition for any understanding of his philosophy – demanded a type of evidence that could not simply be extracted from the text (*Two Treatises*) itself. Thus, the interpretations of Strauss and Macpherson shared a common problem in that they were both dependent upon certain assumptions about the nature of seventeenth-century England and a set of intentions imputed to Locke that assumed significance in relation to that social context, but neither the nature of the context nor Locke's intentions were established by the evidence presented in their books.

To some extent, Wolin (*Politics and Vision*, 1960, ch. 9) skirted around this issue, since his argument was designed less to situate Locke's thought in its proper historical context than it was to present a sketch of what might be called the social psychology of liberalism. Locke's thought, that is, formed an essential element in the reconstruction of a social consciousness compatible with a particular set of social and political institutions (liberal bourgeois society). Ultimately, of course, some historical factors were causally significant with respect to the emergence of this specific *Weltanschauung*, but the relationship of these factors to the formulation of Locke's thought was not clear in Wolin (as it was in Macpherson) nor did Wolin pursue the roots of liberal anxiety – the Weberian ideal type which he employed in his reconstruction of liberalism – into the recesses of Locke's personality and hidden motives (as Strauss had done). Nevertheless, the existence, origins and development of this form of social consciousness seemed to call for some historically grounded explanation – not to mention some account of how that social consciousness was related to the emergence and development of a particular social structure – which was not presented in *Politics and Vision*. These questions certainly cannot be answered through analyses of specific texts in the history of political theory. Yet none of the presumptively historically oriented interpretations offered by Strauss, Macpherson or Wolin advanced beyond the boundaries of that methodological approach, which had traditionally been employed by those interpreters who eschewed historical evidence for philosophical analysis.

Plamenatz's treatment of Locke (*Man and Society*, 1963, Vol. 2) represented a continuation of the philosophical approach, now accompanied by a polemical defence justifying the exclusion of historical evidence. All that was required of an interpreter, Plamenatz argued, was that he/she read the text over and over again until the meaning of the author became transparently clear in the interpreter's mind. Unfortunately, the *Two Treatises* proved a rather recalcitrant example for this approach since, as Plamenatz's predecessors had noted, it was not a profound, consistent or carefully constructed work of philosophy. Riddled as it was with ambiguities and contradictions, Locke's work might never yield a plain meaning. Notwithstanding his methodological pronouncements in the preface to *Man and Society*, therefore, Plamenatz's interpretation of Locke (and of other theorists) is filled with assumptions about Locke's intentions, the expectations and beliefs held by his readers, the nature of English society in the seventeenth century, and so on, which are employed to elucidate the meaning of the text. Yet no references are supplied by Plamenatz to indicate from where he derived these assumptions, no evidence is offered to support them, and there is no conscious defence by Plamenatz of these assumptions relative to others that might have been made. Lacking such evidence, all such judgements are simply the arbitrary impositions of the interpreter, and since they are not to be discovered merely from a reading of the text in question they cannot claim the *only* source of authority sanctioned by this methodological approach. Plamenatz characterized Locke as one of the most abstract political philosophers, but his perspective did not permit him to raise the question of to what extent the 'abstractness' of Locke's argument was due precisely to the failure of interpreters to utilize a context-based approach to the arguments contained in the *Two Treatises*.

Cranston's biography (*John Locke*, 1957), the first in nearly a century, was notable for its failure to shed any light upon the intellectual dimensions of Locke's thought. The predominant conclusion one derives from a reading of Cranston's *Locke* is that he was an exceedingly secretive person. However, drawing upon the recently discovered Locke manuscripts and Peter Laslett's argument concerning the composition of the *Two Treatises*, Cranston's work did extend our knowledge of Locke's activities, especially during the period of his association with the first Earl of Shaftesbury. In an early (1956) article, but much more fully in his introduction to the critical edition of the *Two Treatises* (1960), Laslett saw the association of Locke and Shaftesbury as a fact of central importance to the writing of the *Two Treatises of Government*. Locke wrote that work, Laslett argued, 'for Shaftesbury's purposes' (27). The general proposition that the *Two Treatises* should be read primarily as a political and not as a philosophical work was clear enough, but precisely how this affected one's view of the specific arguments advanced by Locke was less easy to discern. Laslett's dating of the *Two Treatises* as an Exclusion tract appeared to dislodge the long-standing orthodoxy that Locke wrote the work as a defence of the 1689 Revolution, but his misdating of the composition of the *Second Treatise* (see Appendix) made it extremely difficult to determine what interpretative judgements were called into question by his argument, especially since it was not based upon the introduction of any new historical evidence pertaining to Locke's or Shaftesbury's political 'purposes'. Laslett maintained that Locke was not writing as a philosopher 'applying to politics . . . his view of reality as a whole' (x), but since no one had ever imagined that Locke's philosophy and his political theory were entirely integrative systems of thought or stood in a deductive relationship to each other this assertion had little effect upon the supposition that there were serious – possibly irreconcilable – conflicts between Locke's philosophy and his political theory. It is true the reinstatement of Filmer in place of Hobbes as Locke's primary opponent in the *Two Treatises* represented some advancement in the appreciation of the historical and political dimensions of that work, but few interpreters ventured beyond a recognition of that simple fact, as is evident from the persistent indifference they showed towards the *First Treatise*.

Von Leyden's introduction to the *Essays on the Law of Nature* (1954) revived an earlier emphasis upon Locke's hedonistic ethics and the conflict between rationalism and empiricism in his treatment of natural law. Martin Seliger (*The Liberal Politics of John Locke*, 1968) offered a reading of the *Two Treatises* that made Locke an authoritarian liberal, a champion of executive power and prerogative, and a reluctant revolutionary. Seliger called attention to certain neglected passages in the *Two Treatises*, as Kendall in propounding a very different interpretation had done nearly thirty years before, but Seliger's interpretation similarly went far beyond any support provided by the text without introducing any corroborative historical or contextual evidence.

With the appearance in 1969 of John Dunn's *The Political Thought of John Locke*, Lockean scholarship reached a significant turning-point in its evolution. This was due not so much to Dunn's resolution of old interpretative problems as it was to his methodological insistence upon paying attention to 'Locke's *own* meaning' in the *Two Treatises* rather than imposing twentieth-century meanings (for example, Strauss, Macpherson) upon that work (ix). What Dunn sought to achieve was 'a more coherent and historically accurate account of what Locke was maintaining in the *Two Treatises* than has yet been given' (xi). The most important conclusion to emerge from Dunn's study, as he himself noted, was 'the theoretical centrality of Locke's religious preoccupations' to any understanding of his political thought. Although some of Dunn's specific arguments are unconvincing, I do not see how this general point can be contested, and in the context of a more general shift towards an understanding of the historical Locke it will require a formidable argument and a substantial amount of evidence to justify the substitution of another interpretative axis for this one.

Notwithstanding the correctness of Dunn's reconstruction of the theoretical hierarchy of Locke's thought, its operative function in *Political Thought* as a guide to the *Two Treatises* seemed more adapted to evaluating alternative readings of that work than to clarifying Locke's own intellectual or political objectives. For Dunn, the state of nature is purely an ahistorical construct, the nature of legitimate political society is merely a formal exercise in reasoning sanctioning an almost infinite variety of forms of government, Locke's treatment of consent is a case of muddled reasoning, and his discussion of revolution is actually a reassuring endorsement of the legitimacy of the English polity in the 1680s. To say that it is difficult to extract a clear or concise picture of Locke's political theory from Dunn's book is to understate the problem. Moreover, if the *Two Treatises* was written as an Exclusion tract (*pace* Laslett), Dunn observes, it was certainly an ineffective or poorly organized political tract (53).

If, for Dunn, Locke's political views appeared to be more the product of an exercise in deduction from religious premises than a directive for organized action addressed to a particular audience, this was due, in part, to the metaphorical status of 'historical' as a descriptive characterization of his book. In fact, very little historical evidence of any kind is introduced into Dunn's discussion of Locke's thought, and none which serves to elucidate the meaning of Locke's political objectives in writing the *Two Treatises*. For, despite the cogency and effectiveness of the methodological critique mounted in the 1960s against the philosophical, analytical and merely textual approach to the interpretation of political theory in favour of a contextual, historically grounded framework for recovering meanings, the fact remains that no such interpretative reading of Locke's *Two Treatises* was produced. In other words, the failure to present the historical evidence necessary for a reconstruction of the political debate to which the *Two Treatises* was a contribution not only left the notion of 'historical context' without a concrete referential meaning, it also seriously undermined any attempt to gain an appreciation of the political meaning that work might have had for Locke and for his audience. (This lacuna in Locke scholarship I hope to have filled with *Revolutionary Politics*.)

The Locke industry shows little sign of succumbing to intellectual bankruptcy, though it is difficult to forecast the direction of its future development. There now appears to be a secure and historically grounded niche for the message of political radicalism of the *Two Treatises*, located in various ways by Franklin (1978), Tully (1980), Kenyon (1977), Goldie (1980), and in my work cited above. This extension of the political dimensions of Locke's thought rests upon a recognition of the importance of religious beliefs to the structure of Locke's thought. In both respects, therefore, the 'historical' Locke – Locke the seventeenth-century political and religious dissident – has finally achieved a place of prominence within the framework of Lockean scholarship.

BIBLIOGRAPHY

More extensive bibliographies can be found in: H. O. Christophersen, *A Bibliographical Introduction to the Study of John Locke* (Oslo: I Kommisjon Hos Jacob Dybwad, 1930); R. Hall and R. S. Woolhouse, *Eighty Years of Locke Scholarship: A Bibliographical Guide* (Edinburgh: Edinburgh University Press, 1983); and Godfrey Davies and Mary Frear Keeler (eds), *Bibliography of British History: Stuart Period, 1603–1714*, 2nd edn (Oxford: Clarendon Press, 1970).

This bibliography is divided into four sections: (i) works by Locke; (ii) works written before 1900, including reprints published after that date; (iii) books published after 1900; and (iv) articles published after 1900.

(i) WORKS BY LOCKE

The Correspondence of John Locke, ed. E. S. De Beer, 8 vols (Oxford: Clarendon Press, 1976–85).

An Early Draft of Locke's Essay, ed. R. I. Aaron and Jocelyn Gibb (Oxford: Clarendon Press, 1936).

An Essay Concerning Human Understanding, ed. Peter H. Nidditch (Oxford: Clarendon Press, 1975).

Essays on the Law of Nature, ed. W. von Leyden (Oxford: Clarendon Press, 1954).

A Letter on Toleration, ed. Raymond Klibansky and J. W. Gough (Oxford: Clarendon Press, 1968).

Some Thoughts Concerning Education, in *The Educational Writings of John Locke*, ed. James L. Axtell (Cambridge: Cambridge University Press, 1968).

Two Tracts on Government, ed. Philip Abrams (Cambridge: Cambridge University Press, 1967).

Two Treatises of Government, ed. Peter Laslett, 2nd edn (Cambridge: Cambridge University Press, 1967).

The Works of John Locke, 12th edn, 9 vols (1824).

(ii) WORKS WRITTEN BEFORE 1900

[Anon.], *Political Aphorisms* (1690).

[Anon.], *Vox Populi: or, The People's Claim to Their Parliament's Sitting* (1681).

Cobbett, William (ed.), *The Parliamentary History of England*, 36 vols (1806–20), esp. Vols 4 and 5.

Ferguson, Robert, *A Brief Justification of the Prince of Orange's Descent into England* (1688).

Ferguson, Robert, *An Enquiry into the Administration of Affairs in England* (1684).

Ferguson, Robert, *The Interest of Reason in Religion* (1675).

Ferguson, Robert, *A Just and Modest Vindication of the Two Last Parliaments* (1681).
Ferguson, Robert, *A Representation of the Threatening Dangers* (1688).
Ferguson, Robert, *A Sober Enquiry into the Nature, Measure, and Principles of Moral Virtue* (1673).
Filmer, Sir Robert, *Patriarcha and Other Political Works*, ed. Peter Laslett (Oxford: Basil Blackwell, 1949).
Fox-Bourne, H. R., *The Life of John Locke*, 2 vols (1876).
Grey, Anchitell, *Debates of the House of Commons from the Year 1667 to the Year 1694*, 10 vols (1763).
Grotius, Hugo, *The Rights of War and Peace (De Jure Belli ac Pacis Libri Tres)* (New York/London: M. Walter Dunne, 1901).
Hooker, Richard, *Of the Laws of Ecclesiastical Polity*, 2 vols, Everyman's Library (London: Dent, 1907).
Hunton, Philip, *A Treatise of Monarchy* (1643).
King, Peter, *The Life of John Locke*, 2 vols (1830).
Lawson, George, *Politica sacra et civilis*, 2nd edn (1689).
LeClerc, Jean, *An Account of the Life and Writings of John Locke*, 3rd edn (1714).
Macaulay, Thomas B., *The History of England from the Accession of James II*, 5 vols (New York: Thomas Nelson, n.d.).
Neville, Henry, *Plato Redivivus*, 2nd edn (1681); reprinted in *Two English Republican Tracts*, ed. Caroline Robbins (Cambridge: Cambridge University Press, 1969).
Parker, Samuel, *A Discourse of Ecclesiastical Polity* (1670).
Pufendorf, Samuel, *Of the Law of Nature and Nations (De Jure Naturae et Gentium)*, trans. Basil Kennett, with the notes of Jean Barbeyrac (1729).
Sidney, Algernon, *Discourses Concerning Government* (1698).
State Tracts: A Collection of Several Treatises Relating to the Government (1689).
Stephen, Leslie, *History of English Thought in the Eighteenth Century*, 2 vols (1876; reprinted New York: Harcourt, Brace and World, 1962).
Tyrrell, James, *Patriarcha non Monarcha* (1681).

(iii) BOOKS PUBLISHED AFTER 1900

Aaron, R. I., *John Locke*, 3rd edn (Oxford: Clarendon Press, 1971).
Appleby, Joyce O., *Economic Thought and Ideology in Seventeenth-Century England* (Princeton, NJ: Princeton University Press, 1978).
Ashcraft, Richard, *Revolutionary Politics and Locke's 'Two Treatises of Government'* (Princeton, NJ: Princeton University Press, 1986).
Brandt, Reinhard (ed.), *John Locke Symposium* (Berlin: de Gruyter, 1981).
Buchdahl, G., *The Image of Newton and Locke in the Age of Reason* (London/New York: Sheed & Ward, 1961).
Colman, John, *John Locke's Moral Philosophy* (Edinburgh: Edinburgh University Press, 1983).
Cox, Richard, *Locke on War and Peace* (Oxford: Clarendon Press, 1960).
Cragg, G. L., *From Puritanism to the Age of Reason* (Cambridge: Cambridge University Press, 1966).

Cranston, Maurice, *John Locke: A Biography* (London: Longmans, Green, 1957).

Daly, James, *Sir Robert Filmer and English Political Thought* (Toronto: University of Toronto Press, 1979).

Dickinson, H. T., *Liberty and Property: Political Ideology in Eighteenth-Century Britain* (London: Weidenfeld & Nicolson, 1977).

Dunn, John, *John Locke* (Oxford: Clarendon Press, 1984).

Dunn, John, *The Political Thought of John Locke* (Cambridge: Cambridge University Press, 1969).

Euchner, Walter, *Naturrecht und Politik bei John Locke* (Frankfurt am Main: Suhrkamp, 1979).

Feiling, Keith, *History of the Tory Party, 1640–1714* (Oxford: Clarendon Press, 1924).

Fennessy, R. R., *Burke, Paine and the Rights of Man* (The Hague: Martinus Nijhoff, 1963).

Forbes, Duncan, *Hume's Philosophical Politics* (Cambridge: Cambridge University Press, 1975).

Franklin, Julian H., *John Locke and the Theory of Sovereignty* (Cambridge: Cambridge University Press, 1978).

Gibson, James, *Locke's Theory of Knowledge and Its Historical Relations* (1917; reprinted Cambridge: Cambridge University Press, 1968).

Gooch, G. P., *English Democratic Ideas of the Seventeenth Century*, 2nd edn (New York: Harper & Row, 1959).

Gough, John W., *John Locke's Political Philosophy, Eight Studies* (Oxford: Clarendon Press, 1956).

Greenleaf, W. H., *Order, Empiricism and Politics* (London: Oxford University Press, 1964).

Haley, K. H. D., *The First Earl of Shaftesbury* (Oxford: Clarendon Press, 1968).

Harrison, John, and Laslett, Peter, *The Library of John Locke*, 2nd edn (Oxford: Clarendon Press, 1971).

Jones, J. R., *Country and Court: England, 1658–1714* (Cambridge, Mass.: Harvard University Press, 1978).

Jones, J. R., *The First Whigs: The Politics of the Exclusion Crisis, 1678–1683* (London: Oxford University Press, 1961).

Kendall, Wilmoore, *John Locke and the Doctrine of Majority Rule*, Illinois Studies in the Social Sciences, vol. 26, no. 2 (Urbana, Ill.: University of Illinois Press, 1941).

Kenyon, J. P., *Revolution Principles: The Politics of Party, 1689–1720* (Cambridge: Cambridge University Press, 1977).

Lacey, Douglas, *Dissent and Parliamentary Politics in England, 1661–1689* (New Brunswick, NJ: Rutgers University Press, 1969).

Lamprecht, Sterling P., *The Moral and Political Philosophy of John Locke* (1918; reprinted New York: Russell & Russell, 1962).

Larkin, Paschal, *Property in the Eighteenth Century, with Special Reference to England and Locke* (1930; reprinted New York: Howard Fertig, 1969).

Laski, Harold J., *Political Thought in England from Locke to Bentham* (London: Oxford University Press, 1920).

Letwin, William, *The Origins of Scientific Economics: English Economic Thought 1660–1776* (London: Methuen, 1963).

Mabbot, J. D., *John Locke* (London: Macmillan, 1973).

Macpherson, C. B., *The Political Theory of Possessive Individualism* (London: Oxford University Press, 1962).

Martin, C. B., and Armstrong, D. M. (eds), *Locke and Berkeley: A Collection of Critical Essays* (Garden City, NY: Doubleday, 1968).

Meek, Ronald, L., *Social Science and the Ignoble Savage* (Cambridge: Cambridge University Press, 1976).

Ogg, David, *England in the Reign of Charles II*, 2 vols (Oxford: Clarendon Press, 1956).

Parry, Geraint, *John Locke* (London: Allen & Unwin, 1978).

Plamenatz, John, *Man and Society*, 2 vols (New York: McGraw-Hill, 1963).

Plumb, J. H., *The Origins of Political Stability in England, 1675–1725* (London: Penguin, 1967).

Pocock, J. G. A., *The Ancient Constitution and the Feudal Law* (Cambridge: Cambridge University Press, 1957).

Polin, Raymond, *La Politique morale de John Locke* (Paris: Presses Universitaires de France, 1960).

Riley, Patrick, *Will and Political Authority* (Cambridge, Mass.: Harvard University Press, 1982).

Ronalds, Francis S., *The Attempted Whig Revolution of 1678–1681*, Illinois Studies in Social Sciences, vol. 21, nos 1–2 (Urbana, Ill.: University of Illinois Press, 1937).

Sabine, George H., *A History of Political Theory*, 3rd edn (New York: Holt, Rinehart & Winston, 1961).

Schlatter, Richard B., *The Social Ideas of Religious Leaders, 1660–1688* (London: Oxford University Press, 1940).

Schochet, Gordon J. (ed.), *Life, Liberty, and Property: Essays on Locke's Political Ideas* (Belmont, Calif.: Wadsworth, 1971).

Schochet, Gordon J., *Patriarchalism in Political Thought* (New York: Basic Books, 1975).

Seliger, Martin, *The Liberal Politics of John Locke* (London: Allen & Unwin, 1968).

Skinner, Quentin, *The Foundations of Modern Political Thought*, 2 vols (Cambridge: Cambridge University Press, 1978).

Stewart, J. B., *The Moral and Political Philosophy of David Hume* (New York: Columbia University Press, 1963).

Strauss, Leo, *Natural Right and History* (Chicago, Ill.: University of Chicago Press, 1953).

Tuck, Richard, *Natural Rights Theories: Their Origin and Development* (Cambridge: Cambridge University Press, 1979).

Tully, James, *A Discourse on Property: John Locke and His Adversaries* (Cambridge: Cambridge University Press, 1980).

Vaughn, Karen Ivarsen, *John Locke: Economist and Social Scientist* (Chicago, Ill.: University of Chicago Press, 1982).

Viano, C. A., *John Locke, dal Razionalismo all' Illuminismo* (Turin: Giulio Einaudi, 1960).

Von Leyden, W., *Hobbes and Locke* (London: Macmillan, 1981).

Western, J. R., *Monarchy and Revolution: The English State in the 1680s* (London: Blandford Press, 1972).

Weston, Corinne Comstock, and Greenberg, Janelle Renfrow, *Subjects and Sovereigns: The Grand Controversy over Legal Sovereignty in Stuart England* (Cambridge: Cambridge University Press, 1981).

Wolin, Sheldon S., *Politics and Vision* (Boston, Mass.: Little, Brown, 1960).

Wood, Neal, *John Locke and Agrarian Capitalism* (Berkeley/Los Angeles, Calif.: University of California Press, 1984).

Wood, Neal, *The Politics of Locke's Philosophy: A Social Study of 'An Essay Concerning Human Understanding'* (Berkeley/Los Angeles, Calif.: University of California Press, 1983).

Woolhouse, R. S., *Locke's Philosophy of Science and Knowledge* (Oxford: Basil Blackwell, 1971).

Yolton, John W., *John Locke and the Way of Ideas* (Oxford: Clarendon Press, 1956).

Yolton, John W. (ed.), *John Locke: Problems and Perspectives* (Cambridge: Cambridge University Press, 1969).

Yolton, John W., *Locke and the Compass of Human Understanding* (Cambridge: Cambridge University Press, 1970).

(iv) ARTICLES PUBLISHED AFTER 1900

Albritton, R. R., 'The politics of Locke's philosophy', *Political Studies*, vol. 24, no. 3 (1976), pp. 253–67.

Appleby, Joyce O., 'Locke, liberalism and the natural law of money', *Past and Present*, no. 71 (May 1976), pp. 43–69.

Ashcraft, Richard, 'John Locke's library: portrait of an intellectual', *Transactions of Cambridge Bibliographical Society*, vol. 5, no. 1 (1969), pp. 47–60.

Ashcraft, Richard, 'Locke's state of nature: historical fact or moral fiction?', *American Political Science Review*, vol. 62, no. 3 (September 1968), pp. 898–915.

Ashcraft, Richard, 'Political theory and political reform: Locke's essay on Virginia', *Western Political Quarterly*, vol. 22, no. 4 (December 1969), pp. 742–58.

Ashcraft, Richard, 'Revolutionary politics and Locke's *Two Treatises of Government*', *Political Theory*, vol. 8, no. 4 (November 1980), pp. 429–86.

Ashcraft, Richard, and Goldsmith, M. M., 'Locke, revolution principles, and the formation of Whig ideology', *Historical Journal*, vol. 26, no. 4 (1983), pp. 773–800.

Batz, William G., 'The historical anthropology of John Locke', *Journal of the History of Ideas*, vol. 35, no. 4 (October–December 1974), pp. 663–70.

Behrens, B., 'The Whig theory of the constitution in the reign of Charles II', *Cambridge Historical Journal*, vol. 7, no. 1 (1941), pp. 42–71.

Colie, Rosalie, 'The social language of John Locke: a study in the history of ideas', *Journal of British Studies*, vol. 4, no. 2 (May 1965), pp. 29–51.

Cranston, Maurice, 'The politics of John Locke', *History Today*, September 1952, pp. 619–22.

Cranston, Maurice, 'The politics of a philosopher', *Listener*, 5 January 1961, pp. 17–19.

Day, J. P., 'Locke on property', *Philosophical Quarterly*, vol. 16, no. 64 (1966), pp. 207–20.

Dunn, John, 'Consent in the political theory of John Locke', *Historical Journal*, vol. 10, no. 2 (July 1967), pp. 153–82.

Dunn, John, 'Justice and the interpretation of Locke's political theory', *Political Studies*, vol. 16, no. 1 (1968), pp. 68–87.

Furley, O. W., 'The Whig Exclusionists: pamphlet literature in the Exclusion campaign, 1679–81', *Cambridge Historical Journal*, vol. 13, no. 1 (1957), pp. 19–36.

Goldie, Mark, 'John Locke and Anglican royalism', *Political Studies*, vol. 31, no. 1 (1983), pp. 86–102.

Goldie, Mark, 'The Revolution of 1689 and the structure of political argument', *Bulletin of Research in the Humanities*, vol. 83 (Winter 1980), pp. 473–564.

Goldie, Mark, 'The roots of true Whiggism, 1688–94', *History of Political Thought*, vol. 1, no. 2 (June 1980), pp. 195–236.

Goldwin, Robert A., 'John Locke', in Leo Strauss and Joseph Cropsey (eds) *History of Political Philosophy* (Chicago, Ill.: Rand McNally, 1963), pp. 451–86.

Gough, John W., 'James Tyrrell, Whig historian and friend of John Locke', *Historical Journal*, vol. 19, no. 3 (1976), pp. 581–610.

Hundert, E. J., 'The making of *Homo faber*: John Locke between ideology and history', *Journal of the History of Ideas*, vol. 33, no. 1 (January–March 1972), pp. 3–22.

Kearney, H. F., 'The political background to English mercantilism, 1695–1700', *Economic History Review*, vol. 11, no. 3 (1959), pp. 484–96.

Laslett, Peter, 'Market society and political theory', *Historical Journal*, vol. 7, no. 1 (1964), pp. 150–4.

Maclean, A. H., 'George Lawson and John Locke', *Cambridge Historical Journal*, vol. 9, no. 1 (1947), pp. 68–77.

Olivecrona, Karl, 'Locke on the origin of property', *Journal of the History of Ideas*, vol. 35, no. 2 (April–June 1974), pp. 211–30.

Olivecrona, Karl, 'Locke's theory of appropriation', *Philosophical Quarterly*, vol. 24, no. 96 (July 1974), pp. 220–34.

Parry, Geraint, 'Individuality, politics and the critique of paternalism in John Locke', *Political Studies*, vol. 12, no. 2 (1964), pp. 163–77.

Polin, Raymond, 'Justice in Locke's philosophy', in C. J. Friedrich and J. W. Chapman (eds), *NOMOS VI: Justice* (New York: Atherton Press, 1963), pp. 262–83.

Riley, Patrick, 'On finding an equilibrium between consent and natural law in Locke's political philosophy', *Political Studies*, vol. 22, no. 4 (1974), pp. 432–52.

Schochet, Gordon J., 'Patriarchalism, politics and mass attitudes in Stuart England', *Historical Journal*, vol. 12, no. 3 (1969), pp. 413–41.

Seliger, Martin, 'Locke's theory of revolutionary action', *Western Political Quarterly*, vol. 16, no. 3 (September 1963), pp. 548–68.

Simon, W. M., 'John Locke: philosophy and political theory', *American*

Political Science Review, vol. 45, no. 2 (June 1951), pp. 386–99.

Singh, R., 'John Locke and the theory of natural law', *Political Studies*, vol. 9, no. 2 (1961), pp. 105–18.

Strauss, Leo, 'Locke's doctrine of natural law', *American Political Science Review*, vol. 52, no. 2 (June 1958), pp. 490–501.

Tarlton, Charles D., 'Rope of sand: interpreting Locke's *First Treatise of Government*', *Historical Journal*, vol. 21, no. 1 (1978), pp. 43–73.

Thompson, Martyn P., 'The reception of Locke's *Two Treatises of Government*, 1690–1705', *Political Studies*, Vol. 19, no. 2 (1976), pp. 184–91.

Von Leyden, W., 'John Locke and natural law', *Philosophy*, vol. 31, no. 116 (January 1956), pp. 23–35.

Wallace, John M., 'The date of Sir Robert Filmer's *Patriarcha*', *Historical Journal*, vol. 23, no. 1 (1980), pp. 1155–65.

Yolton, John W., 'Locke on the law of nature', *Philosophical Review*, vol. 67, no. 4 (October 1958), pp. 477–98.

INDEX

313